A-U-M
Awakening
to Reality

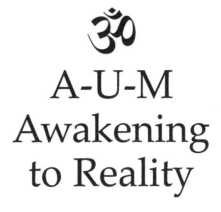

A-U-M
Awakening
to Reality

Dennis Waite

MANTRA
BOOKS

Winchester, UK
Washington, USA

First published by Mantra Books, 2015
Mantra Books is an imprint of John Hunt Publishing Ltd., Laurel House, Station Approach,
Alresford, Hants, SO24 9JH, UK
office1@jhpbooks.net
www.johnhuntpublishing.com
www.mantra-books.net

For distributor details and how to order please visit the 'Ordering' section on our website.

Text copyright: Dennis Waite 2014

ISBN: 978 1 78279 996 2

A CIP catalogue record for this book is available from the British Library.

Design: Stuart Davies

Printed and bound by CPI Group (UK) Ltd, Croydon, CR0 4YY, UK

We operate a distinctive and ethical publishing philosophy in all
areas of our business, from our global network of authors to
production and worldwide distribution.

CONTENTS

The purpose of this work is to present the knowledge to dispel the ignorance, which propagates the illusion that this world has any existence separate from Consciousness. *(Paraphrase of Shankara's statement in his introduction to the text addressed by this book.)*

Many thanks to Dr. Ramesam Vemuri, who carried out a critical review of the manuscript in addition to providing invaluable copy-editing. Our views did not always seem to coincide but his comments and the subsequent discussions that we had to reach an understanding have resulted in a number of significant improvements to the text.

Introduction

(Note that, in many books, the 'Introduction' consists of material that can safely be ignored and many readers may be tempted to skip it to move on to the actual subject matter of the book. This is not the case, here. Some key concepts are introduced which are essential to an understanding of what follows later – so ignore it at your peril!)

Search for Happiness

There is much talk about happiness at present. Even governments have begun talking about it, as though they have suddenly realized that the subject is actually of interest to voters and that their ability to promote happiness in some way might win them the next election.

Of course, we *are* interested! One could say that the search for it motivates our every action, directly or indirectly. Whole books have been written about it. This is not obviously one of them. Certainly I do not intend to say anything about it other than in this short, preliminary section. Yet it will not escape your attention that it is the very first topic that I introduce!

The point I would like to make is that neither governments nor most individuals actually *know* how to make people happy. What we do tend to know is what the specific thing (object, person, status etc.) is *at present* that we *think* will make us happy. What we invariably find is that, irrespective of whether or not we obtain that thing, any happiness gained is only temporary and we eventually move on, desiring and seeking for the next thing that might work.

The naïve view is that, ideally, I would always be free to do what I want rather than often seemingly being forced to do things that I don't want to do. But, on analysis of our experience, we should rather say that I really want to be free of that pervasive idea.

What is actually happening here?

The problem is that what we are actually looking for is the removal of some perceived limitation. We might want a new house if we think the present one is too small, too distant from our job etc., or if we do not have one at all. We might want a new partner if the current one is unfaithful, drunk all of the time etc., or if we do not have one at all. We might want a new job if the present one is too boring, not paid sufficiently well etc., or if we do not have one... You get the idea!

The perceived limitations are either in our body or our mind. If there is no literal limitation, such as a muscular or sensory one, it is usually a thought that: 'I must have X before I can be happy'. And, if you follow this line of reasoning, you end up with the real problem being that I believe that I *am* the body or mind. Since our bodies and minds genuinely are limited, it is no surprise that trying to remove these limitations inevitably causes problems and is ultimately doomed to failure.

So what has all of this got to do with this book? Well, the source text, which will be introduced in the next section, says that who we think we are is actually somewhat wider than this. It looks at our entire life experience through the three states of consciousness – waking state, dream state and deep-sleep state and their corresponding objective 'universes'. There is nothing else in our experience apart from these.

And what it says is that these states are effectively 'masks' that we put on. A metaphor which is sometimes used is that of an actor, playing parts in several plays. The waker, dreamer and deep-sleeper are merely roles that the actor plays at various times. Who he 'really is' is the fourth aspect, called *turīya* in Sanskrit – the actor himself. The waker is not the dreamer, the dreamer is not the deep-sleeper but I am all of these.

The waking and dream roles are inherently fraught with limitations. We play the role of a limited being in a largely hostile universe. The deep-sleep state, on the other hand is a blissful one, in which we experience no limitation whatsoever. But then we know nothing about this directly and can only say on waking up that we 'slept well'.

What can we make of these observations? If these states are 'masks' that we put on, who is the one without a mask? If the perceived limitations of those states are not present when the masks are removed, then it would seem to follow that 'who-we-really-are' must be without limitation and therefore permanently, transcendentally happy. This is indeed the case! This is why the subject of this book is so important. Read on!

Title of this Book

The title of this book may seem to be somewhat outrageous. Whatever the mystical significance of the word **OM** may be, it hardly seems credible to imply that it could tell us anything useful about the nature of reality. This is not at all the case.

It occurred to me that I ought to begin the book with a photograph of some readily identifiable object taken with a fish-eye lens. (This is a very wide-angle lens which 'sees' a 180-degree image and thus, to our eyes, seems to distort the view.) I thought this would serve as a potent metaphor to emphasize that we ourselves never see what is 'really' there anyway.

Of course, we rarely admit this is so. We have always interacted with the world via the senses that we have, supplemented as necessary by spectacles, hearing aids and so on, and we do so very successfully. This is thought to prove to us that we really are seeing the world as it is. However, Western philosophers such as Immanuel Kant have argued that this can never be. Our senses are very specific. Our eyes, for example, only cover a tiny part of the electromagnetic spectrum – we cannot see in the radio or microwave regions at the lower end, or in X-ray and gamma ray regions at the higher end. Even infra-red and ultra-violet are outside of our scope.

Also significant is the 'conceptual lens' through which we

view the world. It is difficult for someone brought up as a Muslim to look at the world from a Jewish standpoint, as we know only too well, and innumerable other examples might be cited.

OM, then, could be thought of as a very specialized lens which enables us to see reality more nearly as it is than through any other philosophical-cultural lens that exists!

Most people in the West will have encountered the word in the context of meditation. They will have seen popular films in which cross-legged, shaven headed, saffron robed or near-naked men (almost invariably!) chant the word in a monotone with eyes closed, in a purposeful manner. And these Westerners would probably regard the practice in a condescending way, considering them to be little better than savages.

But such an attitude is the result of ignorance only. The word has a long history of usage and meaning in Indian philosophies and religions. This book addresses just one of these, namely its use as a profound metaphor in an ancient text called the Mandukya Upanishad. And the investigation which follows on from this really does reveal the truth about yourself and the universe.

The Upanishads occur in Hindu Scriptures called the Vedas. These are massive texts, which were written down thousands of years ago, having previously been communicated by word of mouth. (And much of the content has been lost in time.) Most of the scriptures are concerned with instructions for rituals intended to lead to specific results, such as conceiving a child or going to heaven, but those small elements known as the Upanishads are deeply philosophical texts explaining the nature of reality.

"OM, the word, is everything. All that is past, present and future is OM. And that which is beyond time is also OM." (Mandukya Upanishad, mantra 1. This will henceforth be abbreviated to MU1)

4

This verse opens the shortest and most profound of the Upanishads. It makes what appears to be the most preposterous of statements – what can it possibly mean? And yet, the similarity with a certain other statement, from the King James Version of the Gospel according to John I.1 – *"In the beginning was the Word, and the Word was with God, and the Word was God"* – cannot go unnoticed.

The Mandukya Upanishad consists of only twelve verses. It would be outrageous to claim that such a short text could tell you all about this philosophy (whose teaching is known as Advaita). Fortunately, there are a further 215 verses of explanatory commentary. These are usually attributed to a philosopher called Gaudapada, who lived around the seventh century CE. But the name probably only refers reverently to someone who lived in the region of what is now northern Bengal. And the authorship is much disputed. The so-called Gaudapada *kArikA-s* are in four separate chapters. These are believed to have been written at different times and almost certainly by different people, with the one now known as Gaudapada compiling and editing the material. Some academics think that the first chapter was the actual Upanishad, and that what is now called the Mandukya Upanishad was a short summary of that. Ref. 36 summarizes many of these arguments. It seems that the terms used, and even the claims made, are such that it is not reasonable to think that there was a single author.

[Pedantically, the word *mantra* should be used for verses from the Upanishad, which is in terse, prose format, while the word 'verse' should be used for the *kArikA*. The word *mantra* is usually used in the West for a word or short group of words that is chanted, or mentally repeated, in meditation but strictly speaking it refers to the entire 'sacred' text of the Vedas. I will tend to be rather sloppy in my usage, however!

A *kArikA* is a concise philosophical statement written in verse form, so that it may more easily be memorized. It has been defined as *'that which indicates profound meaning in a few words'* (Ref. 11).]

Based upon words used, references made and so on, the best guesses seem to be that the Upanishad itself was written around 1–200 CE, Chapter 1 300-400 CE, Chapter 2 sometime after 1 and before 3 (!), Chapter 3 400-500 CE and Chapter 4 400-600 CE. And there is also an increasing influence from Buddhism, with many of the terms in the final chapter being specific to Buddhist texts. Swami Tyagishananda (Ref. 6) suggests that it was compiled at a time when Buddhism was in decline and that Gaudapada wanted to use terms with which seekers were familiar in order to persuade them of the truth of Advaita Vedanta. This seems very reasonable. It also explains why this text is so relevant to the modern age in that it mostly uses reason rather than any particular religious dogma to make its points.

Shankara is the name most specifically associated with the teaching of Advaita, since he spent his short life commenting on key scriptures and penning his own elucidatory works, clearly setting down the principles. Also known as Adi Shankara (*Adi* meaning 'first') and Shankaracharya (*AchArya* meaning 'teacher'), he was responsible for establishing four or five monasteries around India, initially headed by his own disciples, and these continue to this day. Shankara has provided a commentary (*bhAShya*) on this Upanishad and the *kArikA*-s. Others have commented on the complete set (Upanishad + *kArikA*-s + Shankara's commentary). One of the main commentators is Anandagiri, who has written what is called a *TIkA*, which just means a 'gloss', especially a commentary on another commentary!

Most writers seem to agree that the material represents the earliest presentation of what is clearly Advaita philosophy, although this conclusion may be based on the traditionally held belief that Gaudapada was the teacher of Shankara's teacher. Mahadevan (Ref. 54) points out that the ideas expressed in the *kArikA*-s bear significant similarity both to those in the Yoga Vasishtha (generally thought to have been written much later – around 1000 - 1400 CE) and to the Bhagavata Purana or Srimad Bhagavatam (somewhere between 500 – 1000 CE).

I will not be addressing any of these authorship issues further. Some of the books listed in the bibliography discuss these topics at length. Nor will I say any more about whether Gaudapada was essentially a Buddhist or the extent to which the author(s) might have been influenced by Buddhist beliefs. Again, some of the references present divergent views on this subject. There is even some dispute about whether the commentary on the Upanishad and *kArikA-s* is even by Shankara but I will leave all these debates for those qualified to write about them and those interested in reading about them and concentrate instead simply upon the content and meaning.

The bottom line has to be that there is much profound wisdom to be found there. It really does not matter who wrote what. Even the fact that some of the points made appear to be contradicted in later chapters can be understood as a 'progressive' teaching, analogous to the way in which Relativity supersedes Newtonian mechanics. The overall commentary is so brilliant that Upanishad and *kArikA-s* are almost invariably studied together and treated as a single work. What I will be doing, however, is addressing the subject matter via topics, rather than sequentially. (N.B. In Appendix 1, however, I do provide a detailed analysis of each of the 12 mantras of the Upanishad itself. This utilizes the Sanskrit text and provides translation and commentary.)

It is interesting to note that not everyone thinks that this work is difficult. Sri Aurobindo says: *"Gaudapada's clear, brief and businesslike verses... presuppose only an elementary knowledge of philosophic terminology... provide the student with an admirably lucid and pregnant nucleus of reasoning which enables him at once to follow the monistic train of thought and to keep in memory its most notable positions. To modern students there can be no better introduction to Vedanta philosophy... than a study of Gaudapada's* kArikA-s *and Shankara's commentary...*" (Ref. 44)

And not everyone thinks that the work is profound. Radhakrishnan, in his classic two-volume work 'Indian philosophy', makes the following astonishing statement: "*The general idea pervading Gaudapada's work, that bondage and liberation, the individual soul and the world, are all unreal makes the caustic critic observe that the theory which has nothing better to say than that an unreal soul is trying to escape from an unreal bondage in an unreal world to accomplish an unreal supreme good, may itself be an unreality.*" And he goes on to point out that: "*If we have to play the game of life, we cannot do so with the conviction that the play is a show and all the prizes in it mere blanks.*" (Ref. 45, extract quoted in Ref. 21)

One serious drawback, for the Western student at least, is that both Upanishad and commentary were written in Sanskrit. This means that most readers have to rely upon someone else's translation. It is exceedingly unlikely that any two translators would produce the same English sentence from a given Sanskrit one and, unfortunately, it is inevitable that the accuracy of the interpretation will be dependent upon the level of the understanding of the writer. And this is not only Sanskrit understanding, but also understanding of the message that is being transmitted. This particular Upanishad is normally only studied after all of the other major Upanishads have been understood. (There are currently 108 Upanishads – many more having been lost – and 10 of these are considered to be 'major', because commentaries have been provided by Shankara, who is acknowledged to have been the greatest Indian philosopher.) Although on the one hand tradition says that one should only study the Mandukya after studying all of the other major Upanishads, one work (Muktika Upanishad) which speaks about all of the Upanishads states that one *only* needs to study the Mandukya in order to attain the highest understanding.

Needless to say, the work is not very well known in the West. Consequently, it is extremely probable that any potential reader of this book will not previously have heard of the Mandukya Upanishad at all and will therefore also be likely to view any claim to its intrinsic worth with skepticism, to say the least.

And no wonder! Here are some of the most radical ideas ever presented, yet backed by the most rigorous logical argument. You will encounter, and eventually endorse, propositions that you would previously not even have countenanced: Your waking experiences are no more real than your dreaming ones! There has never been any creation – you cannot die because you were never born! The fact that you experience separate objects proves that they are not really there!

You may be worried that conclusions such as these are based upon ancient scriptures, with which you will be unfamiliar and would be very likely to reject. This is not a problem! Gaudapada was a stickler for logic and reason. Although he does refer to scriptures, since these were the absolute authority for seekers at the time, he refuses to accept anything unless it can also be supported by our own experience and/or reason. Also, like it or not, it remains a fact that the nature of ultimate reality cannot be fathomed by reason alone. Logic requires distinctness and differentiation in order to function. Accordingly, for some aspects, the sequence has to be: find out what the scriptures say; then subject this to reason and experience.

How this single syllable word, chanted by millions in meditation, can possibly point to such astounding statements as were indicated above provides a fascinating story and may lead to the realization of one's true nature as limitless Consciousness. OM is quite literally the key to understanding 'the answer to the question of life, the universe and everything'.

Brief Note on the Presentation

I wanted to write this book simply because I consider the Upanishad together with its *kArikA* to be possibly the most significant philosophical work ever written. And it seems criminal that it is not better known. But there seemed little point in producing yet another word by word translation, together with a commentary that could only be appreciated by those who already understand the philosophy. Accordingly, I do not intend to go through the work verse by verse and I will also try to avoid the use of unnecessary Sanskrit terminology in the main text. Note that this will not be entirely possible, simply because some of the concepts do not have English equivalents. Therefore, I hope that readers will respect this and be prepared to learn a few Sanskrit words. I will always give an English explanation when a new term is introduced and there is a Glossary at the back explaining all of the Sanskrit terms used (and probably a few which are not, since this Glossary accompanies most of my books).

Also, however, I hope that existing students of Advaita* philosophy (i.e. 'seekers' of enlightenment) will want to read this book. They *will* be interested in verse references, so that they may check the original Sanskrit or translations in other books. Accordingly, where appropriate, I will reference chapter and verse in brackets after relevant sentences. All verses will be covered at some point and the reader may find the associated section immediately by using the Index.

Also, again for the benefit of those who are already familiar with the teaching of Advaita, I will include the relevant Sanskrit terms in brackets following any paragraphs in which key terms appear. Readers who are only interested in the concepts and philosophy may simply ignore both the references and the Sanskrit terms in brackets! (*Note that it is expected that readers of this book will already be familiar with the word 'Advaita'! In the unlikely event that you are not, it refers to the principal non-dual teaching/philosophy of Hinduism, and is based on the Vedas. The word itself means 'not two'.)

My aim is to make the topics understandable to any seriously interested reader, whether or not they have prior knowledge of Advaita. What I will do, therefore, is try to provide a logical order for those topics which are addressed in the Upanishad and in Gaudapada's commentary. I also provide a list of related books in the bibliography, together with a few notes regarding their readability, reliability and difficulty (and availability).

As regards the use of capital letters at the beginning of certain words, this is traditionally done to differentiate the mundane use of those words from the special meaning assigned by Advaita. The very common word that is treated in this manner is 'consciousness'. In this text, in common with most other sources of this teaching, it is written with a capital 'C' when I want to differentiate it from the everyday usage of 'consciousness-unconsciousness' which we use to refer to a person's state of mind. Another word which is sometimes capitalized is 'absolute'. 'Absolute' with a capital refers to the non-dual reality. Similarly, as far as this text is concerned, 'Self' refers to this same reality – who we really are – as opposed to 'self', which is what we call our body-mind-ego.

Another word which I have capitalized in some places is 'Existence'. This is because this word is sometimes used in an analogous manner to 'Consciousness'. 'Consciousness' manifests as *jIvAtman*, the consciousness of *jIva*-s. Similarly, 'Existence' manifests as *paramAtman*, the existence of objects. Consciousness (*chit*) and Existence (*sat*) are 'attributes' of brahman. Since *brahman* is part-less, *chit* = *sat* or *jIvAtman* = *paramAtman*. This is another expression of the *mahAvAkya tat tvam asi* and is explained by Shankara in his text Sri Dakshinamurti Stotram. (But this idea does not occur in Gaudapada's work, so don't worry if you did not follow any of this paragraph!)

Some writers prefer to capitalize other terms such as 'reality'.

My own view is that, if a word is not ambiguous in the way that 'consciousness' and 'self' are, for example, then there is no need for capitalization. There is only one 'reality'. We may mistakenly refer to the waking state as real but that is what it is – a mistake.

I have also decided to give the names of teachers and writers in their Anglicized form only. Since there is no confusion here, it seemed simplest to avoid unnecessary use of ITRANS. Thus, for example, I use 'Gaudapada' and Shankara throughout, rather than the more correct 'gauDapAda' and 'shaMkara'. I also use the Anglicized names of key texts, such as Mandukya (mANDUkya) and Brihadaranyaka (bRRihadAraNyaka) Upanishads.

A (Very) Little Sanskrit Background

Sanskrit is represented in this book by the ITRANS system, which looks peculiar because it uses capitalized letters in the middle of words (and when such a word begins a sentence, it may not have an initial capital). You can safely ignore this and pronounce words mentally in whatever way you like. If, however, you would like to know the correct pronunciation, Appendix 3 on ITRANS explains this briefly. There is also a glossary for explanation of Sanskrit terms.

I have used this system in all of my books because it is the one to which I was first introduced and because it is commonly used on the Internet (historically because it used not to be possible to represent Sanskrit letters in the form in which they are more usually found in printed books). Occasionally a reader will write to me (or even make an adverse review on Amazon!) because they find capital letters in the middle of words distracting and think them unnecessary. Just as an example for why they can be necessary, however, consider the word kArikA. The 'A' is pronounced like the 'a' in 'car' (I.e. long), rather than that in 'cat' (short). I have already explained the meaning of the word but you may be interested to know that, had I written it without the long 'a'-s, as karika, the Sanskrit word would actually mean 'elephant'!

Since one of the main topics of the book relates to the symbol 'OM', which is one of these untranslatable Sanskrit terms, it is necessary to explain the nature of this first, which does involve learning three letters from the alphabet!

The spoken word 'OM' is actually Sanskrit. The written 'OM' is its 'Romanized' representation (i.e. using the English alphabet). In its original language, it actually looks like this:

If you have ever been to India, this character will be very familiar and it also frequently appears on New Age items and jewelry. But this is in fact a special, shorthand representation and the word is actually formed from three separate letters. Only this word, in the entire language, has a special symbol – an indication of how important it is! And, in case you don't know how to pronounce it, it is like the unit of electrical resistance – the ohm. It is not like the computer's read-only memory, ROM, without the 'r'. Also, although it can be written 'aum', the 'au' in Sanskrit is not pronounced like the 'ow' in 'cow'.

Sanskrit is an incredibly logical language and this begins with the alphabet itself. Letters are formed in a very consistent, stepwise manner founded upon the way in which sound is initially made by the vocal chords and subsequently modified by the throat, mouth, tongue and lips. If you open your mouth and cause the vocal chords to operate very briefly without any inter-ference, the most basic sound of all emerges. It sounds like 'uh' and it is this sound that is molded by the rest of the vocal apparatus to make every other sound, letter and word. This basic sound is the first Sanskrit vowel, represented in English as 'a'. In the Sanskrit script (which is called Devanagari), it is written as:

If you now make this basic 'a' sound and allow it to continue sounding as you move the tongue in the mouth, various other Sanskrit vowel sounds are formed. Eventually, dropping the tongue down and closing the lips to make a circle, the sound that is now made is a short 'oo', as in 'cook' or 'book'. (If the sound is prolonged, it becomes more like the 'oo' in 'moon' but this is effectively another vowel – in Sanskrit, the duration of the sound is critical). This short vowel is written 'u' in English or, in Devanagari:

उ

Finally, if you (attempt to) continue to make the basic sound but close the lips altogether, the sound is effectively cut off and just a 'mm' sound is made. This is not a vowel but a consonant, in Sanskrit. It is written 'm' in English or, in Devanagari:

(All sounds have to incorporate the basic 'a' or there would be no sound at all. Accordingly, when the alphabet is spoken, 'a' is always added to the consonant sound. Therefore the 'm' consonant is actually spoken as 'ma' and would be written म . Since we want to use the 'm' sound without any 'a' appended, we have to use the 'tail' sign on the letter to indicate that the 'a' must be omitted.)

So, we have introduced the three letters 'a', 'u' and 'm'. It is these three letters which together make the word OM: a + u + m = OM.

And that is almost all the Sanskrit you need to know for this book although, as already noted, a few Sanskrit words will be used later where there is no English equivalent.

OM = Everything = God

Words are used to refer to objects. In the physical presence of an object, we can simply point to it, although even this may be ambiguous in the absence of any further elucidation. But, when the object is not there, we have to resort to language so that an object and the word that we use to refer to it are effectively inseparable.

If you consider a specific object, say the cat outside your window, you will probably know it by a very specific name – 'Tiddles', maybe. But of course, that is only your own pet-name and most people would simply call it a 'cat'. If you had never seen a cat before but saw this one eating meat, you might have to be more general and call it a 'carnivore'. If really ignorant about these things, and someone told you that it was a mammal, at least you would have some idea of what they were talking about. And the 'class' of mammals comes within the even broader 'kingdom' of animals, as opposed to, say, plants.

So language gives us the capability to speak in general or specific terms about the things that we perceive. If we continued to follow this sort of series back to increasingly more general words, we would have to find a 'catch-all' word to include absolutely everything. That word is OM.

Since the word OM, in a very real sense, 'contains' all possible sounds, it is natural that it should be the word used to designate all things. And, to the extent that a word *is* the thing designated, so OM *is* the entire universe – all that is or can exist.

It is also understandable, by the same sort of argument, why God or *Ishvara* is given the name OM. (*Ishvara* is the Sanskrit word used in Advaita to denote the principal, Creator-Ruler God.)

Since God has no limitations, it seems logical that the name of God ought also to be without limitation. Every 'ordinary' word gives rise to a specific sound or vibration, whereas a humming 'mmm' sound effectively contains all vibrations. The word *praNava* is a synonym for OM and comes from the word *praNu*, meaning 'to make a humming or droning sound'.

God is infinite, without beginning or end. No other word could convey this image so well. Nor is OM language, culture or religion specific. The word 'Amen' has a similar connotation and we can now see how the text from the bible *'In the beginning was the Word...'* fits with this interpretation.

Structure and Content of the Text

The Mandukya Upanishad itself undertakes two 'investigations': 1) into the nature of the Self (both who we seem to be, and who we really are); and 2) into the makeup of the word OM. And it shows how the two investigations mirror each other so that we can appreciate the power of the word (as a metaphor and an object of meditation).

The *kArikA* then proceeds to expand on this and to branch out into related areas of enquiry. The first chapter is normally presented 'interleaved' with the Upanishad itself, since it elaborates upon what is discussed there. Its title is *Agama prakaraNa*.

The word *Agama* can mean "reading or studying, acquisition of knowledge, a traditional doctrine or a collection of these". It also refers to anything handed down by tradition, which in the present context could easily refer to the scriptures (*shruti*) or in particular the Upanishads themselves. The word *prakaraNa* means not only 'chapter' but also 'treatise, subject, treatment, explanation' or even 'book'. The term *'prakaraNa grantha'* refers to those classical, scriptural texts which do not form part of the threefold canon of scriptures (*prasthAna traya*) – Upanishads, Bhagavad Gita and Brahmasutras – but are highly regarded on their own merit. These are usually verse discourses (the word *grantha* means 'tying, binding or stringing together') which discuss some particular topic(s) from the *shAstra*, which is the generic name for the scriptural texts. There are four elements to a *prakaraNa*: *adhikArI* – establishing that the reader is sufficiently qualified to benefit from reading it; *viShaya* – the subject matter itself and its *sambandha* – how the *prakaraNa* relates to that subject; *prayojana* – the purpose or reason why the student should study it in the first place, i.e. what he or she will get out of it.

The entire Upanishads plus *kArikA-s* is also collectively known as the '*AgamashAstra* of *Gaudapada*', and this is the title of one of the commentaries, that by Vidhushekhara Bhattacharya (Ref. 7). Colin Cole (Ref. 11) describes Gaudapada's work as "*a systematic interpretation or explanation of this* (i.e. the oneness of reality) *from the standpoint of absolute non-dualism and as such represents the first of its kind, as far as the extant literature goes, in the tradition of Advaita*". It is thus a tremendously important work from the teacher who is effectively the first in the *guru-shiShya* (teacher-disciple) *sampradAya* (authorized lineage) tradition. (Prior to Gaudapada, the lineage that is recited in the invocatory prayers is mythological and proceeds from father to son, from Narayana or Vishnu down to Shuka, the son of Vyasa or Badarayana.)

Shankara says that: "*This treatise is begun for the purpose of revealing brahman in as much as, by knowledge* (vidyA), *the illusion of duality caused by ignorance is destroyed.*" (Ref. 4) He explains that this is analogous to the way in which someone recovers from a disease when the cause of the disease is removed. In the same way, we are suffering because we are under the illusion that we are separate entities in an alien universe. Once this illusion of duality is removed, we recognize our true Self and thus 'recover' our natural state, as it were. As he says in his introduction to the Upanishadic commentary, this is "*the quintessence of the substance of the import of Vedanta*".

This first chapter addresses the topics of the Upanishad, namely the states of consciousness, the nature of the self and reality. It analyses the various theories that have been propounded regarding the creation of the universe. It looks at how the word OM can be used to illustrate the nature of consciousness. And it shows how meditation on OM can help us to realize the truth.

The second chapter is called *vaitathya prakaraNa*. The seventh *mantra* of the Upanishad effectively provides a description of the nature of reality. (It must be noted here that because reality is non-dual, it is actually impossible to 'describe'. Accordingly, the words that are used in this seventh verse are really only pointers.) This second chapter of the *kArikA* analyses just one of these words in the seventh verse. That word is *prapa~nchopashamaM* and it means that the world is not in itself real. Much more will be said about this in a moment! *vaitathya prakaraNa* means 'a chapter about the unreality' of the universe. (*vaitathya* means 'falseness'.)

There is a very famous metaphor in Advaita which most readers of this book will already have met before. It refers to someone coming across what they believe to be a snake as they are walking through the forest at twilight. The consequences of this encounter are easy to imagine – any or all of the symptoms of fear caused by a rush of adrenaline. The story then goes that someone else comes along with a torch. Shining this on the 'snake' reveals it to be a coiled-up rope. Entire books have been written about this metaphor describing the ways in which it can be used to explain various aspects of the teaching. Here, the simple point is that the snake itself did not exist but, of course, something *did* exist, namely the rope. The illusory appearance of the snake arose as a consequence of the shape and length of the rope, combined with the over active imagination of the observer.

In a similar way, the world is not real in itself. But there is something which is giving rise to the appearance (combined with our over active imagination!) This, then, is the topic of the second chapter. The first half explains how external objects are not in themselves real. The second half presents various theories, from other branches of Indian philosophy, about the nature of reality and concludes with an explanation of the nature of reality as propounded by Advaita.

The third chapter looks at the meaning of the term '*Advaita*' itself (this word also occurs in the seventh mantra of the Upanishad) and is called *Advaita prakaraNa*. Shankara notes that, whereas the aim of the second chapter was to demonstrate the unreality of duality (i.e. the entire universe), the aim of this third chapter is to demonstrate the reality of non-duality. In other words, it sets out to prove that the nature of reality is non-dual. This is necessary because, otherwise, we might conclude like the Buddhists that reality is *shunya* or nothingness. It utilizes reason but also refers to scriptural statements for corroboration.

In this context, another famous metaphor is employed – that of the space which is erroneously thought to be 'contained' inside a pot. In fact, if the pot is broken, the space is totally unaffected and is never contaminated by the contents of the pot. Just as the 'pot space' is never separate from the total space, so the 'individual' self is never separate from the non-dual Consciousness.

The topic of creation is revisited in the context of the concept of *mAyA*, the idea that the world appears in an analogous manner to that of the illusions presented by a magician. Following this, the nature of the mind is examined in its three states of waking, dreaming and deep sleep. This leads on to the discussion of the attitude of mind wherein one effectively becomes detached from worldly enjoyments and rests in knowledge of one's non-dual reality. This is termed *asparsha yoga*, the 'touch-less' *yoga*.

The final chapter examines some of the beliefs of other philosophies that might serve to undermine Advaita – and refutes them. And it analyses yet another famous (Buddhist) metaphor, which also gives its name to the chapter – *alAtashAnti prakaraNa*, the 'quenching of the firebrand'. *alAta* means 'firebrand', while *shAnti* literally means 'peace'. The firebrand was the wooden stick, with one end wrapped in a rag, dipped in oil and set alight for use as a torch at nighttime. A more familiar modern example would be the sparkler – the hand-held firework that throws out lots of scintillating, incandescent particles of iron as it slowly burns down.

When we play with these as children (or as adults with children), we tend to move them around and 'draw' patterns with them. In the dark, when the glowing tip of the sparkler is moved fairly quickly, the persistence of vision of the eyes means that solid patterns seem to form in the air. We may see what appears to be a solid circle, for example. But is there really a circle there? Where does it come from? Does it come from inside or outside the sparkler? And when the firework dies, is the circle 'reabsorbed' into the sparkler?

If you analyze what is happening here, you will find that questions such as these cannot be answered, because they implicitly assume that there actually *is* a circle. In fact, there is no circle – what there is, is simply movement of the sparkler. The circle is what is called *mithyA*, depending for its existence on the sparkler alone. (This is one of the most important Sanskrit terms – there is no corresponding word in English – and much more will be said about it later.) Similarly, the world of objects and people and minds does not exist as a real, separate entity. What is there is simply movement of Consciousness. Also, we must not make the mistake of thinking that the sparkler is the 'cause' of the patterns. There is no cause-effect relationship here because, in order for such a thing to be possible, there have to be two things – and the patterns do not actually exist. (Again, I must keep reminding you that all of this will be looked at more carefully and gradually. I do not expect you to accept any of this... yet! This is just to tell you what you are letting yourself in for and whet your appetite!)

Chapter four discusses lots of different theories of causation and shoots them all down. And there is more discussion on the topic of waking versus dream experience.

Gold Ring Metaphor

Suppose you are about to get married. Your parents have generously offered to provide the wedding ring and they give you a choice of three. The first has been in the family for generations. It is therefore old and relatively worn. The clarity of the original markings has been lost but it is a direct connection through to your great, great grandmother and you know that your parents would like you to choose this one. The second is a very solid and substantial ring, lacking any ornamentation but therefore all the more indicative of the essential meaning of the golden wedding ring – a symbol of eternal love (in the form of the endless circle), of stability and permanence (being the nature of the metal gold) and perhaps the 'endowment of worldly goods' in the form of an expensive gift. The third is a very fashionable and expensive design from one of London's Bond Street jewelers.

Which will you choose? Which 'ought' you to choose? What criteria should you use to decide? You realize that it probably comes down in the end to your own particular upbringing. What are the cultural and personal 'values' that have been inculcated in you from early childhood by parents, teachers, books and television? But, ignoring the temptation to stray into a reflection on the relative arguments in favor of fate or free will, you decide to borrow all three rings and seek advice from an expert – a goldsmith that you just happen to know.

Your friend examines each of the rings carefully through a magnifying lens and declares that each is of the same quality of gold. He then weighs them and announces that, by an amazing coincidence, each is of precisely the same weight as the others. Accordingly, he concludes, they are of equal value and there is no good reason to choose one rather than another.

He sees the dismay and astonishment on your face and so embarks upon a little more explanation. The Bond Street ring, he says, is currently quite fashionable and so people at present are willing to pay much more than it is really worth, simply in order to be seen to be wearing the latest style. In a few years time, there will be new designers in vogue and the old styles will lose their value unless the vagaries of fashion happen to accord the old designer some particular prestige as happened with someone like Fabergé for example. The old ring was not designed by anyone who has since become famous so it is really only sentimentality that would elevate its selling price. The third ring is a simple, plain gold ring. If each were melted down, it would produce the same weight of gold.

From a philosophical point of view, he goes on to say, you must realize that the ring is simply a particular shape in which the gold has been cast; it has no substantiality of its own. Any ornamentation, design, unusual form or whatever does not and cannot change the essential nature. All it can do is to modify the form. So it is pure affectation on our part to assign one particular form a greater value than any other. Yes, you can talk about beauty of design and workmanship and so on, but in the end none of those have anything to do with what is actually there in essence. It is the vagaries of society and their changing cultural values that dictate whether or not something is 'beautiful'. It is unlikely that we would hold the same views as a stone-age cave dweller, for example. You only need to consider that today's famous painters, whose canvases sell for millions, were probably unable to sell enough of their own work to feed themselves in their lifetimes.

This gold ring story is, of course, a metaphor – Advaita uses very many metaphors in its teaching since the essential subject (the nature of reality) is so ineffable. The idea is that, having understood the metaphor, your mind will make an intuitive leap to grasp whatever lies behind the subject that is presently under discussion. So for example, having appreciated the point being made above, we could go on to look at the stages of development of the person. We have the child – physical profile, opinions and personality still developing; immature in all ways but full of potential. Then we have the middle-aged parent, still fit and active with a full, working life; having achieved much with many ambitions still remaining. And later we have the weather-beaten features of the grandparent, prone to illness, forgetful, not able to move about very quickly and with a certain death now on the horizon. These are clearly very different forms of what is actually the same person, albeit at different times. There is no denying that we have the same feeling 'I' throughout our life. Is there a sense in which this 'I' is really essentially the same, in the way that the gold is the same in the different rings? Is it only the outward form which changes, while who-I-really-am remains the same?

In the Mandukya Upanishad, we can use the same metaphor to examine the nature of the three states of consciousness. Here, the states are outwardly so different that another version of the metaphor is more applicable. Instead of talking about three different rings, the metaphor used by Advaita is that of bangle, chain and ring (all made out of gold). Here, the outward forms are quite different. A ring is small and is worn on a finger; a bangle is much larger and is worn on a wrist; and a chain or necklace, worn around the neck is finer but longer still. Similarly, the natures of waking, dream and sleep states are very different. We (think we) know that dreams are entirely imaginary, lasting for a brief time only, while the waking world lasts indefinitely, or at least is seen by us throughout our lifetime (while we are awake!) The sleep state is quite unlike the other two in that there are no perceptions of any kind, imagined or 'real'.

Following on from the earlier analysis, we now realize that the bangle, chain and ring are simply different forms of the same gold; they have no substantiality of their own. Is it possible that the states of consciousness, too, are in some way only 'forms' of something that is the essence of all three? These ideas will no doubt sound very strange but the intention is that they will seem obvious by the time you reach the end of the book!

Reality and Unreality
Much of the discussion in this book will be about what is real

and what is unreal and I do not want to anticipate this. There is, however, a term that is so important that it needs to be understood clearly (and there is no equivalent word in English). It was already introduced earlier but I now want to reinforce the concept.

All of the separate 'things' that we encounter in the universe, including the bodies and minds (and including the one with which you personally identify and call 'me') are not real in themselves – they are only names and forms of the non-dual reality – but, equally clearly, they are not unreal. I can sit on the chair – it is therefore not an illusion. I can drink from a cup – the coffee doesn't pass straight through it onto the floor (despite all that space inside the atom). So, the apparently separate things are neither real in themselves nor unreal.

It is a bit like the metaphor of gold and ring. In the metaphor, it is the gold that is real; the ring is not real in itself – it depends for its existence upon the gold alone and is merely a temporary form of that gold. Advaita says that everything is like this. The world itself, including you and me, is simply a transient form of the eternal reality; the next moment everything will be different. There are not many things at all; the reality is non-dual. Advaita calls this reality *brahman* if speaking in a general sense, or *Atman* if talking about what 'you' really are. The English term which is commonly used is 'Consciousness'. (The word 'Awareness' is used by some, particularly the teacher Nisargadatta Maharaj, to mean *brahman* but I will use 'awareness', if at all, in its ordinary sense.)

Another aspect is that, in order to be 'real', a thing must not be subject to change. If A changes into B, it effectively becomes what it was not to begin with; it ceases to be A. How, therefore, can A be said to have been 'real' if it entails non-existence?

Accordingly, only *brahman*, Atman or Consciousness is truly 'real'. Anything else – world, cup of coffee, tiger, you and me – is not, in itself, real at all; it is only a particular name and form of *brahman,* much as we know that the ring is only name and form of gold.

There is no word in English to describe this peculiar state of affairs. The Sanskrit term is *mithyA.* The universe and everything in it, from the grossest brick to the most subtle imagining, is *mithyA.* These things are not unreal but neither are they real-in-themselves; they have 'dependent reality', depending for their ultimate existence on *brahman.*

That which is 'true' or 'real' is called *sat* in Sanskrit; 'truth' or 'reality' is *satyam.* 'False' or 'unreal' is *asat* (putting the letter 'a' in front of a Sanskrit word usually gives it the opposite meaning). The word *mithyA,* then, means neither real nor unreal, neither *sat* nor *asat.* This is an effective definition of *mithyA* – neither real nor unreal (*sat-asat-vilakShaNa* – the word *vilakShaNa* means 'differing from; not possible to define exactly'). But we do need to be very careful when using words, since there is a natural tendency to understand them in their everyday sense – and this is not always the case! (This is the reason why Advaita has to use so many Sanskrit terms, so that this inherent ambiguity is avoided.) Thus, we tend to use the word 'real' to refer to 'things' that occupy time and space. When speaking of the absolute reality, however, this limited meaning has to be discarded – absolute reality has to be outside of time, space and causality.

Do not worry if you find all of this hard to accept – the Mandukya Upanishad and Gaudapada's *kArikA* will use OM, together with the most rigorous logic, to convince you! The whole of the second chapter is on the subject of the *mithyAtva* (state of being *mithyA*) of the world. (Note that neither the Upanishad nor Gaudapada actually uses the word *mithyA.* The equivalent word that he uses is *vaitathya,* which has already been introduced as meaning 'falseness'.)

The 'bottom line' truth is that everything is *brahman.* Names only refer to forms and in all cases the substrate of the form is *brahman.* In a sense, it could be claimed that it is the very act of naming, of using words, that 'brings about' duality. As Shankara quotes in his introduction to the Mandukya: *"All this phenomenal creation of that* brahman *is strung together by the thread of speech and by the strands of names."* (Ref. 15)

Another one of the Upanishads – the Chandogya – says (VI.i.4): *"Dear boy, just as through a single clod of clay all that is made of clay would become known, for all modification is but name based upon words and the clay alone is real..."* In truth there never was any duality but, in this apparent world into which we are apparently born, it is necessary to utilize language in order to make sense of it. Unfortunately, we end up believing in the effective duality that this creates. We are 'ignorant' of the truth about the reality of ourselves and the world. The only way to remove this self-ignorance is by gaining self-knowledge and it is pointed out by Shankara that: *"This treatise is for the purpose of revealing* brahman *inasmuch as by knowledge, the illusion of duality, caused by ignorance, is destroyed."* (Ref. 4)

In the third chapter, for example, Gaudapada talks about how we artificially 'create' something called 'pot space' when we speak of the space that is temporarily marked off by the present location of a pot. (K3.3 to 3.9 – this notation will be used throughout the book to refer to specific verses; here this stands for *kArikA*-s 3 to 9 in Chapter 3.) Swami Paramarthananda takes the example of a house in order to make the point even more dramatically. He says that when we talk about living in a house, we are actually referring to the space 'inside' the house – clearly we do not live inside the walls or the roof. Yet, when the house is built, what happens is that we simply erect the walls and thereby separate out a part of the space that is already there – the space itself is not created. When the house is later knocked down, the total space is unaffected, still there as it was to begin with. You can see this more clearly if you think of, say, a bottle rather than a house, i.e. something which can be more easily moved. You might think that the bottle 'encloses' a space but, if you move the bottle a meter to the right, the space remains unaffected. Even breaking the bottle does not affect the space. In fact, there is only 'total space', never any actual 'pot space'. Indeed, it is not space which is 'inside the pot' at all but a pot which is effectively 'inside' the space.

Similarly, when we refer to our 'self', what we are actually talking about is the Consciousness that is, as it were, delineated by the 'walls' of the body and mind. The body is certainly 'born', just as the walls of the house are 'built' but, says Gaudapada, just as the space does not actually have anything to do with the walls, neither does Consciousness have anything to do with the body. The body 'marks off' a 'part' of Consciousness and we call this a 'person' but actually, there is only (total) Consciousness and it is not actually affected by the body at all. When it dies, Consciousness continues just as before.

In the metaphor the pot, which seemingly delineates and creates a separate part of space, is called an *upAdhi* – a 'limiting adjunct'. Similarly, the body-mind is the *upAdhi* which apparently gives rise to the individual. Monier-Williams (the standard Sanskrit-English dictionary) gives the definition "*that which is put in the place of another thing, a substitute; anything which may be taken for or has the mere name or appearance of another thing, appearance, phantom, disguise.*"

The mistaken way of viewing the situation accounts for the difficulties found by scientists attempting to 'explain' consciousness. In the case of the pot-space, the space is not actually in the pot at all – it is the pot which is in space. Similarly in the case of the person, Consciousness is not in the brain or body-mind at all – it is the brain that is in Consciousness. (Or, to be more accurate, there is no separate entity called brain or person at all. These are nothing but name and form of the ever-undifferentiated Consciousness.)

These are just some of the radical ideas expounded by Gaudapada and to be addressed later in the book.

So, what has happened to our discussion of OM, you may ask. Well, the point of this seeming diversion into states of consciousness is that the letters of OM *represent* the states of consciousness. The letter 'a' stands for the waker and the waking state; 'u' stands for the dreamer and the dream state; and 'm' stands for the deep-sleeper and the deep sleep state of consciousness. The significance of this, of course, will be entirely lost upon you at the moment but the correspondences, once we begin to analyze them in depth, prove to be awe-inspiring. And it will take us much further than this, into an understanding of the nature of reality itself.

Means of Acquiring Knowledge, with an Emphasis on Inference

Relevance of Scriptures

Advaita is what is called an *Astika* Philosophy, which means that it is one of the Indian philosophies that acknowledge the authority of the scriptures. Many, such as Buddhism, do not and they are called *nAstika*. (The word *Astika* simply means 'there is' or 'there exists'.)

You might find some doubts arising at this announcement. Is Advaita effectively a 'fundamentalist' religion, which is going to point to statements made in some ancient written document for its ideas? Definitely not. The way in which Advaita treats the scriptures is analogous to the way in which we would regard the words of someone for whom we have deep respect and whom we know to be totally trustworthy, with vast experience and knowledge. We trust such a person implicitly. Such trust is called *shraddhA*, usually translated as 'faith', and the words of such a source are given the status of a 'valid means of knowledge' (*pramANa*) in Advaita. This 'valid means of knowledge' is called *shabda*, and is one of the six means recognized by Advaita. It means 'scriptural or verbal testimony'. Swami Chinmayananda says (Ref. 3): *"Vedanta, unlike any other religions in the world, does not allow and accept even a single solid factor which is against reason. Vedanta suffers no blind faith!"*

We never accept scriptural statements absolutely – there is always room for some doubt and questioning until such time as we realize the truth for ourselves. Note that this is in contrast to skepticism. With faith, our natural bias is towards accepting what is said as true; with skepticism, our natural inclination is to think it is probably false. Unfortunately, modern society has inculcated a natural tendency towards the latter.

If you think about it, science often acts in this way for us. We normally rely on our own direct experience as a source for what is actually the case. Direct perception (*pratyakSha*) is our principal means for obtaining knowledge (i.e. through any of the senses, not just sight) and it tells us, for example, that the sun travels around the earth. We see the sun rise and set without any doubt. Yet science tells us that it is not like this; that the earth is in fact rotating and the sunrise is only an appearance. And we all accept those statements. Of course, many learn science at school so that they understand the principles involved. Accordingly, in this example, the claims are supported by knowledge and reason. But what about the Apollo moon landing in 1969? None of us actually witnessed this in person (excepting those astronauts involved, of course). All that we had to go on was some poor quality video footage and the claims of the media. Even scientific understanding may question the likelihood of such an event. For example, one could argue that computers were so rudimentary in the 1960s, that it seems scarcely plausible that they could have been adequate for such a task. Nevertheless, few doubt that a moon landing really did take place.

We should also note that the average person's attitude to scriptures as opposed to, say, science (such as it was) was very different from what it is now. Swami Chinmayananda notes that: *"To them philosophy was a bundle of values-of-life by living which everyone could come to experience the goal of life pointed out by the philosopher; and if a theory had no complete scriptural sanction, they simply did not accept it as an orthodox philosophy."*

T. M. P. Mahadevan explains the relevance of the Vedas as follows (Ref. 60): *"The Upanishads which are the end of Veda (vedAnta) or the crown of* shruti *contain the discoveries made by the ancient seers in the realm of the spirit; they are a record of the declarations made by the sages and are designed to initiate the votary into the secrets of the intuitive or mystic experience. Even as in the sphere of physical science an investigator cannot afford to neglect the researches already made by others in the field, in the realm of the super-physical also a seeker of the truth must take into account the realizations of the sages. The appeal to the authorship of* shruti *means no more and no less."*

In all such cases of 'verbal testimony', we should always subject the information obtained to reason and test it in the light of our own experience. Accordingly, if the sort of statements made on the cover of this book relied only on some ancient texts written in Sanskrit, you could be excused for discarding them without much serious thought. Fortunately, this is not the case. Gaudapada does, indeed, use the scriptures to support his ideas. It would be strange if he did not do so because, in his time, this was how most philosophers operated, deriving arguments from existing scriptural texts to support their own contentions and to refute opponents' views. But Gaudapada also uses rigorous logic to show that his ideas must be accepted, even where they might initially seem to contradict our experience.

This is how Krishnaswamy Iyer summarizes the situation (Ref. 25): *"Vedanta as the science of Reality makes no assertions incompatible with reason or unverifiable by experience. It demands no blind allegiance to any sect or school, and respects no traditions or biblical authority in its search after truth. Its statements are plain and its inferences are drawn from unimpeachable facts within the experience of every human being. To ignore its worth simply because it is ancient, is an aberration of mind, which visits itself with the consequences of its own folly."*

In K2.32, Shankara provides an elaborate commentary which diverges into a discussion on scriptural testimony (*shabda pramANa*). He emphasizes that the scriptures do not tell us about the nature of the Self or reality – since it is attribute-less, this would be impossible anyway. Also, since we *are* the Self, we do not actually need anyone to tell us what the nature is; the Self is, if you like, 'Self-revealing'. The problem is one of ignorance – we do not know who we really are and, to make things worse, we identify with what we are not! Accordingly, the purpose of the scriptures is to remove this ignorance. It does this by revealing what we are not. We are not a doer, enjoyer or even a knower. These are all superimpositions upon the Self, which is what we really are.

When we think that we see the snake, we do know that there is something there; i.e. the existence of something is known. If we had complete absence of knowledge of there being something there, then we would not think there was a snake. What is not known is that this existent thing is a rope. And the particular attributes that are visible trigger our memory to project the imagined snake. We take the attributes of length, coiled, thin etc. from the rope but fail to take the rope-ness; instead, we erroneously superimpose snake-ness. When the light of the torch shines on it, the fact that it is a rope is revealed.

Similarly, the *Atman* is partly known to us – we know that we exist! We take the 'as-though-attributes' of Existence and Consciousness but miss the unlimited-ness. We do not know that we are this *Atman* – the unlimited, non-dual *brahman* – and instead we superimpose imagined attributes of being subject to birth and death, happiness and misery, and so on. We imagine that we are the limited body-mind doomed to a 'nasty, brutish and short' life.

So, in the claim 'I am a *<enter an adjective of your choice>*

person', the 'I am' part is true, while the '<xxx> person' part is false. We already know that 'I am', so we do not need any scriptures to explain this to us. What the scriptures do is to convince us that the rest of the sentence, whatever it might be, is false. Hence the famous quotation from the Brihadaranyaka Upanishad: *'neti, neti'* – 'not this, not this'. The scriptures are the torch that we shine onto our misconceptions. Once all the erroneous superimpositions have been removed, the substrate reality is revealed.

Once we have realized the truth for ourselves, all scriptures become redundant. Mahadevan (Ref. 60) continues: *"The knowledge that is revealed by Scripture must become a matter of experience; only then revelation would have fulfilled its mission. And for one who has realized the integral experience, there is no need to depend upon any external authority in the form of* shruti *or to subscribe to a formal dogma. His wisdom is self-certifying and self-revealed. To him the Vedas are no Vedas."* (It should be noted that the word 'experience' here should not be understood in its usual sense but in the sense of 'directly realized', *anubhava*.

Vedantic Inference
The six means of acquiring knowledge, then, are as follows:

- direct perception (*pratyakSha*);
- verbal authority or evidence (*shabda*);
- inference (*anumAna*);
- comparison or analogy (*upamAna*);
- non-apprehension (*anupalabdhi*);
- postulation or supposition (*arthApatti*).

We will only be interested in the first three of these in this text. The first two have already been mentioned and it is now necessary to provide some details about inference, since this logical tool is used to great effect by Gaudapada.

Inference is a very important tool in the philosophy of Advaita, precisely because of the limitations of direct perception. We are, after all, trying to learn about the nature of the Self and reality, neither of which is amenable to direct perception (I use the word 'neither' at this juncture but it will eventually be seen that they are two names for the same 'thing'). All of our senses are 'turned outwards', as the Upanishad says. They give us information about the world (which includes our body) but can tell us nothing about ourselves, who it is who operates these senses. Just as, however good our sense of sight might be, we still need a mirror in order to see our face, so also we need some sort of mirror in order to find out about ourselves. The scriptures function as this mirror.

We cannot make an inference unless we have gained some prior knowledge from direct perception. We can suppose something to be the case, indulge in speculation or imagination, but none of these will give rise to knowledge. The classical example used in the scriptures to describe the process of inference is that of seeing smoke on a distant hill. We are used to seeing, in the kitchen for example, that when smoke arises it means that the pan has caught fire. We can therefore apply the analogy and infer that there must be a fire on the hill.

The formal logic is as follows:

- There is a proposition (*pratij~nA*), that there is a fire on the hill.
- There is a reason (*hetu*) for making this statement, namely that one can see smoke on the hill.
- We have a prior example (*udAharaNa* or *dRRiShTAnta*), that in the kitchen, where there is smoke there is also invariably found to be fire.
- The effective subject of the discussion (*pakSha*) is the hill.
- The thing that is to be inferred or deduced (called the *sAdhya*) is whether it is on fire or not.

The subject of the discussion has to be something that is already known about – i.e. available from direct perception (*pratyakSha*) – otherwise we would not be able to talk meaningfully about it. Conversely, the fire in this example must *not* be perceptible – otherwise there would be nothing to infer. Finally, the justification (*hetu*) for making the inference – the smoke on the hill – must also be perceptible (and must relate to the hill in question!) or we would not be able to make the inference. The object of the exercise is to prove the existence of the invisible part (the fire) by inference, based upon the similar example of the kitchen (where all of the elements are visible), together with the visible smoke on the hill.

What effectively enables us to make the inference in this example is the knowledge we have from previous direct perception that smoke is invariably accompanied by fire. This is called the *vyApti*, which means the "inseparable presence of one thing in another," "invariable concomitance" or effectively "a universal rule." The *vyApti* has to be proved through direct perception, ideally over many instances. Once this has been done it can be treated as a rule and thereafter we can use it to make inferences in similar situations.

There are two types of inference used in Advaita. There is what might be called scientific reasoning, as was described earlier. Here, we make direct observations using our perceptions and then extrapolate or make inferences in a similar situation where we cannot use our perceptions directly. We can call this scientific inference (Indian logic uses the term *laukika anumAna*, where *laukika* means 'worldly, everyday, common' [*loka* is the earth or world]). Unfortunately, when it comes to the nature of the Self (*Atman*), worldly observations cannot be used to collect data. The only valid source for the data is the scriptures (*shAstra*). Therefore, philosophers tend to make lots of references to quotations in the various *upaniShad-s* and inferences are then made from these. This is called scriptural inference (*shAstrIya anumAna*).

When encountered in the scriptures, and as used by Gaudapada in this work, we do not usually find the detailed breakdown as described above. Instead, the inference is usually abbreviated to, for example, 'wherever there is smoke, there is invariably fire' (*yatrayatra dhUma, tatratatra agni*). The example that prompts us to make the inference is omitted; i.e. it is assumed that we are all familiar with this – hence the justification.

Incidentally, it is worth noting that scriptural texts do tend to be on the terse side. There is good reason for this: they were not originally written, but passed from teacher to disciple by spoken word only – the disciple learned them by heart. Accordingly, verbosity had to be assiduously avoided! The intention was rather to ensure that the disciple remembered all the key points. The extended explanation would then follow as a result of deep understanding, also learned from one's teacher. This procedure was developed almost as an art form in the use of sutras. A *sUtra* is an especially abbreviated verse in which the fewest possible words are used to convey the message. *sUtra*-s function by deriving context, and even words, from earlier sutras in the same work so that very great skill was needed, firstly to write them, and later to understand them! And this emphasizes why it is so important for a seeker to have a skilled teacher who has thorough understanding of the scriptures and the means whereby to explain them. Such a teacher has to be able to 'fill in the missing words' appropriately and pick up on the sparsest references.

Note that philosophers do also use scientific inference for refuting the arguments of those other schools of philosophy which do not accept the authority of the scriptures, since that is the logic which they themselves use. Also, just as it is not possible to use scientific reasoning to discuss the self and reality, it is also not possible to use it to refute statements made in the scriptures themselves. It simply does not apply when talking about that which lies beyond the reach of science.

In the case of scientific inference, the observations upon which the conclusions are based are usually taken as read; it is only the conclusions that may be wrong. This is obviously essential, otherwise the procedure would be pointless and new knowledge would never be gained. Similarly, in order for a scriptural inference to be valid, we must have accepted that the initial premises are true, i.e. we must have accepted the authority of the scriptures.

You now have sufficient background to enable the investigation into OM and the secrets of life to begin!

Cover Image

Finally, you may have been wondering about the image on the cover of this book (and when I was going to tell you what it is)! This hand gesture is called *chin mudrA*, and is associated with a teacher called Dakshinamurti. But that is all I am going to say at present, because you will only really appreciate how it summarizes the entire book, once you have actually read it!

What the Mandukya Upanishad is About

As already noted, the Upanishad itself consists of only 12 mantras. Because it is fundamental, I do translate and analyze this word by word. This involves exposure to lots of Sanskrit and scriptural references, however, and not every reader will want to go into it in this depth. Accordingly, this is 'relegated' to Appendix 1 although of course, since it is effectively the principal subject matter of the book, you really ought to read it! In the main body of the book, I am dealing with the material on a topic basis. So, here, I will first provide just a brief summary of the Upanishad so that there is no doubt as to the essential matter being considered by Gaudapada.

The Upanishad conducts two consecutive investigations – the first into the nature of the Self and the second into the mantra OM as a powerful metaphor for focusing the mind to consider this nature. By utilizing its symbolism, and meditating upon the mantra, the manifestations of the Self as well as its true nature may be more easily understood.

We are told that OM is everything (literally), another name for which is 'brahman'. And we are also told that our own, real 'self' is brahman. So these enquiries into OM and into our Self are necessarily also an enquiry into everything. Knowledge of our Self is the same as knowledge of the nature of reality.

Then it is said that there are actually four aspects to, or ways of looking at, our essential nature. Our direct experience of the Self is through its three manifest 'states of consciousness' – waking, dreaming and deep-sleep. But the Upanishad tells us that the reality of the Self is that which is 'beyond' all of these and is only 'made manifest' in the states, as both that which knows and that which is known.

The word 'beyond', above, is in quotation marks because, although this is how it is often spoken of, the metaphor is misleading. Each state is a manifestation of *brahman-turIya* and this means that the reality of each state *is brahman-turIya*. We do not have to look 'beyond' in order to find this mysterious entity! Swami Paramarthananda uses the expression 'in and through' – "turIya *is in and through the states of consciousness*". But even this is not really correct, implying as it does that there is something else (as though *turIya* might be a liquid that is 'soaked up' by the 'sponge' of each state of consciousness). Whichever state we happen to be in, there is really only *turIya*.

Of course, you will say, I am a waker now, and I will be a dreamer when I go to sleep. But how could I conceivably *be* the waking world; the earth and stars; and, by implication, all of the other beings in the universe, animal and vegetable? It is patently ridiculous! "For a start", you might say: "my body is rather more complex than the chair on which I am sitting and my brain is animated by consciousness."

There is another well-known metaphor in this teaching tradition which says that oceans and waves are not essentially different – both are in fact nothing but water. A wave is name and form of water; an ocean is another name and form of water. We could put this differently and say that water manifesting as the thing that laps against the beach or carries surfers is called a 'wave', while water that manifests as the enormous mass of (seemingly) blue stuff between continents is called an 'ocean'. But there is no actual substance called 'wave', and there is no actual substance called 'ocean'. The only real material is water. Using the terms of Advaita, we can say that the wave and the ocean are *mithyA*, while the water is (relatively speaking) *satyam*. This metaphor is akin to the ring-bangle-necklace and gold metaphor discussed earlier.

And so, to complete the analogy, we could say that I, the individual body-mind, am equivalent to the wave, while the material universe (including all other persons) is equivalent to the ocean. But both these are *mithyA*; they have no substance of their own. In reality, both are Consciousness, the only *satyam*. And I am That.

If you really believe that, you can stop reading this book now; you do not need it! I am going to assume, however, that you don't believe a word of it – but nevertheless may be a little intrigued. In which case, read on!

The first mantra states that OM is everything (*sarvaM*). Therefore, enquiry into it is enquiry into everything. Upon concluding the enquiry, the truth of OM will be the truth of everything. This, in a nutshell, is why this Upanishad is so important!

[It is worth pointing out now, so as to avoid potential confusion later, that we have to be very careful in our use of the word 'I'. Our normal use of the word (in fact, most people's *only* use of the word) refers to the *person* who is speaking the word. And that person almost certainly thinks of him or herself as his/her body and mind. If they are religious, they may also think there is a 'soul', in which case it will be that which is actually 'I'. (Although they might be hard pressed to say what they mean by 'soul'!)

Advaita, however, shows us that 'who-we-really-are' is not the body or mind. There is only Consciousness. This is 'reflected' in the individual's mind and gives the illusion of separate existence through identification with body and mind. This idea was presented through the 'pot-space' metaphor earlier (and is explained in detail in Appendix 3).

Accordingly, we have to consider which meaning of 'I' we are using in any given sentence. In everyday usage, it will be the person; e.g. 'I went to the shop' means that I-the-mind directed I-the-body and I-the-person traveled to the shop. When a sentence such as 'I am That' is encountered, the meaning will be the 'real' I, *Atman* – I-the *Atman* am *brahman*.]

States of consciousness

(MU2) The second mantra of the Upanishad tells us that every-thing is *brahman*. *brahman* is the name given by Advaita to the non-dual, attribute-less reality. The Sanskrit for 'attribute' is *guNa*, so that 'without' attributes is *nirguNa*. The empirical world, of course, seems entirely dualistic – I am separate from you and from all of the objects that make up the universe. As we shall see, this is only how things *appear*, not how they really *are*. Nevertheless, Advaita recognizes this appearance as valid from the empirical standpoint and this is where the concept of creation has meaning. And, at this level, it refers to this same *brahman* as appearing to have attributes; i.e. as 'with' *guNa* or *saguNa*. And this *saguNa brahman* has its own name – *Ishvara*, which we in the West can call 'God', the Creator and the maintainer of the laws of that creation.

[Note that the scriptures do not generally differentiate between *nirguNa brahman* and *saguNa Ishvara*, since in reality there are not two. Practically speaking, for the sake of teaching, it is useful to do so. In this book, I will endeavor always to differ-entiate and the convention will be simply to use the word *brahman* for the *nirguNa*, eternal, attribute-less Consciousness and the word *Ishvara* for the *saguNa*, attributed, 'worldly' form.]

And this mantra goes on to say that this Self is *brahman*. This follows of course, if everything is *brahman*, but it needs reinforcement, since it is most unlikely that I will think that I am God unless my mind is somewhat disturbed! It also follows that the Self is everything so that, by understanding the Self, I will also come to understand everything. (Note that this does not mean being able to understand quantum mechanics or speak Mandarin!)

Finally, it states that this Self has four aspects. And this is the introduction to the examination of the states of consciousness. The Upanishad regards this as being an investigation into the nature of the Self – Self-enquiry or *Atma vichAra*. This is reasonable because, as already noted, the three states of consciousness cover all of our experience. Other conditions such as hallucinations, trance and so on can be absorbed into these three (a discussion of this is given in Appendix 2). We will come to this mysterious 'fourth' aspect later!

Modern Western philosophy, like Advaita philosophy, recognizes three states (*avasthA-s*) of consciousness – waking, dreaming and deep sleep – and the general description of these states is similar in both. There is, however, a very fundamental difference in the treatment of these.

Essentially, Western philosophy takes its stand firmly in the waking state – this, for the typical person, is the fundamental reality. The world, objects, people, time and space are self-evidently real. Although we may not know the reasons for, or the precise mechanisms of dreams, we believe that they are in some way a product of the mind (when it is no longer under 'our' control). Dreams are – equally self-evidently – 'unreal'. They may provide us with diversion, excitement or fear but, when we awake, they are usually forgotten as being of no further interest. Similarly, the deep-sleep state is regarded as another mind-mechanism – one for ensuring that the brain, as well as the body, is rested and made ready for the following day's activities.

Thus, when Western philosophers and scientists consider such topics as 'consciousness', they are primarily concerned with the waking state and historically have given little thought to the other states. This, according to Advaita, means that they can never reach any valid conclusions – they are only looking at a third of the overall picture. If you want the complete picture, it is necessary to take account of all of the data. (In fact, as we will see, even when we take into account all these three states, we are still missing the truth!)

And it is much worse than this. When other philosophers and scientists talk about dreams, for example, everything is considered from the vantage point of the waking state. But the waker does not have dreams (by definition, since he must be awake)! If we call the 'I' that we usually take ourselves to be the 'ego', as modern psychology tends to do ever since Freud, then we really ought to qualify this as the 'waker ego'. The waker ego does not dream – it is the 'dreamer ego' that dreams!

You may need to think about this for a minute. Is it not the case that the nature of the person that you think yourself to be in your dreams can be quite different from your 'real' (i.e. waking) nature? Certainly what you do, where you go, whom you meet etc. can be very different. It is, put simply, a different life altogether, even if some of the characters may appear in both.

And we might argue, if we have not given the subject much thought, that dreams are unreal because only I am aware of the dream world, whereas the waking world is real because lots of others can verify my experience. But this proves nothing. In the dream, also, all of the other dream people will verify that the dream world is real and none of them (and this usually includes myself) knows anything about any other 'waking' world.

This is one of the main themes that Gaudapada addresses and there are paradoxes to be investigated and revelations to be made on the subject later in the book. But, just as an example, ask yourself this question: If the dreams that you had each night continued from where they left off the night before, how would you be able to differentiate dreaming from waking? If you think about it, you may be able to come up with some valid reasons (if not, Gaudapada will give you some later) but you must also realize that these reasons are also from the standpoint of the waking ego!

Advaita says quite clearly that, if you want to understand the nature of consciousness, you must take into account all three states so, before embarking upon our examination of the Mandukya Upanishad and Gaudapada's analysis, we must have an initial look at these states in more detail.

The individual waker is called *vishva* or *vaishvAnara* in

Sanskrit. The former is more common and used by Gaudapada but the latter is used in the Upanishad. Note that I qualify the waker with the word 'individual'. This is because Advaita also uses a similar concept at the universal or 'macrocosmic' level. This will be explained in a moment. The waker (*vishva*) looks out into, and functions at the level of, the gross world (which is called *jagat*). The waking state of consciousness itself is called *jAgrat*, just to add a minor possibility for confusion! The waker is who we normally take ourselves to be. We look to the world for our 'meaning', supposedly to find happiness in the gross objects, people and activities therein.

The individual dreamer is called *taijasa* and the dream state itself *svapna*. Dreams 'happen' in the subtle world rather than the gross, material world of the waker. According to the waker, this subtle world is inside the mind, perhaps 'replaying' or 'assimilating' experiences that happened in the waker's past.

Finally, the deep-sleeper is called *prAj~na* and the deep-sleep state *suShupti*. Deep sleep is characterized by our apparently not knowing anything at all. The typical Westerner believes that we are unconscious during sleep; Advaita denies this. Consciousness is always present (since there is only Consciousness)! It is the senses and mind that are not available in deep sleep. And Consciousness needs the mind in order to be 'aware'. It is analogous to light in this respect. If you were in space, looking away from the sun so that there were no objects to reflect the sun's light, you would be unaware of that light. Similarly, it is the presence of objects, thoughts and feelings etc. that 'reflect' Consciousness.

Our experience takes place on three different planes of consciousness. We could say that there are three different 'experiencers'. In the waking state, we are the waker experiencer. When we are asleep, there are two different states of experience: the dream state, in which we are the dreamer; and the deep sleep state, in which we are the deep sleeper.

In each of these states, there is an experiencer (*pramAtRRi* or *pramAtA*), an experience (*anubhava*), and something which is experienced (*prameya*). The experiencer is the individual waker, dreamer or deep-sleeper; the experienced object is everything else in the related state. Accordingly, we also have to recognize what we might call three objective 'universes' – the 'objects-of-experience' in each of the three states.

These 'experiencing egos' could be thought of as parts that we play in different movies; I play the part of a waker, a dreamer and a deep-sleeper. But, says the Upanishad, I am not actually any of these; the reality is that I am the actor playing these roles.

In each of the three section headings below, the first Sanskrit term is the experiencing 'individual' for the related state and the second term is the experienced 'universe'. For the detailed interpretations and explanations of these, terms as far as the Upanishad is concerned, see Appendix 1 – I will not say much about the macrocosmic (universal) element here.

The Waking State – *vishva* and *virAT*

The first of these 'universes' is the physical world of our waking experience. It is dealt with first, and actually called 'the first' by the Upanishad, because knowledge about the other states depends upon it. Most Westerners believe this world to be objectively real, existing independently of any physical observer. In it, I can be said to be 'identified' with my physical body with its mind and intellect etc. I believe I *am* that body. Of course, a little thought will expose the difficulties with such an idea. My own body now, having been around for quite a few decades, does not look remotely like the one that emerged from my mother's womb and, indeed, has few cells in common with that! And my ideas, powers of reasoning, ability to interpret my environment etc. have all changed drastically over the years. Which body and mind, precisely, is the one that I am?

The first part of the Upanishad, then is addressing the

question of who this Self really is. Notice that I have given the word 'Self' an initial capital letter. If you recall, this is to indicate that I am talking about 'who-we-really-are' as opposed to the more colloquial usage.

This is also one of those occasions in which we need to utilize the correct Sanskrit term, since it is so fundamental. The word for Self with a capital S, or Consciousness with a capital C, is *Atman*, when referring to ourselves and *brahman* (as introduced in the section on 'Reality and Unreality') when referring to the impersonal Absolute. Advaita tells us that we are not the body or mind but the essential Consciousness without which both body and mind would be inert. This is the *Atman*. And this *Atman* is the same as *brahman*, of course, since there are not two things.

So, the tendency is for us to believe we are the waker – *vishva* – with its gross, physical body. And we experience a separate, objective, gross, physical universe, called *virAT* in Sanskrit. My mind is 'turned outward' to perceive and act in this physical world.

The Upanishad uses the word *vaishvAnara* instead of *vishva*. The word *vishva* literally means 'everyone, the whole universe, everywhere' and so on. It is in its philosophical sense that it refers to the faculty which perceives the waking body and world, i.e. the waker. *nara* means 'man' or 'person'; so the word *vaishvAnara* is really just emphasizing the fact that the waking world is seen by everyone alike, as opposed to the dream world which is private to the dreamer. It is effectively the collective name for all human beings in the gross world, all pursuing the objects in that world for their pleasure. (Note that there is understandable confusion over the use of terminology here. I have simplified the issues in this paragraph and look at them in more detail in the translation and commentary in Appendix 1.)

It is the 'first' of the four quarters or aspects because it is the starting point, as it were, for the others. We go from waking into sleep and dream and it is only in the waking state that we can seek an end to our self-ignorance and attain enlightenment (which is simply clear Self-knowledge). It is as a result of our identification of the Self with the body and mind that we associate the material objects of the world with our happiness and fulfillment. We go after things because we mistakenly assume that they will satisfy our desires. In fact, Self-knowledge entails realization of the truth of the limitlessness of our nature.

Furthermore, the waker knows that he dreams and sleeps (or at least thinks that he knows this!), whereas the dreamer and deep-sleeper are unaware of the other two states. The dreamer thinks that he or she *is* awake and the deep-sleeper does not think anything.

In the waking state, I am Consciousness associated with the gross physical body, using the senses and mechanics of that body to interact with, and enjoy (or not) the external world.

There is apparently myself, the knower, and a 'world out there' – the known (which also includes this body that I see and the thoughts and emotions which arise in the mind). But it is instructive to ask ourselves about the existence of this 'world out there'. Does it really exist separate from me, the knower?

In order for us to be able to say that something 'exists', that thing has to be, at some time or other, to at least one conscious entity, an object of knowledge acquired by way of a valid *pramANa*. After all, if X is never an object of knowledge to anyone at any time, ever, how could anyone claim that X 'existed'? Effectively, there can only ever be an 'object of knowledge' if there is a 'knower' to know it. I.e. the existence of an object depends upon there being a knower. Having a 'dependent' existence, not existing in its own right, is how we defined the term *mithyA*, earlier. (Note that there is no intimation at this point of the philosophy of Idealism, which says that there are no external objects at all, and that everything is only 'in our mind'. But there will be more on this later, since some commentators believe that Gaudapada was an Idealist.)

In order for there to be a 'knower' in the first place, I (as Consciousness) have to choose to know something and decide to operate a *pramANa*. I might direct one of my (waking) senses outwards (in the case of the gross world) or I might use my mind to draw inferential conclusions but, whichever is the case, it is Consciousness which is the prime mover, as it were. In the case of dreaming, the same reasoning applies, except that the awareness is directed inwards (using dream senses) towards the dream world created in the mind. In both cases, a 'knower' comes into existence.

In the deep-sleep state, we have to take this one step further because, not only is there neither an objective external world nor an objective internal world, but neither is there a 'knower'. There are no deep-sleep *pramANa*-s and no choice on the part of Consciousness. Both the senses (gross or subtle) and the mind are inoperative; they are said to be 'resolved'. Consequently, no 'knower' comes into existence and I have to conclude that the knower is not an independent entity either. A 'dream knower' springs into existence when we move from deep sleep into dream, and a 'waker knower' springs into existence when we move from deep sleep into the waking state.

It follows that both knower and known are dependent upon Consciousness alone, i.e. the *Atman*. And this dependent reality means that the knower is also *mithyA*. To put this the other way round, I (Consciousness) am appearing as both the knower and the known, both of which are only *mithyA* names and forms of Consciousness.

There is thus only *Atman-brahman* or the 'Consciousness Principle', at all times. In the waking state, I (this 'Consciousness Principle') effectively divide myself into a waker knower and the gross, objective universe. In the dream state, I (this 'Consciousness Principle') effectively divide myself into a dream knower and the subtle, objective world of the dream. In the deep-sleep state, I (this 'Consciousness Principle') effectively divide myself up into a deep-sleep knower and a deep-sleep known universe, both of which are unmanifest but contain the potentiality for both gross and subtle knowers and worlds, respectively. These are all *mithyA*. Who-I-really-am is the non-dual Consciousness, the only *satyam*, called in this Upanishad *turIya*. (This line of reasoning is presented by Swami Paramarthananda in Ref. 5.)

The Dream State – *taijasa* and *hiraNyagarbha*

The common view of the dream state is that it is much inferior to the waking state. The former is unreal, we might say, whereas the latter is real. "It was only a dream", we say, usually with relief, occasionally with disappointment. What we never admit is that, when we make such a statement, we are usually in the waking state. It is the waker who disparages the dream state. (Conceivably, of course, we could make such a pronouncement in a dream, speaking of what was believed to be a [secondary] dream. But, at that time, we would still believe ourselves to be awake.)

The Upanishad does not agree with this view. The word used for the dreamer – *taijasa* – means 'consisting of light'. The dreamer creates the dream world entirely out of the content of his or her own mind. Everything is included, from the body of the dreamer and all of the other characters, the opinions and objectives in the dreamer's mind, and the world inhabited by the dreamer, complete with mountains and elephants, and its own time and space. Everything seems at least as real as the waking world. Rarely do we pause to wonder at this incredible achievement! Indeed, the dream state can certainly be considered to be superior to waking, being more subtle than the gross world of matter in the same way that we consider the mind to be superior to the body. People can manage without limbs and senses but no one can survive in the waking state without a brain and mind.

The dreamer interacts with the dream world through dream sense organs and dream organs of action in the same manner as does the waking ego. The dreamer ego appears to act autonomously, without any interference or even awareness on the part of the usual waking ego (lucid dreams apart). Although everything must seemingly come out of my own (i.e. waking) mind, the dreamer-I may not even act in a manner which is at all 'normal'; e.g. typical waking inhibitions or preferences may not function. The dreamer-I may seem to be an entirely different person. Nevertheless, says Shankara, we remain under the influence of the same desires and fears and simply rework the impressions previously acquired from the waking state.

The Deep-Sleep State – *prAj~na* and *antaryAmin* (*Ishvara*)

Ask most people about their view of deep sleep and they will almost certainly tell you that it is a state of unconsciousness, in which body and mind are resting and recuperating, in readiness for the next period of waking consciousness. It is characterized by a change in the pattern of brain waves from the higher frequency Beta (14 – 21 cycles/sec) to the much slower Theta and Delta (0.5 – 7 cycles/sec). And, although we would undoubtedly acknowledge the importance of sleep, and concede that we cannot survive without it, we probably think that it is the least 'important' of the three states. We might justify this belief by saying that the most important aspect – the sense of 'I' – is not there. In the terms that we are now using, you might want to say that consciousness is absent.

Needless to say, Advaita does not agree with this assessment! In fact, this state is the most important because the delusions of the other two states are absent and Consciousness does not make the mistake of believing that there is a separate world 'out there', whether it be what we take to be the 'real' waking world or the 'made up' dream world. Those worlds are temporarily

49

unavailable so that we exist in what is effectively a non-dual state. We are not 'unconscious' at all but, as T.S. Eliot puts it in 'The Four Quartets', 'conscious but conscious of nothing'. (He is actually speaking of the anesthetized mind, but deep-sleep is similar.)

Douglas Fox argues this way (Ref. 9): "*This is not to be thought of as an absence of consciousness for, if it were, consciousness would never return (on the premise that what does not at any time exist cannot begin to do so). Consciousness of objects* does *return and this proves that some mode of consciousness, the permanent substratum of all others, was present all the time.*"

It is very likely that you will object to this idea. You will argue that you are not aware of anything in deep sleep. Indeed, you might say, any reference to that state is by inference only, after you awake. 'I feel refreshed; therefore I must have had a good period of deep sleep – but I was unconscious and didn't actually know anything at all'. Krishnaswamy Iyer makes the following observation, however (Ref. 25): "*The objection that in sleep we are not aware of subject or object, and therefore that it is an unconscious state, contradicts itself, for we are aware of not having been aware of anything.*"

All of the senses, together with the mind, are inactive and, as the Upanishad puts it, 'everything is undifferentiated'. But Consciousness is there, simply 'illuminating' nothing. We are aware but there is nothing to be aware of, neither objects, nor thoughts/emotions.

The deep-sleep state has no subject-object division, contrary to the waking and dream states. 'Division' or 'manifoldness' in Sanskrit is *vikalpa*. So the deep-sleep state is 'without division' or *nirvikalpa*, while the other two states are 'with division' or *savikalpa*.

You may recognize the first of these words in the context of *nirvikalpa samAdhi*, the state sought after by adherents of the Yoga philosophy (and also the neo-Vedantins of Vivekananda) as being the end-point of seeking, and equivalent to enlightenment. This is not the case. *nirvikalpa samAdhi* is a state of extremely deep meditation in which unity is experienced. Nevertheless, it is a state with a beginning and an end, so cannot be *mokSha* or liberation. Swami Paramarthananda jokes that it is called *nirvikalpa samAdhi* if you are in a sitting position and sleep if you are lying down! And, if you think about it, they do have to be the same – you cannot have two types of non-duality! The bottom line here is that enlightenment cannot be an experience. We are *already* the non-dual Self; we just don't know it. Accordingly, enlightenment has to be simply Self-knowledge.

[*mokSha* means freedom or liberation, i.e. from *saMsAra*, the eternal cycle of birth and death. It is synonymous with 'enlightenment' or 'Self-realization' in modern parlance, although those words are often misunderstood. The fact is that we are already 'free', in that our real nature is *Atman* or *brahman*. The problem is that we are ignorant of this fact and so have to gain Self-knowledge. This is analogous to realizing that the snake in front of us is actually a rope.]

Deep sleep is certainly the most refreshing of states; effectively a state of 'bliss'. *suShupta* literally means excellent (*su*) sleep (*supta*). In Advaita *brahman*, the non-dual reality, is often described as *sat-chit-Ananda* – Existence, Consciousness and Bliss. 'Blissfulness' is our real nature. In the waking and dream states, we are diverted from this by what we believe to be separate, external objects (which we try to obtain or avoid) and by internal thoughts and feelings (which seem to be beyond my control). These are all absent, in an unmanifest state, during deep sleep, so that the natural condition is unimpeded, as it were. There being no knower-known duality, this is the bliss of non-duality.

Another way of looking at this is that, in both the waking and dream states, we experience hopes and fears, brought about by perceived limitations of our bodies and minds. Happiness occurs whenever our perceived limitations are temporarily removed. For example, when we desire something very much, we feel this as a 'lack'; as something which is required for 'fulfillment'. At the moment that we attain the desired object, this lack disappears and we feel whole. This wholeness is experienced as happiness and may last for some time – but is inevitably lost eventually. Attaining objects, status etc. cannot ever affect who we really are (which is already whole and unlimited).

In deep sleep, all perceived limitations are removed because we are unaware of anything 'out there'. Accordingly, we experience unalloyed happiness (bliss). Blissful though this is, it is the bliss of ignorance. There is no knowledge here of our true nature. Although there is no misperception of a separate universe or an unreal dream world, both are effectively present in unmanifest form ready to spring forth on moving to the waking or dream state. It is a temporary state only. Swami Paramarthananda in his commentary on the *tattva bodha* (Ref. 64) compares the deep-sleep state to the actors' 'Green Room'. This is where they go off-stage when they are temporarily not playing any role but they are ready to go back on stage as soon as they are called.

This 'potential' form – as though containing the material for waking and dream states – is why the deep-sleep state is also referred to as the 'causal' state. The 'potential' refers to both subject and object. Whereas in both the waking and the dream states there is a clear 'ego' and an apparent 'external world', in the deep-sleep state there is neither. Both knower and known are unmanifest.

In order that a universe should come into existence, there are two causal elements required: material for the creation and the knowledge and skills to bring it about. (Material cause is *upAdAna kAraNa* and intelligent cause is *nimitta kAraNa*.) The interim explanation for this is that the lord, *Ishvara*, carries out both of these functions. (Note the word 'interim'; the topic will be discussed in more detail later.)

Ishvara is described by the Upanishad as being omniscient (*sarvaj~na*) (i.e. the intelligent cause) and the source of everything (i.e. the material cause). He is Himself the substance of the creation and the universe 'emerges' out of Him and returns to Him at the end of a cycle. (The scriptural teaching is that creation is cyclical, with 'big bangs' and 'big crunches' occurring successively for eternity. Creation is called *sRRiShTi* and the 'crunch' is called *pralaya*.) But note that the universe is not a 'part' of *Ishvara*; nor does it ever become separate from Him. *Ishvara* 'becomes' the world in the same way that gold 'becomes' a ring or a bracelet. The ring and bracelet are always nothing but gold, and the gold itself has not undergone any real change.

[Note that I will tend to use 'He' or 'Him' as the pronoun for *Ishvara* when speaking of 'god-like' properties and 'it' when the word is used in a more general sense. In Hinduism, there are very many gods (*deva-s*) but *Ishvara* is the 'worldly aspect' of *brahman*. Even gods must abide by the rules of creation, whereas *Ishvara* makes and governs those laws. *brahman*, of course, cannot be regarded as a god; there is *only brahman*.]

Ishvara, then, is the material cause of the whole universe. This is in the same way that we might consider a lump of clay to be the potential form for all vessels made of clay. Clay can be thought of as having all the forms in an unmanifest state.

Summary of the Three States

(K1.3 – K1.4) Gaudapada briefly summarizes the three states in these *kArikA*-s. The waker experiences the objects in the gross external world and gains his or her satisfaction from these. The dreamer experiences the subtle, internal world, generated from memory and desires and is satisfied by these. (K4.87) Both states are dualistic. In the waking state, there is perception of actual objects. In the dream state, although there is still perception, the objects are only ideas in the mind. (In this verse from the fourth chapter, Gaudapada uses the term *laukika*, meaning 'worldly', or 'common to all beings', for the waking state. And he uses the term *shuddha laukika* – pure worldly, meaning without objects – for the dream state. These are Buddhist terms.)

The deep sleeper has no experience at all and is blissfully ignorant. The first two are associated with duality and its corresponding pleasures and pain, whilst the third is a non-dual state and is characterized by bliss (*Ananda*) (and ignorance). Shankara comments tersely that these *kArikA*-s have already been explained (under MU3-5).

(K4.88) The deep-sleep state has no contact with external objects (i.e. gross, waking world) nor with any ideas of objects (i.e. subtle, dream world). There is no empirical experience of any kind. Gaudapada calls it *lokottara* in this verse, meaning 'beyond worldly experience' – effectively without either subject or object. But this is the 'causal' state being, as Shankara puts it, the 'seed of all future activity'.

(K4.89) It is through analysis of the three states that we come to know the *turIya Atman* – the Consciousness that is the substratum of all. We investigate the states successively, as was shown by the Upanishad's metaphor of a-u-m. First we know the waker and the objects of the gross universe. In dream, both these are effectively 'merged' and we experience ourselves as the dreamer in a world manufactured by the mind and its *vAsanA*-s (the tendencies we have to act in one way rather than another in a given situation – this concept is explained further when we look at the theory of *karma*). This subtle universe in turn is 'merged' into the deep-sleep state where there is neither knower nor known; only the peace and stillness associated with total ignorance.

I am the 'knower' of all three states, which are 'known'. When we realize the truth of the non-dual Consciousness, *turIya*, that is the basis of all three states, we know that 'I am *Atman*; I am everything'. I become 'all-knowing', not in the sense of knowledge of

mundane *mithyA* objects and concepts, but in the sense of understanding the reality that underlies all appearance. This is enlightenment.

(K1.5) Gaudapada states that the person who knows that all
three experiencers and their objects of experience are really one
satyam (*turIya*) is not affected by anything, even though the
experiences continue. Shankara gives the example of fire, whose
essential nature is heat. This nature is unaffected by fire
consuming its objects, such as wood. Similarly, the knower is
unaffected even when enjoying the objects of experience.

And he adds later in K1.22 that, one who truly understands
that it is *turIya* that is the reality behind the three states is a great
sage and is revered by all human beings.

The 'Fourth' – *turIya*

Many people who know a little about Advaita, but who have not
studied it from the traditional standpoint, have a serious miscon-
ception about *turIya*. They naturally assume that, because its
literal meaning is 'fourth', it must be another state like dream
and deep-sleep. They think that they are supposed to be looking
for a special experience if they are to achieve enlightenment. It is
also likely that they will have read or heard material to support
this viewpoint.

After all, they might argue, the waker (*vishva*) is found in the
waking state (*jAgrat*), the dreamer (*taijasa*) is found in the dream
state (*svapna*) and the deep-sleeper (*prAj~na*) is found in the
deep-sleep state (*suShupti*). Therefore, enlightenment must be
found in the *turIya* 'state'. But this is not how it is.

Both the Yoga philosophy and neo-Vedanta (the teaching
propagated by Vivekananda) imply this. And both speak of
samAdhi as being the key to this. In particular, *nirvikalpa samAdhi*
is thought to be a direct experience of the Self. But of course the
Self is not an experience. Who would be experiencing it? And
experiences have a beginning and an end so that, if this were

enlightenment, it would only be temporary.

So, if this 'fourth' is not a state, then what is it? I can say, while I am awake, that 'I am a waker' and no one (who is also awake) would be likely to dispute this. Also in the waking state, I can imagine myself saying in the dream state that 'I am a dreamer'. But we are already beginning to make mistakes. In the dream state, we do not believe that we are dreaming and, assuming that the topic arose, we would actually still say 'I am a waker'. (Note that there is an exception to this, which I have not found discussed anywhere in the Advaitic literature. That is so-called 'lucid dreaming' and it is discussed briefly in Appendix 2.) In the deep-sleep state, we would all agree that I would not say anything at all.

Accordingly, although I refer to myself as 'I' throughout all of these changing states, we have to concede that the person that I consider myself to be – namely the one who is present in the waking state and able to read this book and think about such things – is not actually present in either the dream or deep-sleep states. So, if I believe that I am a 'continuous' entity who 'experiences' being awake and dreaming, and sometimes goes into deep-sleep, then I have to ask the question: who am I, actually?

The gold ring metaphor continues to be invaluable in discussing this. We can re-form a lump of gold into a bangle, chain or ring. The name and form may change but the gold remains present throughout all of the instantiations. The gold is not something separate.

Similarly, we have the three states of experience. These do not coexist: the waker goes away and is replaced by a dreamer. The dreamer goes away to be replaced by a deep-sleeper. *turīya* is not any one of these, yet it is there throughout all of the instantiations. We could say that *turīya* is transcendent – beyond or other than the three states; and immanent – intrinsic to each of the three states. Gaudapada says (K1.1) that "It is one only (*eka eva*) who is known in these three states." It is the same entity, which we think of as 'I', that can be thought of in three different ways; c.f. the actor playing three different roles.

The word 'fourth' is used, of course, precisely because of the other 'three' states. This mantra implies that (ignorant) people call it 'fourth' because they consider that the other states are real when, in fact, they are *mithyA*.

Another name for *turIya* is *brahman*. So, I am *brahman*. In the second mantra of the Upanishad, we have this very statement, one of the four highlighted 'great statements' (*mahAvAkya*-s) from the Upanishads: *AyamAtmA brahma* – this *Atman* is *brahman*.

To return to the metaphor, we know that bangle, chain and ring are simply name and form of gold; their 'substantial reality' is gold; they themselves are *mithyA*. The gold is not *mithyA*; it is the reality (*satyam*) of each of the different forms.

Similarly, we can say that *turIya* is the substantial reality of the three states of waking, dream and deep-sleep, which are themselves *mithyA*. It is not itself a fourth state but the one *satyam* – absolute reality. It is the 'taking on of name and form' that manifests as the three states. But the essential reality is non-dual.

Absolute Reality (*brahman* or *turIya*) cannot be 'described'. In order for something new to be 'describable' at all, it has to satisfy one or more of five conditions:

- It can be available for direct *perception* via at least one of the senses. Then we can give it a name and refer to it.
- It may be a *species* of something with which we are already familiar.
- It can have describable *properties*, such as color.
- It can provide a describable *function*.
- It can have some describable *relationship* with something that we know.

Since *brahman* doesn't have any of these aspects, we cannot talk directly about it. However, that is not to say that we cannot speak of it indirectly. And this is how the scriptures operate.

Some ways in which they manage to achieve this are:

- Speaking of *brahman* as the 'witness' is analogous to saying that the sky is blue – it is an 'apparent' attribute.
- Speaking of *brahman* as 'existence', 'consciousness' or 'unlimited' (*sat, chit, ananta*). These are 'descriptive' of the essential nature (*svarUpa lakShaNa*) of brahman, to the extent that this is possible.
- Speaking of what *brahman* is not. The example often used is identifying a man by his baldness – the fact that he has no hair.
- Speaking about something else and about *brahman* only by implication. This is what is often referred to as '*neti, neti*', 'not so, not so'. Any attribute would necessarily be limiting, since it would imply the absence of any contrary attribute. When we have finished negating, whatever is left must be *brahman* by implication.

Thus, *brahman* is described by the seventh *mantra* of the Upanishad as *adRRiShTam* – (it is) unseen (this stands for not being accessible to any of the senses); *avyavahAryam* – not amenable to 'worldly' transactions; *agrAhyam* – ungraspable (i.e. inaccessible to the organs of action); *alakShaNam* – without any characteristics; *achintyam* – inconceivable; *avyapadeshyam* – indefinable.

In this Upanishad, then, we are attempting to arrive at an understanding of *turIya*, our true nature, through an examination of those states of consciousness with which we are familiar.

The fact that we are not always a waker, not always a dreamer and not always a sleeper tells us that none of these can be our real nature. Advaita is very clear about the meaning of the word 'real' – it is that which never changes. If a thing, X, changes into something else, Y, then X ceases to be. Therefore X could not have been real. (Other schools of Philosophy in India have different definitions for 'real'.)

Accordingly we have to conclude that waking, dreaming and deep-sleeping are all temporary states, reflecting incidental aspects of our true nature. The waking state is that incidental nature where our mind is temporarily turned outwards to consider the gross world. The dream state is that incidental nature where our mind is temporarily turned inwards to make up a dream world from our memories, desires and fears. And the deep-sleep state is that incidental nature when the mind and senses are temporarily resolved and we are aware of nothing.

If we now ask what it is that remains unchanging throughout all of this, it is Consciousness. (Consciousness is, of course, also present in deep sleep. If it were not, we would not be able to say, on waking, that we know that we were aware of nothing. Also, if it were not present, someone would eventually call for the undertakers to remove the body!). In the waking state, I am the waker; in the dream state, I am the dreamer; in the deep-sleep state, I am the deep sleeper. When each of these temporary assignments is dropped, what remains unchanging throughout is simply 'I am'.

We have already seen that each of the three states of experience can be divided into two: knower and known. In the waking state, the waker, *vishva*, is the knower of the known gross (*sthUla*) universe, *virAT*. In the dream state, the dreamer, *taijasa*, is the knower of the known subtle (*sUkShma*) universe, *hiraNyagarbha*. In the deep-sleep state, the deep-sleeper, *prAj~na*, is effectively knower of the known causal (*kAraNa*) universe, *antaryAmin* or *Ishvara* (though these are in unmanifest form in deep-sleep).

The first part of the seventh mantra says that *turIya* is not a knower, i.e. not the waker, dreamer or deep-sleeper just described, nor any other state that we might envisage. The second part tells us that we are not anything that can be 'known' directly either. In fact, says the Upanishad, our real nature cannot be described at all in any positive sense. The best that we can do is to say what it is not and there is then a possibility that we will realize the truth. This is analogous to the way in which we might finally appreciate that the coiled up rope in the metaphor introduced earlier is not in fact a snake or a stick or a crack in the ground.

The seventh mantra says that *turIya* is not accessible to any of the senses or organs of action and, indeed, has nothing to do with the world of objects at all. *turIya* has no characteristics at all and cannot be spoken or even thought about.

Everything in the three states is 'attributed'. We can describe the knower and known aspects by using appropriate adjectives. What is not usually realized when we do this, however, is that attributes necessarily limit the thing being described. As soon as we say that something is 'X', we automatically exclude it from being 'not X'. So everything in the three states is also limited by virtue of having attributes, or being *saguNa*. The seventh mantra tells us that *turIya* is *nirguNa* – without any attributes at all. It is completely unlimited.

So does this mean that, in order to 'reach' *turIya* from the waking state, we have to somehow get rid of all of our waking attributes? Not at all! *Atman* is *never* attributed. It is always *nirguNa*. Our problem is not that we *have* attributes but that we *think* we have them. We think that we are a man or a woman, a husband or a wife, rich or poor, and so on. It is this identification with these notional attributes that causes all of our problems. All that we need to do is to realize that our true self is not any of these things – that is why it is sometimes called 'Self-realization'. It is simply a question of receiving the knowledge and recognizing that it is true.

In fact, says the Upanishad, *turIya* is the essence of every experience in every state. Although the waker might be replaced by the dreamer, 'I' am present throughout. Even when the mind is unconscious, I am the witness of the 'nothingness' that is experienced. And this is the same 'I' in the past, present and future. The changing aspects belong only to the physical body and world and to the subtle mind and causal factors – and I am none of these. I am unaffected by any of them, whose empirical reality depend upon me alone and not the other way round.

Although we are thus forced to concede that we cannot be waker, dreamer or deep-sleeper alone, we have to recognize that who-we-really-are must be present in all three states. In fact, this 'feeling of I' is the same throughout our lives, regardless of age, experience and knowledge. Effectively, what we have to do is to drop all of the incidental attributes relating to body and mind as 'not me', and aim to recognize that essential reality that is ever unaffected or 'untouched' by anything. (The concept of 'untouched' or 'touchless' is one that will reappear later in Gaudapada's *asparsha yoga*.)

The Upanishad uses the word *prapa~nchopashamaM* to 'describe' *turIya*. This effectively eliminates the three states as having any ultimate value or meaning. The literal meaning is negation (*ama*) of the experience (*pash*) of the universe (*prapa~ncha*). This confirms the status of the world as *mithyA* or *vaitathya* and thereby negates it. This is the subject of the second chapter of the *kArikA*-s.

If the world were real (*sat*), then it could not be negated, since that which is truly existent cannot 'not exist'. And if the world were unreal (*asat*), then there would be no need to negate it. Accordingly, if the world is neither *sat* nor *asat*, it must be *mithyA*.

This mantra also introduces the word *advaitaM*, non-dual, further to 'describe' *turIya*, and this word is taken up as the subject of the third chapter of the *kArikA*-s.

Finally, the *seventh mantra* concludes by saying that all of this is to be understood, implying that it is necessary to remove our ignorance of the truth of the nature of ourselves and the universe if we are to be free (from the eternal wheel of *saMsAra* – continual birth and death, with its concomitant suffering).

Gaudapada comments on this mantra in K1.10. The key point about this *kArikA* is its use of the word *turIya*. The Upanishad itself does not use this word; it uses *chaturtha*, which is the ordinal number 'fourth' (*chatur* is the numeral '4'). *turIya* rather means 'the fourth part' of something which consists of four parts. So Gaudapada is being strictly accurate here and we always use this word when referring to *brahman* in this context.

He says that *turIya* is mighty, and the master or enjoyer of everything, who brings an end to all our troubles (caused by identification with the ego). It is non-dual, changeless, all-pervading and the Consciousness that enlivens everything in the three states but is totally unaffected by any of them.

Investigation into OM

The remaining section of the Upanishad carries out an investigation into the word OM itself. It shows how each part of the word can be equated in a precise manner with the aspects of the Self. Thus, OM can be used as an object of meditation. Providing that we are aware of the exact nature of these similarities, it is then possible to prepare the mind to understand and realize the true nature of the Self. The details of the practical aspects will be covered later, since the Upanishad itself does not go into these and it is necessary for Gaudapada to elaborate.

The makeup of the word OM was explained in the introduction; it consists of three letters: *a*, *u* and *m*. The Upanishad tells us that these correspond to the waking, dream and deep-sleep states respectively. And it explains the reasons for these correspondences – see Appendix 1 for all the details.

The reasoning is that, although our primary aim should be to investigate into the nature of ourselves, as instructed by mantras 1 – 7, many people simply will not have the intellectual capacity to do so. Accordingly, such seekers should begin by practicing meditation, whose purpose is to prepare the mind for the main investigation.

Meditation helps us to still the mind, increase concentration, aids in developing discrimination and dispassion etc. All of this is outside the scope of this book – read one of my other books for this – Ref. 62 or 63. But meditation on OM, providing we are aware of the precise similarities between letters and states of consciousness, also directs the mind towards their meaning. When we think of the *u* of OM, for example, we immediately connect that with the dream state, the dreamer and *hiraNyagarbha* (after we have heard the teaching, of course!)

Thus, both *a* and the waking state are the first in their respective series and also have the quality of 'pervasiveness'. *u* and the dream state are in the middle of their series and can be regarded as 'superior'. *m* and the deep-sleep state have the characteristics of the utensil used for measuring grain and of 'absorbing' what has gone before, ready to recreate it at the next iteration.

[The 'utensil' referred to here is one used for measuring quantities of (usually) barley or rice. The idea is that the grain is visible in, for example, a sack. You pour the grain into the measure and it (the grain) disappears from view. You take the measure over to the cooking pot and empty it in. The grain then 'reappears' in the pot. This reference is from the 11th mantra of the Upanishad, which is analyzed in detail in Appendix 1. Presumably it was a recognizable and potent metaphor at the time that it was written!]

You really need to read the details of all this if you want to make more sense of it! They are given in the analysis of mantras 9 – 11 in Appendix 1. If you are proceeding directly to the main investigation into reality (i.e. reading the rest of the main text of this book) then you do not *need* to understand the meditation aspects. If you intend to practice meditation on OM, then in order to derive the benefits, you will have to understand the associations and so you ought to read the analysis of the relevant mantras.

In meditation on OM, the sound of the mantra, and its letter associations with the related states, are intended only to lead the mind to the silence that follows. This silence is the fourth part of the mantra and is called *amAtra*. This means 'without measure' or 'limitless'. Silence has no beginning and no end. This silence (which is always present, including during the sounding parts of OM) is *turIya*.

There is thus a parallel progression: from waking to dream to deep-sleep to *turIya* and from *a* to *u* to *m* to silence; from gross to subtle to causal to absolute. As we meditate on OM, we can progress from identification of *a* with *virAT*, through *u* with *hiraNyagarbha*, and *m* with *Ishvara* until we rest in silence and recognize that we are that Consciousness-*turIya* which is the substratum of everything.

The benefits of carrying out such meditation, for those who are interested in material benefits, are also detailed by these mantras (MU9 – 11). But it is understood that the true seeker, who is mentally prepared to carry out investigation into the Self (*Atma vichAra*), will not be interested in any material benefits! Meditation on *a*, for the waking state, obtains for the meditator all of his or her desires, since objects in the gross world are the principal attraction for the waker. It also ensures that the meditator becomes the foremost in their field of endeavor. Meditation on *u*, being associated with the mind, increases mental power and knowledge and gains the acceptance of everyone. Meditation on *m* brings discrimination and under-standing of the true nature of things.

Gaudapada also adds (K1.5) that whoever understands the differentiation between subject and object, experiencer and experienced, in each of the three states will be freed from depen-dence upon getting the desired results from his or her actions.

The waker enjoying the gross world is not present in the dream, where the dreamer enjoys an entirely different, subtle world. And neither waker nor dreamer is present in deep-sleep, where the sleeper simply experiences the bliss of deep sleep. They are mutually exclusive and yet I am present throughout. Accordingly these states must be *mithyA* – not absolutely real. Therefore, as Gaudapada puts it, 'I am not tainted by experience'.

Shankara uses the metaphor of fire, which does not gain or lose anything by consuming its own fuel. Similarly, the Self neither gains nor loses anything in terms of knowledge or awareness when it is both the enjoyer and the enjoyed in each of the three states.

Silence – *amAtra*

After OM has been sounded, the lips have closed and the 'm' sound of *ma* has stopped, there is a return to silence. The initial 'o' sound (of *a* + *u*) arose out of silence and now the silence is re-established.

It is certainly true that, when there is sound, there cannot be silence and vice versa – this is what the words mean. But, in a sense, we could say that the silence was never really absent because a sound is audible only against the background of silence just like letters are seen against the background of a blackboard.

If you imagine OM (or anything else) being sounded against a background of white noise at the same volume, what would be heard? (White noise is sound of equal amplitude across all audible frequencies.) If every frequency is already being sounded, how can a new sound of just a few particular frequencies be heard? Or imagine being in a room with noisy machinery all around – a cotton mill springs to mind (I worked for short periods in these during holidays while at university). If someone speaks to you in a normal voice, you simply cannot make out any words; they have to really shout; i.e. they have to increase the amplitude in order to make themselves heard; the frequencies of words at an amplitude less than or equal to that of the background cannot be heard.

The word 'silence' in common usage means 'no sound'. But it is a fact that, in a very real sense, there is always a 'background' of silence out of which any sound 'arises'. It is not that, when sounds stop, silence comes; it is rather that, when they stop, one is able to recognize the silence that was always there. So silence should not be regarded as 'negative sound'; rather it is the 'sustainer' or 'support' of sound.

This is similar to the situation we had with the three states and *turīya*. We consider that 'I' am present in all three states, although the waker, dreamer and deep-sleeper clearly come and go. Thus I have to equate myself with *turīya*, which is the only reality, in the same way that gold is the only reality of chain, bangle and ring. Similarly, *a*, *u* and *m* come and go but the silence which is the background reality of all of them is there before, during and after.

Both *turīya* and *amAtra* can be 'described' in the same way. There have to be quotation marks around the word because, precisely, neither *can* be described! Both are attribute-less, though associated with peace and bliss and non-duality.

In his commentary on the Upanishad, Shankara speaks of the states being identifiable with 'objects', while the parts of OM are identifiable with the 'names' of those objects. One of the key teachings in Advaita is that the naming of something effectively brings that thing into existence. We begin with everything being non-dual and therefore non-separate, not identifiable. It is the act of separating out a form from this amorphous Consciousness and assigning a name to it that 'creates' an object.

We can see this through the metaphors of gold and ring or water and wave. The ocean (which is already a named, separate thing when there is really only water) is one, and then we choose to identify 'waves' as separate entities upon the surface of that ocean.

Accordingly, another correspondence between *turīya* and *amAtra* is that the former actually has nothing to do with the world of objects and the latter has nothing to do with the world of names. It is the result of ignorance that we see both the external and internal worlds as separate and hence assign distinguishing names to objects that are really only separate in our minds. When that ignorance is dispelled and Self-knowledge is gained (enlightenment), there is no more separateness; there is only *turīya*; no more need for names, only *amAtra*.

Comparison of the States – Ignorance and Error

Gaudapada does not actually introduce the famous metaphor of rope and snake until K2.17 but it is helpful for this comparison to make use of it here.

Its value lies in the analysis of what happens when the misidentification takes place. It is the partial ignorance of the rope that is the direct cause of the mistake. Had the light been good, the rope would have been seen clearly and no error would have been made. Also, had the darkness been total, no mistake would have been made then, because the observer would have seen nothing at all. We thus have to differentiate between these two elements – ignorance and error, the former being the 'cause' of the latter 'effect'.

We can now look at the states of consciousness in a similar way. The analogy is that, in the waking state for example, we are partially ignorant of our true nature as *brahman-turīya*-Consciousness. We know that we exist but we do not know what we are. Instead, we take ourselves to be a separate 'person', limited physically by a body, which is prone to illness and doomed to decay, and by a mind with hopes and fears, inadequate intellect and poor memory. And so on! The Self-ignorance is the cause of our subsequent mistake in taking ourselves to be something that we are not and taking the gross world as reality.

The same thing happens in the dream state. The dreamer is usually ignorant of the fact that he or she is dreaming and takes the dream ego and dream world for reality. Of course, we still know that we exist. Both waking and dream states are characterized by this twofold problem of partial ignorance and consequent error in believing that which is only *mithyA* to be reality.

The deep-sleep state is different. Here, there is total ignorance and, since the mind is in unmanifest form, it cannot make any error. We do not take ourselves to be anything that we are not but neither are we aware of what we are. I know neither the world nor my true Self. There is the bliss of ignorance but it is temporary only; we all too soon transfer to the state of waking or dream once more.

And now, to conclude the analysis, we can see that *turIya* can be represented as absence of both ignorance and error. But remember that this is not a state; we are only using concepts to bring about understanding. Once that realization dawns, the concepts are dropped.

This is one of the key elements of the methodology of Advaita and has its own Sanskrit term: *adhyAropa – apavAda*, meaning that a concept or explanation is introduced in order to further understanding but later taken back as not really being the case. Michael Comans (Ref. 13) explains the procedure by saying that *"It is not possible to proceed directly to the unknown without taking the help of the known."*

What is effectively being said here is that, when we are no longer subject to either Self-ignorance or error; when we no longer take ourselves to be a limited, separate entity; then we can be said to have attained the status (not state) of *turIya*. Self-ignorance goes when Self-knowledge is gained, and ignorance being the cause of error, error also goes since there is no longer anything to cause it.

There is a popular story, which illustrates the use and value of *adhyAropa – apavAda*:

A man died and in his will left his 17 elephants to his 3 children, stipulating that they had to be divided as follows: half to the eldest, one third to the second and one ninth to the youngest. Needless to say, they couldn't work out how they could do this without killing and cutting up one or more elephants. Then the inevitable wise man came along, upon his elephant, and said that he could solve their problem. He said he would donate his own elephant to the estate.

So, with 18 elephants, it was now easy: half to the eldest – 9; one third to the next eldest – 6; one ninth to the youngest – 2.

$9 + 6 + 2 = 17$.

Then the wise man took back his elephant and went away.

In the story, the elephant belonging to the wise man is introduced to solve the problem. Once solved, it is no longer needed and is taken away. Similarly, in *adhyAropa – apavAda*, a concept is introduced to provide an interim explanation for a perceived problem. As our understanding grows, there comes a time when what was originally seen as an obstacle to understanding ceases to be so. And the introduced concept can now be dropped, as it is no longer needed.

We can now see how this can apply to something that may seem strange (and is examined by Gaudapada in K1.7 – 10 and elsewhere): why do the Upanishads provide various descriptions of creation if there is not really any creation at all? The reason is that everyone starts off believing that there is a real world so they naturally want to know how it came about. Accordingly, Advaita accepts this as natural and begins by indulging that belief. It introduces the notion of a creator and related ideas of *karma* and so on. Later the concept of a non-dual Consciousness is investigated and, gradually, the mind is taken away from the unhelpful and ultimately mistaken beliefs and refocused on something that will prove more rewarding. Eventually, the provisional notions of creation, *karma* etc. can be dropped, as the mind is now ready to consider ideas which initially would have been rejected out of hand.

To return to *turIya*, who-I-really-am is the reality – *satyam* – and is unaffected by the *mithyA* empirical reality. The clay pot was clay before the pot was made, is clay while it is being used as a pot and is still clay after the pot is broken. It is analogous to the relationship between waker and dreamer. Although the body of the dreamer may be injured in the dream, that of the waker is totally unaffected. Ignorance and error belong to the mind, not to Consciousness. Consciousness 'illuminates' both ignorance and error, just as it 'illuminates' everything else, but it is unaffected by either of them.

The position regarding the apprehension of reality can now be summarized as follows:

vishva	Waking State	associated with ignorance and error
taijasa	Dream State	associated with ignorance and error
prAj~na	Deep-sleep State	associated with ignorance only
turIya	The 'fourth'	associated with neither

The World Appearance

Our normal (unexamined) experience is at odds with the statements made by Gaudapada. We know that we experience duality. For example, 'I' am separate from the 'chair' on which I am sitting – there are (at least) two things here. And yet the word 'appearance' used in the heading of this section indicates that Gaudapada is clearly claiming that this is not the case. As just noted, the waking state is associated with both ignorance and error. Being ignorant of the fact that there is only *brahman-turIya*, we make the mistake of believing that the chair exists apart from me. Being ignorant of the nature of the rope, I make the mistake of believing it to be a snake.

As was mentioned earlier, the second chapter of Gaudapada's work is essentially expanding upon the one word – *prapa~nchopashamaM* – from the seventh mantra of the Upanishad. The word used by Gaudapada – *vaitathya* – is a synonym for *mithyA* and is to be applied to our concept of the universe as a separate entity. The words should be taken to mean that the world is not real *in itself*.

It is important to realize that this is *not* saying that the world is unreal. The world has what we might call 'relative' reality. Or perhaps a better description is 'empirical' reality, meaning that 'for practical purposes' there is a real world. All our behavior assumes that the world is real and Advaita is not suggesting that this should be otherwise.

This practical 'reality' is given a special term in Advaita which is very important – *vyavahAra*, adjective *vyAvahArika*.

But, whilst we can regard the world as dualistic for all practical purposes, the absolute truth, according to Advaita, is that everything is *brahman* – there is only Consciousness. It is like saying that we have cups and plates and mugs and vases and that these have practical value. We can use the mug to contain a

71

drink while putting our sandwich on a plate. But when it comes down to it, there is actually only clay (assuming that all these things are made out of clay for the sake of the metaphor). This absolute truth is called *paramArtha*, adjective *pAramArthika*, in Advaita. Realizing this truth is realizing that we are already 'free' – it is 'enlightenment'; just as realizing the truth of the rope frees us completely from concerns over whether the snake is poisonous.

As Swami Lokeswarananda puts it (Ref. 20): "*Non-dualists sum up their position as follows: Objects and your perception of them are empirical realities. Together these two constitute your waking state. Vedantists recognize this state and are grateful that there is this state, for it makes it possible for them to study the scriptures and strive for Self-realization, the supreme goal of life.*"

For the sake of completion, there are two other 'states' of reality talked about in Advaita. Dreams clearly have a degree of reality, since we do experience them in our (dreaming) sleep (and sometimes whilst awake, where they are called 'day-dreams') but are of no 'practical' value. Accordingly, they are of a 'lower' order of reality and are called *pratibhAsa*, adjective *prAtibhAsika*. Finally, there are things that have no reality whatsoever. Examples encountered in the scriptures are 'horns of a hare' and 'son of a barren woman'. Such things have the status of being utterly unreal or *tuchCham*.

Note that, if we are being pedantic we would have to say that, from the standpoint of the dreamer, the dream world is *vyavahAra* and the waking world *pratibhAsa* or even *tuchCham*. This is because the waking world has no reality at all for us in dream (lucid dreams excepted). In dream, we genuinely believe the dream world to be the empirical reality.

We should also note that experience of both the waking and the dream worlds do not come to an end on the gaining of *mokSha*. As noted elsewhere, experience is no proof of reality. We will still be aware of apparent objects and their separation and may still make use of them for transactions. The crucial point is that we now know that the waking (as well as the dream world) is *mithyA* and it is this knowledge that is the beginning of the end of *saMsAra*.

Another good metaphor for explaining the relative reality of the world as opposed to the absolute reality of *turIya is* that the 'reality' of day and night is relative to your location on the surface of the earth. Day for someone in the UK is not day for someone in the US (and both would be meaningless for an astronaut on the moon!) Accordingly, the 'reality' of this aspect is relative or empirical, *mithyA* or *vyAvahArika*. Absolute reality has no such dependence upon anything relative; it is always, unvaryingly the case.

Unreality of Dream

In order to show that what he is suggesting here is true, Gaudapada begins by comparing the waking state with that of dreams. His intention is first to demonstrate that dreams are *mithyA* and then show by inference that the waking state too is *mithyA*. (Note that it was pointed out above that, while the waking state is *vyAvahArika*, the dream state is *prAtibhAsika*. The word *mithyA* can be applied to both.)

He first points out (K2.1 and K4.33) that all the objects in a dream are, as it were, 'located' in the mind (which is effectively in the body). Since such objects may include entire cities and even worlds beyond the earth, they clearly cannot be real since there is insufficient space in the body to contain them.

Furthermore (K2.2 and K4.34) we may dream of events which, in the dream, last for days or even years, only to wake up and find that mere minutes have passed. We may travel to distant countries (which travel may take many hours or days) but awake to find ourselves still on the same bed; we never awake to find ourselves at the place to which we travelled in the dream. Clearly the time units of the dream do not correspond with waking time, which we believe to be the 'real' time, and distance units of dream do not correspond with those of waking.

Also (K4.35), we may meet a friend in the dream and discuss some topic or other. But if, after waking, we contact this person and ask them about the meeting, they will have no recollection of it. (The friend may even have been dead for many years!) And if we were given something in the dream, we find that we no longer have it on waking.

In our dreams, we move around in a body, which may eat, drink and perform many other activities. Clearly this is not the same body as the one which is lying asleep on the bed (K4.36); on waking, we realize that the dream body was unreal. Indeed, we acknowledge that everything that we perceived in the dream was equally unreal. Those things were being perceived by the mind, yet were quite unreal. In just the same way, says Gaudapada, those things perceived by the mind in the waking state are also unreal. This waking body and world disappear again when we go back to sleep.

Only Consciousness is absolutely real. It cannot be an object of experience because we are That. Therefore, anything that we do experience cannot be Consciousness; cannot be absolutely real. Consequently, we can regard both waking and dream states equally as *mithyA*.

We all recognize these examples and will agree that the dream events and world cannot be real, other than as a mind-manufactured illusion during sleep. But these 'obvious' facts are obvious only from the standpoint of the waker. At the time of dreaming, the 'dream' is taken for waking reality and we would not countenance the idea that we might 'wake up' from that world and discover that it was 'only a dream'.

This reasoned conclusion is also supported by the scriptures. K2.3 refers to the Brihadaranyaka Upanishad (4.3.10), which says that there cannot be real objects such as chariots, with horses pulling them along roads, inside our head when we are dreaming.

We might try to use the argument that 'everyone else corroborates the existence of the waking world' to assert that the waking world is real but this is not reasonable either, because this is also the case during dream; all of the dream characters substantiate that dream-reality, no matter how bizarre it might seem to our waking mind.

In K4.37, Gaudapada explains that our usual assumption is that dream images are projected by the mind based upon impressions gained in the waking state (just like the interpretation of modern science!) The mechanism for this would be that the experiences in waking are recorded in the memory and give rise to *vAsanA*-s. It is these *vAsanA*-s that dictate the nature of our dreams and why the experiences we have there are similar to those in the waking state.

Based on this idea, we (the waker) ascribe a 'real' reality to the waking world which is the now-perceived cause of the dream, which we say is 'unreal'. But only I see the dream. So, if the dream is the 'effect' of the waking world, should I not infer that only I see the waking world also? All of the other dream people proved to be unreal; why not all of the waking people also?

In fact, if we think about it, we only (think we) know that the waking state *is* the waking state by comparing it to the prior state which we now deem to have been a dream. We could just as well say that we experience a succession of dream states, but the current one is always deemed to be a waking state.

Just as an aside here, Western philosophers also have considered the criteria that differentiate dreams from the waking state and Descartes, for example, felt he had hit upon a solution by looking to 'consistency'. He suggested that there was a clear difference in that we cannot use our memory to connect one dream with another over the course of our lives, whereas there is no problem with remembering past waking events. But Arvind Sharma points out in Ref. 28 that philosopher A. R. Manser has refuted this argument as follows: "*Consistency can only be used as a test of a particular experience by waiting to see what happens in the future. It would enable me to tell that I had been dreaming, not that I am now dreaming; for however confident I am of the reality of my surroundings, something may happen in the future that will reveal them to be part of a dream.*" Also, there is no test that we can apply (in the dream) to prove that it is a dream. Any test that we tried to apply would only confirm that the dream was real.

[In fact, studies on the topic of lucid dreaming have shown that this is not strictly true. It is possible to train the mind to recognize key events as signifying dream. For example, during our waking lives, we can cultivate the habit of always looking at our watch twice when we want to find out the time. It is a recognized fact that if we do this in a dream, the watch or clock will not show the same time on both occasions. This observed discrepancy will then alert us to a dream and, thereafter, the dream may become lucid.]

(K4.38) Fortunately, this line of thought need not disturb us too much! Although it has been argued that the waking state can be considered to be the 'cause' of the dream state from the empirical perspective, it makes no sense to consider it to be so from the absolute point of view. If we had been taking the *kArikA*-s in order, we would already have dealt with the topic of creation and shown that there is actually no creation at all. As it is, this is one of the concepts to look forward to! Here, Gaudapada simply asserts that an unreal entity cannot be born or created out of a real entity. A human cannot give birth to a unicorn. Accordingly, we cannot argue that the (assumed) real waking world gives rise to the unreal dream world.

(K4.39) In fact, we see things that are not absolutely real (i.e. *mithyA*) in the waking state, such as rings that are really gold and pots that are really clay and then we go to sleep and dream about such things also. And likewise we see unreal things in sleep – 'impossible' objects and creatures – though, fortunately, those things are no longer there when we wake up; i.e. there seems to be evidence for a causal relationship from waking to dream but not in the reverse direction. But we cannot, on this basis, say that there actually *is* any causal relationship. There are lots of things that we see in the waking state but do not dream about. The point is that an unreal thing cannot give rise to another unreal thing. There can be no connection between waking and dream from the absolute point of view.

Unreality of Waking World

We have no trouble believing that dreams are unreal, but accepting that the waking state is also unreal is rather more difficult. Gaudapada uses the logical reasoning discussed above under 'Means of Acquiring Knowledge, with an emphasis on Inference' to try to persuade us.

The subject of the discussion (*pakSha*) is the waking world. What we want to conclude (*sAdhya*) is that this waking world is *mithyA*. The reason (*hetu*) is discussed shortly (K2.6) and amounts to saying that anything that is not eternally existent is *mithyA*. The example that is used to illustrate this (*dRRiShTAnta*) is that of dream, which has just been shown to be *mithyA*. The argument, then, is that things that we see and feel in the dream are believed (at the time) to be real – if we feel a dream thirst, we have a drink of dream water and are satisfied, as the dreamer. But this is all realized upon waking to be *mithyA*. Similarly, objects seen in the waking state will be realized to be *mithyA* if we consider the situation from the standpoint of *turIya*.

Those who are widely read in Advaita may notice an apparent contradiction in the stand taken by Shankara in his commentary on this verse in the *kArikA* and what he says regarding the appearance of the world in his commentary on the *brahma sUtra*-s. (This is the scripture which summarizes the philosophy of Vedanta and Shankara comments on it, interpreting from the standpoint of Advaita.) This is discussed briefly and explained in Appendix 6.

Commenting on K2.4, Shankara rephrases Gaudapada's statement into the form of a syllogism. He says that the proposition to be established is that 'objects perceived in the waking state are illusory'. The reason (*hetu*) for the inference is 'being perceived'. The example or illustration is that 'objects perceived in dream (are illusory)'. He says (Nikhilananda translation, Ref. 4): "*The common feature of 'being perceived' is the relation between the illustration given and the proposition taken for consideration. Therefore the illusoriness is admitted of objects that are perceived to exist in the waking state.*"

So Gaudapada's first argument as to why waking and dream states are alike is that perception of objects in both states is similar (K2.5). Objects are seen external to the body (the dreambody in the case of dreaming). And, since dreams have been shown to be *mithyA*, the waking world must also be similar. Basically, if we experience something, then it cannot be real, because whatever is 'experienced' is always an 'object'. Only 'I', the subject, am real because I cannot be objectified. The existence of everything depends upon there being a 'knower'. And 'dependent reality' is one of the definitions of *mithyA*. To put this simply, what Gaudapada says is: because I can see the world, it cannot be real! It is only name and form of the non-dual reality.

The second argument (K2.6 and K4.31) refers to what is now widely recognized in Advaita as being the definition for 'real'. This is that, in order to be real, a thing has to exist in 'all three periods of time' – past, present and future. (In fact, the Self is said to transcend all these – *trikAlAtIta* – because time itself is, in a sense, a part of creation.)

Gaudapada says that, if something was non-existent at some time in the past (i.e. was effectively 'born' or 'created') or will be non-existent at some time in the future (i.e. will 'die' or be 'destroyed'), then it is non-existent even now. Conversely, for something to be real, it cannot have been born and cannot die. As

Richard King states, this is effectively a concise definition of *ajAti vAda*, the belief that is key to this entire text – nothing has ever been born; there is no 'creation'.

This claim must not be treated as poetic, metaphorical or ironic but as quite literal. If we consider the example of the clay pot again, the pot did not exist in the past and will not exist in the future. But the clay itself exists throughout and the pot, having been 'formed' by the potter, borrows its existence for a time from the clay. We have to say that, even while it is in the form of a pot, it is clay itself that actually exists and not the pot. This description should bring back the memory of the gold and ornaments metaphor from the introduction. It is one of the ways in which we can define the word *mithyA*. Just as 'pot' is only a name and form of clay, so also the 'world' is only a name and form of *brahman*.

If 'existence' is only the case for a time, then it is only an incidental attribute of the thing and not its intrinsic nature. The intrinsic nature of something cannot change; otherwise it cannot be called 'intrinsic'. Fire is always hot, water is always wet and, says Advaita, real things always exist. As the Bhagavad Gita (2.16) puts it: *there is no existence of that which is unreal and no non-existence of that which is real.*

By analogy, the universe itself has to be *mithyA*. Before the big bang it did not exist and there will come a time when it will cease to exist. It is *brahman*, as its substrate, that really exists throughout. It is *brahman* that is the reality, *satyam*. The universe is only name and form and has no substantial existence of its own.

And this applies to every object – including the body that I usually think of as 'myself'. The body is a gross object (and the mind a subtle object) which did not exist in the past and will not in the future. As Som Raj Gupta points out in Ref. 66: "*It is indeed a pity that human beings should be so rich in intelligence and so poor in sight that they should forget that the body is a* this *and not a* me."

We could define 'real' as something which never changes. In order to change, a thing has to cease to be what it is and become something else; i.e. it would have to become what it is not. Therefore, anything that changes cannot be real, since the act of changing involves non-existence.

(K4.41) Both waking and dream states are unreal, so neither can be the cause of the other. In each state, we see unreal things but think them to be real. When we wake up, we claim that we were stupid to think that the strange and wonderful things we saw in the dream could have been real. And yet we now make exactly the same mistake in the waking state; in terms of the metaphor, we still see ropes and think that they are snakes! (Remember that the snake is not *totally* unreal, because it generates fear in us and there is clearly something present. Yet it is obviously not real either, as we can see for ourselves when we bring the torch. This is one of the definitions of *mithyA* – neither real nor unreal.)

Most people, although willing to accept that dreams are unreal, would baulk at the suggestion that the waking world is unreal also. Accordingly, Gaudapada now presents some of their likely objections. This is standard practice in Advaita texts – an objector posits an objection or query (*pUrvapakSha*) and the teacher responds with an explanation or counter-argument, the conclusion or established viewpoint (*siddhAnta*).

First Ojection to World Being Unreal

The first of these objections relates to utility. The idea is that we can make use of objects in the waking world, whereas those in dream have no use whatsoever. Consequently, although the dream world is unreal, we must grant reality to the waking world. Gaudapada concedes that waking things are useful but, he says, only in the waking world. Although the glass of water may quench our waking thirst, no amount of waking water is going to quench our dream thirst, and vice versa.

Shankara says that waking and dreaming have to be regarded alike in this way. We may have a satisfying meal in dream but wake up hungry. The waking experience contradicts the dream. This is how we normally view things, thinking that the waking state is the reality and the dream unreal. But the situation is precisely the same the other way round. We may eat a satisfying meal before going to bed but then dream that we are hungry. The dream experience thereby contradicts the waking one. Both waking and dream states are alike demarcated by a beginning and an end. Utility is only relative and, consequently, both must be regarded as unreal (*mithyA*).

Second Objection to World Being Unreal

The next objection takes the stance of someone who believes that dreams are real; that the dream world is literally created (by God) for the benefit (or not) of the dreamer. Some actually believe this to be the case; for example, *vishiShTAdvaita* ('qualified' non-dualism), one of the three branches of Vedanta (the other two being *Advaita* and *dvaita*). After all, if the body in which we are born and the sorts of situation we encounter in life are dictated by our *karma* (fruit of past actions, in this and previous lives), why shouldn't our dreams also be similarly directed?

Such an objector states that, since we see things in dream that we have never encountered in waking life, they must be real.

This does not follow. We might for example dream of a location, a city perhaps, that does not exist and that consequently we can never have seen in waking life. Nevertheless, we are familiar with cities, with different types of buildings, transport, people and their dress. It is perfectly possible mentally to construct a city with aspects taken from many different places that we have actually visited in our past. We can even add features from movies that we may have seen, where locations are designed and implemented only on a computer. And we can imagine entirely new, even impossible constructions. If all this were not so, it would be impossible for an architect ever to conceive a new design.

Shankara likens the dream to seeing a snake instead of a rope or a mirage in the desert. What one sees is not really there; the strange objects are merely due to the nature of the dream state itself.

Gaudapada says that, even if our dreams were created especially for us, they would still be *mithyA* for the same reasons already given above. They are experienced, and therefore dependent upon the subject of the experience. And anything which has a beginning and an end must be *mithyA*, since *satyam* is eternally *satyam*. Basically, the dream and everything in it depends upon the dreamer for its existence; i.e. the novelty of dreams is subjective, not objective; it depends upon the dreamer. Only Consciousness, which experiences the beginning and end of all objects, is real.

Anandagiri adds that this 'extraordinary imagination' attribute of the dreamer is only a temporary one, since it disappears on awakening. The intrinsic nature is, of course, Consciousness only. He says it is due to ignorance (*avidyA*) that we see unusual things in dream. And, indeed, it is really no different in the waking state. Those things are also unreal since they have a beginning and an end, as was discussed earlier.

Third Objection to World Being Unreal

And this leads on to the third objection namely that, whereas the dream world is subjective, the waking world has objective reality. It is experienced as external to ourselves, whereas the dream takes place in our mind (K2.9 – 10). But this notion suffers from the same confusion as before. We only recognize that the dream world is 'in our mind' when we are awake; at the time of the dream, it is just as much 'external' as is the waking world when we are awake. We might as well say that the waking world is really non-existent since it disappears when we are in the dream or deep sleep states. At the time of the dream, I experience external objects and events in just the same manner. Their illogicality or even impossibility only becomes apparent on awakening.

Similarly, when we recognize that *turīya* is the reality, we will also realize that the waking world has no objectivity of its own but is just an appearance within Consciousness. The objective reality of the two worlds is entirely relative to the standpoint of the observer. In fact, they are both *mithyā*.

From a 'detached' point of view, both waking and dream are similar experiences. Within the dream, there are 'others' who validate my dream experience. I have conversations with them and I assume (as a dreamer) that they see the same external (dream) world as I do. It is only from the vantage point of having woken up that I am able to see that this world was internally generated and (no longer) has any objective existence.

Of course I feel that I am unable to take a position from outside of this waking world to look at the situation in a similar fashion. And so I call the waking world 'real' and the dream world 'false'. But in fact I do take such a stand every time I go to sleep. In the dream, the waking world is negated and in deep-sleep, both waking and dream are negated.

If we imagine a dream A in which we go to sleep and have a dream B. When we 'wake up' (from dream B into the dream A), we will say that the dreamt dream was 'only a dream in the mind', and that we are now (in dream A) in the real world. Of course, when we 'really' wake up into the waking world, we realize that both A and B were dreams and think that we are now in reality. Except that we are now effectively in dream C!

So long as we continue to believe in the objective reality of a separate world, we have not really woken up! The bottom line, with respect to this third objection, is that the experience of an external world does not mean that the world is real. Of course, we assume that it does, but an assumption is no proof at all.

If objects of both waking and dream worlds are unreal, that must include the people who inhabit them also, including the waker and the dreamer! If this is the case, it is denying the reality of the knower as well as the known. But this makes no sense as there has to be someone who is doing the denying! So who is it who sees or imagines these two worlds (K.2.11)?

This question highlights the danger of choosing the wrong word. Gaudapada actually uses the word *vaitathya* for the word translated here as 'unreal' but this should be regarded as a synonym for *mithyA*. The objects of the world are not unreal. Try walking in front of an oncoming car to demonstrate this! The objects (of both states) have reality relative to that state. What they do not have is absolute reality. Their reality depends upon I, the observer. That is I, the ultimate observer – Consciousness – not I, the separate person, which is equally *mithyA*. I, the waking person, cannot have absolute reality because I disappear, to be replaced by the dreamer or sleeper, when I go to sleep. I, the ego, also has only relative reality.

Gaudapada provides a preliminary answer to this question of who sees the worlds in K2.12, and introduces the concept of *mAyA*, which was mentioned in the introduction. He says that the scriptures tell us that it is the non-dual Self that 'imagines' itself and cognizes objects, by the power of its own *mAyA*. There is only the non-dual Self, or Consciousness. But he is suggesting here that this Self effectively creates a world, together with conscious beings to inhabit it, out of Itself. And, looking out at the world through the eyes of these beings, this Self 'forgets' that it is everything.

In fact, the 'knower' is not the original Consciousness but Consciousness 'reflected' in the mind of the observer. And we should never forget that all of this is really *mithyA*, like the snake misperceived in the rope.

It does, indeed, sound fantastical. And yet this is precisely what happens when I the waker go to sleep and dream! Whilst dreaming, I fully believe that I am in a complex, fully populated world of others; and yet everything is produced in my own mind, by itself, out of itself. The apparent plurality is self-delusion. Relatively speaking the waking world is no different. None of it has independent, substantial reality; it is all only name and form of myself, *turīya*.

Who-I-really-am is not the waker, which is Consciousness identified with this material body and believing in a separate gross universe. Both body and world effectively disappear when I go to sleep. And I am not the dreamer, which is Consciousness identified with the mentally created subtle body and dream world. These creations disappear when I wake up or go into deep sleep. The reality is that I am the Consciousness which is doing the identifying; that which is present throughout all of the three states and which does not change.

When I enter the dream, I (now the dreamer I) forget all about the waker I, believing that I am now completely awake in this mentally created dream world. And when I enter deep sleep, I forget both. All these experiences come and go but I, as Consciousness, remain unchanging as that in which they all arrive and depart. They are transient and their reality is relevant only to the 'I' which temporarily rules in that particular state. I, as Consciousness, am the only absolute reality. Recall again the metaphor of the actor playing several roles.

Another reason why the world has to be empirical and temporary is that how we experience it depends upon the nature of our senses. Even taking just one element – the electromagnetic spectrum – we are directly aware of only a tiny part, namely visible light. We need the aid of specialized instruments to detect radiation outside of those frequencies. If our eyes functioned in the x-ray region, the world that we perceived would seem very different.

And we do not even 'see' the light waves; we are only aware

of interpreted neuronal events in the brain, after the light has impinged upon the retina and been converted into electro-chemical impulses. That which actually 'caused' the light to be emitted or reflected in the first instance can only ever be an inference. We never see the thing itself, only something else, much later, which (we believe) signifies the thing. Anaïs Nin expressed it so cogently: "*We don't see things as they are; we see them as we are.*" The world can only appear as we are capable of perceiving it. And, without any senses, we would not experience it at all.

It is tempting to say that, therefore, we can never know the world as it 'really' is, still being trapped in the mindset with which we have been brought up. This is effectively what the German philosopher Kant said in his analysis along these lines. In fact, what we should say is that the world is name and form of non-dual Consciousness and that the duality that we perceive is imposed by us as a result of our limited instruments and our use of language.

What we observe is dependent upon *how* we observe. The perceived nature of the world depends upon the nature of me, the observer. The observed world is necessarily a relative one. The absolute reality must be different. And everything objective has the same problem. All are changeable and relative. Only one thing is non-changing, non-relative – I as objectless-Consciousness. I, *turIya*, am the absolute reality.

Gaudapada says that the Self (*Atman*) is the creator (efficient cause), creating the world out of itself (material cause) by itself (instrumental cause). This has to be so, since there is nothing else. Of course, if the *Atman* actually underwent a change to become the world, then this would negate the non-dual status; there would be *Atman and* the world. Accordingly, it is 'delusion' only and no real change takes place at all. It is the magical power of *mAyA* which makes it appear as though it has.

[Some philosophers believe that the *Atman* really does make a world out of itself. This theory is called *pariNAma vAda*, the proposition that an actual transformation occurs. The doctrine will be refuted later. What is claimed here is called *vivarta vAda* – apparent transformation, only thought to be real as a result of ignorance; this is the same as what Gaudapada calls *vaitathya*.

The Self, in combination with this power of *mAyA*, is called *Ishvara* and it is He (God) who creates. But *Ishvara*, *mAyA* and the created world are all *mithyA*. The Self remains unaffected by any of this. Creation, and *mAyA*, will be discussed in much more detail below.]

In K2.13-14, Gaudapada puts forward another variation on the external-internal argument as to why the waking world differs from the dream. He says that the *Atman* creates the manifest, external world of objects, which may appear permanent (e.g. mountains) or transient (like lightning). These constitute the so-called 'objective' phenomena. Both are characterized by a perceived existence over a period of time, however short. And we believe that they continue to exist even when I am not actually observing them. I may work away from home and not see it for most of the day but I expect the building in which I live still to be there when I return.

Because of the existence of waking objects at two separate points in time like this, Gaudapada calls them *dvayakAla*, 'two times'. This differentiates waking experiences from dream experiences, the latter being only *cittakAlAH* – lasting only so long as the mind of the dreamer imagines them. This shows that Gaudapada "*concedes to the world of waking relative objectivity and universality which do not belong to the world of dreams.*" (Ref. 54).

The *Atman* also imagines the ideas of the mind – so-called 'subjective' aspects – which exist as mental impressions (*vAsanA*-s) and are not manifest as name and form. These are different from the external objects in that they exist only for so long as the thought lasts and are not perceived by the senses. Dreams are also of this type. Only I can see them and only while they last; I do not expect to go to sleep tonight and continue the same dream that I had last night.

Accordingly, the objector claims that 'reality' has objective existence whereas the inner world of thoughts and dreams is only subjective.

But the same argument as before refutes this suggestion. There is a clearly objective, external world in the dream also, from the vantage point of the dreamer. And I, the dreamer, may have an internal thought in just the same way. Yet this world is shown to have been subjective when I wake up.

Fourth Objection to World Being Unreal

One final idea which Gaudapada puts forward, as an attempt to argue that the world is real and the dream unreal, is as follows: he says that the unmanifest ideas of thought and dream are all 'imagination', whereas the external objects of the waking world are clearly accessible to the sense organs. Only the latter can therefore be real.

This might seem plausible, since we have no difficulty remembering what we saw in the world yesterday (at least before we reach old age!), whereas most people cannot remember the dream they had. Indeed, many claim that they do not dream at all, whereas science has shown that we all do.

But, again, this is not really anything new. The argument above regarding the limited nature of our senses easily refutes the suggestion. The 'visible' waking world is not at all clearly experienced by someone with deficient or absent sight. In fact, someone who was once able to see but is now blind may have dreams in which he or she can 'see' with remarkable clarity! And the dreamer may well have 'internal' dream thoughts, emotions and desires, which can be clearly differentiated from the 'external' world of dream objects.

The objector is still failing to acknowledge that the dreamer's relationship with the dream world is entirely analogous with the waker's relationship to the waking world. Each world seems real in its own sphere; each seems unreal to someone in the other state. Gaudapada says that the external dream world, as seen through the dream sense organs is perfectly real while the dream lasts.

Accepting the World as *mithyA*

Gaudapada accepts that, despite the barrage of logical arguments that he has put forward, most people will still find it difficult to accept that the world is *mithyA*. Accordingly, he revisits the dream-waking comparisons again in subsequent chapters so as to reinforce the view. As I am attempting in this book to deal with topics systematically, these later points are discussed here. Apologies for any seeming repetition, but I am assuming that most readers will still be skeptical!

The fundamental point with which we cannot argue is that, in dream, our own mind creates the seemingly real world of the dream, with its endless complexity of objects and people. This world has all the characteristics that we equate with the waking world when we are awake. It seems to be outside of our (dream) body and mind; it appears to have objective reality; objects within it seem to have functionality and we can perceive them clearly through our (dream) sense organs. Yet, when we awake, we are certain that this dream world was *mithyA* – a complete fabrication of our mind.

Therefore, the fact that an unreal world can exhibit all of these convincing properties means that, when we observe these aspects in the waking world, we cannot thereby conclude that it is real. In fact, just as the dream world is negated when we wake up, the waking world is effectively negated when we go to sleep. We are forced to conclude that the waking world is also *mithyA*. This does not, of course, mean that it is completely unreal. On the contrary, it is very real while we are awake. But then so is the dream when we are asleep – ask someone who has nightmares if you find this difficult to accept! If you take the standpoint of *turIya*, all the states are seen to be *mithyA*.

The absolute reality is that there is only non-dual *brahman*. At the individual level, the mind projects a dream world. This is taken as real by the dreamer but seen to be *mithyA* by the waker. At the cosmic level, the macrocosmic Mind projects a waking world. This is taken as real by the waker but seen to be *mithyA* if one takes the standpoint of *turIya*. (Of course, 'one' cannot literally 'take the standpoint of *turIya*'! The truth is that there is *only turIya*; 'one' and any intellectual 'standpoint' can only be *mithyA*. But the mind is capable of making this leap of understanding.)

Also, there are not two things in *turIya* – mind *and brahman*. The mind seems to be separate as a result of *mAyA*, just as the rope appears to be a snake as a result of ignorance. But the reality is that the mind *is brahman*, just as the snake *is* the rope. Therefore, whether we say that mind projects the universe or *brahman* projects the universe, it amounts to the same thing. As Gaudapada pointed out in K2.12 above, *brahman* imagines itself and the world by the power of its own *mAyA*. This applies equally to waking and dream worlds. Consciousness is the real substratum of both. (The 'individual' power of *mAyA* is called *nidrA*.)

It must be noted that there is, of course, a practical difference as regards 'waking up'. On waking from the dream, the dream world disappears. On becoming enlightened (equals 'waking up' from the presumed separate waking universe), the world does *not* disappear. This can be rationalized as following from the observation above that the waking world is a projection of the cosmic Mind, not the individual mind. Nevertheless, the world is now known to be *mithyA*.

The summary position so far is therefore as follows. Both waking and dream worlds have these characteristics in common:

- both are objects of experience (*dRRishya*)
- both are transient (*anitya*)
- both are finite (*parichChinna*)

It follows that neither can be absolutely real, yet they are clearly not unreal. They are therefore both *mithyA*.

Falsity of Waking and Dream Objects

Gaudapada next presents another argument, using the analogy of dream, to demonstrate that the waking world is *mithyA*. Both dream and waking states are characterized by three aspects: the witnessing consciousness, the mind, and the objects of perception.

In our dream experience (K4.63 – 4.64), the dream-mind is the perceiver of the creatures and things about which we dream. But, on waking, we realize that all of those things had no existence separate from that dream-mind, which was itself an object of the dreamer's perception. The dream-mind is subject to the dream-world but object to Consciousness. The dream world cannot be separated from the dream mind; what is perceived in it depends upon the dream senses. And clearly the dream mind had no existence at all separate from the dreamer (Consciousness). Dream mind and dream world are both *mithyA*.

Similarly (K4.65 – 4.66), the waking world is object to (and therefore dependent upon) the waking mind. It was argued earlier that a thing which is never perceived in any way by anyone at any time cannot be said to exist. The world depends upon our perceiving it! Similarly, the waking mind is object to (and therefore dependent upon) the witnessing Consciousness. Accordingly, both the waking mind and the world are also *mithyA*.

Shankara says (K4.67) that objects and mind are interdependent in both the states. We can only say that there is a mind in relation to the objects or thoughts that it perceives or conceives. And, as pointed out above, objects cannot be said to exist until a mind perceives them. Each effectively exists only by virtue of the other and thus neither can be said to really exist; there is no proof of any independent existence. The example he gives is that of a pot. We cannot have a 'pot thought' without having first perceived or conceived of one, yet we cannot cognize that a thing is a pot without the thought of a pot.

Swami Lokeswarananda puts it thus (Ref. 20): "*Nothing really exists if it does not exist independently. The knower and the known do not exist separately. That is why, according to non-dualism, the knower, known and knowledge are not separate entities. They are one and the same.*"

Anandagiri adds that we cannot therefore distinguish which is the means of knowledge (*pramANa*) and which the object of knowledge (*prameya*). The existence of each is dependent upon the other and there is no means of knowledge for either's independent existence. We can actually see this for ourselves, in that both world and mind are resolved in the deep-sleep state and are manifest once again on waking. (Similarly with respect to the dream world and dream mind in dreaming.) Neither the minds nor the objects are present all the time, so neither is *satyam*.

The only reality, *satyam*, is Consciousness, the witness of all. It is this alone which reveals the existence of objects and mind alike. It alone is present throughout waking, dream and deep sleep, and is called *turIya*.

Gaudapada next gives three examples to illustrate that there is no real birth or death of people and objects that we see in our waking lives.

(K4.68) All 'things' – from the smallest individual atomic particle to the universe itself – appear and disappear in just the same way as do corresponding objects in dream. Dream objects suddenly appear when we begin the dream and just as suddenly disappear when we sink into deep sleep or wake up. While in the dream, we validate the existence of all the objects using our dream senses, matching them up with known objects in our dream mind. Yet all is imagination only.

(K4.69) Magicians in the time of Gaudapada were clearly brilliant illusionists and, just as with the rope trick described later in 'Theories of Creation' (K1.7-9), were able to baffle an audience with amazing skills. Here, it is suggested that they could conjure up creatures, making them appear and disappear. But this is only seen while the magic lasts. The performer of the magic can be seen as a metaphor for *Ishvara*. It is suggested that *jIva*-s in the world are similarly born and die but have no real existence. [*jIva* is the term used for the 'individual soul', the 'essence' of the person, the 'embodied *Atman*'.]

(K4.70) Finally, he says that incantations and medicines cause artificial creatures to seem to be born and die. This is said by some commentators to refer to the '*siddha*-s' – those yogis who had carried out esoteric practices for many years and developed special powers. It might also be thought of as referring to drugs – perhaps especially to those of a psychedelic variety – which are able to delude the subject into imagining all manner of things.

All of these 'causes' are able to produce the effect of seemingly bringing into existence creatures and objects that are not really there but nevertheless appear to be real. Ultimately, they are only products of the mind and, says Gaudapada, the *jIva*-s of the waking world are no different. They have no real birth or death either; no absolute reality.

He concludes (K4.71) with a repetition of the verse K3.48, the concluding statement in the third chapter on the non-dual nature of *turIya*. This is an adamant, unwavering statement of *ajAti vAda*: No *jIva* is ever born, is ever originated; not ever in any manner. The absolute truth is that nothing is ever born. There is no 'cause' which could produce such an 'effect'.

Swami Chinmayananda points out that Gaudapada is effectively being much stricter than Shankara in his teaching. Shankara propagated the *paramArtha-vyavahAra-pratibhAsa* differentiation for the 'degrees' of reality. This was, of course, a teaching strategy to enable students to approach the absolute truth gradually, in the style of *adhyAropa-apavAda* already discussed. But Gaudapada makes no such concessions and insists on revealing the truth from the outset. Dream equates to *pratibhAsa* and waking to *vyavahAra* and both have been shown to be *mithyA*.

Also, since the Upanishad and the earlier *kArikA*-s make it clear that *turIya* (*brahman*) cannot be a cause at all, standing 'outside' of space, time and causality, it cannot 'produce' anything. There is, in any case, only *brahman*; anything 'else' would be duality.

Criticism of Dualists

There is no denying that the world appears to be real. It is no surprise that we start off believing that we are separate entities in a dualistic universe. Nor is it surprising that many believe this universe to have been created by a God. Although not exactly explaining all that we find inexplicable, such a belief does at least allow us to blame some entity for all of the apparent injustices in life, offer thanks when events turn out as we desired, and maybe even pray in advance that they do.

But it is also understandable that many others become dissatisfied with the never-ending search for happiness through material means and look for a means to escape this apparent cycle of *saMsAra*, the never-ending roller-coaster ride of birth and death, which ultimately goes nowhere. Advaita offers such a means – the Self-knowledge that my real nature is unaffected by the events of life or even by life itself, which is no more significant than a movie to be enjoyed.

Here, Gaudapada criticizes the dualists, who refuse to acknowledge the truth of Advaita and continue blindly on their unending path. He begins (K3.17) by saying that, although the dualists believe that theirs is the correct approach, in fact they contradict each other. This is inevitable. It was pointed out in the introduction that philosophers such as Kant showed that one person can never perceive the world in exactly the same way as another. It is even more difficult when it comes to concepts, since each person has such widely differing family, environmental and educational backgrounds. Dualistic religions attempt to enforce rigid views, which will inevitably conflict with those of others, and history shows that this leads to violence.

Shankara adds that they do not have the support either of the Vedas or of correct reasoning, unlike Advaita. Also, they often violently condemn anyone holding contrary views, because of their attachment to their own philosophy. Advaitins do not do this. One does not attack one's own limb because it is injured and does not function properly. So why should we attack those who, through ignorance, have formed wrong views about the nature of reality? The *Atman* is unaffected by either attachments or hatred. Advaita accepts all religions as *adhyAropa* stages on the path to Advaita. All 'relative' truths are fine, because they are only relative! Unfortunately, the related believers think that their relative truth is absolute – this is what causes all the problems.

Also (K3.18), Gaudapada points out that the dualists believe that the dualistic world is the real effect of a dualistic cause, whereas for the Advaitin, the world is an apparition only since the non-dual reality cannot undergo change. The world is not an 'effect' of any process or cause. A real creation is not possible. Since it is undeniable that we perceive a separate world, it must be the case that there is an apparent creation only.

The Dvaitin believes he or she has *real* problems and we should sympathize with them in their delusion! After all, we were in this position not so long ago! Also, we should not feel threatened by someone who is deluded.

Shankara gives a story as a metaphor. He says we should imagine we are riding an elephant in rut (i.e. one which is very excitable and potentially dangerous). Suppose we encounter a man who is standing on the ground but thinks that he is also on an elephant and challenges us to try to attack him. Shankara says that we would ignore the man, since we know he is mad, and feel sorry for him. Similarly, knowing that the one with the dualist views is also *brahman*, his own Self, the Advaitin feels compassion and does not argue with the Dvaitin.

Advaita does not deny the appearance of duality. Experiencer-experienced duality is as though an effect of the Advaita cause but is never separate from that cause; it is *mithyA*. One of the metaphors for this is a garment. Advaita does not deny the existence of the garment but says that it is not separate from the cloth out of which it is made. Similarly, the cloth seems to be real but is actually *mithyA*; the 'reality' of the cloth is the cotton or other material out of which it is made. Duality is fine… as long as we realize that it is only a name and form of the non-dual substrate, which is the only reality.

This non-dual substrate, *brahman*, only appears to undergo change to become the dualistic universe (K3.19). For the sake of 'explanation', the concept of *mAyA* is introduced as the magical 'force' through which this happens. Alternatively, we can say that we perceive a dualistic world as a result of ignorance, in the same way that one might see double because of a physical defect in the eye.

A cause cannot become an effect without undergoing change –and *brahman* is changeless. If there were a real modification, says Gaudapada, then the infinite would become finite and this is not possible (because then it would not be infinite). Modification would also make it subject to time. (K3.20 and K4.6) Being immortal, this would make it mortal, which is also a contradiction. That which is born must inevitably die. Shankara adds that 'mortal' means 'time bound', whereas 'immortal' means 'timeless'. That which is within time cannot become outside of time. Consequently, there could never be any *mokSha* for the *jIva*, if one accepts these dualistic concepts.

Another possible explanation for the appearance of duality might be that the *jīva* is a 'part' of *brahman*, which has become separated, and has to 'merge' again to attain *mokSha*. But, as we have seen, *turīya* is that non-dual reality which is the all-pervasive substrate of the apparently separate states. It does not have parts so that, in reality, there cannot be any separate *jīva*-s.

What is immortal can never become mortal and vice versa (K3.21 and K4.7). One's essential nature can never change in any way. If I were really mortal, nothing I could do would ever make me immortal. Fortunately, since my real nature is in fact immortal, I need not do anything at all. All that needs to happen is for me to get rid of the false notion that I am limited. This is what we call 'enlightenment'.

When we shine the light of a torch on the 'snake', we automatically realize that it is a rope. You cannot and need not do anything to gain *mokSha*. You are already free; you just have the erroneous belief that you are bound. What is required is to shine the light of knowledge on the mistaken understanding brought about by the darkness of ignorance.

As Swami Paramarthananda puts it: "*Liberation is freedom from the idea that I have to become liberated.*" (Statements such as this might remind one of the 'teachings' of some of the modern, Western 'neo-Advaitins'. And, indeed, one might paradoxically regard Gaudapada as the original 'neo-Advaitin'. The crucial difference is that Gaudapada draws his teaching from the timeless Vedantic scriptures and backs up his statements with rigorous logic. In contrast, the modern 'teacher' makes similar statements without any reference or reasoning and expects the naïve seeker to understand. It is often doubtful that even the speaker understands.)

The dualist, believing that he is mortal, thinks that it is possible to do something and thereby become immortal (K3.22 and K4.8). One last point regarding this is that, if it were possible, it would be an event in time. Implicitly, it would not be permanent and would therefore be liable to future loss. The Advaitin says that this is not real *mokSha*.

jIva is Never Born
Pot Space Metaphor

(K3.3) When we say that we have 'built a house', we tend to think that we have created the various room-spaces in which we live, sleep and wash etc. But of course we have not really done this at all. All we have done is erected some walls and a roof and it is these which demarcate and separate the space that was already there in an unlimited form.

The space itself is totally unaffected by what we have done. Before the house was built, there was space – a single, total space stretching to infinity in all directions (assuming that the universe is unlimited for the sake of this metaphor). We have erected these walls but the space outside and inside has not changed. And when the house is destroyed, whether by natural or man-made forces, the space will still be there, and will remain quite unaffected by the entire process. What we do – and it is this which causes the confusion – is to give the newly delineated spaces names, such as 'kitchen', 'bedroom' etc. This is another very clear example of how it is that the 'naming' of things brings about what we believe to be duality. In fact, there is only ever the non-dual and really undivided total space.

If we are being strictly correct, we cannot say that one room contains more space than another. When we say that one house is bigger than another (because we do live in the space, not in the walls), what we really mean is that the walls are higher or the shapes marked out by the rooms are larger. Or we could say that there is more *air* in one room than another (although we would then have to start being pedantic and say 'at the same temperature and pressure')! Perhaps we really ought to say that there are more bricks in this house! (See commentary on K3.6 below.)

Gaudapada uses the traditional metaphor of clay pots. We talk about the space in the pot as though it was associated with the pot but this is not how it is. If we move the pot, the space remains where it was – the pot moves through space and occupies a different part of it when it comes to rest. What moves with the pot are its contents. If the pot is empty, the air inside will move with it. If a jar previously contained perfume, we might say that the 'space' smells sweet but it is actually the air which smells, probably tainted by the clay itself which has absorbed some of the scent molecules.

The *jIva* is compared to the 'pot-space'. We think that we are separate entities because of the body-mind that seems to limit us, just as the boundary of the clay pot seems to delimit a specific pot-space. But the *Atman* is like the total space. It is quite unaffected by the individual bodies and the individual minds. The body is like the pot which appears to designate a particular part of space but does not really do so. The mind reflects Consciousness making us think that it is a separate entity. (This concept – *chidAbhAsa* – will be mentioned later and is explained in detail in Appendix 3.)

When a new 'pot-space' is 'created' by the potter's throwing a new clay pot, we can see that nothing has really happened as far as the space is concerned. Before, there was the total space, and after, there is total space. The only difference is that there is now some clay occupying part of it and seeming to delineate a separate portion. 'Pot space' is a mistaken notion. 'Pot space' is never created; it is the physical clay pot which is 'as though' created. (Of course, this is not created either as we saw in the gold-ring-bangle-necklace metaphor.)

Similarly, no *jIva* is ever 'created'. Matter, in the form of sperm and eggs, performs its mechanical function, grows and evolves (from the empirical viewpoint). Consciousness (*Atman*) was there before and after. It reflects in the mind of the new *jIva* but is quite unaffected by all this. When the body dies, it is still there just like the space of the house when the walls are knocked down.

Gaudapada identifies five mistakes that we make when thinking about the *jIva* and matches them with mistakes that we make in thinking about the pot space. K3.3 introduced the metaphor and effectively addresses the idea that pot-space or *jIva* is born or created.

K3.4 says that, when the pot is broken, the space within ceases to exist as an apparently separate entity. In fact, as already stated, it never was a separate entity. Moving the jar around never moved a discrete space around; rather it was the jar itself which was moved within space. If the jar was full, the contents moved with the jar; if the jar was empty, the air inside moved with the jar. Space was always unaffected. Some translators use the word 'merge' here, saying that the pot-space 'merges' with the total space when the pot is broken. This is misleading, for the reason just given.

Similarly, many teachers and writers say that, on gaining Self-knowledge (becoming a *j~nAnI* or 'gaining enlightenment'), the *jIva* 'merges' into *brahman*. The same applies here. The only change that takes place is that the intellect realizes the truth – that there is only *brahman*. There has always only been *brahman*, so there can be no change in reality. The seeming change is all at the level of the empirical world, which is *mithyA*.

The correct way of looking at the destruction of the pot is that, following this event, we can no longer refer to a 'pot space'; i.e. all that happens is that we stop calling it by the name that we (mistakenly) gave it in the first place.

In K3.5, Gaudapada looks at the notion we have that we are in some way inadequate or less than perfect. Obviously there are endless ways in which we do this. We feel that our body, mind and intellect are deficient and would like to rectify this. What is happening is that we are identifying with the 'container' rather than the *Atman* that we really are.

This is analogous to the way that we might say that the pot

space is contaminated, with dust, smoke or other impurities. Especially if the pot is empty and smells bad, we tend to think that the space in the pot smells. Of course, it is the air or the material out of which the pot is constructed that smells.

More generally we say that one person is happy, another miserable and so on. Shankara uses this notion to argue against the beliefs of the Sankhya and Yoga-Vaisheshika philosophers. [These are three of the other major philosophies which were prevalent in India at the time that Gaudapada was writing. The beliefs of Yoga and Vaisheshika are very similar so they were often grouped together.] The Sankhyas believe that there are many *jIvAtma*-s. And they attempt to argue that, if there were only one *Atman* then, if one *jIvAtman* is happy, then all should be. But this is to confuse the pot-space with the pot. It is like arguing that, if one pot smells bad, then all pots should smell bad. Gaudapada says that it is therefore not the case that, if one *jIvAtman* is associated with happiness, then all are.

[The word *jIvAtman* is often used to refer to the 'embodied' *Atman*, i.e. Consciousness associated with a body-mind. The word *paramAtman* is often used to refer to Existence associated with the universe, or the 'macrocosmic Consciousness'. This sort of breakdown is useful in the intermediate, *adhyAropa* stage of teaching, when these things seem to be different entities. In reality, of course, *jIvAtman* and *paramAtman* are the same; Consciousness and Existence are different 'aspects' of the non-dual *brahman*.]

Of course, the *Atman* cannot be associated with anything, not even happiness, and Gaudapada makes this clear in K3.8. Here he uses another metaphor – that of children thinking that the sky is sometimes dirty or contaminated. In the same way, it is ignorant people only who think that the Self can be tainted by impurities (such as happiness!). [Note that one should not confuse the 'happiness' of the *jIva* with the *Ananda* of *Atman*. The latter should rather be understood as *ananta*, referring to its 'unlimited' nature.]

The body, mind and intellect of *jIva*-s are analogous to the material out of which the pot is made. The *Atman* is non-dual, like the total space. Gaudapada actually speaks of *jIva*-s being 'polluted' by happiness, drawing attention to the fact that happiness is only a temporary attribute of the 'container', and not a property of *Atman*.

(K3.6) The fourth mistake that we make is to think that the space and *Atman* can have specific attributes. Thus the kitchen is such by virtue of the items that are stored there and the functions we perform – using a casserole dish in an oven to cook food, for example. The 'kitchen space' has nothing to do with any of this. The attributes that we erroneously assign to the space are name, form and function. As already noted, the shape (or form) is defined by the walls. The name and the function are arbitrary – there is no reason why we cannot watch the television in the kitchen (and apparently many do these days).

Similarly, attributes that we assign to the *Atman* are really applicable only to the gross, subtle or casual bodies. There are many such attributes (though all are *mithyA*) but only one *Atman*. Some bodies are fat, some disabled etc. Some minds know how to speak Mandarin and many do not. If a pot smells, we do not need to do anything to the space. This can be demonstrated by taking the pot away and the space where the pot was standing no longer smells. Similarly, we do not need to do anything to ourselves in order to become perfect. The *Atman* is already perfect and nothing can be done to it anyway. All that is required is to remove the mistaken notion in the mind that I am limited in whatever way – I am really unlimited.

(K3.7) The fifth mistake is to think that the pot space is a 'part' of the total space and that we ourselves are a 'part' (or a modification) of the supreme Self or *paramAtman*. There is a tendency to think that there is a space 'inside' the pot and a different space 'outside' the pot. But as has already been noted, it is the pot which is in the (total) space, not the other way round. Space cannot have parts.

(K3.9) Gaudapada concludes that the Self is like space in all these respects. The *jIvAtman* is not born, does not die, is not 'impure' in any way, has no attributes (good or bad), and is not a part of a 'total' Self. Nor does it travel (from body to body in reincarnation). Indeed, it is everywhere always, so there is nowhere else for it to go. This leads on to the next topic of causality because the fact that the *jIvAtman* is not born means that it is not an effect. This, in turn, means that *paramAtman* is not a cause. There is only the *Atman*, falsely divided into *paramAtman* and *jIvAtman*, and it is beyond time, space and causality.

Scriptural Negation of *jIva*

The analysis of the pot-space metaphor provided a logic-based refutation of the notion that a *jIva* is ever born. Gaudapada next turns to utilizing scriptural references to refute it.

The introduction already addressed the question of the value of scriptures in Vedanta and why we should give them credence. All seekers who follow a reasonably formal, traditional route for the teaching of Advaita will inevitably come to the conclusion that scriptures, when interpreted by a qualified *sampradAya* teacher, can be trusted. Such a teacher is one who has Self-knowledge and has studied those scriptures (with a *sampradAya* teacher) for many years. (And who has a high level of understanding of Sanskrit.)

The point is that much of what is learned from the scriptures is not directly accessible to experience; it is known by certain intuition once one's knowledge has reached the necessary level. Accordingly, it is necessary to acquire the input for this from a source other than experience. Gaudapada shows that it is possible to achieve this by reason alone but it is nevertheless extremely valuable to be able to show that others, too, have reached the same conclusions.

The ultimate difference between Vedantic scriptures teaching Advaita and biblical scriptures teaching about God's administration of earthly matters is that the former can be validated for oneself (whilst still alive)! Accordingly, innumerable people have realized the truth of Advaita in their lifetime, whereas the best that a Christian could say is that he or she 'firmly believes' in the truth of the tenets of that religion, the existence of God and so on. And the difference between knowledge and belief is vast.

According to Advaita, the testimony of the Vedas (*shruti*) sublates the knowledge that we gain from perception. Just as we see the sunrise, but science tells us that this is because the earth is rotating, we see duality but the scriptures tell us that the world is *mithyA* and only Consciousness is ultimately real. The duality of the world has transactional validity (*vyavahAra*) only.

[The word 'sublate' is not a common one in English. It refers to the mental event in which one's understanding is suddenly radically revised as a result of some new experience or piece of knowledge. For example, shining a torch on the 'snake' or walking up to the mirage-water 'sublates' the earlier knowledge and supplants it with the knowledge that the snake is a rope and the water is only sand. The Sanskrit term for sublation (sometimes also spelled 'subration') is *bAdha*.]

In K3.11, Gaudapada gives the first of several references to other Upanishads to show that they also support what he says (and has concluded through reasoning). This first reference is to the Taittiriya Upanishad (2.1-2.4) and the metaphor of the five sheaths.

Basically, these verses say that the *Atman* is as though enclosed in a series of sheaths like the sheath of a sword. These are 'made up of' such things as 'food', since the physical body is constituted of the food that we eat. They become successively more subtle until we uncover the innermost one (of bliss) and find the *Atman*. But the metaphor is another device to lead us from the *mithyA* things (body and mind etc.) that we think we are to the non-dual *Atman* that we really are.

The sheaths, as with the world, have no existence separate from *Atman*. It is like the pot-space metaphor. The space 'inside' the pot' is the space 'outside'. There is only 'total' space. The Self 'inside' the body and other sheaths is called *jIvAtman*; the Self 'outside' is called *paramAtman* or *brahman*. The Taittiriya and other Upanishads tell us that 'this *Atman* IS *brahman*' (or *jIvAtman* = *paramAtman*). Since this is the case, the *jIvAtman* cannot have been created or have been 'born'; and *brahman* is not a creator.

Swami Chinmayananda points out that this verse also corrects a possible misunderstanding on the part of the seeker. Having learned that the world is effectively a product of *mAyA*, we will hopefully conclude that the world is unreal (only name and form of *brahman*). But there is a danger that I may still feel that my body, mind and intellect etc., are real, since it is clear that 'I' must be real. But this is not the case. Those 'sheaths', too, are equally *mithyA*. It is only the *Atman* that is ultimately real, and the entire world, *including* all bodies and minds, depend upon it for their apparent existence.

(K3.12)The next reference that Gaudapada makes is to the Brihadaranyaka Upanishad (2.5). We already met the concept of microcosmic and macrocosmic in the Mandukya Upanishad itself. In this section of the Brihadaranyaka, it is stated that Consciousness in both is the same, i.e. *jIvAtman* = *paramAtman*. Again, the metaphor of space is used and Gaudapada says that the space in the earth and that in the stomach is the same. The conclusion is the same as before. It is like the wave and the ocean; these are superficially different but in reality one and the same water.

(K3.13) In general, wherever the identity of Atman and *brahman* are spoken of in the scriptures, this attitude is praised; wherever difference is suggested, such an idea is condemned. One can only conclude that non-duality is the correct viewpoint.

Swam Paramarthananda elaborates on this topic, and it is a

useful aside. He points out that there are many passages which speak of concepts (such as creation) which are dualistic. And of course there is an entire branch of Hindu philosophy (*dvaita*) that bases its dualistic beliefs on the Vedas. A skeptic could justifiably claim that Gaudapada was 'cherry-picking' data which supports his arguments.

He responds to this potential criticism by pointing out that, in those places where difference is stated, there are invariably other statements which censure such a view. For example, the first few mantras of the Mundaka Upanishad, book 2 section 1, describe how everything is created from *brahman*, including (2.1.7) all of the gods, celestials and, specifically, human beings. But, if you carry on reading, 2.1.10 effectively contradicts this (*adhyAropa-apavAda*) and explains that the world is *brahman* alone and the one who knows this 'resolves the knot of ignorance'. Non-duality alone is reasonable, says Gaudapada.

The Katha Upanishad (also 2.1.10) says that '*whoever sees difference between what is here* (jIvAtman) *and what is there* (brahman) *goes from death to death* (i.e. remains in *saMsAra*)'.

Shankara says that, although it is natural for ordinary people to believe in duality, this is only because of their faulty reasoning and because they have turned away from the scriptural authority (or, nowadays far more likely, never come across it in the first place). He says that, contrary to how it appears initially to these people, the identity of *jIva* and *Atman* is '*rational, easily under-standable and proper*' (Ref. 21).

(K3.14) If one should wonder why the Vedas talk about duality at all, it is only to provide interim explanations for the seeker who is not yet ready to accept the final truth of non-duality. And practices such as *upAsana* are provided for them as 'stepping stones' to lead them to the point at which full under-standing may be gained. The other helpful metaphor in this context is that of the pole-vaulter. He or she needs the assistance of the pole in order to reach the bar which has to be crossed. But the pole has to be left behind if the vaulter is to cross to the other side without dislodging the bar. Similarly, many seekers need the initial help of teaching that it is not ultimately true; i.e. material that involves duality. Once their understanding has matured, it has to be dropped.

[*upAsana* is meditation, conducted as a practice to prepare the mind prior to Self-inquiry. It literally means 'adoration, worship' and may appear to take this form if the object of meditation is a deity. But meditation on OM as instructed by the Mandukya Upanishad and *kArikA*-s is more relevant here.]

Another good metaphor used in the scriptures is that of the scaffolding that is initially erected when building a house. Until such time as the walls and upper floors have been at least partially completed, the scaffolding is needed. But we would not dream of leaving it there permanently, after the house has been finished.

Causality

From an everyday perspective, the concept of causality seems intuitively obvious. X happens and triggers subsequent events – Y, Z, and quite possibly A and B as well; A and B then bring about more events in turn. And so it goes on. The phone rings, whilst I am deep in thought. This startles me and I turn quickly, knocking the cup of tea off the desk, breaking the cup and staining the carpet. Suddenly all that I had planned to do must be dropped while I attempt to return to the status quo.

As soon as one starts to look into a presumed cause-effect situation in detail, things begin to get very complicated very quickly. Even language cannot be trusted: 'if A happens, then B *must* follow' might relate to an injunction, obligation, inference, physical necessity, logical necessity, to name some that spring to mind. A road accident might be 'caused' by driving too fast, an uneven road, a design fault in the car, inattention, weather conditions, back-seat driving or something else, depending upon whom you ask. Causes might be 'necessary' and/or 'sufficient' or 'instrumental'. There are entire books written on the subject! And you very soon have to start thinking about free-will, too!

But you will have already realized by now that philosophers are never happy simply to accept the way that things *seem* to be! Here, Gaudapada is principally interested in inquiring into causality in the particular case of 'making' something; i.e. the cause of an object which has been produced from something by someone (we are gradually working up to asking whether the universe is 'created' or not). If we return to the gold-ring metaphor, we know that the goldsmith began with a lump of gold and produced the ring by making use of specialized tools together with heat, and employing his acquired skills. We say that the lump of gold is the material cause of the ring, while the goldsmith is the efficient cause.

Refutation of Other Philosophies

Chapter 4 of the *kArikA*-s is largely concerned with refuting other theories of causality and creation. It is called *alAta shAnti prakaraNa* – the 'chapter on the quenching of the firebrand'. The 'firebrand' refers to the metaphor of the whirling, burning torch that appears to draw patterns in the air. I used a firework sparkler in the introduction instead.

The whirling of the firebrand generates what seem to be real circles and patterns of light in the air, albeit they do not last very long. Similarly, we might say that the vibrations (*spandana*) of the mind produce what appear to be the separate objects of the world, and these seem to last rather longer. It is the purpose of the scriptures to bring the mind to stillness, as it were, so that the mistaken interpretations of perception are quelled and the world is realized to be name and form of non-dual Consciousness. This is then analogous to the way that the appearance of patterns is dissolved by stilling the movement of the firebrand.

The firebrand metaphor had previously been used in Buddhist texts to explain the concept of 'vibrations of the mind', particularly by *vij~nAna vAda* Buddhists. Gaudapada uses lots of Buddhist terminology in this chapter and it is reasonable to conclude that he is specifically aiming to 'quench' them with his arguments, using their own phraseology to help to do so. [*vij~nAna vAda* is effectively the philosophical belief of Idealism; the belief that objects are actually just ideas in the mind. The word *vij~nAna* literally means intelligence, knowledge, the act of understanding.]

Firebrand is also a word used to describe someone who is very passionate about a cause or belief (usually a trouble maker) and in this chapter Gaudapada attacks such people and discredits them. Unfortunately, it is most unlikely that this meaning is in any way implied – this western usage is relatively modern, around the fourteenth century possibly – but maybe the Sanskrit word had similar connotations.

satkAryavAda vs asatkAryavAda

You may have heard the story (probably apocryphal) about how Michelangelo, when asked how he was able to create such phenomenally lifelike statues, denied that he actually created anything new. He claimed that he was able to sense the already-completed form within the stone and all he needed to do was to chip away the excess material around it.

This is effectively the theory of satkArya vAda, which is the proposition (vAda) that the effect (kArya) is already pre-existent (sat) in the cause. Adherents claim that an effect must already be potential in the cause; otherwise it could not come out of it. They would say that, in the case of the statue, the stone was veiling the form of the statue and Michelangelo was effectively removing the veil.

This belief is held by the sAMkhya philosophers, propounded by the sage Kapila, who claim that the world evolved from prakRRiti , i.e. is a transformation or modification (pariNAma) of some primeval 'stuff'. Thus, another name for the belief is pariNAma vAda. (K4.3)

The nyAya philosophers, originated by Gautama around 300 BC and further developed by Kanada into the vaisheShika philosophy, claim that this is not a sensible idea. They ask: if the effect is already there, then what does it mean to produce it? It is like saying that the stone and the statue are at one and the same time both different and identical. This is clearly contradictory.

Although admitting that there must be an inherent relationship (samavAya sambandha) between cause and effect, the actual result is produced solely as a result of the creative act. [samavAya means a constant and inseparable conjunction between an attribute and substance, such as between 'blue' and 'Lotus' in the particular example of a 'blue Lotus'; sambandha means relationship.] Their theory is, unsurprisingly, called asatkArya vAda – the effect is not pre-existent in the cause.

The sAMkhya-s object to this 'creative act' explanation. To say that the effect is not inherent in the cause is tantamount to claiming that something comes out of nothing, which is clearly nonsensical (K4.4). They argue that this would imply that any given cause could produce any effect and not a very specific one. Chipping away at the stone, for example, might be the means of preparing our next meal and Michelangelo's next creation might come from leaving a bucket of water underneath his bed when he goes to sleep.

Furthermore, the *nyAya* concept of *samavAya* does not make any sense on analysis. If we say there is a relationship between cause and effect, this 'relationship' cannot be the *same* as cause and effect. If it were, there would be no things to relate, nor anything doing the relating. Nor can the relationship be different from cause and effect. If it were, there would have to be two more relationships, one between cause and *samavAya* and another between *samavAya* and effect. And so on, ad infinitum.

Thus it is that the *nyAya*-s and *sAMkhya*-s contradict each other's theory and the Advaitin need not do anything in the way of argument (K4.5). Gaudapada ridicules them both. He says that the *sAMkhya* view amounts to saying that what already exists can be born, while the *nyAya* view is that a non-existent thing can be born; and both propositions are impossible. An existing thing cannot come into existence when it already exists and a non-existent thing can never come into existence either. It also contradicts the law of conservation (of mass-energy) which states that mass-energy can neither be created nor destroyed. If a non-existent thing could be created, this would amount to matter coming out of nothing. [Note that Theoretical Physicists continue to speculate about all of this and no doubt will continue to do so!]

The confusion arises here because of language. We give something a name for convenience and, as a result of constant use, we take it for granted that the word refers to some separately existing thing. The classic examples that are quoted in the scriptures are clay-pot and gold-ring-bangle etc. When the potter makes a pot out of a lump of clay, the resultant object clearly has a new function. It can hold a liquid so that we can use it as a drinking vessel, for example. But we quickly forget that the pot is not a new thing in its own right. In the beginning, it was simply a lump of clay. Now, it is clay shaped into a more useful form. If we break it, it will still be clay, albeit now in pieces with little use at all.

The Chandogya Upanishad (6.1.4 - 6) says that any product is only a new word: *"just as, through a single clod of clay, all that is made of clay would become known, for all modification is but name based upon words and the clay alone is real..."* (This is known as the *vAchArambhaNa shruti* – meaning 'depending on mere words or some merely verbal difference' – and is a very important text in Advaita.) The making of the pot is simply changing the form of the clay and giving it a new name.

In the same way, then, when the world and the *jIva* come into being, all that is happening is that *brahman* is acquiring new forms and new names to go with them. But, before, during and after, all that actually exists is *brahman*.

As will be seen, the Advaitin agrees with both the Sankhya and the Nyaya philosophers (when they contradict the other)! The birth of an existent thing is negated and the birth of a non-existent thing is negated. Gaudapada's contention is the simple and logical conclusion – *nothing* is ever born! Having established this theory of *ajAti vAda* by means of his opponents' own disputes, he then briefly revisits the fallacies that ensue from adopting the standpoints of these dualistic philosophers. K4.6 – K4.8 are essentially repetitions of K3.20 – K3.22 respectively. (See 'Criticism of Dualists' above.)

The Absolute is eternal. It cannot be the 'cause' of anything, since that would involve change and contradict its eternal nature. 'Immortal' *means* 'changeless'.

In K4.9, Gaudapada lists the four characteristics by which

things can be classified to describe their essential nature:

sAMsiddhikI – this refers to those aspects which are acquired
but which subsequently never go away. A trivial example
would be knowledge of multiplication tables or alphabet;
svAbhAvika – refers to inherent characteristics, such as the
heat of fire or sweetness of sugar;
sahaja – this relates to innate capabilities, for example the
ability of a bird to fly as soon as it leave the nest;
akRRita – natural tendencies, such as that of water to flow
downhill.

Things cannot change any of these essential characteristics
without changing their 'nature' and effectively becoming
something else.

The Self, Atman – turIya, is the essential nature of everything.
It is not subject to change (K4.10). It is free from birth, growth,
disease, old age and death. No one feels that he or she can ever
die. We secretly think we are 'invincible'. People say this about
others who have 'died': "he thought he was invincible." But we
also no longer see these people so we convince ourselves that,
logically, we must also die. What we do not appreciate is that it
is only the gross body that perishes. We identify with that and
therefore think that we will also perish. Our ignorance of our
true nature leads us to make this mistake and suffer the consequences of this delusion – this is an aspect of saMsAra.

Swami Paramarthananda tells the story of a game played by
children on an unsuspecting newcomer to their group. They use
saliva to press a coin onto the new child's forehead so that it
sticks. And they tell him that he can hit himself on the back of the
head to make the coin fall and, if he can do this with three hits,
he can have the coin. So they then press the coin to his forehead
for perhaps 10-15 seconds and then, unbeknownst to the child
they actually take it away. But it feels to the child as though the

coin is still there and he proceeds to hit himself increasingly harder on the back of his head trying to dislodge the non-existent coin. Even when he is allowed further tries, he is doomed to continue to fail because there is no coin there to fall.

Similarly, saMsAra can be thought of as our repeatedly hitting ourselves on the head, lifetime after lifetime. The coin will never fall because it is not there. We have conditioned ourselves to think that we are limited and need to seek freedom but we are already free. He says that the other children can demonstrate that there is no coin by holding up a mirror for the dupe to see. Vedanta is the metaphorical mirror that can be held up to enable us to realize that we are *Atman*.

Refutation of sAMkhya Theory

Having said above that Advaita need not bother to refute sAMkhya, since the arguments between them and the nyAya-vaisheShika philosophers effectively nullify each other, Gaudapada then goes on systematically to destroy the sAMkhya view regarding creation. The reason for this is that, in Gaudapada's time, sAMkhya was one of the most powerful philosophical systems and had to be taken very seriously indeed. It also has many similarities with Advaita so that there is a real danger of confusing the two systems.

It was pointed out above that Sankhyans believe that an effect pre-exists in the cause but in a different form, as in the example of Michelangelo's statues. The 'creation' of the statue therefore consists of converting the 'causal' form into its already existing 'effect'. (Of course, one assumes that they would not deny that this also requires quite a bit of skill!) This would also apply to a tree and a seed: the tree already exists in the seed but in causal form. And, paradoxically, the seed already exists in the tree! Effectively, therefore, they say that cause and effect are essentially different forms or states of the same substance.

As was illustrated in the Introduction, Advaitins claim that bangles and chains are simply differing names and forms of gold and this is effectively the same theory. The key difference relates to how this is applied to the 'creation' of the universe itself. The *sAMkhya* philosophers do not treat this any differently. They believe that the 'causal state' of the universe is something called *prakRRiti* or *pradhAna* (primary nature or matter) and that there is an actual creation which transforms this *prakRRiti* into the world. And they say that, whilst *prakRRiti* is eternal (*nitya*), its product, the universe, is transient or non-eternal (*anitya*).

Gaudapada proceeds to point out the fallacies in their logic. He says that their reasoning can be summarized by the following statements:

1. The effect is the same as the cause.
2. The cause (*prakRRiti*) is eternal.
3. The effect (*universe*) is non-eternal.

From the first two statements, the effect equals the cause and therefore must also be eternal. But this contradicts the third statement. Alternatively, from the first and third statements, the cause equals the effect and must therefore be non-eternal. But this contradicts the second statement (K4.11-12). Logically, if *prakRRiti* and the universe are the same (different forms of the same substance), either both must be eternal or both must be non-eternal.

sAMkhya also refers to *prakRRiti* as the root cause, *mUla kAraNa*, of the universe (*mUla* means 'root' or 'origin') and, in keeping with its claimed status of 'eternal', they say that *prakRRiti* is itself causeless. Now the Sankhyan concedes that *prakRRiti* is not available to perception (*pratyakSha pramANa*) so that he arrives at his postulation of its existence as a result of inference (*anumAna pramANa*). But, as can be seen from the discussion of *pramANa*-s and logic in the Introduction, in order to be able to make an inference we need experiential data. We can infer the existence of a fire on the hill because we have experienced the invariable existence of fire in connection with smoke. If we now look at the situation with respect to effects and causes, says Gaudapada (K4.13), we have to say that all our experience points to the conclusion that every cause is itself the effect of another cause. Our parents were themselves children; trees came from seeds which themselves were produced from an earlier tree; and so on. So the conclusion that we reach is that every cause has a beginning (i.e. was the effect of a prior cause). Hence, the very idea of a 'causeless cause' contradicts our data. In order for the Sankhyans to make such an assertion, they must provide a *vyApti* – a rule that has been derived from actual examples that we might witness ourselves. And he is unable to do this. His inference is fallacious and, based upon our own experience, is a logical contradiction.

The only way out of this is to admit that *prakRRiti* is not eternal, not beginningless. But, if you do this, you then have to ask 'what is the cause of *prakRRiti*, since it is *mUla* no longer?' You cannot say that X is the cause because, if you do, Gaudapada will ask what is the cause of X, since a beginningless cause is a contradiction. So you cannot postulate *any* root cause for the universe and, if you are unable to establish a cause, you cannot talk about an effect either. Or, to be more specific, if you have no root source for the creation, you cannot actually talk about a 'creation' at all. The word itself presupposes a creator. In fact, you have to acknowledge that there is no creation at all. This is the theory of *ajAti vAda* and is that put forward by Gaudapada.

Refutation of *Dvaita* Theory of *karma*

The *dvaita* philosophers take the theory of *karma* to be the explanation for the creation of the world. In order to understand the theory, some basic concepts are needed (these are provided below in slightly more detail than needed to understand what follows but it is useful for reference):

saMskAra - whenever an action is performed with the desire for a specific result (whether for oneself or another), *saMskAra*-s are created for that person. These accumulate and determine the situations with which we will be presented in the future and will influence the scope of future actions. The accumulation of *saMskAra*-s dictates the tendencies (*vAsanA*-s) that we have to act in a particular way. There are three 'types' of *saMskAra* – *AgAmin* (or *AgAmika*), *saMchita* and *prArabdha*.

AgAmin is that type of *saMskAra* which is generated in reaction to current situations and which will not bear fruit until sometime in the future. It literally means 'impending', 'approaching' or 'coming'. It is also called *kriyamANa*, which means 'being done'.

saMchita, literally meaning 'collected' or 'piled up', is that *saMskAra* which has been accumulated from past action but has still not manifest.

prArabdha literally means 'begun' or 'undertaken.' It is the fruit of all of our past action that is now having its effect. There are three types of *prArabdha karma* – *ichChA*, *anichChA* and *parechChA* (personally desired, without desire and due to others' desire).

puNya – literally 'good' or 'virtuous' is used to refer to the 'reward' that accrues to us through the performing of unselfish actions.

pApa – literally 'bad' or 'wicked' but is used in the sense of the 'sin' that accrues from performing 'bad' actions, i.e. those done with a selfish motive.

anAdi – beginningless. This is a term which is encountered at various times in Advaita. It is, for example, used to describe 'ignorance' (*avidyA*). In the context of this discussion, it is said that the process of *karma* is also beginningless. Since the concept is probably unfamiliar, it may seem rather strange. Here are a couple of points about it from Arvind Sharma, which may help (Ref. 28):

- *"When we say that a thing comes into being at a definite point of time, we imply also that there was 'non-existence' of that particular thing prior to that moment. And this 'non-existence' is obviously beginningless. But it ceases as soon as the thing comes into being."* (Of course, Gaudapada will deny that a thing can ever come into being!)
- In respect of dreaming – *"Once the person has commenced dreaming, is it possible for the person to know* in the dream *when the dream began? In the dream, one can keep track of the time through a dream clock but one cannot say, in terms of the dream time, when the dream began, for the beginning is itself part of the dream. In this sense, clearly the dream is* anAdi *and, by analogy, the universe."*

The theory, then, says that we collect *saMskAra*-s, or *puNya* and *pApa*, as a result of every action we perform in life where the action is motivated, rather than simply being in response to the need. (*karma yoga* is the practice of learning to act only in such a manner as does not collect any *saMskAra*.) Those accumulated *saMskAra*-s that are not cancelled out by 'right action' by the end of our life will determine the body and conditions for a subsequent life; i.e. rebirth occurs into that body and those conditions which are most suitable for exhausting the *karma*.

The essence of all of this is that the theory states that the bodies that we now have are effectively determined by the *karma* resulting from our past lives. Conversely, the *karma* that we accrue in this life (together with unused *saMchita* from previous lives) will determine the body that we 'get' in our next life. Or, to put it in its most basic form, *karma* (from previous lives) is the cause for the (present) body and the body is the cause for the next batch of *karma*.

Of course traditional Advaita, too, teaches the theory of *karma* to begin with but, as with all of the rest of the teaching, once the student has understood and benefited from it and is ready to move on to a more advanced understanding, that teaching is rescinded and a more sophisticated explanation provided. The Mandukya Upanishad and *kArikA* represent the highest teaching of Advaita, which is why all of these explanations are now being rejected. (This process of teaching is called *adhyAropa-apavAda*, as already explained.)

What Gaudapada now demonstrates is that the theory cannot withstand logical scrutiny. He first shows that neither *karma* nor the body can be the root cause (*mUla kAraNa*) for the creation. The theory of *karma*, as noted above, says that the rewards and punishments are the karmic effects that accrue from the actions performed by the body; i.e. *karma* is the effect and the body is the cause. But the body that we have is said to be the effect resulting from (the cause of) previous *karma*. If, says Gaudapada, *karma* brings about the body but also that body is the cause of the *karma*, then how can either be beginningless? (K4.14) It is the perennial question of 'which came first, the chicken or the egg?' For one of them to come first, it would be necessary for the creator to assign either bodies or *karma* on an arbitrary basis and this could not be reconciled with the theory (or with the concept of an impartial God).

The next possibility is that *karma* and body are regarded as mutually cause and effect; the effect is the origin of the cause and the cause is the origin of the effect (K4.15). This is patently meaningless since causes have to come prior to effects if they are to be called 'causes' at all. It would also lead to such ludicrous consequences as its being possible for a son to be the father of his own father.

So maybe *karma* and body originate simultaneously? (K4.16) Fine, says Gaudapada, but in that case, neither can be the cause of the other. And he asks whether, in the case of an animal with two horns, one horn could have caused the other. Furthermore, if they did originate simultaneously, then what was their cause? So, if the Dvaitin is to maintain his original premise that *karma* is the explanation for creation, he is obliged to say which came first, or which caused the other. This he is unable to do. Two things, each dependent upon the other for its production, can never have a cause-effect relationship points out Shankara (K4.17). Whichever one you take cannot be the *cause* of the other because it is *dependent* upon that other for its own production.

The next possibility that Gaudapada considers is that *karma* and body do have a mutual cause-effect relationship but in the form of a chain (K4.18). Thus, *karma*1 causes body2; body2 causes *karma*3; *karma*3 causes body4 and so on. But numbering them in this way implies that *karma* is the first in the chain. You could equally well say that the order is: body1 causes *karma*2; *karma*2 causes body3; body3 causes *karma*4 and so on. The point is that, in this variant of the explanation, you still have to specify which comes first – you haven't solved anything.

Shankara (in his commentary on K4.20) then takes this one step further. He says that we could get around this by saying that the chain is 'beginningless' (*anAdi*). This is similar to what we see with respect to chicken and egg or tree and seed (although science would now rationalize these through genetics and natural selection). This is also the explanation that is provided within Advaita, albeit it is only provisional within the context of the *adhyAropa-apavAda* teaching method. But he also goes on to say that using an analogy such as seed and tree does not answer the question as to which came first, *karma* or body. It simply transfers the problem to asking whether tree or seed came first in the analogy.

Saying that the chains of *karma* and body or of seed and tree are beginningless does not mean anything if you analyze it, because the 'chain' does not actually exist separate from the 'links'. If you take away *karma* and body (or seed and tree) from the 'chain', there is nothing left. We have already shown that *karma* cannot be the original cause (because *karma* results from the actions of a body) and the body cannot be the original cause (because bodies are 'chosen' on the basis of past *karma*). And to say that it is the chain itself that is 'beginningless' has no meaning. So the entire theory has no foundation and has to be discarded.

In any case, says Shankara, you cannot use an example such as seed and tree to 'explain' the karma problem, because that example itself has not yet been satisfactorily explained. Gaudapada is using this as an illustration or metaphor only and not as a reasoned argument.

Swami Paramarthananda, in his discourse on the Mandukya Upanishad and *kArikA*-s (Ref. 5), goes on to provide additional arguments. He says that, even if you allowed that there *could* be such a thing as a beginningless chain, this would not solve the problem because the next question would be whether or not this chain was endless. If you say that it is also endless, then this would mean that *saMsAra* itself was endless and it would then follow that all of this teaching is a waste of time since nothing that you do or learn can ever bring an end to *saMsAra*. If, on the other hand, you say that the chain does have an end, namely freedom from *saMsAra* (*mokSha*), then this will mean that *mokSha* has a beginning in time. Advaita says that we are already free; we just do not know it. Enlightenment is that event in time when the ignorance falls away and we realize that we have always been free. So the idea that *mokSha* itself could be an event in time is in contradiction to the teaching of Advaita. Moreover, if it has a beginning in time, then it will also end at some future time. Nothing in time is ever eternal, by definition, not even the universe itself. A *mokSha* that begins and ends is no *mokSha* at all; it would be no better than going to heaven and having to return to a human birth again later.

So Gaudapada concludes (K4.19) that the Dvaitins are unable to back up their claims with any logical reasoning. Their confusion shows that these 'intelligent' philosophers (he calls them, sarcastically) have not thought through their arguments regarding the theory of *karma*. And Gaudapada asserts, as he did with his analysis of *sAMkhya* philosophy, that whichever way you look at it, there can be no creation. Shankara says (K4.21) that the fact that one is unable logically to make sense of the idea that there is a cause for creation is the clearest indication that there is none. In everyday experience, there is never any problem in pointing to the cause of anything that is actually 'born'.

Therefore, nothing is ever born, whether out of itself or out of something else, and whether it is itself existent, non-existent or both (K4.22). Shankara elaborates on this by taking the example of a jar produced from clay. (Gaudapada has effectively gone through most of this when refuting the *sAMkhya* philosophers earlier but Shankara visits them again here for the benefit of the Dvaitins.) He says that the jar can obviously not be born out of itself – it cannot be its own cause. If it already exists, it doesn't need to be born. If it doesn't yet exist, then there is no form out of which it could be born. Also, it cannot be produced from, say, a cloth; i.e. from another thing altogether. And it could not be produced by somehow combining jar and cloth.

Of course, Shankara goes on to say, we do speak of a jar or pot being produced from clay and we could even watch this taking place on the potter's wheel. But the idea of something being 'born' or 'created' is mistaken. And he refers again to the *vAchArambhaNa shruti* that was mentioned in the initial discussions regarding the *sAMkhya* and *nyAya* philosophers. Here, in the Chandogya Upanishad, it is pointed out that, although the word 'jar' is new, no actual new thing has been created. "All effects are mere names and figures of speech." Accordingly, since there is only actually clay at all times, it is not meaningful to talk about cause and effect.

If something already exists, it cannot be born again. A non-existent thing (the perennial example in the scriptures being the 'horns of a hare') cannot be produced (although modern geneticists would no doubt be prepared to have a go). And you cannot associate such contradictory ideas as 'existent' and 'non-existent' with a thing so that the final option also makes no sense.

Therefore, whether you are talking about the birth of a jar or the birth of the universe, you are forced to conclude that there can be no birth at all. The Dvaitin's idea of 'beginninglessness' cannot withstand Gaudapada's analysis (K4.23). An effect is a product and therefore must have a beginning or birth. And a cause produced from an effect would also have to be treated as an effect and would also have a beginning. For something to have no beginning means that it has no birth. So, if he maintains that, in the case of creation, cause and effect are beginningless, he is effectively proposing *ajAti vAda* himself!

When we say that something is beginningless or 'birthless' (K4.29), this means that 'not being born' is its intrinsic nature. It cannot, therefore, change into something else. Any seeming birth or creation must be due to *mAyA* and be apparent only. *brahman* is changeless and, since cause and effect involve change, *brahman* cannot be a cause of anything.

The conclusion of this discussion is extremely important for a consideration of *mokSha*. Gaudapada points out (K4.30) that, if *saMsAra* were beginningless, it could never end; and, as a corollary, if liberation had a beginning in time, then it would not be eternal – i.e. it would come to an end.

Shankara posits a possible objection to this conclusion. This is that we could consider liberation as being analogous to the total destruction of something, like a pot which had a beginning when it was made. Such destruction would be endless, even though there was a beginning. We could regard liberation as being destruction of *saMsAra*. But he says that this does not work because it contradicts the disputant's claim that liberation has a positive existence. If it has not, then it cannot have a beginning. A non-existent thing cannot have a beginning, like the classic example of 'horns of a hare', or the more modern example of a squared circle.

So *mokSha* cannot be an event in time. We are always free. This is why we should really always use the term 'Self-knowledge', rather than such words as 'enlightenment', 'awakening' or 'realization'. All of such words imply something happening in time – before we were bound, after we are liberated. This is not the way it is.

Many modern seekers believe that this 'enlightenment' is an experience, brought about by such things as a Zen koan or by an idea heard or read. It happens suddenly and there is a flash of realization and afterwards, we live in a state of heightened awareness in which everything is seen as one.

In fact, *saMsAra* is an illusion. It is simply a mistake that we make as a result of Self-ignorance. As a result of hearing this teaching, questioning everything until we have no further doubts about its truth, and then continually reflecting upon it (reading, writing, discussing, listening, teaching etc.), Self-knowledge is established and we recognize that we always have been, and always will be *brahman*. This is *mokSha*.

Refutation of Buddhism

We saw above how Gaudapada allowed the *sAMkhya* and the *nyAya-vaisheShika* philosophers each to refute the other so that he did not really need to add much to the argument. He now makes use of the idealist (*vij~nAna vAda*) Buddhist to refute the contentions of the realist branches (*bAhyArtha vAda*) of Buddhism.

Nothing was written down about the beliefs of the Buddha whilst he was still alive, and by the time that attempts were made to do this, several hundred years later, his supposed teaching had already developed different branches having contradictory doctrines. Now it is impossible for anyone to gain significant understanding without long study. Since my knowledge of the subject is minimal, I offer here Swami Paramarthananda's simplistic breakdown (Ref. 5) as being adequate to understand

Gaudapada's approach in these verses, even if this is an inauthentic source.

He (Paramarthananda) divides Buddhism into the two main branches of Hinayana and Mahayana. According to the Oxford English Dictionary, the former comprised the orthodox schools of early Buddhism. The tradition died out in India, but it survived in Sri Lanka, Burma, Laos and Thailand as the Theravada School. The Mahayana branch still survives today and is the main School in China, Tibet, Japan, and Korea.

The essential difference for Gaudapada's purpose is that Hinayana Buddhists believed that there is a real, external world which is different from the observer. The Hinayanas consisted of two further branches – *sautrAntika* and *vaibhAShika*. The former believed that the existence of the world was proven by the fact that it was accessible to our senses, *pratyakSha pramANa*.

The latter believed that it required the proof of inference, *anumAna pramANa*.

The Mahayana branch, on the other hand, claim that there is not a real, external world, saying that it has no more reality than a dream. The Mahayanas also have two further branches – *yogAchAra* or *vij~nAna vAda* and *madhyamaka*. The former accept the existence of a separate observer. Like Advaita, they say that the world does not exist separate from this observer, which is Consciousness. The world therefore is *mithyA*. The crucial difference in their belief is that they deny that Consciousness is unlimited, eternal, unchanging etc., claiming instead that it is a fleeting entity, arising and dying in every moment. Gaudapada will dispense with them shortly! The *mAdhyamika*-s, on the other hand, deny that there is an observer at all! Another name for their belief is *shunya vAda* – 'emptiness' belief.

In K4.24, then, Gaudapada effectively presents the view of the *hInayAna*-s. He says that we are aware of sights, colors and sounds etc. and there must be a cause for these. The only explanation is that there actually are objects out there which are giving rise to the perceptions. We experience red, blue and green as distinct. This would not be possible if there were only consciousness and no objects. Consciousness itself is pure awareness; it does not have an internal variety of attributes. Consequently, the red and blue percepts cannot be distinctions of, or in, consciousness itself. Therefore objects must exist and they must be separate from consciousness. Shankara uses the example of the colorless crystal that seems to take on the color of an adjacent object. If there were no adjacent object, it would remain colorless.

Furthermore, we not only have awareness of perception, we also have awareness of different emotions. Sometimes, for example, we experience the pain of a burn. There must be a cause for this and, again, this must be something outside of consciousness, namely a hot object.

All of this provides sufficient proof, says the *hinayAna*, for the existence of a separate, external world.

In response to this (K4.25), Gaudapada uses the *mithyA* explanation given above in the gold ring metaphor and in 'Reality and Unreality'. The ring that we claim to see is actually only the name for a particular form of gold; the pot is the name for a form of clay and cloth for a form of threads. We utilize names for forms of more basic substance because of the practical utility but this does not mean that there really are such objects. The ring and bangle have no weight or value of their own – these derive from the gold alone. And all the properties of the gold come from the nature of the atoms and their lattice structure. The atoms, in turn, depend upon the properties of protons, neutrons and electrons and so on. Ultimately, there are no objects – all depend upon the ultimate substrate Consciousness.

In (K4.26) Gaudapada says that Consciousness does not make contact with any real, external objects nor even with the appearance of objects. There are no real objects and the so-called appearances are not separate from the mind. This is how the *vij~nAna vAda* Buddhist argues. In order for 'contact' to take place, there have to be two things. The so-called objects reduce down to Consciousness as already demonstrated; similarly, mind and its thoughts. There are no two things to make contact; there is only Consciousness. Although he does not mention it at this point, here is his concept of *asparsha yoga* – the idea of 'touch-less-ness'. Consciousness is ever aloof and untainted by any other thing, because there is no other thing. (K4.27) Consciousness never came into contact with objects in the past, does not do so now and never will.

This raises an interesting question, which is now addressed in (K4.27). How do we explain mistaken perception if there is no real object? In the classical example, already discussed many times, if there is no real rope, how can we think that it is a snake? Surely, if we are mentally imagining or projecting the thing, we must already know what it is we are projecting? Don't we determine in practice that we were mistaken in thinking that it was a snake by taking a torch and shining light on an actual thing and realizing that its appearance now no longer matches the mental impression that we had? If there were no real object, this would not be possible.

Furthermore, if we misperceive a rope as a snake, there must be such a thing as a snake somewhere, sometime, in order for us to be able to have that misperception; i.e. we must have dragged the image of something once seen in reality, out of our mind, and confused it with the real rope presently perceived in front of us. For every error, there must be a corresponding real, external object somewhere.

But, says Shankara (speaking on behalf of the *vij~nAna vAdin*), the object cannot be the 'cause' of any mistake because, as just discussed, there is no contact of 'mind' with 'object'. It is the nature of mind to appear as objects; there is no separate cause. When the mind is present, there are objects; when it is absent, there are no objects. Sometimes the mind appears as a 'real' rope and sometimes as a 'mistaken' snake. If we compare this to the dream, we cannot categorize the train that we see in the dream as 'real' but the elephant that we see as 'false'. They are both part of the dream and equally *mithyA*. Furthermore, if there is no real object to begin with, how can it be meaningful to speak of mistaking it for something else?

The bottom line, as far as refuting the realist Buddhist is concerned, is that the experience of external objects does not prove their separate existence. Although it undoubtedly appears as if there is an external world, we find on analysis that this does not exist apart from the observer. We are bewitched by names into thinking that they refer to actual substances, when they really only denote a convenient form. The only real 'substance' is Consciousness.

Having sided with the *vij~nAna vAdin* to refute the *hinayAna* Buddhists, Gaudapada has to show how they themselves are mistaken in their concept of the 'momentary' nature of Consciousness (*kShaNika vAda* or *kShaNabhaNgavAda*). This he does in K4.28. He does this only by a short, almost casual statement – 'Consciousness is not born' – and we rely upon Shankara for a more extensive explanation.

The Advaitin agrees with the *vij~nAna vAdin* that 'things', including the mind, are not born. There are no external objects in reality, whether gross or subtle. Consciousness 'appears' as objects; all of them are *mithyA*. A world is never born, does not exist, and is not subject to destruction.

But Consciousness is not actually 'born' as the objects either, since they do not really come into existence at all. This is not what the *vij~nAna vAdin* says. He says that Consciousness itself is not an eternal, unchanging existence. On the contrary, there is an endless series of momentary Consciousness-es. Because this series is continuous, the Advaitin makes the mistake of thinking of it as one, non-dual whole.

The Advaitins answer to this is simple: how can he know this?

If Consciousness is born and dies every moment, there is nothing to witness any arrival or departure so we could never be aware of either continuity or discontinuity. The very fact that we have 'experiences' (that last longer than a pin-prick) proves the continuity. Thoughts may come and go but the Consciousness that witnesses them does not.

More generally, the phenomenon of memory relies implicitly upon there being a continuous consciousness. The Brahmasutra (II.2 25) uses this argument against the *kShaNika vAda* theory. Reading this book would be impossible without memory and a continuous consciousness. If 'consciousness 1' reads the first syllable of a word and 'consciousness 2' reads the last syllable, then 'consciousness 3' would be asking 'why on earth I am sitting in front of this page; I don't know how to read anyway'. Memory and recognition are only possible if the consciousness that has the present experience is the same as that which had the past experiences.

(Other nonsensical results are entailed in the theory, too. For example (Brahmasutra II.2.21) points out that origination and destruction would have to be the same unless it be conceded that things last for longer than a moment.)

Gaudapada has now refuted the philosophies of three of the four systems of Buddhism. He does not mention the *shunya vAda* of the Madhyamika. The Brahmasutra (II.2.26) points out that 'Existence does not come from non-existence or non-entity'. The Madhyamika claims that the world has come out of nothing but this is quite contrary to our experience. Pots come from clay and yoghurt from milk. If what the Buddhist claims were true, anything could come from anything, since the non-existence of X is the same as the non-existence of Y.

Also, in his commentary on Brahmasutra II.2.32, Shankara is almost sarcastic in his denouncing of their position. He says that we need not bother too much about arguing against them since their own reasoning gives way on all sides like the walls of a well dug in sandy soil. There is a theory (of *shunya vAda*) and they – the Madhyamika Buddhists – are stating this theory. Shankara says: "*O shunya vAdins! You must admit yourself to be a being and your reasoning also to be something and not nothing. This contradicts your theory that all is nothing.*" (Ref. 22)

George Thibaut's translation is the most scathing of Buddhism in general: "*Buddha, by propounding the three mutually contradictory systems, teaching respectively the reality of the external world, the reality of ideas only, and general nothingness, has himself made it clear either that he was a man given to make incoherent assertions, or else that hatred of all beings induced him to propound absurd doctrines by accepting which they would become thoroughly confused.*" (Ref. 81) This is perhaps rather unfair, since it was his disciples who were responsible for interpreting his teaching and writing it down in the various, conflicting ways.

Nothing Can Come into Existence (K4.53-56)

In these four verses, Gaudapada concludes unequivocally that the concept of cause and effect does not stand up to logical analysis. The argument actually follows on from an inquiry using the metaphor of the firebrand. See 'Firebrand metaphor – only consciousness is real' below. This concludes that there cannot be any cause-effect relationship between Consciousness and the world and that therefore the world cannot have been created.

(K4.53-4) In the section 'Unreality of Dream' above, the four possible causal relationships were identified in K4.40. It seems to me that Gaudapada is here attempting to bring us back to that by a short reference, rather than repeating the whole argument. But the point he wants to make is that *brahman* or Consciousness cannot be either cause or effect in any of the four relationships. This is because, in order for there to be any relationship at all, there have to be two separate things. And this can never be the case where Consciousness is concerned because there is *only* Consciousness.

It was shown in the Introduction that 'things' in the world can always be established to be only forms of something more basic – tables are really wood etc. This was the first definition that was given for the term *mithyA*. So-called objects in the world are only Consciousness, which appears to assume empirically separate forms by virtue of the names that we give them.

Accordingly, we cannot say that *brahman* 'causes' or 'creates' the world. In reality, there is no world. These 'forms' (which appear to be separate because we 'name' them) are never actually other than *brahman*. Nothing new ever comes into existence. And, since there is only *brahman*, there is not anything other which might be the cause of *brahman*. The 'bottom line' is that the very concept of cause and effect is mistaken; there is no such thing as 'causality' in reality. It is only those seekers who realize this ultimate truth that can gain *mokSha*.

(K4.55-6) In the next two verses, Gaudapada highlights the dangers of continuing to believe in causality. Our attachment to the concept is associated with the notion that we are 'doers' and 'enjoyers'. We act with the expectation of a causal result and that we will reap the consequences of our actions. We expect that good actions will bring us merit and rewards for the future (future lives if we believe in reincarnation) and evil actions will bring future punishment.

Shankara says that it is because of our obsession with such ideas that they continue to arise and we continue to expect rewards and punishments for our actions. Once we realize that reality is non-dual and there is no causality, the belief structure breaks down, effectively freeing us from *saMsAra*. I use the word 'effectively' because what we actually realize is that there was no *saMsAra* to begin with. The scriptures often refer to the 'dream tiger' metaphor. If we are having a nightmare, in which we are being chased by a tiger, we are very likely to wake up. On waking, the tiger does not 'go away'; we realize that it was never there to begin with.

An Aside Discussion of the Sanskrit in these Four Verses

(You may safely ignore this short section if not interested! It would appear in a footnote if I was using them.)

Sanskrit is an incredibly flexible language. If you look up a word in a Sanskrit-English dictionary, you can usually find many, seemingly quite different, possible meanings – the one to be used depends upon the topic and context of the sentence. Also, there is no punctuation within sentences and the subject and object may appear anywhere. You have to pay careful attention to endings of nouns and verbs in order to understand what is meant. All of this reaches further levels of complexity when authors write in verse and select words and positions in the sentence to suit the needs of poetic meter.

I mention all this because verses 4.53 and 54 are clearly difficult to understand because of these factors. Depending upon which translation is used, the meaning can be quite different and one gets the impression that no translator was really able to understand clearly what Gaudapada was trying to say. It is not that the underlying intent is in doubt – Shankara and Anandagiri make this much clearer – but the specific point being made by Gaudapada is not so obvious!

Another problem is that the word 'chitta' in the 54th verse is usually translated as 'mind', or sometimes more specifically as 'memory'. But this does not really make a lot of sense in the context, although several translators attempt to force it to do so, including Swami Chinmayananda (Ref. 3), Swami Nikhilananda (Ref. 4) and Som Raj Gupta (Ref. 66). Swami Gambhirananda (Ref. 15) and Swami Paramarthananda translate it as 'consciousness' (*chaitanya*) and this makes far more sense. The former points out that Anandagiri equates *chitta* with the supreme Self. Swami Dayananda retains the translation of 'mind' but makes it very clear in his commentary that the mind *is* Consciousness.

A third Sanskrit confusion is that the word *'dharma'* is used in the plural in two different senses in verses 53 and 54 (and neither of these bears any relation to the usual meaning of this word!) In 4.53, it refers to the Self but, because Gaudapada is talking about the real Self of individuals in the world, it is translated as *'Atmans'* (plural). In 4.54, the same word is used to refer to external objects in the world.

All of this aside will give you some understanding of why this particular text is so difficult and only usually taught to advanced students. Although it would appear strange that highly respected Swamis can translate and interpret the verses in apparently different ways, this is not in fact a problem. As long as both verses are taken together, the same conclusion is reached.

Summary

K4.40 summarizes the four possible causal relationships (note that this verse occurs in the section where Gaudapada is arguing that the waking state cannot be the cause of the dream state, K4.35 – 39. I have transferred it to this section, since it is applicable to causality in general and, at the point where it actually occurs, causality has not yet been discussed):

a) An unreal thing might give rise to an unreal thing (this is effectively the standpoint of the Buddhist *shunya vAdin*).

b) A real thing might give rise to a real thing (this is the *satkArya vAda* of the *saMkhya* philosopher).

c) A real thing might give rise to an unreal thing (another school of Vedanta held this position).

d) An unreal thing might give rise to a real thing (this corresponds with the *asatkArya vAda* stance of the *nyAya-vaisheShika* schools).

c) has already been refuted. a) and d) also makes no sense – something that is unreal cannot come out of anything, real or unreal; and nothing can come out of something that is unreal. b) and d) have been refuted above. There is no further possible cause-effect relationship so that we have to conclude that, from the perspective of absolute reality, there can be no such thing as causality.

The fact of the matter is that a cause-effect relationship requires two separate entities, one as the cause and one as the effect. This is never the case when we look at each stage of a 'manufacturing' process. When we 'make' a ring out of gold, we have the same substance at the end as we had at the beginning; it only has a different shape and function. In fact, there are never 'two things'. There is always only Consciousness, to which differing forms we assign ever new names and mistakenly think that something new has actually been created.

Creation

This is the topic most often associated with Gaudapada's work, with elements of the discussion occurring in all four chapters, despite the fact that it does not occur explicitly in the Upanishad itself. He introduces the subject in K1.6 although K1.6 – 9 are ostensibly commentary on the sixth mantra of the Upanishad, which talks about the macrocosmic aspect of the deep-sleep state – *Ishvara*. He addresses only the second part of this mantra, which says *"This is the source of everything; assuredly the place of the arising and dissolution of all beings."* (See Appendix 1 for details.)

He says that it is clear that there has to be a source for everything that exists and concedes that, effectively we have to acknowledge that *Ishvara* is that source, as claimed by the Upanishad. Before embarking on a detailed consideration of all that this entails, beginning with some of the theories that were around at the time, it is worth pointing out where all this is going to lead: there is and can be no such thing as creation!

To return to the bangle, chain and ring metaphor yet again, we can change the bangle into a chain. We might therefore be said to be 'creating' a chain out of a bangle. But all we are doing is changing the form of the substrate – gold. We cannot create or destroy the gold. (Note that any discussion of nuclear fusion or fission would be going beyond the bounds of this metaphor! Advaita has nothing to do with physics or chemistry.)

Given that true 'creation' is not possible, all that we can suggest is that everything already exists and always will exist. If something 'appears' when it seemingly was not there before, we are obliged to say that it *was* there before, but in an 'unmanifest' state. An example of this given in the scriptures is a tree 'appearing' from a seed. Here, we now know that the 'unmanifest' form is the DNA in the nucleus of the seed; all of the instructions for making the tree are contained in encoded form, ready to be activated when food, water and light are provided. Another way of putting this is to say that the tree was in 'causal' or 'potential' form in the seed. Similarly, as far as the universe is concerned, we could say that everything was in a potential form prior to the big bang. But it would be wrong to say that nothing 'existed'.

Note that the DNA explanation is clearly only possible in the light of scientific knowledge not available in ancient times. And, more significantly, DNA is still strictly speaking 'manifest'; it is just that it requires quite powerful microscopes to establish this! And it has to be remembered that this is only a metaphor! It is not being suggested that the 'code' for the universe is held in some sort of pre-Bang computer (where would such a thing be?). It may actually be more helpful to think of the universe being 'created' as a result of our own ignorance, in an analogous way to how we 'manufacture' a snake out of what is really only a rope.

Shankara adds that everything has to have a substratum. Continuing with the rope-snake metaphor, prior to our seeing the snake, we could say that the snake had its existence as the rope. We would never see the snake if it were not for the rope. Similarly, everything in the world, prior to its appearance, has to have its existence in a cause. This cause we give the name of Ishvara (or prANa, as this is called in the kArikA). This is why we are able to say 'All this is brahman' – one of the famous sayings (mahAvAkya-s) of the Upanishads. The appearance itself, of course, is only name and form of brahman and is therefore mithyA.

A note of warning must be issued in respect of this assignment of Ishvara as a 'cause' for the universe. We have already seen above that the very notion of 'causality' is meaningless on analysis. The idea also tacitly assumes that there was a time 'before' creation. Since the concept of time is something only empirically meaningfully within the context of a universe, it is a mistake to think of a 'time' before creation at all. There is some anticipation here of the conclusions to be drawn below!

Theories of Creation

Gaudapada just briefly mentions some of the other views on this, without going into any detail or offering any arguments against them. Some people are creationists, believing that the universe is a demonstration of God's power or glory, while others think that is only an illusion or a dream. (K1.7) Shankara cites the example of people witnessing a magician performing an illusion such as the Indian Rope Trick. In the version described by Shankara, the magician appears to climb the rope, engage in a fight with limbs being chopped off and falling to the ground! It is supposed that the one who climbs the rope is unreal, because the real magician remains hidden from view on the ground. The audience just enjoys the spectacle; they know that it is a trick and only naïve children would think that it is real.

V. H. Date (Ref. 18) interprets Shankara's commentary (with a little artistic license) as follows: he likens the three states of waking, dream and deep-sleep to the illusory rope standing up in the air. And he likens *vishva*, *taijasa* and *prAj~na* to the unreal magician who appears to climb the rope. The (real) magician who performs the trick (presumably through mass hypnosis!) is different from both; he is the only reality – *Atman* or *turIya*.

Shankara says that, similar to the lack of interest in how the trick is done, true seekers are only interested in *turIya* and not in theories about creation (which 'serve no purpose').

Anandagiri points out that the view that creation is a dream differs from the *mithyA* view of the Advaitin. The *vishiShTAdvaitins*, for example (a philosophy – so-called 'qualified non-dualism' – propounded by Ramanuja) believe that the dreams are real while we are dreaming them. And, in waking life, illusions are similarly real while they last. If they were not real, they would not be able to register as real in our awareness. So these creationists are proposing that the creation may be like this sort of dream – real while it lasts.

Others think that God just *wants* to make a universe (K1.8) in the same way that a potter might decide to make a particular piece of pottery.

The second half of this verse refers to the notion that 'creation is brought about by time' but most of the commentators make no attempt to explain what is meant by this, other than suggesting it refers to astronomers and astrologers. Bhattacharya (Ref. 7) points to mantra 1.2 in the Shvetashvatara Upanishad, which seems to explain it better than anything. This says that: *"Time, the inherent nature of things, design, chance, the elements, primordial matter, individual awareness — these are to be considered as the cause (of the universe). But not even a combination of these can be the cause, for they are themselves effects."* (Ref. 41) It seems to me that this can be understood as evolution and Darwinian selection; i.e. it all 'just happens', as the result of natural change as time goes on, with God taking no part in either its initiation or development. (Obviously such a meaning was not explicitly intended by the writer!) But the key point to note is that there is no explanation here as to how the universe came into being in the first place.

The other, more frequently encountered 'explanation' for creation is that it is for God's enjoyment or sport (K1.9). The word *lila* may well have been encountered even by those who have never heard of Advaita. It means 'play', 'amusement' or 'pastime'. But Gaudapada immediately rejects this, asking how it could possibly be that the absolute Consciousness, which is entirely unlimited, complete and in need of nothing, could have desires to satisfy. Desire is synonymous with limitation. Swami Chinmayananda (Ref. 3) gives the analogy of someone who has just enjoyed the most sumptuous meal imaginable and is entirely replete being offered some new dish of food. There will not be the slightest interest, no matter how tasty this might seem at some other time.

The 'explanation' that creation is for God's enjoyment raises another paradoxical point. We know that there are wars and famines, and suffering in the world for all sorts of reasons. How could we explain this if we accepted a God who creates for His enjoyment? He would have to be a sadist! Consequently, the Lord could have no motive for creating the world. As Gaudapada puts it: *"What possible purpose could there be for Him whose desires are always in the state of fulfillment?"*

So what explanation does Gaudapada offer? Much more will be said about this below but, at this point (K1.9), he simply says that what appears to be the creation is simply His very nature. The consensus seems to be that Gaudapada is saying here that, as far as the phenomenal (*vyavahAra*) is concerned, we can say that *mAyA* is the 'cause' of creation. (In fact, he refutes every view of creation later and some commentators think that this view here is simply another one of the many theories he is listing and rejecting. To avoid any danger of being misled, this is probably the safest policy!)

In respect of the view that creation is His nature, Swami Chinmayananda has a metaphor; this time it is the ocean with its waves. He says that we cannot say that the waves are 'created' by the ocean but rather that it is simply the *nature* of the ocean to have waves on its surface. They are restless and in a continual state of flux while, deep down, the vast body of the ocean is totally unaffected by them.

More will be said about *mAyA* later. But, briefly, it is the word derived from the idea of magic (a *mAyAvin* is a magician or conjurer). It is often spoken of as though it were a positive force wielded by God to delude us into believing in something that is not there. But that is not a fair explanation, implying either entertainment or deception. Gaudapada does not actually use this word here anyway but simply says that creation is *svabhAva* – His natural disposition, in the same way that heat is the nature of fire.

But this does, on the face of it, entail a similar problem to that above regarding suffering; it will mean that God too owns all of this suffering. It is difficult for us to conceive that He could be 'all-bliss' while simultaneously having all the suffering of the world.

The explanation is that the world is *mithyA*. Just as we (our waking selves) are unaffected by any suffering that might take place in our dreams, so the non-dual reality is unaffected by apparent suffering in the world. The dream is *pratibhAsa*; the gross universe is *vyavahAra*; the reality is *paramArtha*. A metaphor encountered in the scriptures is that of a person in the bright sunlight casting a shadow. The shadow might 'collide' with a wall or 'fall into' water but the person casting it (as well as the shadow itself) is totally unaffected by it.

Creation According to Scripture

Having briefly looked at the sort of theories that are usually considered in respect of the creation of the universe, Gaudapada now begins his demolishing process by seeing what the scriptures say. His own methods are primarily to use reason and logic so that there can be no argument. Traditionally, however, especially with respect to aspects that are outside of our own direct experience, teachers refer to what is said in the scripture. This source is believed to contain answers to those questions which cannot be answered by recourse to perception and inference. The scriptures contain truths which were 'revealed' to ancient sages and have been passed down from teacher to disciple ever since.

Such an approach is anathema to many people, especially any that have come across so-called fundamentalists, who believe literally in what is said in the Bible, for example, irrespective of how ridiculous it might seem to modern science. But the attitude taken here is quite different. Gaudapada actually states (K3.23) that we should only accept anything that is stated there if it is also supported by reason. The intended meaning of the word 'faith' is that we put our trust in something (that we have good reason to trust) *provisionally*, until such time as we can verify it ourselves.

Shankara also makes the point (in his commentary on K3.15) that scriptural statements such as these are not intended to be taken literally; they are figurative only. And he cites the example of the supposed discussion amongst the 'senses' as to which was the most important. [Prajapati (their father) suggests that each sense should depart the body in turn so that they can find out. The loss of speech, sight, hearing and mind each had the effect of the body's registering their respective absence but carrying on without them. But as soon as *prANa* (the breath) prepared to leave, all the others realized that they could not survive without it and acknowledged that *prANa* was the most important.] Shankara says that the story is obviously only intended to be taken figuratively; we should not imagine that the texts intend us to believe that the senses converse or have a father! The texts on the creation of the world should be regarded similarly.

The other example that Shankara uses is that of 'cooking food'. The point is that whatever is being prepared may not be edible initially, e.g. rice grains. So, when we say 'I am cooking food', it is a figurative expression, being cognizant of the fact that, by the end of cooking, it *will* be edible. Thus, for example, when the scriptures speak of the 'difference' between the *jIva* and *brahman*, it is figurative only – this position is not different from what we believe already. It is done in the knowledge that the later teaching will show their identity.

Nevertheless, Gaudapada maintains that the 'bottom line' teaching of the scriptures is that there has never been any creation. Accordingly, before attacking the notions of creation using logic, Gaudapada wants to show that the scriptures themselves also support what he is about to say.

He begins (K3.23) by pointing out that, on the face of it, there seem to be statements in the scriptures for both sides, namely some that state there is a real creation and some which say that it is only apparent. Most of the Upanishads seem to have something to say, often going into elaborate details as to sequence and mechanism. Consequently, we have the situation where the Dvaitins (dualists) claim that creation is real, whereas the Advaitins say that it is apparent only, like the worlds we create in our dreams. Of course, we (Advaitins) may acknowledge that some scriptures do seem to say that creation is real but we can argue that it is part of the *adhyAropa-apavAda* teaching device.

Irrespective of this, however, the main point is that scriptural statements cannot be taken out of context. The whole section in which a statement occurs must be read before drawing any conclusion. Shankara gives the example of the 'sheath' model used in the Taittiriya Upanishad. Here a statement is made that the sheath made of the vital force, *prANamayakosha*, is the *Atman*. This, of course, is nonsense. But the next verse says that, well actually, *Atman* is not this sheath but the mental sheath, *manomayakosha*. No it isn't! And so on. The entire section has to be read together to get the whole story.

Then Gaudapada makes the point, mentioned above, that we should never accept what is unreasonable; we always have to analyze the whole and apply reason. When a scriptural text makes a statement regarding the creation of elements, people etc., but later makes another statement to the effect that there is really no creation, then we have to conclude that the 'creation' to which it referred initially is only an apparent one. An apparent creation is equivalent to no creation at all. There is no denying that we see a seemingly separate world but it is a *mithyA* world, being only name and form of *brahman*.

Gaudapada gives four examples of statements from the Upanishads to the effect that there is no creation (despite those Upanishads having previously said otherwise).

In K3.24, he refers to Katha Upanishad 2.1.11 – *"there is no diversity here* (in the creation)" and the Brihadaranyaka Upanishad 2.5.19 – *"the supreme being is perceived as manifold on account of* mAyA". And he refers to the Taittiriya Aranyaka 3.13.1

(the part also known as Purusha suktam) – "*unborn, he (brahman) appears in many ways (by the power of* mAyA*)*". (This is part of the Yajurveda – the four extant Vedas are massive texts which contain all of the ritual and mystical aspects as well as the philosophical Upanishads. The Aranyakas are called the 'Wilderness Books' in English, the name being given because, according to Wikipedia, they contain dangerous rituals which had to be performed in the wilderness! The word *AraNyaka* means 'forest'.)

Gaudapada is effectively pointing out here that, because the Upanishad has made it clear that *turIya* is changeless, has nothing to do with the world and is itself unborn, it therefore cannot really produce anything. Therefore, the world must be an appearance only, as in a magic show. Consequently, it follows that there can be no real creation at all. Thus, his theory of *ajAti vAda* (the doctrine that nothing whatever has been 'born') follows from these scriptural extracts as well as from the logical reasoning which he is about to give.

In K3.25, he references quotations from two more Upanishads. The Isha Upanishad (twelfth mantra) says that "*They who worship the Unmanifested enter into blinding darkness, but those who are devoted to the Manifested enter into greater darkness.*" (Ref. 15) The detailed analysis of this mantra is not relevant here. The point is that the word 'Manifested' refers to *hiraNyagarbha*, which is the first stage in the model of creation being referred to. This *kArikA* says that by effectively negating *hiraNyagarbha*, the quoted reference is thereby negating the whole of creation. The word used for *hiraNyagarbha* is *saMbhUti*, which means 'the most powerful'. Anandagiri gives the analogy of the best wrestler being defeated by a challenger. As a result of this, the challenger automatically becomes the best himself; there is no need to fight anyone else. [Note that I have not said anything about *hiraNyagarbha* in the main text. See Appendix 1, mantra 4 for details if you are really interested. It is a confusing topic and, to my mind, an unnecessary one!]

The other reference is to Brihadaranyaka Upanishad (3.9.28.7) which asks about the cause for the (re)birth of man: *"Who should again bring him forth?"* Gaudapada says that this is denying that there can be any real cause for creation. Shankara again refers to the rope-snake metaphor, saying that the snake has not been created by anyone; it simply arises out of ignorance and disappears as soon as this is dispelled. Similarly, there is no cause or origin for the person (the 'embodied Self' or *jIva*). And he points to another scriptural reference which states effectively the same thing: *This intelligent Self is neither born nor does It die. It did not originate from anything, nor did anything originate from It. It is birthless, eternal, undecaying, and ancient. It is not injured even when the body is killed.* Katha Upanishad 1.2.18 (Ref. 15).

The next *kArikA* (K3.26) points to the well-known phrase in Advaita *'neti, neti'*, meaning 'not this, not this' (strictly *'neti'* means 'not this way', 'not in this manner', or 'not thus.'). This also comes from the Brihadaranyaka Upanishad and is used to negate all of those things that we might think ourselves to be.

At the beginning of the related section of the Brihadaranyaka (2.3.1), it is stated that *"brahman has only two forms – gross and subtle, mortal and immortal, limited and unlimited, perceptible and imperceptible."* (Ref. 32) Simplistically, therefore, when the Upanishad repeatedly utters the pronouncement *'neti, neti'* in later mantras, the first *'neti'* negates the gross aspects of the universe, i.e. tangible, material aspects (*mUrta prapa~ncha*), such as the physical body. The second *'neti'* negates subtle aspects (*amUrta prapa~ncha*), such as the mind and intellect. (*'mUrta'* refers to 'shape' or 'form.') Whatever we can experience, see or think cannot be who-we-really-are, since there is always a subject witnessing these things. I am the consciousness-witness which remains when there is nothing to experience, as was seen when discussing the deep-sleep state in the analysis of the Upanishad above.

Recognizing what we are not, in this way, we realize what we are. When the delusion of the snake is removed, the truth of the rope is known (as long as we do not then think it is a crack in the ground!) Once all Self-ignorance is removed, Self-knowledge is revealed.

The Brihadaranyaka Upanishad 3.9.26 says: "*The Self is that which has been described as 'Not this, not this', It is imperceptible, for it is never perceived; undecaying, for it never decays; unattached, for it is never attached; unfettered, for it never suffers and it does not perish.*" (Ref. 32)

Shankara explains that this mantra thus negates all duality, which is only superimposed on the *Atman* as a result of ignorance. Anything that we can grasp mentally has a 'birth' and can be negated. Mantra 7 of the Upanishad says that *turIya* is *agrAhya* – not 'graspable'; it has no attributes or characteristics at all. He says that the earlier descriptions of a dualistic creation were only the means (*upAya*) to lead to realization of the true nature of reality, which is the end (*upeya*). Ignorant people unfortunately tend to take the means as the end itself.

Ironically, and apparently ridiculously, it is possible to make the statement that: "*after rejecting all the* mUrta *and* amUrta *forms of the Atman* (I.e. all the 'obvious' things, like 'I am the body' and 'I am the mind'), *and negating all the superimposed duality, what remains is the Atman.*" (Ref. 21) Anandagiri makes this statement as his comment on K3.26. It is remarkable how similar this is to the statement by Conan-Doyle's Sherlock Holmes that I have been quoting in all my books: "*when all has been investigated and rejected, whatever remains, however improbable, must be the truth.*" Anandagiri goes even further: "*all that falls into the class of comprehensible* (dRRishya) *is established as unreal.*" I.e. whatever you can understand is false; what is real will always be beyond comprehension!

But, lest you should give up at this point, the import of this must be realized. You should never confuse means with ends. And it is not that, for example, you should make the mistake of the neo-Vedantins and think that the *nirvikalpa samAdhi* that it is possible to attain after many years of practice in meditation is what is meant by enlightenment. You should not think either that what is said by the Upanishads is the absolute truth. Words exist only in the empirical realm; the absolute truth is forever ineffable. This teaching is provided to lead you and point you in the right direction. The final leap is up to you. To quote the penultimate paragraph from Wittgenstein's 'Tractatus Logico Philosophicus': "*My propositions are elucidatory in this way: he who understands me finally recognizes them as senseless, when he has climbed out through them, on them, over them. (He must so to speak throw away the ladder, after he has climbed up on it. What we cannot speak about we must pass over in silence.)*" And, in case you should think that Wittgenstein is being extraordinarily insightful and original, here is what Gaudapada said over a thousand years earlier (K4.60): "*That which is indescribable by words cannot be discriminated as true or false.*"

The means to the end does not itself have to be real. The 'dream tiger' metaphor was mentioned a few pages ago. The tiger may not be real but nevertheless serves to wake you up!

(K3.15) Gaudapada effectively summarizes all this in an earlier verse(!). He acknowledges that there are various descriptions of creation in the scriptures. He refers to 'earth, iron and sparks', which abbreviated terms acknowledge the fact that there are differing descriptions in various Upanishads. (The earth and iron examples are from the Chandogya Upanishad 6.1.4 – 6.1.6 and the sparks from the Brihadaranyaka 2.1.20.) Shankara says this is a device to make the intellect realize that *jIvAtman* is identical with *brahman*. First of all, the scriptures tell us that the world and *jIva*-s have been created. This naturally begs the question of who created them and prompts us to say that *brahman* is the cause. Further analysis, however, shows us that there is no world or *jIva* separate from *brahman* and we are forced to conclude that they are not an 'effect' of *brahman* at all'. The reality has to be beyond both cause and effect – and non-dual. There is no 'multiplicity'.

Shankara even suggests that the fact that there are many different versions of the creation is evidence that they are only a provisional explanation, to be taken back later as our understanding grows. He says that there would have been one single, consistent, version in all the different sources if creation had been true and the world a reality. It is not possible to imagine any other useful purpose for them otherwise.

(K3.16) Gaudapada goes on to say that the scriptures, out of compassion for seekers' differing levels of attainment, enjoin them to meditate on such ideas as part of their mental preparation. Students need to be 'high grade' before they are able to take on board the concept of non-duality as a credible reality. He segregates those who are not yet ready into low and medium grades and implies that both need to begin with an effective belief in duality and follow the sorts of practices stated in the earlier portion of the Vedas – the *karmakANDa*. Eventually, they will graduate to readiness for the true teaching.

The low grade students worship a personal god (who is regarded as a 'product' of *brahman*); medium grade worship *nirguNa brahman* as the cause itself; but high grade students know that they themselves *are brahman*.

Creation According to Reason

Having looked at some of the statements from the scriptures, and confirmed that the message here is that there is no real creation, Gaudapada now turns to a consideration of what reason tells us on the matter.

The topic of Causality is not dealt with in depth until Chapter 4 of the *kArikA*-s but we are attempting to address topics in some sort of logical sequence so that Causality has already been covered by the section above. Nevertheless, it is impossible to talk about the origin of creation without asking about the cause of the world so that some overlap is inevitable. And Gaudapada speaks about this in Chapter 3. So I will briefly revisit some of the arguments so that his logical reasoning is not interrupted.

Firstly (K3.27), if the universe that we see is a 'creation' and has effectively been 'born', then there has to have been a creator or original cause. Gaudapada says that we only have two alternatives – either this creation is real or it isn't. We certainly see it and interact with it but it could be like the illusion of the rope trick produced by the magician or like the snake that we believe to exist when there is really only a rope. Once we are aware of the rope or the magician, we can appreciate the illusion for what it is without taking it for reality.

If we accept that the world is not real, then we have to accept that there must be a real substrate (i.e. *brahman*) for the world illusion because we cannot have an illusory effect from a non-existent cause. When we see the rope trick, we know that there must be a magician behind it. The cause has to be real. But there is no 'birth' or creation here, since the effect itself is not real.

The other possibility is that the world is real, in which case a real creation will have to have taken place. If we claim that *brahman* is the creator, then this will be the cause for the world as effect. But this would mean that *brahman* would have to be subject to change, since the movement from cause to effect has to involve change. (If it didn't, and the effect was identical with the cause, then nothing would have happened.) This would contravene all that has been discussed so far.

We have seen that 'I' am the unchanging witness of myself as child and then youth, through to middle and old age. I am the witness of myself as waker, dreamer and deep-sleeper. The point here is that the changing is only known from the standpoint of the changeless. If the witness changes with the witnessed, then no change is seen. The very concept of change is only meaningful against a changeless background. (See the description of *ekAtmapratyayasAraM* from the seventh mantra in Appendix 1.)

This means that, if there is a real creation and the creator necessarily changes, then this creator would also be subject to birth and death. This is explained in the Advaita Makaranda, a short text on Advaita by Lakshmidhara Kavi, who probably lived around the fifteenth century AD. He states that all witnessed things are subject to the 'six-fold modifications' (*shad vikAra*) whereas the witness is changeless (*nirvikAra*). These six stages of change (identified by Yaska around the sixth or fifth century BC) are: birth (*jAyate*), existence (*asti*), growth (*vardhate*), maturation (*vipariNamate*) decline, (*apakShiyate*) and death (*nashyati*).

If *brahman* were subject to change in this way, itself being born, then it would be an effect also and would require another cause to produce it. It would not be real according to Advaita's definition of 'real' (that which is the same in all three periods of time). So we would be caught in a problem of infinite regress (the logical error called *anavastha*), with there being no 'first cause'. Think of yourself, being the son or daughter of parents who were themselves son and daughter of parents, who were themselves…

Furthermore, *brahman* would also be subject to death. Being subject to birth and death means being subject to *saMsAra* and all that this entails. Clearly none of this would make sense. As it says in the Bhagavad Gita (2.20): "*It is not born, nor does it die. After having been, it does not cease to be; unborn, eternal, changeless and ancient. It is not killed when the body is destroyed.*" (Ref. 65). Accordingly, *brahman* cannot be the real cause of a real creation. It can only manifest a *mithyA* universe.

So the reasoned conclusion is that the birth of the universe is only illusory, for which we postulate the power of *mAyA* as an interim explanation. (But "*Magical effects prove the existence of a real magician*", as Anandagiri puts it.)

Gaudapada next states (K3.28) that a non-existent creation could not be born either in reality or as a result of *mAyA*. And he cites the example often used in the scriptures of the son of a barren woman (*vandhyAputra*). Since a barren woman is, by definition, one who cannot have children, the son of such a person is a contradiction in terms. So, the analogy that such a person cannot be born either in reality or as a result of *mAyA* is a good one. This *kArikA* is refuting the belief of the *nyAya* philosophers and also the *shunya vAda* of the Madhyamika Buddhists. A non-existent thing cannot produce either a real or an unreal universe.

The concept of *mAyA*

Other Indian philosophies at the time of Gaudapada accepted the reality of the world and were therefore obliged to have some explanation for its creation. In the next section, we will look at some of these, together with the arguments Gaudapada uses to show them to be untenable. But clearly there does seem to be a real world so that Advaita, too, has to account for its appearance even though denying its reality.

In order to accept *brahman* (or *Atman* from the individual's perspective) as non-dual, the only plausible explanation for creation would seem to be that I (the non-dual Consciousness) 'imagine' the world and all its objects by my own power. This power is called *mAyA* and the explanation is one of the interim ones used by Advaita. This is effectively what Gaudapada says (K2.12), but he doesn't explain in that verse what this *mAyA* is. In K2.19, he adds that the Self is imagined as innumerable different, and separate, objects, and is deluded thereby.

Unlikely though this might sound, you only have to think how, in a dream, you believe yourself to be the dreamer, and think that you (the dreamer) are really awake, to see that the idea is not so ridiculous. When we don't know what an object really is, our mind forces it into something that can be explained. Thus, the coiled-up rope is actually seen as a snake; we have no doubt about it and act accordingly. When we lose sight of *satyam* (what is real), we mistakenly raise *mithyA* to the level of *satyam*. And, of course, this applies to everything in the universe – the only reality is 'I' the observer.

Because of our ignorance, it appears as though things come into existence and are later destroyed (K4.57). This is what we term *saMsAra*. This verse follows on from the metaphor of the firebrand, which will be discussed later when we look at the nature of reality. The essential description was already given in the introduction. Gaudapada is saying here that the appearance of the world is no more real than the patterns generated by the whirling firebrand. Nevertheless, for the one who believes in this appearance, the problems experienced in the world seem to be endless and he or she suffers accordingly – this is *saMsAra*. In reality, everything is *Atman*, which has never been born and cannot be destroyed – it is changeless. The one who denies this is equivalent to the person who runs away from the rope, firmly believing that it is a snake. Though ignorant, this person nevertheless refutes the assertions of the person who has realized the truth.

(K3.10) Following on from the verses relating to the pot-space metaphor, a reader who is alert might pick up on what may seem to be false reasoning. Gaudapada said that it is not the pot-space that is born but the pot itself. The space is one and unchanging and it is just a name that we give to the volume delineated by the pot. Similarly, it is the body that is born and not the Consciousness which seemingly is contained within it.

But, we might point out, if a body is born at all, this means that the world is created, which we are now attempting to deny. Gaudapada accepts that this is how things appear but then worlds seem to be born in dream, also. And he has already pointed out that trying to claim such things as utility and tangibility for the waking world carries no weight because these apply to the dream world also while we are dreaming. What he argues is that there is only a 'seeming' world and, this has come about via a 'seeming' creation. The 'explanation' for how this is done is the power of *mAyA*.

Non-origination applies not only to all objects in the world but also to all *jIva*-s, including myself (as a person). There is no real 'birth' of anyone (K4.58). It is just like the gold-ornament metaphor that was discussed at the outset. We can say that a ring or a bracelet has been 'created' but in reality all that we have done is change the shape of something that already existed and given it a new name. There is no cause-effect relationship here at all because there are not two things to have a relationship! There is only gold, before and after.

We can say that *brahman* (or, to be more accurate, *Ishvara*) uses the power of *mAyA* seemingly to create the world and populate it with objects and living things, just as the magician deludes us into thinking that he or she has made someone disappear or sawn them in half. But the section on Causality showed that there can be no such thing as cause and effect and there is a clear danger here of thinking that there really is something called *mAyA*, which is responsible for the appearance of the world. But this has to be yet another *adhyAropa-apavAda*, interim explanation, and *mAyA* must be taken away again once our intellect is ready. If there were really such a power, which *brahman* employed, then that would mean that there were (at least) two things. *mAyA*, too, has to be *mithyA*.

Swami Chinmayananda says that the world of objects is "*a delusion-created delusion; a non-existence-created non-existence. The world-of-objects, therefore, can have only as much Reality as the eldest daughter of a barren-woman's-son! Her marriage celebration is certainly an impossibility since her father is an unborn non-existent entity.*" (Ref. 3)

In K4.59, Gaudapada says that the illusory plant, which emerges from an illusory seed (in a dream for example) is neither permanent, nor capable of being destroyed (since neither really exists). Both are *mithyA*. And all objects and beings in the world should be considered in the same way because, from the stand-point of absolute reality, they are also *mithyA*. All time-related adjectives cease to have any meaning – birth, death, eternal, transient etc. – because everything has *brahman* as its substrate and *brahman* is outside of time. We can speak of *brahman* as being eternal but even that is a time-related adjective.

Once we have realized that the snake is a rope, there is no further need to inquire into the nature of the snake – is it poisonous, quick to attack, is there an antidote etc. Similarly, the one who has understood that the world is *mithyA* need no longer be concerned about analyzing and trying to understand it (K4.60). It is very much like our ceasing to worry about the outcome of the dream after we have woken up.

The world is nothing but *brahman*. But, since this is without attributes of any kind, we cannot provide any description. This is the meaning of the term *anirvachanIya*, which is sometimes used. Since we cannot say anything about it, we should remain silent! And here is the link to *amAtra* symbolizing *turIya* – the silence that follows the a-u-m of *OM*.

Nature of Reality

Popular Belief

In this section, Gaudapada briefly lists some of the views on the nature of reality that were prevalent at the time. These are really only passing references. One gets the impression that he was being intentionally dismissive, deliberately using only one or two words for each, possibly even in a sarcastic manner. He really did not consider them worthy of more attention. Each of the 9 verses is effectively divided into 4 parts so that a total of 35 different beliefs are addressed (the final part is a comment on all of the others). Since the allusions are much abbreviated, it is not possible to derive a lot of information from them; we have to rely on the commentators to give us a few more details. And of course most of these 'theories' seem naïve and unsophisticated to us now. You can safely ignore this section if not interested; it is only included for completeness!

Some of the early views relate specifically to creation.

1. (K2.20) There were the Pranavid or Vaisheshika philosophers, who believed that the cosmic mind (*hiraNyagarbha*) or a distinctly separate *Ishvara* created the world.
2. The Charvaka philosophers were the ancient equivalent of the modern materialists and believed that everything was formed from a combination of the four elements of earth, air, fire and water. (The scriptures refer to five elements – those above together with space or ether – but the Charvakas did not accept the authority of the Vedas.) Quite how inanimate 'elements', even ones as powerful as these, could create the universe without the benefit of an intelligent cause is not explained.
3. The same argument applies to the Sankhyas, who say that the world is born out of the three 'qualities' of primal

nature (*guNa* of *prakRRiti* or *pradhAna* – *sattva, rajas* and *tamas*). (Don't worry if you do not know what these are.) These attributes are inert – without Consciousness – so have no 'intelligence' to create anything. Consciousness 'belongs' to the other element of Sankhya the 'soul' or 'spirit' – *puruSha*; but these are entirely detached and do nothing. These philosophers say that the three *guNa*-s are in equilibrium prior to creation and that a disturbance of this balance triggers the pluralistic universe. (A precursor of Catastrophe Theory perhaps…) Why there should be a disturbance if they are in equilibrium is not explained. There would have to be a cause (and a cause for that cause etc. ad infinitum).

4. A branch of Shaiva philosophy believed that three fundamental principles of reality created the world. These are Shiva (equivalent to *Ishvara*), *Atma* (meaning the *jIva*-s) and *avidyA* (ignorance). There are some similarities with Advaita but making Shiva and *Atma* different would render one of them inert.

5. There is another school that believes in three principles (K2.21), namely the three states already discussed here – waking, dream and deep sleep. These states, contrary to the Advaitin understanding presented in the Mandukya, are believed to be real and somehow to be responsible for the creation. But even the commentators seem unsure of what is intended.

6. The next quarter-verse references those who regard objects of enjoyment as the reality. This is another variation of the materialist stance. The Sanskrit word for sense object is *viShaya* and interestingly the word *viSha* from which it derives means 'poison' or 'venom'. The senses generate desire, leading to attachment, anger, jealousy etc. and ultimately death (according to the Bhagavad Gita)!

7. The next part refers to those whose reality and aim in life is to go to heaven – the *loka*-s, the planes of reality beyond the world.

8. Some religious sects believe that the Gods to whom they refer are real and that they must propitiate them in order to be rewarded with the satisfaction of their desires.

9. The *mImAMsaka* philosophers believe that the Vedas themselves are the ultimate reality (K2.22). They follow the guidance contained in the first part of the Vedas, called the *karmakANDa*, relating to rituals. They do not accept the concept of *Ishvara* and think that simply chanting mantras (which have the power of gods) will achieve their aims in life. Of course, according to the Advaitin, even the Vedas are *mithyA*. They are only sounds in a particular order.

10. Next for condemnation are those who think that ritualistic sacrifice is the only reality, again following the prescriptions provided by the Vedas. Performed correctly, these are the cause of creation itself, they say. Since these rituals are performed by a priest, using mantras and objects offered to gods, they are necessarily a combination of things and there is no single causal factor.

11. The Sankhyas agree with Advaitins that *Atman* is not a 'doer'. But, as stated above, their creation stems from a second principle called *pradhAna* (nature), and they believe that the *Atman* 'enjoys' this creation (or, pedantically, *Atman*-s, since they believe each individual is an *Atman*). But an enjoyer *Atman* would no longer be unchanging and liberation would cease to have any meaning. Moreover, the *Atman* would be dependent upon the objects for its enjoyment.

12. The reference here is even more obscure than most, being to food or even cooks (according to Anandagiri). It probably refers to certain scriptural passages in the

Taittiriya and Chandogya Upanishads which relate to everything being established in food (*anna*). Or it may refer again to the materialist viewpoint of enjoying the good things in life, because there is no afterlife.

13. (K2.23) This verse could be said to be considering philosophies according to how they perceive the 'size' of the *Atman*. Also, they all believe that this *Atman* undergoes actual transformation (*pariNAma*) in order to become the world. The key word in the first part is *sUkShma*, meaning 'subtle'. Again, there are various opinions as to what this might be referring. The consensus seems to be that it is an allusion to the 'atomic' theory of the *nyAya-vaisheShika* philosophers. They believe that the *Atman* has the size of an atom. But our consciousness does not seem to be so minutely located!

14. The materialists believe that our gross body is the reality and this is indeed the feeling that most of us have. However, consciousness is not felt in limbs severed from the body. Also, although the body is still present, there is no consciousness in it when we are under anesthetic or dead. According to Swami Chinmayananda (Ref. 3), there are 3 groups of materialist in Hindu philosophy: one group thinks that the physical body is the *Atman*, one that the sense organs are, and one that the mind is the reality. Professor Dave (Ref. 21) also notes that the Jain philosophers believe that *Atman* is the size of the physical body.

15. The next key word is *mUrta*, which literally means 'manifest', or 'embodied'. This refers to the idea of a personal god being the ultimate reality; *Atman* taking the specific form of a scriptural god, such as Krishna with his flute or Vishnu with a discus. Swami Dayananda says (Ref. 69) that such forms are specified solely for the purpose of giving our minds something to concentrate on for meditation purposes (*upAsana*).

16. The last part of K2.23 refers to *amUrta*. This may simply mean those who do not believe in a personal god or it may refer to the *shunya* or 'void' of the Buddhists or it may mean 'formless'. Gaudapada will address those who think that the world has come out of nothing later!

17. The first key word in the next verse (K2.24) is *kAla*, meaning 'time'. It is thought that this indicates the astronomers and/or astrologers, who believe that actions must be carried out only when the time is auspicious. But this makes no sense. Apart from the fact that there is past, present and future, time can also be divided up into periods from microseconds and less to centuries and more. It might also be a reference to such scriptural statements as Bhagavad Gita 11.32, where Krishna says: *I am Time, the mighty cause of world destruction, who has come forth to annihilate worlds.* (Ref. 70)

18. Some believe that space, rather than time, is the reality. Gaudapada refers to them here as 'knowers of directions', and Anandagiri says that this refers to those known as Svarodayas, who study the 'science of breath'. The link is not at all obvious! Som Raj Gupta (Ref. 66) says that 'in the pre-modern world', men used to perform rituals which had to be carried out facing a particular direction, and that this enabled them to control and predict events. Clearly, direction did have significance. For example, the stone images of Dakshinamurthy in Shiva temples are always installed facing south. This is ostensibly because the southerly direction was regarded as pointing the way to death. Thus, choosing to face this way was showing that realization of the Self overcomes death. (Dakshinamurthy is the aspect of Shiva as a teacher, and the name actually means 'one who is facing south'. He will be mentioned again later.)

19. The next key quarter of this verse refers to *vAda*-s. Some

translators suggest that this means 'dialog' or 'dispu-
tation', but the explanations for this are not persuasive.
More likely, it is used in the sense of 'discourse' or
'doctrine' and intended to refer to the various mystical
beliefs, analogous to the 'New-age' 'systems' of today.
Swami Chinmayananda refers to *'dhatuvadins and
mantravadins, who conjure up magic through crystals,
chanting, herbs etc.'*

20. The *bhAvana-kosha* philosophers, Cosmologists or
Geographers, referred to in the last quarter of K2.24
believed in the absolute reality of the 14 mythical worlds
in stories of the time – 7 'heavens' and 7 'hells'. Of course,
no one has ever seen these (and lived to tell the tale) and
there are others who favor a different number.

21. K2.25 first refers to those who believe everything is determined by the mind (*manas*). Swami Paramarthananda
talks about psychology and the 'unconscious' but of
course Gaudapada could not have meant these. This
could be another materialist or epicurean allusion to
those who recognize that the mind is the seat of
experience and pleasure and that this is the key reality.
Alternatively, it might refer to the *naiyAyika* philosophers, who value reason and logic above all else.

22. Next there is a reference to intellect, *buddhi*, rather than
manas. Swami Paramarthananda thinks that this refers to
the *yogAchAra* or *kShaNika vij~nAna vAda* branch of
Buddhism. This is a subjective idealist philosophy; they
believe that Consciousness is the only reality so that there
is similarity here with Advaita. However their concept is
that Consciousness is 'momentary' (the meaning of
kShaNika). Gaudapada will tackle this idea later! Swami
Satchidanandendra, on the other hand (Ref. 29), thinks
that it is the next reference – *chitta* or memory – which is
associated with this Buddhist school. And he says that

intellect refers to the Sankhya philosophers (again). Swami Chinmayananda points out that equating any aspect of mind with reality is stupid, since mind, intellect, memory are all dormant during deep-sleep so that reality would have to be suspended!

23. As noted above, Swami Satchidanandendra believes that the reference to memory or chitta in the third part of this verse refers to the *yogAchAra* Buddhists and Swami Chinmayananda agrees.

24. The last reference in K2.25 is to *dharma-adharma*. This is the moral code detailed in the first part of the Upanishads (the *karmakANDa*) and it is the *pUrva mImAMsaka* philosophers who follow the rituals and injunctions in this. But what we should and should not do changes according to culture over time and things that change cannot be reality.

    Alternatively, this can be understood as relating to the law of *karma*, whereby merit (*puNya*) is accrued from performing 'good' actions and sin (*pApa*) is accumulated from 'bad', both destined to mature at some future time and give us pleasure or pain respectively.

25. In K2.26, Gaudapada specifically addresses those philosophers who, believing that the observable universe is the ultimate reality, attempt to identify the laws or principles that define it. This might be compared to science dividing matter up into chemical elements, sub-atomic particles or the four fundamental forces of nature (weak, strong, electromagnetic and gravitational). The first part says that some philosophers claim there are 25 categories constituting reality. These are the Sankhyas again. I am not going to itemize them!

26. The Yoga philosophers (whose principal exponent was Patanjali) have these same 25 with the addition of *Ishvara* or God. The Sankhyas do not accept Ishvara, although they do recognize the authority of the Vedas.

27. Some say that there are 31 categories. This is thought by Anandagiri to refer to one of the four branches of Shaivism philosophy, called *pAshupata*-s, although careful research of these reveals that they actually had 36 (Ref. 3). Professor Karmarkar in Ref. 17 thinks the number refers to the principles mentioned in the Bhagavad Gita 13.5 – 6 but Professor Dave in Ref. 21 is not convinced!

28. And Gaudapada concludes by saying that some hold that there are an infinite number of categories! Anandagiri says that the fact that all these philosophers fail to agree on the number indicates their ignorance of the true nature of reality.

29. Ordinary, 'worldly' people (*laukika*-s) (K2.27) are overly concerned with the world in their life, and believe that they can derive happiness from this.

30. Some feel that the four stages of life established in Hindu society (*Ashrama*-s) are the significant factors. Here is the brief definition from John Grimes' dictionary of terms (Ref. 71): *There are four stages* (Ashrama) *of life's journey. They delineate the individual's vertical ascent to liberation. These four are: the student stage* (brahmacharya), *the house-holder stage* (gRRihastha), *the forest-dweller* (vAnaprastha), *and the renunciant* (saMnyAsa). *These emphasize the individual aspect of one's personal development. They are stages of strife when selfishness is slowly but steadily rooted out.*

    But this is simply a scheme for delineating one's spiritual progress; the stages have no intrinsic meaning. Just as the *Atman* is neither waker dreamer nor deep sleeper, it is not any one of the *Ashrama*-s either.

31. The next keyword is *lai~NgA*, which relates to the gender of words – male, female and neuter in Sanskrit. According to Anandagiri, this represents the philoso-

phers who were known as Grammarians, with their belief, called *sphoTa vAda*, that the spoken letters and words effectively brought the world into existence. But the gender of words is arbitrary and words themselves are merely a means for communication.

32. The last group in this *kArikA* are those (a branch of Vedantins) who believe that there is a higher and a lower reality (*brahman*). Of course, the Advaitin speaks of *brahman* 'with attributes', *apara brahman* or *Ishvara*, as an intermediate teaching (as already discussed, *adhyAropa-apavAda*). But this group believes in its absolute reality. This would mean that there are two *brahman*-s, which would lead to all sorts of contradictions and nonsense. Swami Paramarthananda says that their 'higher' *brahman* would be the causal factor, *karaNa brahma* or *Ishvara*, while the 'lower' would be the effect, *kArya brahma*. But one of the main purports of this entire work is that reality is beyond cause and effect – *kArya-kAraNa-vilakShaNa*.

Furthermore, the non-dual, indivisible, partless *brahman* could never be separated into a causal, higher *brahman* and a lower, effect brahman.

33. The final verse (K2.28), in this catalog of miscreants, returns to those who are interested in the nature of creation in relation to reality. There are three elements to this: creation itself, *sRRiShTi*; final dissolution, *laya*; and the steady state in between, *sthiti*. Again, there are slightly differing emphases on interpreting this. Swami Chinmayananda says that the verse refers to those philosophers who follow the guidance of the scriptures called Puranas and that there are three groups of these. Swami Dayananda, on the other hand, thinks that it refers to the specific gods who are worshipped; those gods being responsible for creation, maintenance, and destruction. Thus, the creation reference is either to those

who believe that the world is continuously being created (Ref. 3) or to the creator god, *brahmA* (Ref. 69).

34. The dissolution reference is either to those who believe that the world is continuously being destroyed (Ref. 3) or to the god responsible for destruction of the universe, Rudra-Shiva (Ref. 69).

35. The sustainer reference is either to those who believe that the universe is a steady state (Ref. 3) or to the god responsible for maintaining it, Vishnu-Narayana (Ref. 69).

36. Whichever interpretation is chosen, the final pronouncement is the same. As Gaudapada puts it: All these ideas are nothing but imaginations in *Atman*. In Consciousness, there is neither creation, nor sustenance, nor destruction – all are *mAyA*.

In any case, it would make no sense to have one of these three without the others. As discussed elsewhere, something cannot come out of nothing, so creation must refer to manifestation of that which is already unmanifest. This, in turn, implies that it must have existed before for some sustained duration. At a micro level, all three are going on continuously, whether we are talking about particle physics or cellular biology.

Origin of Belief

Most beliefs that we hold are not ones that we have arrived at as a result of our own critical deliberations or rationalization from experience. Rather, we hold a belief because this is what we were told by someone in whom we trusted. As a small child, we rely on our parents to teach us all of those things about the world that we need to know in order to survive. That we do survive proves to us that what we were told was true. Accordingly, there is a natural tendency for us also to believe all of the other things that we are told, which we cannot verify for ourselves later.

Next, our teachers at school and the books that we read

provide yet more information that is not directly verifiable. We learn to be more skeptical as we grow older and not take for granted the truth of everything that we hear. This may apply especially to adverts, newspapers, TV and politicians! Nevertheless, many of those early influences remain in place and are not questioned. This is especially the case regarding religious views. A child brought up in the Muslim faith rarely becomes a Christian! Far more common is that people hold onto inculcated beliefs to a fanatical extent, leading to discrimination against others and worse.

Even an adult, intelligently pursuing spiritual understanding, is in danger of being misled if not very careful. Since one begins without spiritual knowledge, one is obliged to go to a teacher who (one has reason to accept) does have it. If such a teacher is not accessible, we may resort to reading books that we think might provide it. This is how an unscrupulous, or merely misguided, guru can lead many others astray. If such a guru is charismatic, plausible, persuasive etc., a seeker may be easily carried away, if he or she does not retain a degree of intellectual detachment and use their reason to question everything. Once attached to a particular religion or philosophy, there is a tendency to become increasingly attached by seeking out more teaching within that movement and thereby corroborating and reinforcing the belief.

But, says Gaudapada, this does not matter in the end. Just as *Atman* (*turīya*) is the substratum of the three states of consciousness, so it is the essence of all of these erroneous beliefs. It is the *Atman* which gives life and power to them all. The false ideas are effectively superimposed upon the *Atman*, just as the snake is superimposed upon the rope. Despite the deception, the truth is still there. The snake *is* the rope in reality; the false philosophy *is* the non-dual *Atman* in reality. Thus, *Atman* literally 'supports' the idea and thereby effectively 'protects' the believer. The believer's misplaced faith in the wrong philosophy is ultimately faith in *Atman*, even though he or she does not know it. That faith will eventually lead them to the truth.

Advaita
Advaita is different

It might be thought that Advaita must also suffer from the same defects as other faiths. Why should the reader believe the ideas presented here? The difference is crucial: whereas all of the philosophies mentioned above (and many others not mentioned) have 'objects' – ideas, gods, rituals or whatever – as their basis, Advaita deals only with the subject Consciousness. All objects are *mithyA*; only the ultimate subject, *Atman*, is *satyam*. Just as people imagine the rope in the dark to be a snake, or a crack in the ground etc., so the various philosophies imagine *Atman* to be states of consciousness, senses, body-mind etc.

We all begin with the attitude that 'reality is out there' and 'I am trying to find out what it is'; 'I am insignificant and limited in so many ways while something else, separate from me, is all-encompassing and eternal'. This is the stance of science also. All are mistaken. It is like the dreamer, believing that the dream world is vast and separate. Yet, when the dreamer awakens, it is discovered that this world was entirely a projection of the mind and not at all alien. Similarly, when Self-knowledge dawns, we realize that the waking universe is also non-separate from me, the *Atman*; that I am not even the waking person that I thought I was.

All other philosophies and religions maintain the subject-object duality. Whilst this view is held, the subject is inevitably at the mercy of those objects and dependent upon them for its peace. We seek out some aspects and try to avoid others. Insecurity is inevitable. Religions even maintain this duality in the afterlife, with a separate god in heaven ensuring that an element of limitation continues forever.

Gaudapada says that duality is only an appearance, like the

magician's illusions. It is like the appearance of sunrise and sunset. We know that the earth actually rotates about its axis, thereby giving an illusion that the sun is orbiting the earth. But, even knowing this, we still see the sun appearing to rise and set and we refer to the times recorded in the newspapers. Everyone is happy to refer to those events as if they were real. The continuing experience does not negate our knowledge.

We should not conclude that the seeming duality is real, just as we would be mistaken in believing in the reality of the mirage. The appearance of multiplicity is a delusion, a superimposition upon reality made by our minds as a result of ignorance. As long as the ignorance continues, we will be forced to suffer the associated ups and downs of *saMsAra*. Once Self-knowledge is gained, we will no longer be deluded by the appearance of an apparently separate world. We can acknowledge that the world is *mithyA*, while *turIya* is *satyam*.

Furthermore, it is only after realizing the truth of this that one is able to interpret correctly the statements of the Vedas. This is why one needs to seek out a teacher who can use both reason and scriptures to explain what has already been realized. Advaita begins where other religions and philosophies leave off. They function as mental preparation but can only continue *saMsAra*. Religions claim to lead to liberation; Advaita recognizes that we are already free.

Why Does Advaita Teach Duality?

(K4.42 – K4.43) Advaita also teaches about creation and many *jIva*-s striving for liberation. If duality is only an appearance, why does it do this?

This has effectively already been explained when the concept of *adhyAropa-apavAda* was introduced above. Even the spiritually inclined are reluctant to accept ideas such as *Advaita* and *ajAti vAda* to begin with. The reasons for this are the same as those given in 'Accepting the World as Unreal' above. We are aware of the world through all of our senses and we interact with people and things in it constantly. The things seem to behave in a recognizable, lawful and predictable manner. Scientists and philosophers study and categorize this world. Everything about it reinforces our conviction in its reality.

Furthermore, the world initially provides the sense of 'meaning' in our lives. This is not simply the basic needs of food, clothing and housing but interaction with other people – love, friendship and status. Whilst we might be willing to accept the ideas of Advaita in a metaphysical sense, the psychological aspects prove more problematic. If the more radical ideas are presented too soon, the seeker is likely to be put off and drop Advaita altogether.

Thus it is that the initial teaching of Advaita assumes duality and teaches the creation of the world, *karma*, reincarnation and so on (not that these latter two appeal to Westerners of course). The teaching has to begin at the level of understanding of the seeker. Although a true seeker is already mature in outlook and mentally receptive to these ideas, he or she is inevitably conditioned by the seeming duality so that the teacher has to begin with topics which are familiar. Only when a student has been studying for some years and has become familiar with concepts such as *mithyA*, does it become natural to begin to emphasize the non-duality of 'everything'. Then, there is no further need for the security of a supporting world and relationships because he or she knows that there is only *brahman* in reality and 'I am already perfect and complete'.

Gaudapada says that teaching in this way, with initial acceptance of dualistic ideas, does not cause any problems in the long run. Even if those erroneous ideas are temporarily reinforced, those who hold them will eventually come round to the truth.

The Delusion
Mistaking the Self

(K2.16) In the preceding verses (K2.4 – K2.15), Gaudapada demonstrated, using the dream analogy, that the waking world, too, must be *mithyA*. External objects have no more reality than the objects imagined by the mind in dream. The things that we see and do in our waking life – the 'external' world – generate feelings, desires and fears in our minds. And it is the memory of these that bring about our dreams, the 'internal world'. Thoughts, in turn, dictate how we respond to external events in our waking lives.

There seems to be a cause-effect relationship between the *jIva* and the perceived external and internal worlds. But, everything being *mithyA*, what is the connection here; which is cause and which is effect? Effectively, say Gaudapada and Shankara, the *jIva* is imagined first (in the *Atman*), in the same way (i.e. as a result of ignorance) that a snake is imagined in the rope. Then are imagined the world of objects 'necessary' to enable the *jIva* to function. These constitute the 'knowledge' of the *jIva*, which then leads to memory and therein begins the cycle of apparent cause and effect.

The *jIva* has thoughts and desires, motivating actions which have results. All of these are retained in memory and dictate future action, now in expectation of repeating desirable results or avoiding results that were previously unpleasant. Thus, the *jIva* imagines one element to be a 'cause' and another to be the 'effect'. Desires lead to action, then to results and karmic consequences, which eventually trigger rebirth and the process begins again.

See Appendix 7 for further discussion on this verse and, in particular, the theory that there is only one *jIva* – *eka-jIva-vAda*.

Rope and snake metaphor

(K2.17 – K2.18) Gaudapada finally (officially) introduces the rope-snake metaphor to illustrate how *Atman* can be 'imagined' as the various objects (and/or *jIva*-s) of the world. Because of ignorance, in partial light, we make the mistake of thinking that the rope is a snake (or a crack in the ground, or a stick etc.) Similarly, I the *Atman*, *turIya*, because of ignorance, make the mistake of thinking that I am a separate *jIva*, doer, enjoyer, reaper of *karma* and doomed to *saMsAra*. In total darkness, I do not see the rope so there is no problem about mistaking it for a snake. In deep sleep, I am not aware of *Atman* so I do not mistake it for this body-mind with all its attendant shortcomings. The problem arises when there is partial light or partial knowledge. In waking and dream states, I know there is something but not that it is *Atman-turIya*.

In the partial light, I imagine a snake; in the partial knowledge, I imagine the world. When I shine a torch onto the snake, it is revealed as an inanimate rope. When I inquire into the nature of the world, using the light of Advaita, Self-knowledge reveals the world as name and form of *brahman* – my own Self.

Note that, as with all metaphors, this should not be taken too far. Even if we are told that the perceived snake is, in fact, a rope, we still have some doubt and probably want to shine some light on it and verify this for ourselves. In the case of the *Atman*, however, there is no object for us to see; we ourselves are the *Atman*. Accordingly, it is rather that the words of the scriptures and the teacher, together with reasoning and our own experience, cause us to realize this already existing truth.

As soon as the rope is seen, there are no further imaginings of snake or crack. Similarly, the teaching eliminates the mistaken notions about the self – the *neti, neti* of the Brihadaranyaka Upanishad – and it is then known that 'I am That' and that 'All there is, is *brahman*'.

Magic Elephant

(K4.44) The magical illusion of the rope trick, in its spectacular Indian version, was described earlier. Apparently there was another trick, equally incredible, that was performed in ancient India. This was the conjuring of a full-size elephant, not only visible to onlookers but which could even be ridden! This therefore satisfied the major criteria for existence that we usually apply to objects in the world: we can perceive it and make use of it. And yet, implies Gaudapada, we do not claim that the elephant is real, since we know that this is a trick performed by an accomplished illusionist. Why, therefore, should we believe that the world is real?

For those who do not accept that such a realistic illusion is possible, we can equally refer again to the dream. Whilst in the dream, we see the elephant and it behaves in all of the ways that a waking elephant behaves. We (the dreamer) may ride on it or even fly on it and believe it to be perfectly real.

Duality
How does Duality come about?

(K4.72 – 3) It is not that there is *really* duality, then; it is just that we insist upon *believing* that there is. It is certainly true that we perceive duality and all of our actions in the empirical universe take it for granted. But that does not make it a fact. Just as gold takes on the form of ring and bangles, so Consciousness takes on the form of *jIva* and *jagat*, living and inert 'objects'. There seems to be a subject, an object and a relationship, which we call 'experience' but all of this is what Gaudapada calls *chittaspandita* – 'vibration or constant movement of Consciousness'. As soon as this movement stops, there is the silence and non-duality of deep sleep, just as there is the literal silence when the sounding of OM ceases.

There is eternally no connection of Consciousness with anything; no perception of, concern for, attention to 'things' in the world. Here, Gaudapada is using the adjective *nirviShaya* instead of *asparsha*, but it means the same. There is no contact or touch of Consciousness with anything, just as we might say that there is no contact of water with the wave. There is nothing other than Consciousness, so that there is no meaning to words such as association, relation or attachment.

Accordingly the empirical world, which we merely perceive and experience, does not exist as an independent reality. It matters not how many schools of philosophy assert its reality. It is *mithyA;* 'apparently real', as a result of Consciousness in motion. The world has the same status, from the vantage point of absolute reality, as the dream has from the vantage point of the waker. Other philosophies are unable to accept this as they believe the waking world to be absolutely real.

The Delusion of Duality

There is a perennial problem regarding discussions in Advaita because many of the questions that are asked result from confusing absolute and empirical reality. There is 'how things appear to be' and there is 'how things really are'. Knowing that the pool we see in the desert is only a mirage may prevent us from getting excited at the prospect of a drink but does not stop us from seeing what seems to be water. Knowing that the earth rotates about its axis, therefore presenting a changing face toward the sun, does not prevent us from seeing the sun 'rise' and 'set'. So it is that we still see a world and separate objects, irrespective of hearing convincing arguments from Gaudapada to the effect that there really is no world at all.

We have to use concepts that are later retracted in order to bring about an understanding of the nature of reality. Gaudapada admits that even the 'bottom line' statements regarding ultimate reality, such as that 'no one has ever been born', have to be dropped. It is simply not possible to speak about *brahman*. The adjectives that we use – even those in the seventh mantra of the *upaniShad* – are not ultimately valid. They are only words that we use in *vyavahAra*. For example, we say that *brahman* is 'changeless' but from the standpoint of absolute reality, there is no such thing as 'change', so that the word 'changeless' is meaningless. All words, even such ones as 'Consciousness', 'real', 'eternal', become redundant.

A metaphor that one may use is that of 'day and night'. These are useful and meaningful from the standpoint of someone living on the earth's surface (apart from the Polar Regions!) but, for someone living on the sun itself, they have no meaning at all.

This is why the Mandukya Upanishad refers to the silence following the sounding of OM as representing *turIya*. We can say nothing at all about reality and have to remain silent.

Here (K4.74), Gaudapada is specifically referring to the use of the word *aja*, unborn, to describe the *Atman*. It is since other schools of philosophy say that the Self is born, that Advaita needs to say that it is unborn in order to contradict them. But it is only a concept and there are no concepts in *paramArtha*. Even the word *Advaita* cannot be used.

(K4.75) Most people are unwilling to accept the claims of Advaita; they are far too enamored of the material world, driven by desires and ambitions to obtain more things and to be admired or even envied by others. Even though the reality is that there are no others, they persist in this drive in the mistaken belief that it will bring happiness or a sense of fulfillment in their lives. Once it is realized, however, that there is no duality, this brings an end to the vain search and, there being no further cause for rebirth, the *j~nAnI* is not reborn.

Gaudapada uses the word *abhUta* for those things to which we are attached. Literally, this means 'whatever has not been or has not happened'. They do not really exist and yet they continually distract us from the only reality! And, for that attraction, Gaudapada uses a word that carries many subtle meanings, all of them relevant. He says that the reason for *saMsAra* is '*abhinivesha*'. Monier-Williams gives the meaning as 'determination or tenacity' but Swami Chinmayananda says it is much more: "*an intense mental preoccupation with an ardent faith in a false*

knowledge sustained and nurtured by a totally laughable ignorance."
And it *"spells the ruin of the individual who maintains this belief."*
Som Raj Gupta gives perhaps the best translation (Ref. 66) with
'infatuation' – an intense, short-lived passion, which ultimately
makes us look foolish. And we can understand how this is so. It
is effectively our own creation: we mistake what we perceive, as
a result of ignorance; then we give names to those forms,
believing what is actually our own Self to be separate, possibly
threatening entities. It is really no different from our dreams,
where the entire world comes out of our own mind and yet we
run in fear of the imagined monster.

(K4.76) The only remedy is knowledge, which removes the
ignorance that brings about the error. In the absence of Self-
knowledge, the *jIva* thinks he is born and reborn. As noted
elsewhere, the course of *saMsAra* is that I believe I have been
born into a body, in which I move about in the world, performing
actions which result in the accumulation of *karma* or *saMskAra*. It
is this which is the cause of rebirth. Here, Gaudapada classifies it
into three types: good (*puNya*), bad (*pApa*) and mixed (*mishra*) or
intermediate (*madhyama*). ('Intermediate' might be, for example,
a 'good' action carried out for basically selfish reasons.) The good
takes me to heaven, the bad to hell and the mixed results in
rebirth.

But Gaudapada has already shown that the notion of
causation is not logically sustainable. The causes themselves are
delusions resulting from ignorance. Accordingly, he asks, if there
is no cause, how can there be an effect?

Reality
Firebrand Metaphor – Only Consciousness is Real
(K4.45) There is no doubt that there appears to be a world, and
people seem to be born and die. The events reported in the
newspaper and seen around us every day seem to be more real
than our dreams. But Gaudapada says that all is appearance

only, brought about (since we seem to require an explanation!) by *mAyA*. He is about to explain to us that it is simply the seeming movement of Consciousness that appears to bring into existence the entire world of so-called creation. In reality, however, nothing is ever born. Consciousness remains still and unmoving, without duality of any kind.

(K4.46) It is only as a result of ignorance that we perceive duality and hence develop desire and fear for imagined objects in an apparent world. No *jIva* is ever born; there is no death. All is simply the apparent movement of Consciousness but, failing to realize this, we fall subject to *saMsAra*. All we need to do is gain the knowledge of Advaita and be no more deluded by the appearances.

(K4.47) He then introduces his metaphor of the firebrand (*alAta*), which was mentioned in the introduction as the more familiar 'sparkler' in children's fireworks, to illustrate this.

The metaphor is deceptively simple. The firebrand, or torch, or stick with a glowing tip stands for Consciousness. When the firebrand is moved, lines and patterns seem to be created – these patterns represent the world. When Consciousness 'vibrates', a subject perceiver and perceived objects seem to be created. Shankara points out that, of course, Consciousness is not really moving or vibrating. (Since there is only Consciousness, there is nowhere it could move to!) The apparent motion is due to ignorance or *mAyA*.

(K4.48) When the glowing tip stops moving, the patterns also stop; the firebrand, complete with still glowing tip, just sits there without any 'appearances' being created. Similarly, when Consciousness is not 'vibrating' (i.e. when the mind is still, in deep sleep), there are no appearances of forms of any kind; we simply rest in stillness and peace. Because there are no patterns when the firebrand is still, we have to conclude that the firebrand itself is not the cause of the patterns. Similarly, when Consciousness is still (in deep sleep), there is no world.

Accordingly, Consciousness itself cannot be the cause of either the waking or dream worlds. It has to be the movement, which is the 'cause' in each case, and the patterns and forms are the 'effect' of this movement. Without the moving firebrand, there are no patterns; without vibrating Consciousness, there is no world.

The next 4 verses (K4.49 – K4.52) ask where the patterns/ world come from when they appear and where they go to when they disappear. (K4.49) when the firebrand is in motion, the patterns do not actually 'emerge' from it but then neither do they come from anywhere else. Similarly, when the motion stops, the patterns do not actually go back into the firebrand, but then neither do they go anywhere else. It seems to be inexplicable. (As mentioned in the introduction, we ignore the actual explanation – namely persistence of vision – for the purposes of the metaphor. It is assumed that this explanation was unknown to the originator.)

Anandagiri points out that, if the movement were the efficient cause and the firebrand itself the material cause, the patterns that are made should continue to exist after the movement has ceased. This is in the same way that, in the case of a potter making pots, when the potter is no longer present, the pots he has made do not disappear.

The fact that the appearances do not come out of the firebrand, says Shankara, means that they are not actually substances. Only something that is real can 'come out of' or 'go into'. The appearances relating to both the firebrand and to Consciousness cannot, therefore, be real. But they are clearly not unreal, since we cannot deny their appearance. Accordingly, they have to be *mithyA*. The 'existence' of the patterns belongs to the firebrand; the 'existence' of the world belongs to Consciousness, in the same way that the existence of the bangle and the ring belongs to gold.

Shankara explains that, whereas the patterns are associated

with the firebrand because of movement, this is not the case with the world and Consciousness. Consciousness is not really moving or vibrating. Accordingly, we cannot actually establish the nature of this relationship. What we can say is that the firebrand is associated with the patterns even though these appearances are unreal. Similarly, Consciousness is associated with the world and the *jIva*-s even though these appearances are also illusory.

The metaphor is also particularly apt for other reasons. There is only one glowing tip, whereas the patterns generated are multiple; i.e. the tip can be considered to represent *Advaita*, the patterns *dvaita*. Also, the glowing tip is self-evident, requiring nothing else to reveal it, just like Consciousness.

Furthermore, as Swami Dayananda indicates in Ref. 69, if we examine any point in the pattern (e.g. perhaps we could use a high-speed camera to 'freeze' the motion), we would find that there is nothing there other than the single tip of the glowing firebrand. Similarly, if we could examine any aspect of the (waking or dream) world in an analogous manner, we would find that there is nothing there other than the non-dual Consciousness.

Truth of the Self/Reality

K2.32 is possibly the most important verse in the entire *kArikA*-s. It makes a succinct and unequivocal statement about the nature of the apparent world: *"There is no birth or death (creation or dissolution); no one is bound, striving to become free, or already liberated. This is the ultimate truth."*

There cannot be any of these things for the simple reason that there is no duality. There is only *turIya* – the *Atman* – and this is already unlimited, part-less, Existence-Consciousness, *satyam-j~nAnam-anantam*. And I am That. The seeming bondage, and consequent need for liberation, is a superimposition resulting from ignorance, having no more reality than the misperceived snake on the rope. In the metaphor, the rope is real and provides the substrate on which the unreal snake is projected by the mind. Similarly, *brahman* is the real substrate on which the *mithyA* world is projected. And *brahman* is the real substrate of *Ishvara*, the projector, and 'me', to whom the appearances appear.

It should also be noted that, when we say that brahman is 'not X', this does not mean that brahman has the *property* of 'not-X'. When we say that the rope is not a snake; the rope does not thereby acquire an attribute of 'non-snake-ness'. When we say that the *Atman* is 'unlimited', what is really being said is that it does not have limitation as an attribute. In other words, *Atman* cannot be described in terms of any finite (limited) property.

Also, whereas the snake disappears once it is seen that the thing is really a rope, the world does not disappear. An appropriate analogy is that, despite realizing that the pot is really clay, we may still continue to use it to hold our coffee; it does not suddenly metamorphose into a lump of earth. The Sanskrit terms are *artha-adhyAsa* for the former and *j~nAna-adhyAsa* for the latter. In the case of the world, we do see it but we erroneously conclude that it is therefore real. It is this conclusion which must be negated, not the seeing of the world itself. The world is empirically real (*vyAvahArika*), unlike the snake (which is *prAtibhAsika*).

The mind interprets what we see as duality, rather than realizing there is only *brahman*. We can say that it is the mind that causes us to see duality where there is none. This can be seen by the argument that: when the mind is inactive, as in deep sleep or under anesthetic or in a (*samAdhi*) trance, we do not perceive duality. But when the mind is active, as in the waking or dream state, we do perceive duality; i.e. mind is – duality is; mind is not – duality is not. (This is called *anvaya-vyatireka* logic – co-presence and co-absence of the mind with the main term, duality.) [Just so that there is no confusion, it is Self-ignorance that causes the mind to interpret what is seen by the senses as

177

dual. Once Self-knowledge has been gained, what is seen is no different but is now known to be non-dual, and my Self.]

Shankara puts forward a possible objection to this idea saying that, just because we cannot see objects in the dark but can when we shine a torch on them doesn't lead us to conclude that the torch causes the objects. Neither do the eyes cause them, although a blind man is unable to see them. He responds to this by pointing out that, in both those cases, the people involved can still feel the objects, or detect them by some other means, even though unable to see them. But in the case of duality, without the mind it is not possible to detect duality in any way.

Sri Satchidanandendra makes an important point here (Ref. 29). He says that, when talking about the mind and duality in this way, we have to be careful not to think that the mind is somehow separate from duality. The mind is part of duality or, as Gangolli puts it: *"It is rational and proper to decide, determine that mind and duality are one and the same."* And he reminds us of the meanings implicit in the word 'Advaita':

1) nothing else similar to it (reality or *Atman*) exists;
2) another entity apart from it does not exist;
3) there are no distinctions or divisions within it.

It is the mind that imposes all seeming duality.

Shankara takes the opportunity to make it clear that what Gaudapada is saying here should not be confused with Buddhism (although the Buddhist beliefs are explicitly refuted later). The *vij~nAna vAda* Buddhist (otherwise known as *yogAchAra*) says that everything exists only as moment to moment manifestations of the mind. In essence this philosophy states, like Advaita, that everything is Consciousness but, unlike Advaita, that Consciousness is not continuous. Everything is born and dies in a moment, with the next moment being entirely new. Here, Gaudapada is saying that nothing is born or dies; it is only name and form of an eternally existing Consciousness.

The *shunya vAda* Buddhist, on the other hand, says that nothing ever exists at all in reality. It is equivalent to the philosophy of nihilism. We say that the empirical world is *mithyA*, having a real substrate, which is Consciousness. How, in any case, can someone claim that there is nothing? Who would be making that claim?

[I have, along with Gaudapada himself, condemned the *mAdhyamika* Buddhist concept of *shunya vAda* several times. This is really without the benefit of any real understanding of the philosophy. In mitigation, I would like to point out that Buddhist philosophers will almost certainly not agree with Gaudapada! Douglas Fox, for example (Ref. 9) prefers the translation 'emptiness' rather than 'nothingness', and he says it points to 'truth-beyond-conception'. The idea is that these philosophers felt that the mind was doomed to failure in its attempt to seek the 'ultimate truth'. So the *mAdhyamika*-s philosophy is rather devoted to demonstrating that all systems of thought inevitably lead to contradiction. When the mind gives up, the wordless truth will be recognized. Accordingly, in this view, the approach bears some comparison with Advaita and the claims that Gaudapada was, or at least began life as, a Buddhist do not seem so farfetched.]

All of the adjectives that I apply to myself throughout this life are superimpositions, imagined attributes applied to the *Atman* out of ignorance (K2.33). There is no exception to this. Whether I am talking about my body, mind, intellect, abilities, desires or anything else – all are untrue. Ironically, it is the mistaken belief in statements such as 'I am old' or 'I am stupid' that helps prevent the realization of my true nature. The seeing of myself as a body or mind is precisely analogous to the seeing of the snake on the rope. Just as I see 'something' and make the error of thinking it is a snake, so I know that 'I am' but make the error of superimposing these limited ideas of body and mind on the substratum of pure 'Existence' – *brahman*.

Reality is that which is left when everything that is *mithyA* has been rejected. There is nothing but Consciousness and everything else has to be dropped in order to appreciate this. Reality cannot even be defined as 'non-dual', since any definition is limiting and, for us, only a concept or a word used within *vyavahAra*. Accordingly, such words and concepts are themselves *mithyA*. As Swami Chinmayananda puts it: *"Truth of Reality is the basis for both the concepts of the non-dual and the plurality. Consciousness or Awareness that illuminates these two concepts is one and the same."*

Just as there has to be something (i.e. the rope) as the substratum for the snake that I imagine that I see, so there has to be something as the substratum for the *mithyA* world and *jIva*. The non-dual reality is effectively 'imagined' as this necessary substrate, a logical necessity to explain the world appearance. Or, another way of looking at this seemingly paradoxical state of affairs, is that once we have negated the appearance, the reality loses its status as substrate. The concept of Advaita, and the word itself, are thus also *mithyA*. Even 'Consciousness' is meaningless when there is no 'non-Consciousness'.

(K2.34) This dualistic world, although having the non-dual *Atman* as its substrate, cannot be said to be identical with the *Atman*, just as the snake is clearly not the rope. After all, ropes do not cause us to take fright and run away. But neither world nor snake has an independent existence; without their respective substrate, they would not appear in the first place. Accordingly, the world has the peculiar ontological status of being neither separate from *Atman*, nor non-separate. (Note that the fear that arises is not caused by the assumed-snake alone. The appearance is linked with memories of danger from poisonous fangs etc.)

We have already seen that, if we examine 'things' more and more closely, we are forced to devise the term *mithyA* to describe their seeming separateness. They are like the dream, which seems real at the time but is seen to have been less than absolutely real on waking. Moreover, if we accepted the world as absolutely real, we would have to reject Advaita. Matter is not conscious so that, even if matter were undifferentiated, there would still be at least two things. (Remember that 'things' cannot meaningfully be said to exist unless there is a conscious entity to perceive them.)

But we cannot deny the appearance of the world and life compels us to act as though duality were the reality. We are forced to postulate the magical power of *mAyA* to account for it.

In his commentary on this *kArikA*, Shankara touches on the logic of the concept of 'difference'. Clearly, it is potentially a very important topic since, if it could be proven logically that the idea of 'difference' is incoherent, it would effectively demonstrate the non-dual nature of reality. Numerous post-Shankara philosophers have looked into this and formulated involved arguments. There is extensive material in the post-Shankara texts of *brahmasiddhi, iShTasiddhi, tattvashuddhi, khaNDanakhaNDakhAdya* and *chitsukhI/tattvadIpikA* but, having looked at these, they seem too impenetrable to study in detail. (No references are given for these – you really don't want to read them!)

One of the arguments claims that, for knowledge to arise, there has to be a *pramANa* and this certainly sounds reasonable. But it then goes on to claim that, since difference cannot be located in either A or B, there is no *pramANa* and therefore there cannot be any knowledge of it. But a *pramANa* is not required. We have *pratyakSha pramANa* for the knowledge about A and the same for B. The intellect is then able to discriminate and conclude that A is not the same as B. This 'not the same' is what we call 'difference'. I feel that this is one of the sorts of issues that Wittgenstein must have looked at. It is a case of our use of language generating a seeming problem which is really not there at all.

It seems to me that we can happily accept 'difference' as being an empirical fact of life without doing injury to the concept of Advaita at all. Words mean whatever we define them to mean –

and we all know what is meant by the word 'difference'. As evidence of this I can truthfully say that, in all the 30+ years that I have lived in this house, I have never tried to enter my neighbor's house by mistake. And, when I go to sleep at night, I always do so in the bedroom and not the kitchen.

If I go into my living room, I see a brownish shape directly ahead and a greenish one to the right. Then I put on my spectacles and they resolve, respectively, into a table and a plant. The table has a bulge in the middle which, on closer examination, is seen to be a book. If I pick this up and open it, I further discover that there are many different pages, and each is filled with many different words. The plant has leaves which are clearly green. But, if I examine one of these leaves through a powerful microscope, I find that this green is not at all uniform, being constrained to just some of the many different structures within the leaf.

This is one way of explaining the meaning of the term *mithyA*. The point is that it becomes impossible to isolate that characteristic that differentiates one 'object' from 'another'. By removing petals and stamens etc., we cannot find in which part the 'flowerness' resides. And a flower, reduced to its subatomic particles looks pretty much the same as a paperclip. Every seemingly separate thing is ultimately nothing other than name and form of Consciousness. Basically, all words relate to empirical, not absolute reality! And apparent 'difference' is seen to be nothing more than a practically useful fiction.

Another approach could use the rope-snake metaphor and claim that any (seemingly separate) thing that we see is not what it appears to be. We are making a mistake, as a result of our ignorance. Just as we think the rope is a snake, so we think that there is a book, a table, a room, a house etc. In fact there are not many things here at all. There are no 'things' at all; there is only *turlya-brahman*. This error (superimposing a mistaken or illusory entity onto the actual, real thing) is called *adhyAsa*. This term is so important in Advaita that Shankara's introduction to his commentary on the Brahmasutras is devoted to explaining the concept.

[It must always be remembered that all of these explanations are themselves concepts which are being assimilated by the mind and both concepts and mind are equally *mithyA*. Understanding how it is that a real Consciousness functions in this process involves a (*mithyA*) concept called *chidAbhAsa*, the 'reflection' of Consciousness in the mind. This is not explained in this text so I have covered it in Appendix 3.]

Reality for Awakened jIva

A favorite topic on the Advaitin discussion group (http://groups.yahoo.com/group/Advaitin/) (where I am one of the moderators) has been what exactly happens when a person is enlightened or 'gains *mokSha*'. A popular, although somewhat incomprehensible, belief is that the world somehow 'disappears'; that, for the *j~nAnI*, there simply is no longer any duality. Quite how the *j~nAnI* (apparently) continues to eat, drink and converse is not adequately explained by those who hold such a view. But Gaudapada approaches it from a different and even more dramatic angle.

Prior to my enlightenment, I make the mistake of identifying myself with the body-mind, believing myself to be a separate entity. This is the result of my Self-ignorance – not realizing that I am the unlimited *Atman*. Gaudapada says that this ignorance is beginningless (*anAdi*) (K1.16). At the dawn of Self-knowledge, I recognize that I am not the waker, dreamer or deep-sleeper but the non-dual *turIya*.

As to whether or not the world then disappears, Gaudapada effectively asks: how can it disappear when it didn't exist to begin with? *"If the visible world actually existed, there is no doubt that it might stop (i.e. disappear) (as soon as j~nAna was gained). (But) this (apparent) duality is merely mAyA (and) the absolute truth is non-dual."* (K1.17)

The world does not disappear because it never existed in the first place! What actually goes away is the mistaken belief that there was a world. Shankara begins his commentary with a supposed objection. The previous verse states that the *jIva* realizes *Advaita* when he 'wakes up' from 'sleep', i.e. dispels self-ignorance. If one can only realize *Advaita* when duality has gone, then how can there be non-duality while the world still exists?

Shankara answers this by pointing out that this would only be a problem if the world actually exists to begin with. And he refers to the inevitable rope-snake metaphor: To speak of the snake disappearing when knowledge of the rope is gained is incorrect. Since the snake never existed in the first place, it cannot go away. Similarly, the world never existed, so to speak of it going away upon enlightenment is wrong. A non-existent thing neither comes nor goes away. (The world is, of course, *mithyA*, being neither real nor unreal but having *brahman* as its substratum.) So, what actually goes away upon obtaining *j~nAna* is not the perceived dualistic universe but the error (*bhrama*) that we made in thinking that there *was* a dualistic world.

And, of course, the *j~nAnI's* supposed body-mind-intellect is equally a part of this supposed dualistic world. So the *j~nAnI* him- or herself does not go away either!

If it were the case that, upon gaining *j~nAnam*, the (now) *j~nAnI* no longer perceived a dualistic world, (and thus no longer used a mind and senses to communicate with it etc.) then this would be a clear break with what had gone before. And so *mokSha* would become an event in time. But the fact of the matter is that all (apparent) *jIva*-s are already free and unlimited, being not other than *brahman*. The problem is that they do no know it and make the error of thinking themselves to be separate and limited. Upon realization, all that goes away is this mistake. The *j~nAnI* sees the world as *brahman* and never sees any appearance or disappearance. He continues to see this *brahman*-world and continues to interact with it whilst in the body but (and of course this but makes all the difference) he now knows that it is all an appearance only. He knows that the world is *mithyA* and nothing detracts from the *turIya* status.

Swami Chinmayananda points out (Ref. 3) that the first line of the mantra says, in effect: *"The universe does not exist; if it existed it would disappear (on being enlightened). It does not disappear, therefore it does not exist".*

Paradoxically, the very same argument applies to the (apparent) duality of the knowledge that brings about enlightenment. After all, it is the result of being taught the wisdom of such scriptures as this that triggers the 'enlightenment event' (*akhaNDAkAra vRRitti*). But we cannot say that Self-knowledge eliminates the duality of guru and disciple for the same reason as above: there was no duality there before. Again, it is analogous to asking if the snake goes away once the rope is known. There is no knower-known duality to be eliminated; what goes away is the mistaken belief that there was a duality to begin with. (K1.18)

Richard King sums this up nicely (Ref. 14):

"K1.18 is an attempt to circumvent one of the greatest paradoxes of a non-dualistic soteriology– if duality is an illusion how is it that the dream is not broken by the first enlightened being? This presents no real problem for the Gaudapada-kArikA for the following reasons:

1. *Duality as* mAyA *is not in conflict with non-duality as the ultimate reality* (paramArtha) *since the former is merely an appearance of the latter.*
2. *The idea of a liberated individual is an erroneous one; no* jIva *is ever liberated, since no* jIva *has ever entered bondage."*

Outwardly, nothing changes – what was there before is still there. Both the *j~nAnI* and the *aj~nAnI* still see the world; the *j~nAnI* knows it to be non-dual. The sunrise metaphor applies again. Or, for a change, the earth is felt to be steady and unmoving despite the fact that we know it is rotating rather quickly, and travelling around the sun at a rate of knots. Combined with the fact that the entire galaxy is moving and the universe expanding, this means that the earth is anything but stationary!

Self Knowledge

The mind and Its 'Death'

(K3.31 – K.32) Everything that we perceive, we perceive through the senses; everything that we 'know', we know through the mind. Consciousness functions through the mind – the concept known as *chidAbhAsa*, explained in Appendix 3. When the mind is inactive – for example, in deep sleep or under anesthetic – we are conscious of nothing. It is the mind that effectively imposes duality on the non-dual. We see the forms and, by naming them, it is as if we create separate things where there is really only *brahman*. Once this apparent duality is imposed, all of the negative emotions of desire, fear, attachment, anger and the rest follow. It is the mistaking of the really non-dual as dual that brings into existence all of our problems, which Advaita summarizes as *saMsAra*.

Having recognized that it is the mind that is the effective source of our problems, it is only natural to conclude that, by somehow 'getting rid of' the mind, we will solve those problems. This is the concept called *manonAsha*, which found favor with Ramana Maharshi in particular, who is claimed to have stated that this should be the aim of the seeker; (*manas* refers to mind in general; *nAsha* means loss, destruction, annihilation, death.) Once we have 'destroyed the mind', it is said, there will be no more duality.

Gaudapada does not use the word *manonAsha* but *amanIbhAva*. This means 'the state of not having perception or intellect' and comes from the Maitri or *maitrAyanIya* Upanishad (VI.34). It is worth quoting some of what is said there (Ref. 80):

Having made the mind perfectly motionless, free from sleep and agitation—when he passes into that state where the mind itself vanishes, then is that the highest place... The mind alone is to

187

mortals the cause of bondage and liberation; cleaving to objects of sense, it is only for bondage; when it is void of all objects it is called liberation.

The way that Gaudapada puts it is that, when the mind ceases to function, duality is no longer perceived – and this we know from our own experience in deep sleep. But clearly this is not quite the same. There is *never* any duality – this is the truth. But, in our ignorance we believe that the perceived duality is real; just as we believe the mirage water is real. Once we gain the knowledge, we realize that our belief was mistaken, even though we still see the duality or mirage.

When the knowledge dawns that the world, *including the mind,* is only *mithyA*, this is the figurative death of the mind. As Swami Paramarthananda puts it, *"A wise mind, which does not see real duality, is as good as no mind".* Anything that we previously thought to be a problem is so no more, because we know that it is not real. We do not have to destroy the dream world; we just need to wake up; *manonAsha* should not be thought of as 'death of the mind', which is not at all the case. It should be understood as the intellectual recognition that the mind is unreal, from the vantage point of absolute reality.

I have included an essay on *manonAsha* at Appendix 4 for those who want to read more about this topic.

Enlightenment

The *jIva* continues to mistake the world of duality for reality, until such time as the ignorance that brings about this erroneous perception is displaced by Self-knowledge. This is an event in the mind, triggered by a thought (called the *akhaNDAkAra vRRitti*). Subsequently, it is known that, despite the continued appearance of duality, it is all *mithyA* and the reality is non-dual Consciousness alone.

This event is also said to eliminate all of the *saMchita saMskAra* (that which has accumulated from past actions but not yet begun to fructify), and to stop the production of any future *AgAmin saMskAra*. This is because it is now known that there is not really a 'person' performing actions – the 'hitherto person' now knows that he/she is *brahman*. There does still remain the *prArabdha saMskAra*, however. It is this that was the 'cause' for the person and it continues to have its effect until it is all 'used up' and the body-mind dies, no longer to be reborn.

The alert reader will spot seeming contradictions in the above paragraph! If there is 'no longer a person', how can there be someone who 'knows' that they are *brahman*? This incongruity arises because we are on the borderline between empirical and 'would-be' absolute statements – the *vyavahAra-paramArtha* distinction that plagues attempts to discuss Advaita. It has already been pointed out that our problem is one of Self-ignorance. When this is displaced by Self-knowledge – an event in the mind – then that mind realizes the following: 'As a person, I was only reflected Consciousness. In reality, I am that non-dual, un-reflected Consciousness; I have never been an individual. What happened was that reflected Consciousness in the mind identified with ideas of separation, suffering etc. Now that identification has ceased.'

Nevertheless, that body-mind continues to function at the empirical level until its natural death (when *prArabdha saMskAra* has been exhausted). To all outward appearances (i.e. other 'persons'), it will appear as before, although its behavior may change. Consciousness will still be reflected in that mind and will operate according to the idiosyncrasies of that mind; i.e. there will still be preferences and aversions, although the response to the outcomes of these will likely be attenuated. And the body-mind will still be available seemingly to perform such actions as teaching Advaita to seekers. And, to return to the apparent anomaly, there will still be a mind (or 'person') to 'know that I am brahman'.

(K4.77) The implication of this 'explanation' is that this knowledge will arrive for a seeker at some future date and *saMsAra* will continue until that time; i.e. that liberation occurs at a point in time. If this is the case, then how can my real nature be *brahman*, which we have said is eternally unlimited? If I really am *brahman*, then I must already be free now. And such is the case. Gaudapada says that Consciousness is ever birthless and free from cause. We may well perceive duality, birth and death of animate and inert objects but this is a mistake, like the rope-snake.

We are never really bound – *saMsAra* is also *mithyA* – and therefore there is not really any event in which we gain liberation. It is analogous to the dream. At the time of the dream, we may believe ourselves to be assailed by all manner of problems but, on waking up, we are not 'freed' from those problems – the dream problems were relevant only in the context of the dream.

So enlightenment does not make us free – we were already free; limitless *brahman* before and after. Enlightenment is simply the removal of the mistaken notion that we were limited. To dispel this ignorance, all that we need is Self-knowledge; we need to know that 'I am not the limited body-mind; I am *brahman*'. And it is not the case that, following receipt of this knowledge, we need to go away and meditate upon it so that we may 'experience' its truth for ourselves. The knowledge is not 'indirect' but itself is 'enlightenment'. There is no need to 'do' anything.

Knowing *brahman*

(K3.33) Having seen that there is no creation, that both the world and the *jIva*-s are *mithyA*, one might wonder how it is possible to discover and know the truth about the Self and reality. Gaudapada says that this knowledge is not the same as what we understand in the context of knowing things in the world.

What we usually call knowledge involves a knower and

something else, distinct from the knower, as well as an instrument for 'channeling' the knowledge. For example, when I say that I know the tree in my garden, I consider that I the subject am different from the tree object, and my eyes are the usual instrument for acquiring this knowledge. This knowledge involves thinking and possibly imagination and is likely to lead to mistaken identity.

In the case of *brahman*, *brahman* is both subject and object and requires no instrument, since it is self-illuminating like the sun. If the sun were sentient, it would not need another source of light in order to 'see' itself. I know that I exist, requiring neither a means of perceiving this nor another source to tell me. My existence is self-evident; there is no thought or imagination that I might not exist; no possibility of error. In this sense, *brahman* **is** pure knowledge, 'devoid of imagination and unborn', as Gaudapada puts it. Knower and knowledge are the one, non-dual *brahman*.

This does, of course, beg the question as to why we are suffering *saMsAra* and need to study the scriptures in order to gain *mokSha*. The answer is that, although we are already free, we do not realize it. Our mind is filled with misconceptions regarding the nature of ourselves and the world. We think that we are separate, limited entities living in an alien world in which everyone and everything is potentially out to get us. It is necessary to study Advaita to remedy this situation. What this does is help us to remove those misconceptions. Once they are removed, I realize that I am the *Atman*, which has always been there and always will be, since there is nothing else.

Shankara explains this very clearly in the Swami Madhavananda translation of the Brihadaranyaka Upanishad (Ref. 32):

The knowledge of brahman *means only the cessation of the identi-fication with extraneous things (such as the body). The relation of identity with It has not to be directly established, for it is already there. Everybody already has that identity with It, but it appears to be related to something else. Therefore the scriptures do not enjoin that identity with brahman should be established, but that the false identification with things other than That should stop. When the identification with other things is gone, that identity with one's own Self which is natural, becomes isolated; this is expressed by the statement that the Self is known. In itself It is unknowable—not comprehended through any means.*

Lest there should be any doubt here, it is worth repeating that everyone already *is brahman*. But most are ignorant of this fact. At the same time, since *brahman* is 'self-evident', it is impossible not to know *brahman*. No one will ever deny that 'I exist and am conscious'. The difference between a *j~nAnI* and an *aj~nAnI* is that the *aj~nAnI* still has misconceptions and believes that he/she is a separate, suffering entity subject to *saMsAra*. The *aj~nAnI* still identifies with the waking, dreaming and deep-sleep states, whereas the *j~nAnI* knows he/she is *turIya*. To return to use of metaphor, the *aj~nAnI* still runs after the mirage, believing that there is water there to quench his or her thirst. The *j~nAnI* sees it but knows that it is only an illusion.

This point also must be very clear. There is always only Consciousness. There are no separate *jIva*-s in reality, no world in reality. From an empirical point of view, there *seem* to be separate *jIva*-s and there *seem* to be objects. This 'seeming' is despite the reality and has nothing to do with any consideration of *mokSha*, Self-realization, enlightenment or whichever term is preferred. (From the empirical point of view), Self-ignorance initially obscures this knowledge. Teaching, from scriptures and guru, may reveal the truth and the Self-ignorance may be dispelled. This event occurs in time, in the mind, and reveals the knowledge that all this is *mithyA*, i.e. teaching, scriptures, *guru*, world, *jIva*-s; that Consciousness/brahman is the only reality and 'I am That

Consciousness'.

'Outwardly', nothing has changed. From the point of view of reality, all is (still) *brahman*. From the empirical standpoint, the world and the *jIva*-s continue their appearance as before. The difference is that the mind of the *j~nAnI jIva* now knows the truth. Gaining Self-knowledge doesn't 'end' duality in any way – there never was any duality to begin with. Self-knowledge is *knowing* this fact, not in any mere intellectual sense but with the same certainty as I know that I exist – the same certainty because it is essentially the same knowledge, bereft of every conceivable contradictory notion.

(K3.34 – K3.35) Knowing *brahman* means knowing that there is no duality. In these two verses, Gaudapada explains that this is not the same as the person in a deep-sleep state, who also does not see duality. In fact, such a person does not see anything at all, whereas the *j~nAnI* does still perceive duality but knows that it is *mithyA*. But this is not the point that he wishes to make.

The crucial difference is that, although there is no manifest duality in the deep-sleep state, it is all there in potential form and (seemingly) becomes manifest as soon as we move into the dream state or waking state. Thus, the one who does not yet have Self-knowledge, moves forever through the three states, only intermittently 'experiencing' non-duality (and not actually appreciating it anyway).

The word 'experiencing' has to be in quotation marks here because, of course, one cannot experience non-duality since, by definition, there is not an 'experiencer' and an 'experienced object'. And this emphasizes the fact that the *samAdhi* (of Yoga philosophy and the neo-Vedantin branch of Advaita begun by Swami Vivekananda) is no better. One can enter the trance-like state of meditation called *samAdhi*, wherein there is no experience of duality but, inevitably, one comes back out of that state eventually. It is not the same as Self-knowledge, in which it is always known that the reality is non-dual despite the appearance (or not) of duality. The *j~nAnI* may seem (to an *aj~nAnI*) to act as though the world is real but the *j~nAnI* knows that it is only seeming movement of name and form of what is always non-dual *brahman*.

In deep sleep, the mind is resolved. We are unaware of the world of duality so it causes no problems. But inevitably we wake up and all of our perceived problems are still there. They must have been there too, during sleep, in what Shankara terms 'seed form'. It was a temporary respite only. With Self-knowledge, it is known that there is no 'other' at all. Knowing that everything is *brahman*, there can be no fear. This knowledge is there on waking from deep-sleep so that the reappearance of duality causes no problems at all. Once it is known that the coiled snake in the shed is only a rope, there is no more fear.

In contrast to the mind in sleep, Shankara uses the word *niruddha* to describe the mind when it knows that the world is *mithyA*. This word literally means 'held back' or 'restrained' or even 'closed', 'suppressed'. Shankara is using it in the sense of 'controlled', not liable to be excited by either desired or feared eventualities. (He also uses the word *nigRRihIta*, which means 'held down or back, caught, checked'.) He describes it as 'tranquil, like a fire without fuel'. Any potentially disturbing thought or action simply does not arise since the truth of non-duality has been realized. This is in stark contrast to the non-disturbance in deep sleep, for the dualistic thoughts leap up again immediately on waking.

Seeing everything as *mithyA* means that it is known that the mind, too, is *mithyA*. This has the effect of rendering it impotent – the *manonAsha* described earlier. Gaudapada says that the mind becomes the fearless *brahman*, with the all-pervading light of knowledge.

(K3.36 – K3.38) *brahman* cannot be known in any objective sense – it is nameless and formless. This harks back to OM in the Upanishad – it is the silence that follows *a*, *u* and *m*. Gaudapada says that it is birthless and without sleep or dream indicating that, although it is the ever-present background and reality of all three states, it is not subject to the limitations of any of them; neither the ignorance of the deep-sleep state, nor the mistaken projections of waking and dream states. *bahman* itself is the non-dual substrate of all projections and has in itself no attributes. It has not undergone any change in appearing as the world. It is we who project duality onto it, just as we project a snake onto what is really a rope. And we are that same *brahman*.

Once this is known, there is nothing further to be done. The neo-Vedantin followers of Swami Vivekananda claim that, once you have gained the knowledge that everything is *brahman*, you then have to practice in order to convert the 'theory' into a reality. But the knowledge and the essential nature of oneself are the same thing. We already were *brahman* before; we just did not realize it.

In K3.37, Gaudapada reminds us of the seventh mantra of the Upanishad. The Self, he says, has nothing to do with speech – 'speech', here, represents all of the sense organs. Nor does it have anything to do with the organs of mind (thought, intellect, memory, and ego). It is tranquil, unchanging and without fear; the eternal light of consciousness.

He also uses the word *samAdhi* to describe *Atman*. This refers to the fact that it is as a result of control of the mind, and concentration, that the *jIva* is able to realize the truth when he hears it from the teacher. It could also be said to 'bring together' the knower and the known. This usage is quite different from that of Yoga, in which it is used in the sense of a deep meditation in which the mind becomes very still and awareness of the outside world is attenuated. What is called *savikalpa samAdhi* is a state in which there is still awareness of a distinction between knower and known; that differentiation has dissolved in *nirvikalpa samAdhi*. Swami Dayananda says (Ref. 69) that *"The difference between this* samAdhi *and the* yoga samAdhi *is in* yoga *there is the fear you may lose it."*

(K3.38) The gaining of Self-knowledge does not entail any acceptance or giving up. Either of these would imply change and *brahman* is changeless and part-less. Consequently, there is nothing that can be accepted or given up. There cannot even be any thoughts in *turIya*, since these can only take place in the mind.

Gaining knowledge of *brahman* amounts to becoming *brahman*. Previously I thought that I was limited, having been born into a body that is always less than perfect with a mind that invariably struggles at times; desiring some things and fearing others, feeling that my happiness depended on their outcome. Now, I know that I am unlimited and unborn. This body and mind, together with all other bodies and minds and the world itself, are only *mithyA* names and forms of my Self. I am without limit and unaffected by anything else, because there is nothing else.

Even this knowledge is name and form of *brahman* so that it is perfectly reasonable and true to say that this knowledge itself is also unborn. The paragraph above said that gaining knowledge 'amounts to becoming *brahman*'. But of course I always was and will be *brahman*. Nothing **really** changes. All that happens is removal of ignorance.

(K3.39) Knowing that I am *brahman* and that there is only *brahman* goes along with knowing that this world that I see, and all of the 'others' living in this world are *mithyA* – they are 'all' only *brahman*. I am everything – there are no 'others'. This is clearly a realization of infinite significance. The normal state of affairs is that I depend upon others for everything in life, from food, clothing and security to perceived happiness, status etc. Most people's raison d'être depends upon others. This knowledge entails the acknowledgement that I can no longer do this – and, for the ignorant person, this means insecurity. Thus, many seekers are afraid of recognizing this truth because of that reason.

Gaudapada calls this non-relationship with anything (because there are no others) *asparsha yoga*. The word *sparsha* literally means 'touching', so that some commentators call this 'touchless yoga'. Shankara says that it is so called because it is devoid of *sparsha*, a term which indicates all relations. Anandagiri says it is *Advaita Anubhava* – non-dual experience. (Ref. 54).

It is interesting to note that the very word 'relationship', in Sanskrit, entails bondage. The word for 'relationship' is *sambandha* and this is effectively two words – *sam*, meaning 'connected with, together with', and *bandha*, meaning 'bondage, binding, chain, attachment to the world'.

Gaudapada probably derives the word *asparsha* from the Bhagavad Gita. In Chapter 5, verse 21 talks about how one acquires the bliss that is one's Self by being unattached to external objects and uses the word *sparsha* to refer to objects that are 'contacted' (via the senses). Verse 22 says that, although we initially get pleasure from this contact, it invariably leads to sorrow and wise people avoid such contact. Accordingly, the notion of *asparsha yoga* embodies the idea of renouncing sense pleasures in the knowledge that they bind us to the *mithyA* world.

Both Swami Chinmayananda and Richard King point out the paradoxical nature of the term 'Asparsha Yoga' since the first word emphasizes that there can be no relationship while the second is about the union of two things (yoga means 'joining together' or even 'contact with'!). V. H. Date (Ref. 18) suggests that "asparsha *indicates that* brahman *cannot be touched by anything else, but that* yoga *indicates that* brahman *can touch everything else.*"

Colin Cole summarizes the meaning as follows (Ref. 11):

On the philosophical level, the term implies the realization of non-duality, i.e. of turIya *or* brahman. *In this sense it could be called the 'non-dual yoga' or the 'yoga of the non-dual'. On the level of religious practice, the term refers to the discipline, path, method or process whereby the* sAdhaka *attains this condition of being one with Ultimate Reality. [sAdhaka means 'seeker'.]*

Michael Comans' view (Ref. 13) is that it is not a practice for attaining enlightenment at all. It follows *from* Self-knowledge. It is the abiding in the knowledge of the non-dual Self (*j~nAna niShTha*) and it is a 'practice' to the extent that it means maintaining the mind in this attitude.

(K4.78) Once I know the truth – that there is only the birthless, causeless *brahman* – I also realize that the world and all of the things that I previously sought to acquire or avoid have no separate reality. I know that they can neither harm me nor bring happiness. In effect, I attain to a 'state' without either desire or fear. These only exist when I mistakenly believe myself to be limited. (Gaudapada uses the word *padam* here, presumably referring back to the Upanishad itself and to the 'fourth' *pada* – *turIya* – which is not a state at all.)

(K4.79) As long as I continue to believe in the existence of an external world, I naturally pursue happiness there. Gaudapada uses the word *abhUtAbhinivesha*, which Swami Gambhirananda translates as 'a conviction that duality does exist', even though there is no such thing in reality. I see something that I find desirable and set about obtaining it. Enlightenment entails the realization that all these objects are *mithyA*. Their essential nature is also my essential nature – I already have everything! Once I appreciate this, all such pursuits naturally come to an end.

What is actually happening here is that I first realize that I am not the waker-dreamer-deep sleeper. Those are states, seen to be effectively only roles that I play. Only then, can I appreciate the *mithyAtva* of the worldly objects also. From the standpoint of the waker, those objects still appear to be real – *mithyA* sees *mithyA* as *satyam*. Just as the dreamer needs dream water to satisfy his dream thirst, so the *mithyA* waker needs *mithyA* objects in the world to satisfy his desires. Enlightenment is the spiritual equivalent of waking from a dream and realizing its unreality.

(K4.80) Instead, we become unattached to anything, unperturbed by events, ever serene and remaining uninvolved in external appearances, knowing them to be unreal. The knowledge that everything is *brahman* makes me immune to discomposure because I know that all is non-different from my Self, which is ever the same, non-dual Consciousness.

Whilst in dream, I take the dream world, which is entirely a creation of my own mind, to be real. On awakening, I know immediately that it was a dream and I automatically drop any concerns I might have had about what was happening, no matter how exciting or frightening. The same applies with respect to gaining Self-knowledge and the waking world. Despite its continuing appearance, I know that it cannot affect who I really am.

(K4.81) Nor am I any longer attached to the three states of consciousness, since I now know that they are *mithyA*, with *turIya* as their real essence. This intrinsic nature is 'self effulgent' – it is Consciousness, and it is this that animates the inert body during waking, the mind during dream and the vital forces during deep sleep and unconsciousness. And it is this that is the essence of the objects in the world, the dream objects in the dream and the peace and ignorance of deep sleep.

(K4.85) The knower of *brahman* knows that there is no birth, life, death; beginning, middle or end. What then, asks Gaudapada, is left for us to desire? Nothing – desire is the wish for something else, which might fulfill my sense of limitation. Knowing that I am unlimited, such a wish is impossible.

(K4.86) One who has gained Self-knowledge, and thus 'knows' *brahman* is naturally disciplined and humble. The peace and tranquility that 'describes' *turIya* – *shantaM, shivam, AdvaitaM* from the seventh mantra – are an inevitable consequence of establishing this knowledge. [See section on 'Knowledge and the Fruit of Knowledge' below, for differentiation between *j~nAna* and *j~nAna niShTha*.] All the striving that characterizes our day to day existence as a 'person' comes to an end. The struggle was to eliminate perceived limitations and, now I know that I am unlimited, there is nothing to achieve. The body may continue with its aches and pains; the mind may continue with its preferences and dislikes. But I know that I am neither body nor mind, and none of these 'disturbances' to name and form affect me, Consciousness. The ego is still there to some degree, but it is now like the mirage – I see it but I know that it is not really there.

Problems and Misconceptions

(K4.82) The senses necessarily register duality. When we see, hear, smell, taste, feel some 'thing', this thing is perceived as something other than our self the perceiver. This is how they have evolved to function, so as to forewarn and protect the body-mind. This has been our experience from birth, so it is hardly surprising that it should be so difficult for us to accept that this is not really how things are; that this duality is only in the perception and not in the reality. Even after we have read about this in books such as this, even if we read the scriptures or listen to a qualified teacher repeat this over and over again, it is difficult for us to reject the evidence of our senses upon which we have relied for so long.

This is why it is very difficult for anyone to gain Self-knowledge – the truth of non-duality. Thus it is, says Gaudapada, that happiness is concealed and misery made manifest.

The body-mind of a *j~nAnI* continues its 'life' in this world until the exhaustion of *prArabdha karma*. (See the section 'Reality for the Awakened *jIva*' above.) This is of no concern to the *j~nAnI*, who no longer identifies with the body-mind but, during this time, the process of perceiving duality and habitually reacting to this still takes place in that body-mind. Every transaction requires us to play the role of *vishva*, the waker, even if we know that there is really only *turIya*.

According to Swami Dayananda's *sampradAya*, the *j~nAnI* may well still behave outwardly as an *aj~nAnI* and effort may still be required, repeatedly to re-establish the knowledge of the truth. This continues until the knowledge is firmly established (*j~nAna niShtha*). This interpretation is discussed later in the section on 'Knowledge and the Fruit of Knowledge'.

(K4.83) What happens, then, is that we intellectualize about who we really are, attempting to rationalize our existence and experience. Philosophers have provided various theories and, here, Gaudapada effectively ridicules them by summarizing them in a way which illustrates how they contradict each other. He uses a Buddhist, logical device called *chatuShkoTi* (meaning 'four points') or tetralemma. This states that, regarding the truth of a proposition X, there are 4 possibilities: true, false, both or neither. (It is actually more complicated than this – see, for example, the page on 'catuskoti' on Wikipedia – but this is not the place for such a discussion!)

Gaudapada says that a man 'of inferior intelligence' tries to define the Atman in one of four ways:

- The Atman exists (*asti*), is distinct and separate from the body, and is the actual 'knower' and 'enjoyer'. He is therefore subject to change. This is the position of the *nyAya-vaisheShika* philosophers.
- The Atman, which is the same as the intellect, arises in each moment to observe a thought-perception and dies in the next as the thought subsides. There is no permanent, enduring Atman at all and thus it can be said to not exist (*nAsti*). This is the belief, *kShaNika vij~nAna vAda*, of the *yogAchAra* branch of Buddhism. Since things have no continuity, not existing from one moment to the next, there can be no such thing as 'change'. (Shankara says that the philosopher who says that Atman does not exist is the

vainAsika Buddhist. This word means something like 'annihilationist' and may be being used in a generally derogatory sense. It is Anandagiri who says it refers to the *vij~nAna vAdin*.)

- The Atman both exists and does not exist (a*sti-nAsti*). It exists as a separate entity from the body but is destroyed when the body dies. There is change during life, no change after death. Objects are separate and have no Atman. The Jain school of philosophy holds this view.
- There is no Atman at all; everything ends in destruction (*nAsti-nAsti*). This is the belief of the *madhyamika* branch of Buddhism and is called *shunya vAda*. Nothing has any meaning (or alternatively, 'nothing' is the only thing that has any meaning).

(K4.84) But the Atman is not a thing which can be thought of at all; it is beyond all conceptualization and ideas such as these are doomed to fail to give any insight into the truth. Until they are dropped, the Atman will remain hidden. Conversely, one who has realized the Atman will be immune to all such concepts. Advaita uses concepts as part of its initial teaching but makes it clear from the outset that all concepts must ultimately be dropped.

(K4.96) Self-knowledge is not knowledge *of* anything; it is not objective in any way. Shankara says it is like the light and heat in the sun; it is steady and unborn, unrelated to anything else. It is 'unattached' or 'touch-less', like the sky or space; hence Gaudapada's concept of *asparsha yoga*. This is in contrast to the everyday, Realist philosopher's belief that knowledge arises when one perceives an object or conceives an idea. Self-knowledge is self-evident (when realized) so that we should not really speak about knowledge *of* Consciousness; Knowledge *is* Consciousness.

When speaking about the *j~nAnI*'s perception of the world, the scriptures and teachers often use the word 'witness' (*sAkShI*). This carries connotations of being 'detached', just observing everything and everyone but not becoming involved. But this is still a dualistic concept – 'I' and 'other'. What has to be realized is that we are trying to convey a *pAramArthika* concept of 'I' and a *vyAvahArika* concept of 'other'.

This is a mistake on two fronts. Firstly, you cannot have 'concepts' from the standpoint of absolute reality – that would be duality! Secondly, you cannot mix levels of reality. To speak of an absolute-reality witness perceiving the world is the same as claiming that a waker can see and involve him or herself in a dream. Accordingly, what is meant by 'witnessing' is perceiving the world just as before, but with the major difference that I now know that my real nature is on a higher level of reality; that who-I-really-am is non-dual Consciousness, while the world is *mithyA* appearance only, albeit with that same non-dual Consciousness as its substratum. There is still a relationship between me, the observer, and the perceived object at the empirical level. But, in reality, there is no relationship between 'I' the absolute reality and any apparent thing at the empirical level. There is no relationship because there is no separation and no second thing to which to relate.

Practical Aspects

OM – The Four Aspects of Consciousness

The first part of the Upanishad, up to the seventh mantra, was concerned with *Atma vichAra* – investigation or inquiry into the nature of the Self or *Atman*. We saw that the *Atman* could be regarded as being made up of four aspects – the *mithyA* waker, *mithyA* dreamer, *mithyA* deep-sleeper and the real *turIya*.

The second part of the Upanishad, from the eighth mantra up to the end, conducts an investigation into the syllable OM. This is also seen to consist of four aspects and it is possible to utilize in meditation exercises what will be seen to be a remarkable correspondence, in order to aid in realizing the truth of the prior analysis of *Atman*. Ultimately, as mentioned before, only knowledge can remove ignorance so that meditation per se can never bring about enlightenment. But, by using the sounds as pointers to or reminders of what has previously been learned and fully comprehended, the understanding can be strengthened until it becomes firm. This forms an important part of *nididhyAsana*.

As was pointed out in the introduction, the word OM is made up of three letters – *a, u* and *m; a* is the fundamental sound that pervades all other letters. When you open your mouth wide and allow the vocal cord to vibrate, the sound that emerges is *a*. And this basic sound is effectively present in all others, just being colored and molded by the shape of the mouth and the position of the tongue and lips.

When the lips close to form a small opening, with *a* continuing to sound, what emerges is the sound *u* (an abbreviated 'oo' sound as in 'root', not as in 'door' or 'blood'). And, midway between *a* and *u*, the sound that is a combination of these two is 'o', as in 'toe'.

When the lips are completely closed, the sounding is stopped, as it were, leaving the vibrating lips sounding the letter *m*.

When the sounding of the vocal cord ceases altogether, we have silence. Just as silence is the inevitable 'background' to all sound, so Consciousness is the inevitable background of all states, waking, dreaming or sleeping. In Sanskrit, the length of vowel sounds are stipulated as part of the language. The 'short' vowels, such as *a*, *i* and *u* are one measure or *mAtra*, while the 'long' vowels, such as *A*, *I* and *U* are two measures.

The Upanishad highlights the correspondences between the *mAtra*-s of OM and the states of consciousness but does not go into any details as to how to carry out any meditation. Gaudapada is a bit more helpful! He first suggests (K1.2) that we can think of *vishva* as being located in the right eye. This is not meant literally, of course. In order to be able to carry out meditation effectively, it is helpful to concentrate the attention on a specific location. The waking experience is epitomized by use of the physical senses to direct the attention outwards to the external world. Sight is the most important of the senses, with by far the most sensory input arriving through the eyes. And traditionally the right eye is considered to be the dominant one. Accordingly, it is most reasonable to nominate this location to symbolize the waker and to concentrate the meditative mind on the letter *a* of OM. (Note that we never attempt to use *a* as a mantra. It is always OM that is sounded or repeated in the mind. It is just that, when meditating on the *vishva* association, we focus the mind on the *a* sound while chanting OM, actually as 'a-u-m'.)

The dream-experience is totally within the mind, with both subject and object being 'located' there. So there is not really any other contender for the point of meditation for *taijasa* and the letter *u*. Shankara points out in his commentary on this verse that, having looked intently at an object in the waking state, one can still see it clearly on closing the eyes, as though seeing it in a dream. And the dream itself is similar to the waking state, thus proving that the dream-Self is not other than the waking-Self. (Note that he is referring to the *Atman*, here, not the ego.)

The location for *m* and *prAj~na* is the 'space within the heart'. There may well be some confusion here for some seekers. This is because this location is also the place where the ancients believed the mind resided and, when sages such as Ramana Maharshi use this terminology, we should automatically understand 'mind'. Shankara says that all the senses become collected in the *prANa* – the 'vital forces' that animate the body – and the symbolic residing place for this is the space in the heart. The logic for this derives from other scriptural sources, as is often the case with such commentaries. Here, the key discussions are in the Chandogya Upanishad (4.3.3 and 6.2.1) and the Brihadaranyaka Upanishad (4.2.2, 4.4.6, 5.6.1). But this material is outside the scope of this book.

Swami Chinmayananda (Ref. 3) has another way of thinking about this. He says that, whereas the head is regarded as the seat of logic and reason, the heart is traditionally thought of as the seat of the emotions, with feelings such as love and justice. Thus, he feels that true intellect is only available when reason is tempered by love and that therefore the unmanifest Consciousness will be found in the heart.

karma and *bhakti yoga*

Many (if not most) Westerners tend to think that there are several 'paths' to enlightenment and that any one of them, or any combination of them, will be efficacious. This is quite mistaken. The very word 'path' is itself misleading. What is to be 'reached' is Self-knowledge and the obstacle to this is Self-ignorance. The only way to resolve this is what is usually called *j~nAna yoga* – the yoga of knowledge – or, more popularly in the West, Self-inquiry. And the process for achieving this is *shravaNa*, *manana* and *nididhyAsana*. Here is how I summarized these in my book 'Advaita Made Easy' (Ref. 79):

1. Hearing the truth from a qualified teacher or (very much second best) reading about it in such works as the Upanishads. This is called *shravaNa*, resulting in a basic understanding of the subject matter.
2. Reflecting upon what has been heard. This is the stage of *manana*, the purpose being to remove any doubts, and resolve any conflicting explanations we may harbor about the teaching.
3. Meditating deeply upon the essence of what has now been fully understood until there is total conviction. This is called *nididhyAsana*. It has the effect of eroding all of the bad habits we have acquired in respect of our dealings with the world, seeing separation, having desires for objects etc.

In theory, hearing (or even reading) a statement of how things are could be sufficient. It is simply a matter of eliminating false notions. I am already *brahman*; there is nowhere to go, nothing to be done, nothing to wait for, no experience to be obtained. I already know that 'I am' (I am conscious and I exist); it is just that I mistakenly think I am 'something' (a body, a mind, a man, a woman etc.). Once I have heard that there is *only* Consciousness-Existence, it follows immediately that I am That.

All so-called paths other than *j~nAna yoga* may be helpful in preparing the mind to receive the knowledge but they can never themselves remove the ignorance, because action is not opposed to ignorance. Accordingly, *karma yoga*, which means the yoga of action, is not a pursuit which will itself lead to enlightenment.

The other major 'path' is thought to be *bhakti yoga* – the yoga of devotion. In fact, this is a mistaken name. *bhakti* is rather an attitude of trust in the teacher and love for the teaching itself, and it is a natural aspect of all spiritual pursuits. When we are referring to devotion in the context of worship of a god and all the practices of ritual etc. that go with this, the correct term is upAsana.

In K3.1, Gaudapada refers to those seekers who pursue upAsana yoga rather than j~nAna yoga. He says that they should be thought of as wretched or pitiable (kRRipaNa) because he believes that he is a creature born into a real world and has to attain to an unborn brahman after he dies. He does not use his intellect to conduct Self-inquiry and discover his real nature. Bbrahman cannot be the object of such a person's meditation. Bbrahman is that which enables the meditation to take place. The non-miserable one who has gained Self-knowledge knows that he (and the world) is the unborn brahman always.

The problem is simple. A devotee worshipping a god or an idol or even a concept is still trapped in duality and duality brings with it all of the misery of saMsAra. Such a person still believes in the efficacy of action. He or she believes that paying homage to a god will bring rewards and failure to do so is a sin, bringing demerit.

But the entire process of karma, saMskAra, saMsAra etc. brings with it all of the negative aspects of fear, worry, misery and pain. Change and time may occasionally bring good times but will inevitably also bring the bad. This is intrinsic to duality. Old age and death are the inevitable outcome for the body. We have to realize that our true nature is turIya – changeless and beyond time, cause and effect.

(K3.2) In contrast to the jIva who indulges in worship of an objective God, and is therefore 'pitiable', brahman is itself the opposite of this (akArpaNya). Gaudapada has shown above that there can be no creation at all; that the reality is non-dual and birthless, has no parts and is eternally the same throughout, never changing. Although it appears that there is a separate world, it is only mithyA. The 'seeming to be born' is only like the snake being apparently born from the rope. In reality, nothing has ever been born – ajAti vAda.

Shankara references the Chandogya Upanishad (VII.24.1) as

effectively defining the nature of 'pitiableness' (i.e. the finite) as being *"where one sees something else, hears something else and understands something else"*. If there is a second thing, then we are necessarily limited. *Bbrahman* (which I truly am) is unlimited because there is no second thing. Everything that we see is only name and form of *brahman* and is *mithyA*. *Bbrahman* is the only reality, *satyam*. It seems that *brahman* is the cause and that the world is the effect but, since the world is *mithyA*, the causal status of *brahman* is also *mithyA*.

Knowledge and the Fruit of Knowledge

You now know all about *adhyAropa* and *apavAda* and acknowledge that all of the teaching is only interim, to be used to lead us to the final understanding and then discarded. The corollary to this is that, in principle at least, *any* teaching could be used for this purpose. If it works, it is valid. So it is hardly surprising that there are other methodologies altogether, which can have the same ultimate purport, e.g. Zen Buddhism, Taoism, Kabbalah etc. (I don't have any personal knowledge of these other systems but understand that their essential teaching is non-dual.)

As far as Advaita Vedanta is concerned, the finer details of the teaching differed from one teacher or branch to another, both before and after Shankara. Some modern-day proponents tend to adhere to some elements and some to others that are apparently contradictory. None of this matters in the final analysis but does tend to lead to some quite heated discussions on the Internet!

Two of the key aspects where views differ are in regard to what exactly happens in practical terms when Self-knowledge is gained, and what precisely brings it about. Thus, some believe that listening to the guru alone (*shravaNa*) is the trigger. Maybe we have to ask a few questions at some point – *manana* – but ultimately, we hear something explained and the veil is lifted, as it were. Others believe that this alone is insufficient, that we have

to go away and meditate upon what has been heard –
nididhyAsana – so as to assimilate it fully.

(And some think that we have to somehow 'live' what we have
heard until an 'enlightening' experience occurs in a flash of
'realization'. Hopefully, having read this book, you understand
that no experience could remove the ignorance that is the cause
of our not appreciating that we are already free!)

There is also another related aspect upon which views differ.
Many seekers believe that Self-knowledge brings with it such
things as total peace, fearlessness, permanent happiness and so
on. Indeed, it is probably not unreasonable to suppose that these
are their principal objectives when they begin seeking. It is
convenient to differentiate between the Self-knowledge itself –
j~nAna – and what we might call the benefits of gaining that
knowledge. These are called the 'fruits of knowledge' by some
teachers – *j~nAna phalam*.

A term for someone who has gained Self-knowledge and
whose physical body has not yet died (some others believe that
true Self-knowledge only occurs with death!) is *jIvanmukta*. (The
abstract noun for 'liberation while living' is *jIvanmukti*.) Some
people use the terms *j~nAnI*, meaning someone who has Self-
knowledge, and *jIvanmukta* interchangeably. And some people
differentiate the two, in the sense that a *j~nAnI* has Self-
knowledge but not *j~nAna phalam*, while the *jIvanmukta* has both.

Another diversion and further complication is now necessary.
This is in respect of the mental preparation which any seeker
must undergo if he or she is to be able to take on board all of this
teaching. Shankara set down the various elements that are
involved in his concept of *sAdhana chatuShTaya sampatti* – the
'fourfold accomplishments.' Very briefly, these are discrimination, dispassion, desire for liberation and the 'six-fold discipline'. This latter comprises aspects such as control of the mind
and senses, patience and trust. The idea is that a mind that is
unruly will be unable to listen clearly and examine the material

in a neutral manner. It will not be amenable to understanding or to benefiting emotionally from such understanding.

Thus, prior to (or in parallel with) studying Advaita, one has to acquire a degree of mental equanimity by following the practices of *sAdhana chatuShTaya sampatti*.

Those who teach that the fruits of knowledge may not immediately accompany Self-knowledge itself claim that the primary causes for the two are different. They claim that it is *shravaNa* which brings about Self-knowledge. In order for this to be able to happen at all, the seeker must have followed *sAdhana chatuShTaya sampatti* to some reasonable level. If the attainment is insufficient, then no amount of study will succeed; the mind will constantly be throwing up objections or simply being distracted by other things.

And this 'school' teaches that the fruits of knowledge are the result of *sAdhana chatuShTaya sampatti* in combination with the knowledge, rather than a result of the knowledge itself. There is thus the possibility (which is considered to be an impossibility by some other schools!) that a seeker might become a *j~nAnI* but not gain the fruits of knowledge. Thus, if a seeker has not done sufficient *sAdhana chatuShTaya sampatti* preparation, he cannot gain either knowledge or fruits; if he is fully qualified from *sAdhana chatuShTaya sampatti*, then he will gain the fruits at the same time as he gains Self-knowledge. Note that, in keeping with the traditional teaching, it is possible for someone to have gained the qualifications in a previous lifetime! (Of course, that teaching is for beginning students, not for those who have advanced to Gaudapada's level and know that there is no birth, let alone rebirth!)

If the seeker has a 'middling' mental preparation, it is possible to gain Self-knowledge but not the benefits. In this case, such a person will be a *j~nAnI* but not a *jIvanmukta*. This analysis is the scheme taught by Swami Dayananda and his disciples, and which I also accept. Swami Paramarthananda says: *"We look on (mental equanimity etc.) only as a secondary benefit because improving your mind is not the primary aim of Vedanta. The primary aim is telling you that you are not the mind! It is incidental that the mind gets refined, improved."* (Ref. 5)

Subsequent to gaining the knowledge, such a person will then (naturally) continue to assimilate the knowledge and is very likely to talk or write about it (as I am doing), read or listen to further teaching or themselves take up teaching. Such activities constitute what was referred to as *nididhyAsana* above. By such methods, the fruits of knowledge will eventually come and the *j~nAnI* will become a *jIvanmukta*.

In the scriptures, there are many explanations for how the world and *jIva*-s were created despite the fact that, in reality, there never was any creation. This is because of the need to lead seekers gently towards the ultimate truth rather than alienating them from the outset.

Similarly, the scriptures tell us that *mokSha* brings total happiness, peace of mind and fearlessness. After all, this is a major motivation for bringing people to *Advaita* in the first place. But what changes on realizing the truth is not the appearance but our understanding of what is real and what is *mithyA*. Just as we now know that the world is only empirically real and cannot harm us, so we now know that feelings of anger, fear, sadness etc. are *mithyA* and do not really affect us. But equally, just as we still perceive duality, so we still have negative feelings unless our *sAdhana chatuShTaya sampatti* disciplines have inured us to these.

The reason for that long diversion is that the final verses of the third chapter of the *kArikA*-s deals with what has been called here *nididhyAsana*, although Gaudapada talks about 'control of the mind' (*manonigraha*) in the *kArikA*-s. And the different commentaries give quite different interpretations of what Gaudapada is saying there and what he means by the word *manonigraha*.

Because this is not intended to be an academic book but a readable one (!), I am not giving any further details here – you can see a longer version of this section at my website – http://www.Advaita-vision.org/knowledge-and-the-fruit-of-knowledge/. There is also an interesting follow-up discussion at http://www.Advaita-vision.org/gk-iii-40-and-some-misconceptions/. The interpretation presented in this book, which is based upon Swami Paramarthanda's, is not the strict, traditional one but it is in accord with reason. Since reason is stated by Gaudapada himself as being the criterion which must be applied to all scriptural statements (K3.23), I feel quite justified in using this interpretation.

To summarize, the following points explain the relevance of 'mental preparation' to Self-knowledge and, separately, to the so-called 'fruits of knowledge':

1 The seeker must have a minimum level of mental accomplishments (*sAdhana chatuShTaya sampatti*) in order to be able to conduct Self-inquiry successfully.

2 When Self-ignorance is dispelled, I immediately know that '*brahman* is the non-dual reality', 'the world is *mithyA*' and 'I am *brahman*'. There is no delay. This is *mokSha* (knowing that I am ever free, and already was even though I didn't know it before).

3 Having ceased to have any identification with the body-mind, I know that 'who-I-really-am' is not 'affected' by events that impact the body-mind. Accordingly, this results in qualities such as humility (as mentioned by Gaudapada in K4.86).

4 However, the extent to which the *mind* is affected by desire/fear and the outcome of actions depends upon the degree of accomplishments (*sAdhana chatuShTaya sampatti*).

5 If the degree of attainment was sufficient for the successful outcome of Self-inquiry but not for complete 'peace-of-mind' etc., then further *nididhyAsana* must be done.

6 The term *j~nAna phalam* is actually a misnomer. It should be called *sAdhana chatuShTaya sampatti phalam*!

7 Self-knowledge is about knowing that I am not the mind, not about gaining peace of mind!

This analysis is also supported by Bhagavad Gita 6.27: "*The yogin whose mind is peaceful, whose passions are calmed, who is free of evil, and has become one with* brahman, *attains the highest bliss.*" (Ref. 70) I.e. both mind control and Self-knowledge are required. [yogin in the Gita does not refer to followers of Yoga but to all seekers.]

In K3.39, Gaudapada says that 'ordinary yogins' would not be able to assimilate the teaching. Shankara assumes this refers to those without knowledge of the Vedanta. Anandagiri says that the 'changeless Existence, Consciousness and Bliss' is attainable by those having correct knowledge – 'dull-witted' persons do not make any effort to know it. The clear implication here is that one must be 'sharp-witted' in order to be willing and able to follow this teaching.

Investigation into the translations of K3.40 reveals many nuances. I solicited a totally unbiased translation from a Sanskrit scholar and here is the result: "*For all Yogis, fearlessness, the removal of misery, knowledge of the self, and everlasting peace are contingent upon the control of the mind.*"

Appealing to reason again, it would seem that Gaudapada is effectively saying that seekers require mental disciplining both to be able to assimilate the teaching (and gain Self-knowledge) and to get rid of misery. V.H. Date's translation (Ref. 18) supports this: "*Fearlessness, destruction of misery and absolute peace as the result of the realization of the Brahman, depend upon the control of the mind, whatever may be the kind of yogin.*" And Shankara adds in his commentary: "*Moreover, even Self-knowledge depends on mental discipline*".

(K3.41) Next, Gaudapada states in what this disciplining consists. He compares the effort involved to that of emptying an ocean by removing one drop at a time with a blade of grass (a story which also occurs in several other scriptural texts). It is obviously meant to convey the fact that the mind is easily distracted and disciplining it requires constant vigilance and being prepared to continue for a long time before results are seen. The word that he uses – *nigraha* – carries the sense of restraint. Bhagavad Gita 6.25 says that the mind of the seeker should come to rest *'little by little, with the intellect firmly held'* (Ref. 70).

(K3.42) He emphasizes the need to quell desires and enjoyment of pleasures and avoid the state of 'pleasurable sleep-like repose'. (We can surmise that he is referring to the *samAdhi* state here.) The method of mental discipline, spoken of with reference to 'Yogins', corresponds to the method of meditation specified by Patanjali in his Yoga Sutras and it makes sense to read those verses as instructions for how to carry out such meditation successfully (not covered here).

Thus, in warning us against sleep, Gaudapada is not telling us never to go to bed but saying that falling asleep during meditation is one of the most significant problems. Swami Chinmayananda also suggests that Gaudapada might be referring not to ordinary sleep but rather to the trance-like state sometimes experienced by meditators which, though it might be enjoyable, is not conducive to proper practice. In this condition, one can feel oneself becoming increasingly drowsy and the mind begins to drift uncontrollably. This is the opposite of what we are trying to achieve!

Common sense provides remedies for this: don't attempt to meditate when tired, after a meal, when worrying about a current problem in life and so on. Aim for a time when there will be no external distractions and the mind is alert.

(K3.43) Attachment to any object invariably results in misery and pain, even if in the short term it may bring happiness. Accordingly, we should avoid such attachments, remaining 'detached'. Also, we should remember the teaching that the world is *mithyA*, and the real substratum is the birthless *brahman*. We already are perfect and complete, and there is nothing external which could provide this. It is the very belief in the reality of the world that opens the door to problems. By seeing that acceptance of duality is actually harmful, we should actively cultivate aversion for objects rather than desire, says Shankara.

(K3.44) These are the two main distractions for us in this practice – sleep or day-dreaming, and attachment to objects. We have to aim to avoid both! Wake yourself up if you find yourself falling asleep, and discipline the mind to prevent attention being caught by passing ideas or objects of attraction. Gaudapada explains that this occurs when the mind is associated with *kaShAya*. This literally means 'stain' and is that negative state of the mind in which latent desires 'take over' our thoughts. Gangolli (Ref. 29) translates *sakaShAya* as *'embedded in or associated with the seed of latent impressions of previous pleasures or enjoyments'*. The objective is a mind in equilibrium, tranquil and dispassionate. This has to be a natural condition though, not forcibly restrained, or it will not work. When we are not asleep, or otherwise distracted, the mind has a tendency to succumb to either day dreams or *kaShAya*. We need to be aware of this and be vigilant.

(K3.45) With practice, and avoiding the main problems by following this guidance, one will eventually succeed in attaining the prolonged stillness of meditation, undisturbed by whatever external or internal events might unfold. But herein lies another problem. One is liable to become attached to the enjoyment of this condition! This is the condition known as *rasAsvAda*, which literally means 'savoring the juice'. All pleasures are potentially addictive and this is no different. Shankara says that all such pleasure is false and a result of ignorance. Consciousness itself is beyond such impermanent and meager indulgence.

(K3.46) If we manage to avoid these various pitfalls, and bring the mind to a totally detached stillness, then it is said to 'become' *brahman*. Of course this should not be interpreted literally, since everything is always *brahman*. What it means is that it reflects Consciousness perfectly, just as a mirror polished to remove the minutest imperfection reflects light perfectly. (See Appendix 3 on *chidAbhAsa*.) Practically speaking, all is now clearly seen as my Self; nothing is believed to be separate.

(K3.47) The next verse clarifies this. We ourselves are already free, and unlimited bliss already exists as our own nature. Gaudapada refers to the eternal peace (*shAntaM*), used to describe *turIya* in the *seventh* mantra of the Upanishad. Thus, the mind does not 'become' *brahman*; it already is *brahman*. Its nature is indescribable because there is nothing with which it is connected or can be compared.

(K3.48) The final verse of the chapter is the key message of Gaudapada, already mentioned above (it is repeated verbatim in K4.71). This is that nothing is ever born, because there is no cause which could ever produce any effect. *Bbrahman* is the only reality and notions of time, space and causality belong only to the *mithyA*, empirical world. All of the 'practices' are intended only to bring us to this realization and are themselves no more real than the world.

It is worth noting here that Gaudapada does not formally accord any reality to the world and the *jIva*. His is a *pAramArthika* viewpoint throughout. It was Shankara who allowed them empirical existence and effectively introduced the *paramArtha* – *vyavahAra* – *pratibhAsa* split when teaching about our experience and knowledge. Thus it is that today's 'neo-Advaitins' are not really 'new' at all!

Meditation on OM

(K1.23) Gaudapada reminds us that *a* stands for the waking state of experience, so that meditating on OM with the mind giving attention to the letter '*a*' will attune us to that aspect. As

Shankara puts it, we will 'become' *vaishvAnara*, the 'cosmic waking Self', leading to the enjoyment of all objects. The details of this are given in the ninth mantra of the Upanishad (see Appendix 1).

Similarly, attending to the letter '*u*' in our meditation 'leads' to *taijasa* and mantra ten tells us that this will increase our mental powers and bring respect from everyone. Swami Nikhilananda construes this as meaning that we realize the world as forms of thought, like the world we see in dreams.

Attending to *m* leads to *prAj~na* and, according to the eleventh mantra, we assimilate and understand the workings of the universe, becoming one with *Ishvara*.

There is thus an effective progression from gross to increasingly more subtle. The *a* is merged into *u* and then into *m*. The gross world of objects is seen to be produced by naming the ideas in mind, as we do in dream; then we realize the deep-sleep state as the causal state for all, with both waking and dream emerging out of this as effect.

When our meditation attains to the silence following the letters (and the background to them), there is nothing more to 'achieve'. As the twelfth mantra tells us, "*It is transcendental, without any worldly existence, blissful and non-dual; It is the Self*". We have progressed from gross to subtle to unmanifest duality and finally to non-duality. The three states manifest at various times of the day. The silence never manifests; it is what is always there when our attention to what is seemingly outside or inside is allowed to fall away. But it is not something to be comprehended in the way that this is normally understood because the mind and senses no longer operate here, in the same way that the letter sounds of OM resolve into the silence.

(K1.24) Therefore, the advice that Gaudapada and Shankara give is to attend to the separate sounds and intermittent silence of OM, and to allow the mind to dwell on their separate meanings and common features – and nothing else.

Metaphorically, the waking state of *a* 'merges' into the dream state of *u* and then into the deep-sleep state of *m*. All are then withdrawn into the silence of *turIya*. The fruit of such meditation infinitely surpasses the mundane satisfaction of worldly desires.

(K1.25) As outlined in the introduction, OM is essentially *brahman*, the ultimate reality, so that one who concentrates the mind in this way goes beyond worldly concerns. By dwelling mentally on the sounds of OM and the silence in between, the mind as though becomes identified with *brahman* (as opposed to identifying with one or more of the myriad of distracting and unreal objects in the *mithyA* world). As such meditation progresses, all thoughts other than these subside until nothing remains but those related to the mantra. As Gaudapada puts it, there can then be no fear anywhere. Fear comes when there is a second thing (which is perceived as threatening). There is no second thing; there is only *brahman*. Consequently, there is nothing to fear.

(K1.26) The *praNava* symbol is the ideal representative word for *brahman* because it symbolizes both the *saguNa* aspects (through the sounds a, u and m) and the *nirguNa* aspects (through silence). Meditators can begin, inevitably, with the states of consciousness assuming most importance. Over time, attention can be shifted increasingly towards the silence and the reality which this represents. Gaudapada says that *omkAra* (the syllable OM) is outside of cause and effect, having no second thing inside or outside.

(K1.27) There is, in this sense, no sound other than OM (just as there is no ring, necklace, bangle other than gold). Similarly, there is no world other than *brahman*. As Gaudapada puts it, OM is the beginning, middle and end of everything – their birth, maintenance and destruction. But there is no real modification; these apparent changes are illusory. The world 'emerges' from *praNava/turIya-Atman* in a way that is precisely analogous to the way that the snake appears on the rope or the mirage on sand.

We need both metaphors. In the case of the rope, the snake is no longer seen once we know that it is a rope but, with the mirage, we still continue to see the water even after we discover that it is only sand. The snake perception is our own error; the mirage is a metaphor for *mAyA* – *Ishvara's* manifestation. And we need the latter to provide an empirical explanation for the continued appearance of the world, despite having gained Self-knowledge. This continued appearance poses no problem for Advaita, whether or not you choose to accept the notion of *Ishvara* as reasonable from the empirical standpoint. We know that, in reality, there is no world, no *Ishvara*, no *jIva*.

Just as OM (pedantically the *amAtra* or silence 'part' of OM) is the essential 'substance' of all sounds, so *turIya* is the essence of all states, gross, subtle and causal. There is nothing that you can think of that is not *brahman* or, to put it another way, everything and every thought is *brahman*.

Gaudapada uses the word *vyashnute*, from the verb *vyash*, meaning 'to attain'. Swami Lokeswarananda says (Ref. 20) that this comes from the root *ash*, meaning 'to eat'. This reinforces the idea that the teaching has to go beyond mere intellectual under-standing; it has to be as though 'eaten', so that its realization effectively becomes a part of us. Once it has been completely assimilated in this way, we know immediately that we are free.

(K1.28) We should regard OM as *Ishvara*, dwelling in our mind – the Consciousness that enlivens us and pervades everything. Knowing this means the end of all sorrow, the end of *saMsAra*, eternal freedom.

(K1.29) The one who understands OM in this way is a true sage because he knows the truth about the nature of reality. Those who fail to appreciate the silence of OM – the non-dual substratum, Consciousness – remain mired in the three mundane, *mithyA* states of consciousness and continue to be limited by these.

Summary of What Should be Done and Benefits

(K2.35) The purport of all that has been said is simply that we must realize the truth for ourselves. It is no use just reading the material cursorily and saying "isn't that interesting"; we need to know beyond doubt that, regardless of appearances, the world is not real and cannot harm who we really are. The procedure is (theoretically) straightforward:

1. Discipline the mind (*sAdhana chatuShTaya sampatti*) so that it is optimally available to receive the knowledge in the succeeding stages. We have to be able to concentrate and discriminate, without distraction from worldly issues of any kind.
2. Listen to the scriptures explained by a qualified teacher (*shravaNa*);
3. Ask questions to clarify doubts (*manana*); eventually, one should be able to answer all questions oneself. (One has to guard against arrogance, smugness etc. in the interim stages, where concepts may have been intellectually grasped but the total implications have not yet been integrated. One must assiduously avoid answering questions which one does not fully understand!)
4. Review the teaching in any way that seems appropriate until it has been totally assimilated by the mind (*nididhyAsana*). Scriptural phrases such as 'becoming *brahman*' are figurative – one already is *brahman*. But the final 'understanding' is more than merely intellectual; it is knowing that it is true with 'every fiber of ones being', to bring in another figure of speech.

To some degree, acquiring this prerequisite degree of 'preparedness' and gaining Self-knowledge go hand in hand. In order to begin to study Vedanta, we require mental stillness, control and focusing ability. Only then are we able to give attention to the teaching, without being easily distracted and so on. But also, as understanding grows, realization that the world has less than absolute reality enables us to reduce our attachment to, and dependence on, things of the world for our happiness and peace of mind. Ultimately, we are able to let everything "be" without exercising value judgments, knowing that the appearances are *mithyA*, dependent upon *brahman* for their existence.

Dispassion (*vairAgya*) is one of the four requirements and this only matures in someone who, through discrimination (*viveka*), recognizes the difference between real and unreal.

And, of course, we have to be interested and want to learn about the truth. If we still have material ambitions and desires in life, and feel that their satisfaction might bring happiness, then pursuing this teaching is unlikely to prove fruitful. This is *mumukShutva* – the over-riding drive for freedom from suffering and from the limitations of life. Whilst the usual concerns of life continue, we will remain trapped in the illusion of duality and continue to be subject to the attachment, fear, anger, hatred etc. that this entails.

Provided that these preparations have been made and the skills are developed in parallel with listening to the teaching, then there will inevitably come a time when, hearing some message from the scriptures such as 'You are That' (*tattvamasi*), the truth will be directly realized (*aparokSha j~nAna*). Without the qualifications, the message may be heard but its full implications will not be appreciated. Swami Satchidanandendra gives the analogy of having a perfect pair of spectacles for reading. If the person wearing them is blind or cannot read, the sentence will not be understood (Ref. 29).

(K2.36) Once we have 'got the message' and realize the truth of the teaching, we need to continue to remember this in all that we think and do – this is the essence of *nididhyAsana*, as described earlier. Also, warns Gaudapada, we should conduct ourselves in life 'as though we are an inert object'. By this, he means that we should not broadcast this knowledge. Advaitins do not prose-lytize or proclaim! By all means answer questions when asked but do not offer the teaching to all and sundry – they will almost invariably think that you are either mad or extremely gullible. If their entire life's commitments depend upon world appearances being real, they will not appreciate being told about the *mithyA* status of the world!

(K2.37) The way of life of the Brahmin (literally one possessing sacred knowledge, i.e. knowledge of Self) – the Indian scholar or priest – around the time of Gaudapada involved four 'stages' or *Ashrama*-s. He began his life as a student or *brahmacharya*, unmarried, religious and chaste. He then married and had a family – this is called the period of the 'house-holder' or *gRRihastha*. He then retired from life with its pursuit of pleasure and wealth and became a so-called 'forest dweller' or *vAnaprastha*. He then lived the life of a hermit and continued his religious studies. The final stage was called *saMnyAsa* and involved complete renunciation. He relied entirely on charity for food and clothing and spent the remainder of his life in meditation and control of the senses. The practice still continues, albeit to a much lesser degree of course, up to today.

It was generally accepted that the serious seeker would follow this path and finish his life as a *saMnyAsin*. Gaudapada says here that a *saMnyAsin* is no longer bound by the ritual practices followed by a *gRRihastha*. Nor does he seek praise or devotion from others for his accomplishments. He is unconcerned about where his shelter and food come from, happy to trust that these will be provided when needed. (Wandering ascetics were always treated with respect in ancient India and householders willingly provided them with alms as a sacred duty.)

Shankara says that the *saMnyAsin* knows him or herself is always the unchanging *Atman* but that, for ordinary activities such as eating, he or she effectively re-identifies with the body for that purpose.

(K2.38) Once the truth has been realized, and it is known that both oneself and the external world are nothing other than name and form of *brahman*, one has 'become one with reality' and will naturally remain always mindful of that knowledge, and take no further interest in any dualistic phenomena. The unenlightened tend to believe that they are their mind. Since the mind changes, they think that 'I' change also. Sometimes I may think that I know the truth and feel positive and happy about this. Then something happens that upsets this false knowledge and I become pessimistic again. The truly enlightened are steady in their knowledge and remain unaffected in the face of adversity. They know that 'I', the *Atman*, is unchanging and that is my real nature. They look on everything with equanimity, knowing that it is their own Self.

chin mudrA

Now that we have almost concluded the unfolding of the *kArikA*-s, we can return to that cover image! The 'hand-sign' is not actually mentioned in the Mandukya Upanishad, nor by Gaudapada, though it is highly relevant. As I mentioned in the introduction, it is a gesture associated with the Sage who is said to be the first teacher of Vedanta – Dakshinamurti. As such, he was the head of the teaching *sampradAya* and did not himself have a teacher – i.e. he was already fully enlightened. He is also identified with the God Shiva. It is called *chin mudrA* or *j~nAna mudrA* (more usually *chin*), where *chin* means Consciousness and *mudrA* means sign.

It is often said that Dakshinamurti taught through silence. Of course, this would not make any sense. Silence can be interpreted in innumerable ways, few of which are likely to convey useful knowledge! But, once we have the knowledge, a symbol can convey a world of information, reminding us through memory of what we have previously learned. Witness the vast amount of knowledge which is now conveyed to you through the word OM.

The hand position shown on the cover of this book is another symbol of this sort. And it is highly relevant to the same knowledge.

Here is the symbolism:

- The thumb represents *paramAtman*. There is some reasoning behind this. The scriptures speak of *paramAtman* as residing in the space in the heart (*hRRidaya*). By this, we were expected to understand 'mind', since it used to be thought that the mind was contained in the physical organ of the heart. Since the heart is about the size of a fist, it was reasonable to think that the space inside was about the size of a thumb.

- The forefinger represents the individual or *jIva*. It could also be thought of as the ego or sense of myself. It is common in many cultures to use the forefinger to point out personal opinions and also to threaten or criticize others whose views differ from 'mine'.

- The second finger represents the gross body, *sthUla sharIra* or waker.

- The third finger represents the subtle body, *sUkShma sharIra* or dreamer.

- The fourth finger represents the causal body, *kAraNa sharIra* or deep-sleeper.

- The first finger is normally held in association with the other three, indicating our identification with the body and mind.

- All four fingers depend upon the thumb for their strength and ability to do practically anything. It is this feature which distinguishes us from other animals and gave humanity its great advantage in manipulating objects.

- When the index finger is moved to touch the tip of the thumb, it separates from the other three, indicating realization that I am not in fact these bodies at all. In forming an unbroken circle with the thumb, it is recognizing that *jIvAtman* and *paramAtman* are one, unaffected by the three *mithyA* states of consciousness.

Removal of Obstacles

This section completes the coverage of the verses in the *kArikA*-s. (Traditionally, it would have occurred rather earlier!)

It is quite usual at the beginning of scriptural texts to have verses which offer up respectful salutations to a god, asking that the teacher and students may be granted health and that any obstacles be removed for the duration of the teaching so that this knowledge may be passed on. More is said on this in Appendix 1 regarding the *shAnti pATha* which begins the Upanishad itself. In the *kArikA*, such verses occur, unusually, at the beginning of the fourth chapter. (This fact is used by some to argue that the fourth chapter is an entirely separate work, not written by the same person responsible for the other chapters.)

In K4.1, Gaudapada offers up prayers 'to the one who is the greatest amongst all bipeds', who is effectively the first guru, being (already) fully enlightened. Shankara assumes that Gaudapada is talking about Lord Narayana (*nArAyaNa*), which is one of the names for Vishnu. (In Hinduism, the trinity of Gods who are relevant to creation comprises Brahma the creator, Vishnu the preserver and Shiva the destroyer.) Gaudapada was traditionally supposed to have studied in the Badrinath valley in the Himalayas and it is Narayana who is associated with that location. [Another name for this 'first guru' is Dakshinamurti, as was just discussed with reference to *chin mudrA*.]

But the complexities of the myriad of Hindu gods and their relationships are not relevant to this book (all being *mithyA*!). The significant point is that Gaudapada is acknowledging the 'original teacher' and the uniqueness of the situation of already having the knowledge that 'resembles space', in being without limit. He says that this knowledge is also non-different from the object of knowledge; i.e. the Self that is to be known is non-different from Self-knowledge and non-different from the Self that knows this.

There is a subtle difference between the already-known Self-knowledge of the first teacher and the 'realized' Self-knowledge of everyone else, all of whom are disciples of a teacher. This is that, from the point of view of everyone else, what is learned from the guru is that I, the *jIvAtman*, am really identical with *paramAtman*. What is already known by the first teacher, however, is that I, the *paramAtman*, am identical with *jIvAtman*.

(K4.2) Having given thanks to the teacher, Gaudapada then gives thanks to the knowledge itself. He refers to the 'methodology' as *asparsha yoga* – the 'relationless' yoga already described. It is devoid of any relations because there is nothing else with which the non-dual could have a relation. The synonymous adjective used elsewhere is *asa~Nga*, which means 'free from ties, having no attachment or interest in'. He praises the knowledge because of a number of characteristics:

- it brings joy to all beings (*sarva sattva sukha* – here *sattva* means a living or sentient being, not *sattva guNa*). This is in contrast to practices such as austerity which, though it may be a valuable means to an end, is scarcely joyful.
- it is beneficial or wholesome (*hita*). Again, some things may be very enjoyable, such as cream cakes, but do not do us any good in the long run.
- it is free from dispute or argument (*avivAda*) because it does not contradict any other system of knowledge (*aviruddha*). This is because it deals with the nature of absolute reality, whereas other philosophies and religions are concerned with empirical reality.

Gaudapada salutes this knowledge that has been taught by the scriptures (*deshita*).

Conclusion

(K4.90) Gaudapada says that there are four things to be known:

- There is the thing to be avoided or given up (*heya*). This is no minor entity but effectively everything that we have previously considered to constitute the realm of experience, namely the three states of waking, dream and deep-sleep. They are to be given up in the same way that we 'give up' the snake which is misperceived on the rope. The first of these states, of course, incorporates the entire universe of gross objects. Practically speaking, Gaudapada does not mean that we should stop eating, drinking and sleeping; simply that we should always remember that these states are *mithyA*. Nothing and no-one (including our own body and mind) is real in itself; it is only name and form of Consciousness.
- The thing to be known or realized (*j~neya*) is *turIya* itself, the only reality.
- In order to come to appreciate this, certain qualifications are needed as already discussed above; these are the 'thing to be attained or reached' (*Apya*). This includes all relevant psychological, spiritual, attitudinal traits, not just *sAdhana chatuShTaya sampatti*. Shankara refers to the 'virtues' practiced by sages after they have renounced the three principal desires (for wealth, children and happiness). These desires may be key ones but represent all other desires. Until these are given up, the desire for liberation cannot become predominant. Specifically, Shankara mentions wisdom, childlike innocence and silence. 'Wisdom' means the ability to exercise intelligent discrimination; innocence means lack of egoism and openness to the teaching; silence means reflection, meditation and

nididhyAsana, i.e. no discussion!)

- Finally, those thoughts and impressions that obstruct the above have to be rendered ineffective (*pAkya*) so that we can gain maturity. This includes all hopes, fears, attachments, aversions etc. Those which are immoral/unethical have to be eliminated; those which merely indicate individual preference can be (will be!) retained but must not be allowed to divert us from our aims. (*pAkya* literally means 'cooked' and alludes to the fact that seeds, once cooked, can no longer germinate.)

Apart from that which is 'to be known', the rest exist only 'as imagination, resulting from ignorance', says Gaudapada.

Up to a point (usually governed by reason), you can accept whatever feels right regarding 'explanations' of the nature of *brahman* or how things 'really' are. The reality is that *brahman* is outside of space, time and causality so that such questions ultimately have no meaning. The 'bottom line' is that there has never been any creation and there is no seeker or liberation; there is *only brahman*. The world that we seemingly inhabit has its seeming laws and is empirically real but, in the end, it is has the same relative reality as dream has from the vantage point of waking. You can accept whatever reasoning helps you to move towards that final understanding but, in the end, those explanations have to go as well.

To put this in another way, who you think you are and the world that you think you inhabit have no real existence; both are *mithyA*. Who you really are (and what the world really is) is complete, unlimited, immortal – and non-dual. You are *brahman*.

(K4.91) All *jIva*-s are, by their very nature, eternal, all-pervading, beginningless, stainless etc., just as space is ever-present regardless of day or night, and unaffected by stars and planets, clouds or lightning. Gaudapada goes on to explain that we should not be confused by the use of the plural '*jIva*-s' here, either. In fact, there is never any plurality at all, in any degree. There are no subject-object or part-whole relationships. The seeming distinction needs to be made lest we should fall into the trap of thinking that, once one person is enlightened, all will be.

There appears to be multiplicity at the empirical level but *turIya* is strictly non-dual. Another metaphor is the splitting of white light into many colors by a prism; the mind acts as a prism for reality. It is the concepts of time, space and causation which bring about the illusion of duality. These do not exist in *turIya*.

(K4.92) These *jIva*-s appear to be objects of cognition but that is empirical appearance only, no more real than the snake perceived on the rope. Just as light is the nature of the sun, so Consciousness is the nature of *jIva*-s. And the certainty with which we should know this is the same. How can anyone doubt that the sun shines and is independent of any other light? One who knows this is qualified and 'attains' immortality. Seeking to discover oneself by looking outside and conceptualizing is as if the sun were to look for another source of light in order to see itself. In fact, everything 'other' is an illusion and conceals the truth.

The trouble is that we continually superimpose limitations on ourselves. Instead of recognizing that I am non-dual Consciousness, I claim that I am a man, woman, teacher, doctor, father, fat, stupid and so on. But the sun is always there, even when it seems to be obscured by clouds.

(K4.93) In fact, just as the sun has always shone, so has the *jIva* always been free. Accordingly, this 'attaining immortality' is only getting what one already has. The real nature of 'all' *jIva*-s is, as the seventh mantra of the Upanishad put it, *shAntaM* (peace, tranquility), *shivam* (pure, supreme Bliss) and *advaitaM* (non-dual). There are not actually *jIva*-s (plural) at all but only non-dual Consciousness appearing as the world and its population of the living as well as the non-living. The reality is that nothing has ever been born or created; there is only one pure 'substance'.

It follows that all our efforts to attain liberation are super-fluous. What can be gained is simply the knowledge that we are already free. There is a beautiful metaphor which illustrates this. Here is how I related it in Ref. 77:

It is an extension of the story about the lady who is looking every-where for her necklace but then realizes that it has been around her neck all the time. This version has the lady discovering her loss after returning from visiting a friend, to whom she had been showing the necklace. She realizes that she must have left it there and runs out into the street and all the way back to her friend's house only to have the friend point out that the necklace was around her neck the whole time. The question we should now ask is: was it necessary that the lady make the effort of going round to her friend in order to find the necklace?

Clearly she already had the necklace but, equally clearly, she did not know that she had it. And this is the key point of the metaphor. We already are free but we do not know it. We imagine that we are not free, and therefore we suffer. The effort of sAdhana *and* j~nAna yoga *is to acquire the knowledge that will remove the false notion that we are bound.*

Enlightenment is for the mind. The self-knowledge that destroys the self-ignorance takes place in the mind. It is the 'person' that seeks enlightenment and the person discovers that the 'finding' includes the realization that there never was a 'person' in reality.

We do not have to do anything to escape from the seeming bondage of *saMsAra* because it *is* only a 'seeming'. In theory, we can stop being 'seekers' because we already have (are) that which we are seeking. (In practice, we still have to realize this.)

It all seems paradoxical because of the impossibility of speaking about reality. Words can only operate in duality; the non-dual can have no attributes. When I use the word 'I', I am speaking from the vantage point of a 'person' or an ego as if 'I' am a separate individual self. The speaker is an inert body-mind enlivened by Consciousness. Non-dual Consciousness does not make any statement – how could it speak without a body-mind (and to whom would it do so)?

All statements made by those proclaiming themselves (or being proclaimed) as *j~nAnI*-s are by 'persons' at the level of the world. And this is not absolute reality.

(K4.94) As long as we continue to believe in the reality of the world, we will continue to suffer and strive to relieve this suffering in the various ways already discussed, forever failing to realize that we already have everything that we really want. (There is also a suggestion that Gaudapada may be criticizing dualistic philosophers here; serious thinkers who let their preoccupation with empirical experience lead to a firm belief in multiplicity.)

Separation of subject and object is the false belief that causes all of our problems, and therefore a dualistic outlook is certain to propagate these. People who hold such views are considered to be wretched and pitiable (*kRRipaNa* – can also be translated as 'narrow minded'), says Gaudapada. Shankara adds that they are also miserly, since they do not utilize their human birthright to discover the truth. (Only humans have the intellect and discriminatory ability to gain *mokSha*. Even the gods in Hindu mythology have to be reborn in human form in order to do this.)

(K4.95) Those who have conducted Self-inquiry and realized that which is unborn and always the same – the *turIya* that is the reality behind the three *mithyA* states of Consciousness – have attained the highest wisdom. It is beyond the understanding of ordinary people. Those who attempt to reproduce the 'path' that such enlightened ones have followed are trying to track the marks left by the 'footprints' of birds in the sky, says Shankara.

This metaphor alludes to the fact that birds do not leave tracks because they are not following any path themselves; there is no trail to follow. The Mundaka Upanishad (3.2.5) says that the knowers of reality 'become everything'; how could anyone follow such a path? That which removes the ignorance is itself a thought, which disappears after it has fulfilled its function. Swami Dayananda asks which path the pot followed when it realized that it was clay.

Outwardly nothing has changed post realization. To the aj~nAnI, the person who is now a j~nAnI looks just the same. Conversely, to the one who is now a j~nAnI, the world looks just the same as it did before; the big difference is that it is now known to be literally the same! The delusion of duality is now gone. It is the understanding which has changed, not the appearance.

(K4.97) So long as one believes in duality, birth and change, in the slightest degree, there is no possibility of gaining mokSha. Such beliefs entail all of the negative emotions that result from perception of difference, viz. attachment, fear, desire, envy and jealousy, anger etc. Such feelings are inherent in saMsAra and they prevent one from ever realizing the non-dual nature of the Self.

Here, Gaudapada is warning the seeker that any residual belief that the empirical world is a reality (i.e. that a universe has been created and that jIva-s really exists as separate entities) will condemn him to saMsAra. One has at least to countenance the possibility that the world is mithyA if one is to be able to dispel the ignorance that veils Self-knowledge.

(K4.98) It is possible that the believers in duality may raise an objection based on the implication in the above verse that there exists an actual "covering" that veils the true Knowledge. So Gaudapada immediately leaps to defend this possible criticism. No jIva is ever really covered by ignorance. There is not really any bondage or saMsAra and no need for any mokSha to provide release. This follows, of course, from what has gone before. If no jIva has ever been born, no jIva can really be bound! The problem is simply that, the moment I think I am born, I must accept the consequences of feeling limited and (hopefully!) seek liberation. If all goes well (and I find a good teacher), I will discover that I was mistaken, that the *jIva* is *mithyA* and my real nature is *turIya*, ever pure and free. It will then be figuratively said that I have gained *mokSha* or the truth has been *revealed*, but I will simply have understood my real nature. All *jIva*-s have this potential to realize the truth.

(K4.99) When we looked at the metaphor of 'pot space' and 'total space' earlier, it was concluded that space does not actually have anything to do with the pot at all. When we move a pot from A to B, the space that was 'in the pot' does not move; rather it is the pot that moves in space. Space is ever unaffected by any object. Here, Gaudapada says that Consciousness (and hence knowledge, which is the same as pointed out in K4.96 under 'Problems and Misconceptions') is like space in this respect and never contacts objects. It has nothing to do with the knower-known-knowledge relationship. (There can never be any relations when there are not two things.) The *j~nAnI* knows this but the same applies to the *jIva* who is still ignorant – it is a fact whether it is known or not.

Just in case we have forgotten the earlier discussions, Gaudapada reminds us that this denial of the existence of separate objects is not the same as the Idealist position of the Buddhists, who believe that the world exists in the mind only. For the Advaitin, the mind, too, is *mithyA*! Only Advaita teaches the limitless and eternal, non-dual nature of Consciousness.

(K4.100) Gaudapada concedes that it is difficult to grasp this understanding. Its profundity is immense, like the ocean. Being without attributes, it cannot be 'learned' in the same way as knowledge of a language or a science. It can only be 'known' by being. We are not the waker, the dreamer nor the deep-sleeper. We are That which is the substratum of them all – *turIya*. Gaudapada concludes: *Pure and free from multiplicity, we offer our obeisance (to turIya) as best as we can.*

We are obliged to do the best we can to speak about the reality that is beyond speech because only by doing so may we wrest the mind from its dualistic pursuits and bring it to rest in eternal peace. Hopefully this book has succeeded in some small measure.

Appendix 1

Translation of and Commentary on the Upanishad

Note that this Appendix is a detailed analysis of the 12 mantras of the Upanishad, looking at the meaning of Sanskrit terms, ambiguities, academic discussions etc. There are quotations from various translations and commentators. Although I attempt to make the whole thing readable, you should only read it if you are interested in this level of detail! This is why the material is relegated to an Appendix.

shAnti pATha and Introduction by Shankara

The Upanishad itself begins with a *shAnti pATha* – a traditional prayer for peace, for conditions conducive to uninterrupted study and for the blessing of the gods towards that end, recited before the lessons commence. There is a specific prayer for each of the Vedas. The Mandukya belongs to the *atharva veda*, which uses the prayer beginning with *OM bhadraM karNebhiH*.

ॐ भद्रं कर्णेभिः शृणुयाम देवाः । भद्रं पश्येमाक्षभिर्यजत्राः ।
स्थिरैरङ्गैस्तुष्टुवाᳵसस्तनूभिः । व्यशेम देवहितं यदायुः ।
स्वस्ति न इन्द्रो वृद्धश्रवाः । स्वस्ति नः पूषा विश्ववेदाः ।
स्वस्ति नस्ताक्ष्यों अरिष्टनेमिः । स्वस्ति नो बृहस्पतिर्दधातु ।
॥ ॐ शान्तिः शान्तिः शान्तिः ॥

AUM bhadraM karNebhiH shRRiNuyAma devAH | bhadraM pashyemAkShabhiryajatrAH |
sthiraira~NgaistuShTuvA{\m+}sastanUbhiH | vyashema devahitaM yadAyuH |
svasti na indro vRRiddhashravAH | svasti naH pUShA vishvavedAH |
svasti nastArkShyo ariShTanemiH | svasti no

bRRihaspatirdadhAtu |
|| *AUM shAntiH shAntiH shAntiH* ||

The idea is that one offers up prayers to the gods, so that they may look favorably upon this study and grant that both student and teacher should remain healthy and alert for the duration. Some presentations of the Upanishad and *kArikA-s* omit lines 3 and 4 while others omit the invocation altogether; maybe because they are impatient to get to the substance of the Upanishad itself. Grant us patience (*titikShA*) might usefully be added to the invocation!

bhadraM karNebhiH shRRiNuyAma devAH – Oh, Gods! May we hear auspicious (words – i.e. those words to come in what follows – *shRRiNuyAma* has the same root as *shruti*; *shru* means to hear from a teacher, study or learn).

bhadraM pashyemAkShabhiryajatrAH – grant that we may see that which is auspicious, oh (Gods who are) worthy of worship (*yajatra*)!

sthiraira~NgaistuShTuvA{\m+}sastanUbhiH | *vyashema devahitaM yadAyuH* – grant us long lives (*Ayus*), with strong (*sthira*) limbs (*a~nga*) and bodies (*tanU*), (in order that we may) praise you!

svasti na indro vRRiddhashravAH – may the great God Indra (*vRRiddhhashravas* literally means 'possessed of great swiftness') grant us (*naH*) good fortune (*svasti*)!

svasti naH pUShA vishvavedAH – may the omniscient (*vishvavedas*) sun God grant us good fortune! (*pUShA* is another, less-common name for *sUrya* and should be understood as *Ishvara*)

svasti nastArkShyo ariShTanemiH – May the limitless *tArkShya*

237

grant us good fortune! According to Wikipedia, *tArkShya* is the name of a mythical being in the *RRigveda*, described as a horse 'with intact wheel-rims' – *ariShTanemiH*. This means it has no restriction in movement. It is also identified as a bird-like creature (*garuda*, meaning an eagle) in the Mahabharata. Some translators seem to translate this as 'Vayu, the god of swift motion' also; or maybe there is an alternative version of this prayer.

svasti no bRRihaspatirdadhAtu – May *bRRihaspati* afford (*dadhAtu*) us success.

shAntiH shAntiH shAntiH – All prayers tend to end with these three words, which ask for freedom from obstacles to receiving the teaching. (*shAnti* means 'peace'.) Obstacles may arise in three ways:

- from the gods, in the form of catastrophic and unavoidable events such as natural disasters. These are called *Adhidaivika* – related to or proceeding from supernatural or divine agents.
- from other humans who create problems or prevent us in some way. These are called *Adhibhautika* – related to created beings.
- from our own shortcomings, be it physical or mental. These are called *AdhyAtmika* – proceeding from bodily and mental causes within oneself.

OM is spoken at the outset of all prayers and scriptures both as an effective 'name' for God and as a symbol for the aim of the study – freedom from ignorance, i.e. enlightenment or *mokSha*. In the case of this Upanishad, of course, it is also the very subject of the study, representing all states of consciousness and reality itself.

Following this Vedic 'invocation for peace', Shankara adds two further verses before the Upanishad commences.

प्रज्ञानान्शुप्रतानैः स्थिरचरनिकरव्यापिभिर्व्याप्य लोकान् ।
भुक्त्वा भोगान्स्थविष्ठान्पुनरपि धिषणोद्भासितान्कामजन्यान् ॥
पीत्वा सर्वान्विशेषन् स्वपिति मधुरभुन्गमायया भोजयन्नो ।
मायासंख्यातुरीयं परममृतमजं ब्रह्म यत्तन्नतोऽस्मि ॥

praj~nAnAnshupratAnaiH sthiracharanikaravyApibhirvyApya lokAn
|
bhuktavA bhogAnsthaviShThAnpunarapi dhiShaNodbhAsitAnkAmajanyAn | |
pItvA sarvAnvisheShan svapiti madhurabhungmAyayA bhojayanno |
mAyAsaMkhyAturIyaM paramamRRitamajaM brahma yattannato.asmi | |*

Without a word by word breakdown, there is no way that I am able to attempt a translation of these verses so the best I can do is to appraise and present the essence of those translations I have been able to find (Prof. J. H. Dave, Ref. 21; Swami Nikhilananda, Ref. 4; Swami Gambhirananda, Ref. 15. None of the other versions present Shankara's invocation.) I sometimes wonder if it is actually possible to translate some of these Sanskrit 'sentences' found in the scriptures into meaningful, grammatically correct English sentences on a one to one basis. They are apparently so long and tortuous that it must take even someone with a good understanding of the language a significant time to understand. It seems that only as a result of familiarity with and a deep understanding of the scripture itself, acquired over many years of learning with a *shrotriya* teacher, can someone read a verse such as the one above and then tell us immediately what it means. The translations given by Nikhilananda and Gambhirananda are definitely not good English! And Professor Dave does not even attempt a straight English rendering.

In the overall *shAnti pATha*, we are asking for dispensation to be allowed to begin and complete the study of this Upanishad without encountering any problems or interference. In these two verses, Shankara is not only giving thanks/asking for blessings (the invocation is to *brahman* in the first verse and *turIya* in the second) but he has clearly already studied the entire work and makes references to both content and conclusions. Accordingly, his invocation functions also as a 'curtain raiser' for what is to come, albeit that one presumes we are not really expected to understand yet what he says!

In the waking state, *brahman* pervades everything in the universe and thus is the 'enjoyer' of all gross objects, moving or unmoving. (Note that *brahman* is called '*praj~nAna*' here, from the *mahAvAkya* '*praj~nAnam brahma*' – Consciousness is *brahman*.) This 'enjoyment' is through the 'rays of' consciousness reflected in the mind of man (*chidAbhAsa*). In the dream state, *brahman* experiences the variety of seeming objects that are brought into existence by desire in the mind (memory). In the deep-sleep state, both gross and subtle objects (of waking and dream states respectively) are absorbed and *brahman* experiences bliss alone. In this way, through the power of *mAyA*, *brahman* makes us experience these three *mithyA* states. From the standpoint of *mAyA*, this *brahman* is called the fourth (*turIya*) and is the highest (*parA*), immortal (*amRRita*) and unborn (*aja*). I bow to this *brahman*..................................... 1

Thus, Shankara is telling us that it is *brahman* himself who, as a result of *mAyA*, seemingly becomes the enjoyer-*jIva* in the three states of existence. This is the topic or subject matter (*viShaya*) of the Upanishad. More generally, of course, this fact boils down to telling us that *brahman* and *jIva* are the same (*tat tvam asi*) – the *jIva* is only a reflection of Consciousness. This is the *viShaya* of Advaita itself. Since *brahman* is *paramamRRitamajaM*, we, too, are not subject to birth or death either. Our belief in *saMsAra* is due to ignorance only and the purpose (*prayojana*) of the Upanishad is to dispel this ignorance.

यो विश्वात्मा विधिजविषयान् प्राश्य भोगान् स्थविष्ठान् ।
पश्चाच्चान्यान् स्वमतिविभवान् ज्योतिषा स्वेन सूक्ष्मान् ॥
सर्वानेतान्पुनरपि शनैः स्वात्मनि स्थापयित्वा ।
हित्वा सर्वान्विशेषान्विगतगुणगणः पात्वसौ नस्तुरीः ॥

yo vishvAtmA vidhijaviShayAn prAshya bhogAn sthaviShThAn |
pashchAchchAnyAn svamativibhavAn jyotiShA svena sUkShmAn
||

sarvAnetAnpunarapi shanaiH svAtmani sthApayitvA |
hitvA sarvAnvisheShAnvigataguNagaNaH pAtvasau nasturIaH
||

turIya identifies with and enjoys the gross universe (*virAT*) in the
waking state. It enjoys the subtle world of its own mind
(*hiraNyagarbha* at the cosmic level) in the dream state. And it
withdraws everything into itself in the dissolution of the
universe (*pralaya*), where it is known as the 'unmanifest'
(*avyAkRRita*), the causal level of Ishvara. (On the gaining of Self-
knowledge) all of this is discarded and he realizes that he is the
fourth, free of all distinctions. May this *turIya*, that is without any
attributes, protect us 2

Again, I would like to point out that the above 'translations'
are my understanding based on the few commentaries that I
have seen. If any Sanskrit scholar is reading this, please email me
to point out any errors and suggest a better rendering! (A word
by word translation into English of Shankara's complete works
would be invaluable but I do not think such a thing exists.)

Mantra 1

हरिः ॐ ।
ॐ इत्येतदक्षरमिदं सर्वं तस्योपव्याख्यानं भूतं भवद्ः भविष्यदिति सर्वमोंकार एव ।
यच्चान्यतः त्रिकालातीतं तदप्योंकार एव ॥ १ ॥

hariH OM |
OM ityetadakSharamidaM sarvaM tasyopavyAkhyAnaM bhUtaM
bhavadH bhaviShyaditi sarvamoMkAra eva |
yachchaanyatH trikAlAtItaM tadapyoMkAra eva || 1 ||

> *OM iti etad akSharam –* Thus, this syllable OM
> *idam sarvaM –* (is) all this.
> *tasya upavyAkhyAna –* The explanation begins with this:
> *oMkAra –* the syllable OM (is)
> *iti eva –* thus truly
> *sarvaM –* everything –
> *bhUta –* past,
> *bhavat –* present
> *bhaviShyat –* (and) future.
> *yat cha anya –* and what is other than
> *atIta –* transcending these
> *trikAla –* three time periods
> *tat eva –* even is that only
> *oMkAra –* OM
> *api –* as well.

The syllable OM is everything. The explanation follows (with this Upanishad). All that is past, present and future is OM. And, whatever is beyond the three periods of time, that too is only OM.

At first sight, this opening mantra seems incomprehensible. Is it really saying that OM literally *is* everything, the entire

242

universe? It certainly seems so. *idam sarvaM*, 'all this' can only refer to everything that is in front of one, available to the senses.

If you listen to the wonderful three-CD musical interpretation of this Upanishad by Pandit Jasraj (Ref. 31), you will find the spoken mantras are taken from the translation by Sri Purohit Swami and W. B. Yeats and this majestic version is even clearer:

The word OM is the Imperishable; all this its manifestation. Past, present, future – everything is OM. Whatever transcends the three divisions of time (i.e. the unmanifest), that too is OM. (Ref. 30)

Some translations are even more explicit, to avoid any possibility of doubt. Swami Lokeswarananda (Ref. 20) 'translates': *OM is this phenomenal world."* and points out that *"OM stands for brahman, as both cause and effect."* (One presumes that he actually means *Ishvara*, here, since *brahman* is *kArya – kAraNa - vilakShaNa* – beyond cause and effect – as the *kArikA-s* will later make clear!

The word *akShara* can mean 'imperishable' but is also used to refer to a syllable, letter or sound. But, in this context, it has the connotation of *brahman*. Anything created has a beginning in time and will therefore also have an end – it is perishable. *brahman*, being prior to creation, is imperishable. It may manifest forms but essentially remains always the same. Accordingly, there is already the implication (which will be made explicit later) that OM, in the sense of being immortal (*akShara*), *is brahman*. Also, the 'past, present and future' refers to the *vyAvahArika* manifestation of the world of space, time and causality; that which 'transcends time' is the unmanifest *pAramArthika*. 'Both' are, of course, *brahman*; OM refers to every-thing.

So, it seems reasonable that we should use OM as a *symbol* for *brahman* but the *mantra* seems to be saying much more than this – why? The key to understanding this is the *vAchArambhaNa* sutras from the Chandogya Upanishad. (Note that the

Mandukya Upanishad is the last one taught traditionally, so that you would be expected to know all the others very well by this time!) In Chapter 6 of the Chandogya, Svetaketu asks his father to explain how the Vedas can teach us about unknown things (i.e. the Self) by talking about things that we do know. In VI.1.4, the father tells Svetaketu:

O good looking one, as by knowing a lump of earth, all things made of earth become known: All transformation has speech as its basis, and it is name only. Earth as such is the reality. (Swami Gambhirananda translation)

And then the next verse uses the well-known metaphor of gold and gold ornaments. Everyone who has made more than a passing study of Advaita will know that chains, rings and bangles are all only name and form of gold. But the argument is much more subtle than this. How is it that, by knowing that gold is the material cause of the ornaments, the different products become known? Shankara points out that this objection is not valid because the product is *not* different from the cause. The Upanishad makes the following crucial point: it is effectively the *naming* of (giving a label to) the discrete forms (which are all actually the same substance) which 'creates' the supposed, new object. The phrase '*vAchArambhaNaM vikAro nAmadheyaM*' is repeated many times in the chapter to emphasize that all objects have no substantive other than *brahman*. *vAchArambhaNa* is a Vedic form of *vAgAlambhana*, which means it depends upon mere words or on some merely verbal difference. *vikAro nAmadheyaM* means that the *vikaraH*, transformation, is *nAmadheya*, (just in) name only.

In the metaphor, rings and bangles etc are *mithyA*, while the gold alone is *satyam*. The rings and bangles are *always* gold and nothing but gold. It is by the very act of putting a name to a specific form that we con ourselves into thinking that we have a separate, distinct object. And, of course, in the wider context everything in the world is *mithyA* and *brahman* alone is *satyam*. There are no separate things; there is only name and form of *brahman*. In a very real sense, we can say that the name IS the object; without the word, there would not be any separate thing. That which we 'bring into existence' by naming would otherwise simply be part of the 'background'. So name and form are inseparable; and both are *mithyA*.

Now, it is simply a matter of combining this understanding with the analysis of OM that was carried out in the section 'A (very little) Sanskrit background'. There, we saw that all sounds (and therefore all words) are 'contained' in the word OM. OM 'contains' all sounds in the same way that *brahman* 'contains' all forms. Since name effectively *is* form, therefore OM effectively *is* every 'thing'. As Shankara puts it in Swami Gambhirananda's translation (Ref. 15):

As all these objects that are indicated by names are non-different from the names, and as names are non-different from OM, so OM is verily all this.

And the reason that this is so important is explained by Shankara:

The necessity of understanding their identity arises from the fact that (once this identity is established,) one can by a single effort eliminate both the name and the nameable to realize brahman that is different from all.

According to Shankara, the syllable OM (*oMkAra*) is both the form and the expression of *Atma*. The sound OM pervades all spoken words (which are just 'modifications' of OM). Similarly, the named 'things' are the illusory appearances of *Atma* and are not different from their names.

Thus it is said that OM is everything, as expression OM and the expressed Atma are not different. The name and the nameable are one only... ultimately only one entity, devoid of subject-object relationship, of distinction (of the name and the nameable) is established and all modifications are found as unreal. (Ref. 21)

Note that, of course, *brahman* cannot *literally* be OM – this really would not make any sense. It is rather that *brahman* can be realized through the analysis of OM that is carried out in this Upanishad and *kArikA-s. brahman* is the substratum, the essence of all that appears as this world and it is being represented by the name OM. The name and form of any object are effectively the same. Any name is 'contained' in the all-encompassing symbol OM. Therefore it makes sense that OM is an effective pointer to *brahman,* itself.

It should also be mentioned that OM corresponds to what is spoken of in the Bible as 'In the beginning was the Word'. Creation is said (in the philosophy called *sphoTa vAda* rather than Advaita) to have begun with the vibration of the word OM (spoken by the *saguNa* creator). Again, this is a perfect analogy. All sounds (words) come out of (are part of) the syllable OM. Similarly, all of creation (objects) come out of (are part of) *Ishvara.* The metaphor often used for this is the spider building its web out of its own substance. *Ishvara* is both the efficient and material cause of creation. Every 'thing' is a part of *Ishvara* and an 'effect' of *Ishvara's* 'cause' – the effect being a 'manifestation' of the cause (*vivarta vAda*). (*Ishvara,* of course, has to be prior to creation. He is not Himself created, being not other than *nirguNa brahman* in reality.)

This, of course, is all from a *vyAvahArika* standpoint. As has been pointed out in the main text, there is not really any creation at all. All is always and only *brahman* from the standpoint of absolute reality. This is the final truth (*ajAti vAda*).

Mantra 2

सर्वं ह्येतद् ब्रह्मायमात्मा ब्रह्म सोऽयमात्मा चतुष्पात्॥ २॥

sarvaM hyetad brahmAyamAtmA brahma so.ayamAtmA chatuShpAt
|| 2 ||

sarvaM etad – Everything here
hi – (is) certainly
brahma – *brahman*.
ayam AtmA – This *Atman*
brahma – (is) *brahman*.
saH ayam AtmA – This very *Atman*
chatuShpad (= *chatur* + *pAda*) – (has) four aspects.

Absolutely everything is brahman. This Atman is brahman and has four aspects.

In the first mantra, OM was said to be everything. (How this is so will be analyzed in mantras 8 – 12.) The Upanishad now asks what is the nature of this Self, *Atman*; mantras 2 – 7 make this enquiry.

In this second mantra, it is being said that this 'everything' is *brahman. brahman is* Existence – hence the *'sat'* in *sat-chit-Ananda*. OM was the 'name' given to 'everything'. Both OM and 'everything' are only name and form of the real 'substrate', which is *brahman*. The world is *mithyA, brahman* is *satyam*. Only after this has been realized, can *brahman* be (as it were) 'known', since *brahman* is the reality upon which all of this appearance takes place. We can therefore find out the truth about everything either by investigating into the nature of OM or by investigating into *Atman-brahman*. Both investigations will lead us to the same understanding, but the direct investigation into our own nature is the 'fast track' whereas the analysis of, and meditation on, OM is for those of weaker intellect.

Shankara's commentary begins by stating that the name and the thing named are one – name and the object named are not separable. I.e. OM *is* everything.

If this were not said, the circumstance that knowledge of a thing is dependent upon the name of the thing would appear to suggest that the oneness of names and objects is only metaphorical. The object of establishing the unity of things and names is none other than the possibility of doing away with both of them, by a single effort, thus simultaneously realizing brahman as distinct from both. (Ref. 2)

This statement can be understood by reference to the *vAchArambhaNa* sutras of the Chandogya Upanishad, discussed above.

The emphasis on 'this, here' (*hi etad* – *hi* means 'indeed' or 'certainly') is made in order to differentiate 'this', which is closest to me, from 'that' which is further away. Swami Chinmayananda points out (Ref. 3) that 'this *Atman*' can never be referred to as 'that' because it is our very Self and can never be away from us. So that reality which is my Self is 'responsible' for both the feeling of 'I' in this body-mind as well as for the universe which it seemingly experiences. Both are manifestations of *brahman*.

ayamAtmA brahma is, of course, one of the four most famous statements (*mahAvAkya-s*) from the Upanishads. It signifies the realization that who-I-really-am is that same *brahman* that has previously been stated as being everything. Shankara suggests that the speaker will put his hand on his heart as these words are spoken, referring to the Self 'within'. (Naturally, we should acknowledge that the Self is everywhere and does not literally reside in the 'cave within the heart'.) Having said that everything 'out there' is OM and *brahman*, it is now being said that this *Atman here*, i.e. I myself, is also *brahman*. This Self-realization is directly intuited (*aparokSha*) rather than being indirectly inferred or deduced (*parokSha*). It is known as a fact; there is no need for reasoning. Indeed, it is always available for direct knowledge; it is just that we usually need a guru to point out the obvious, which has become obscured by lots of misleading notions!

So, since *brahman* is everything, and I am *brahman*, it follows that 'I am everything'. By carrying out an investigation into my Self, I can come to know everything – the nature of reality itself. This follows because everything and the knower of everything are dependent upon Consciousness itself and I am That. Both knower and known are *mithyA*. Only 'I', Consciousness itself, am *satyam*.

The word *chatuShpad* refers to the four aspects of this Consciousness, i.e. the three 'states' of Consciousness – waking, dreaming and deep sleep – and that reality which is the 'background' to all states. [As an aside, it can be noted that Advaita pedantically recognizes 5 states of consciousness: waking, dreaming, deep sleep, unconsciousness and death. In unconsciousness, the person cannot easily be awoken by the usual means; in death he cannot be awoken at all! So these two 'extra' states have to be different from the usual three. Shankara discusses unconsciousness, the 'swoon' state, in BSB III.2.10. See Appendix 2 for further explanation.]

The word *mithyA* means dependent reality, consisting only of name and form. The waking state, *jAgrat*, consists of gross name and form (*sthUla nAma-rUpa*) – the appearance of this material universe. This can be thought of as the gross knower-known (this knower is called *vishva*) dependent upon me, the *sthUla Atma*. The dream state, *svapna*, consists of the subtle name and form of the dreams projected by my mind (*sUkShma nAma-rUpa*). This is the subtle knower-known (this knower is called *taijasa*), dependent upon me, the *sUkShma Atma*. And the deep-sleep state, *suShupti*, consists of the causal or unmanifest name and form. Because they are unmanifest, there is no knower-known distinction but these are similarly dependent upon me, the *kAraNa Atma*. (The causal, undifferentiated consciousness is called *prAj~na*.)

I am, as it were, acting as *sthUla Atma* in the waking state, *sUkShma Atma* in the dream state and *kAraNa Atma* in the deep-sleep state. When I am not acting any part, I am simply myself. This non-acting condition is called *turIya* and, though referred to here as one of the four parts, is not in fact a part or a state at all – it is the reality, in which I can be called *turIya Atma*. In *turIya*, there is no knower-known differentiation or distinction of any kind. *turIya* is the *satyam*, reality; the other three *pAda-s* are *mithyA*.

Shankara says that the Sanskrit word *pAda*, when used to refer to the three states, is in the instrumental case of the noun, i.e. it carries the sense of 'that by which something is attained', *sAdhana*. When used to refer to *turIya*, however, it is in the objective case, carrying the meaning of 'that which is achieved' – *sAdhya*. It is clearly not incidental that the word *sAdhana* also refers to the spiritual disciplines we need to follow in order to attain Self-realization. [The word *pAda* also means 'foot' and *chatuShpad* means a 'quadruped'. Shankara is careful to point out that, here, this meaning should not be used – the *Atman* does not have four legs or feet, like a cow!]

Mantra 3

जागरितस्थानो बहिष्प्रज्ञः सप्ताङ्ग एकोनविंशतिमुखः स्थूलभुग्वैश्वानरः प्रथमः
पादः ॥ ३ ॥

*jAgaritasthAno bahiShpraj~naH saptA~Nga ekonaviMshatimukhaH
sthUlabhugvaishvAnaraH prathamaH pAdaH || 3 ||*

   prathamaH pAdaH – The first aspect (of the Self)
   vaishvAnara – is *vaishvAnara* (or *vishva*).
   jAgaritasthAna – (This is) the waking state
   praj~na – (and it is one in which one's) knowing awareness
   bahis – (is) turned outwards.
   sapta a~Nga (*a~Nga* literally means 'limb') –(This aspect has)
   seven divisions *ekonaviMshatimukhaH* – and nineteen interfaces (with the outside world) (*viMshati* is 'twenty' and *ekona*
   is 'one less than'; *mukha* literally means 'mouth' or 'opening').
   sthUlabhugvaishvAnaraH – *vaishvAnara* (is) the enjoyer (*bhug* =
   bhuj = *bhoktA*; experiencer, enjoyer) of the gross world.

The first aspect of the Self is vaishvAnara. *This is the waking state in
which one's awareness is turned outwards to the external world.*
vaishvAnara *has seven parts and experiences the universe via 19
interfaces.*

Mantras 3 – 7 carry out an investigation into the nature of the
Self (*Atma vichAra*) and 3 – 6 look specifically at the waker,
dreamer and deep sleeper, while 7 is the mantra which
'describes' *turIya*, our true Self. The reality is that I am the
unassociated *Atman* but in the several states (*avasthA-s*), I
associate myself with gross, subtle and causal name and form
and believe myself to be the waker, dreamer and deep-sleeper,
respectively. These states are all *mithyA*.

Before explaining the detail of this mantra, I want to highlight the possible confusion regarding the use of the term *vaishvAnara*. I haven't encountered anyone suggesting that there is confusion but it certainly seems that way to me! The more usual term for the individual waker is *vishva*, while the term normally used for the macrocosmic or universal aspect is *virAT*. Now, of course, 'I' am all of these in reality. In the case of the waking world, 'I' as Consciousness, *Atman*, am the waking observer and knower of the external world. But I am also the known universe of objects – *sarvaM khalvidam brahma*, as it is said in the Chandogya Upanishad (All this, verily, is *brahman*). Accordingly, it is true that I am the waker, *vishva*, but it is also true that I am the macrocosmic *virAT*.

However, you might think that at this stage in the Upanishad, it would be unreasonable to suppose that the disciple understands all this. And if he does, there would seem to be no point in analyzing the states in the first place. Furthermore, the next mantra speaks of the second *pada* being *taijasa* and the fifth and sixth mantra describe the third *pada* as *praj~nA*. These are the dreamer and deep-sleeper 'I' from the individual point of view.

Accordingly, it might seem to be more than a little incongruous to speak of the individual dreamer and sleeper but of a universal waker. And Swami Sivananda is quite unambiguous in his commentary:

The text here gives a description of vaishvAnara *or* vishva *and not the* virAT. virAT *is the universal or the macrocosmic aspect of* Ishvara *and* vishva *is the individual or microcosmic aspect. The sum total of all* vishva-s *is* virAT. *jIva is a microcosm of the great macrocosm.* (Ref. 22)

But some commentators point to the word in its universal sense. Prof. J. H. Dave (Ref. 21) says:

vishva, *who is called* saptA~Nga *is now explained as described in* prashna *Upanishad and this* vishva *(Atma in the waking state) is identified with* vaishvAnara, *the Atma of the universe, in the manner explained hereafter.*

And later:

vaishvAnara *means one who leads all creatures in various ways, or he is all beings (the different creatures experience pleasure or pain according to their meritorious or evil acts and this* vaishvAnara *is the giver of the rewards of their acts – that is why he is called* vaishvAnara)... *he is the* Atma *of all the beings as seen in the aggregate in the sense of* samaShTi *and also called* virAT.

It seems that the allusion to the seven limbs etc, which is taken from the Chandogya Upanishad (and described below) is perhaps to blame. Swami Krishnananda's commentary on this *'vaishvAnara vidyA'* portion of Chandogya actually has headings of 'Air as the breath of the *Universal Self'*, 'Space as the body of the *Universal Self* etc. clearly indicating that the term *vaishvAnara* is used in its macrocosmic sense.

Swami Sharvananda reconciles this to some degree when he says (Ref. 6):

The gross macrocosmic aspect of the Universal Soul is called virAT *and the microcosmic is known as* vaishvAnara. *The Upanishad describes here only the* vishva *or the* vaishvAnara *and not the* virAT. *Thereby it tacitly alludes to the fact that the same Atman who is viewed from the individual standpoint as the individual soul is also the Universal Soul.*

But if you read Shankara's commentary carefully, it becomes clear that the apparent confusion is quite deliberate. *vishva* is definitely the individual and *virAT* is definitely the *samaShTi*. *vaishvAnara* therefore makes us think and hopefully realize that I am both. It is intentionally pointing to the apparent duality by speaking of the individual but referencing the Chandogya description of the cosmic and therefore saying that the reality is non-dual.

Professor Dave's commentary also draws on the notes from *kUranArAyan* of the *vishiShTAdvaita* school, *madhva* and *shrinivAsa* of the *dvaita* school and *puruShottama gosvAmi* of the *shuddhAdvaita* school, as well as Shankara's, but it is not always obvious whose comments are whose! At any rate, it is explained there (by someone!) that:

> *The intention is to state that there is no* bheda *(difference) between* adhyAtma *(individual) and* adhidaiva *(relating to gods). Thus the first quarter mentioned in connection with* vishva *is also of* virAT, *the totality of the gross universe.*

And Shankara's comment clarifies:

> *And in this way alone the non-duality can be established by the cessation of the entire illusory phenomenal multiplicity; and further that one* AtmA *is realized as abiding in all beings as also all beings are seen as abiding in* AtmA.

If we dealt with only the individual waker, we would have an assumed separate world and hence no possibility of non-duality. So it is as well to establish from the outset that, when we speak of whichever state – gross, subtle or causal – we are intending to refer to the individual, subjective aspect *and* the universal, objective aspect also. *jIvo brahmaiva nAparah* – I am not other than *brahman.*

The Sanskrit derivation of *vaishvAnara* is from the words *vishva*, meaning 'all, whole, entire, universal' and *nara*, meaning 'man, humanity'. The idea is that we (in the waking state) are continually looking 'outwards' towards enjoyment of external things, turning away from an investigation into the inner self. We go after things because we mistakenly assume that they will satisfy our desires. In fact, the only thing that will bring realization of the truth of the already-existing limitlessness nature of ourselves is Self-knowledge.

vishva is identified as the 'first aspect' because the waking state is the one in which we begin and carry out our investigations. We think that it is the waking state that is primary and the others are merely supportive, allowing the mind and body to recuperate so as to allow us to return to the fray. It is only later that we realize that the waking world is only the gross aspect.

At the macrocosmic or *samaShTi* level, I am the known world of gross objects, while at the microcosmic or *vyaShTi* level I am the individual knower of this world. This is analogous to the way in which, in my dreams, I divide myself as it were into the dreamer and the dreamed universe. But, whereas the dream world is constituted from my own mind, the waking world is made up of the five elements (*pa~nchabhUta-s*) – ether, *AkAsha*; air, *vAyu*; fire, *tejas*; water, *ap*; earth, *pRRithivI*. Therefore who-I-really-am, the *Atman*, seemingly divides into the subjective *vyaShTi* knower and the objective *samaShTi* known, in the gross waking state.

This knower experiences the known universe via nineteen interfaces, There are five sense organs, or organs for acquiring knowledge – *j~nAnendriya-s*, through which data enters from the outside: sight, *chakShus*; hearing, *shrotra*; taste, *rasana*; smell, *ghrANa*; touch, *tvak*. There are five organs of action – *karmendriya-s* – via which we interact with and impact upon the outside world: speech, *vAk*; grasping, *pANi*; movement, *pAda*; excretion, *pAyu*; generation, *upastha*. There are five aspects to the vital force – *prANa* – that maintain the body in a functional state: the air itself in the lungs etc, *prANa*; that associated with excretion, *apAna*; that which governs the circulation of blood in the body, *vyAna*; that controlling digestion, *samAna*; that directing the vital force upwards, *udAna*. Finally, there are the organs of mind: *manas* is responsible for managing data input/output and the emotions; *buddhi* controls the intellectual and discriminatory functions; *chitta* refers to the subconscious and memory aspects; *ahaMkAra* is the ego element. 5 + 5 +5 + 4 = 19.

The reference to 'seven limbs' derives from Chandogya Upanishad 5.18.2. "*Of that very* vaishvAnara-*self who is such, heaven indeed is the head, sun is the eye, air is the vital force, sky is the middle-part of the body, water is the bladder, earth indeed is the two feet, sacrificial alter is the chest, kusha-grass is the hair,* gArhaptaya-*fire is the heart,* anvAhArya-pachana-*fire is the mind,* AhavanIya-*fire is the mouth.*" (Swami Gambhirananda translation)

Precisely how this maps onto seven limbs is a bit unclear (Swami Lokeswarananda in Ref. 20 even finds 'nose' from somewhere!) but the consensus seems to be that these seven are:

- heaven – the word used in the text is *sutejas*, which means 'very bright, splendid'. This represents the head.
- sun – the word used is *vishvarUpa*, which means 'manifold, various or multicolored' or literally 'form of everything'. This represents the eye.
- The remaining five limbs are the five elements. Air, *vAyu* (the breath);
- space or ether, *AkAsha* (the body);
- fire, *tejas* (the mouth – fire is traditionally associated with *vAk*, speech);
- water, *ap* (the lower belly or bladder);
- earth, *pRRithivI* (the feet).

Mantra 4

स्वप्रस्थानोऽन्तःप्रज्ञः सप्ताङ्ग एकोनविंशतिमुखः प्रविविक्तभुक् तैजसो द्वितीयः
पादः ॥ ४ ॥

svapnasthAno.antaHpraj~naH saptA~Nga ekonaviMshatimukhaH
praviviktabhuk taijaso dvitIyaH pAdaH | | 4 | |

dvitIyaH pAdaH – The second aspect (of the Self)
taijasa – is called *taijasa*.
svapna sthAna – (Its field of action is) the dream state.
antaHpraj~naH – (Consciousness is) turned inwards (as
opposed to the waking state in the previous mantra, where it
was turned outwards).
sapta a~Nga – (As with the waking state) (it has) seven
divisions
viMshati mukhaH – (and) nineteen interfaces.
praviviktabhuk taijaso – *taijasa* is the enjoyer (*bhug* = *bhuk* =
bhoktA; experiencer, enjoyer) of the private, internal world
(*pravivikta*).

The second aspect of the Self is taijasa. *This is the dream state in which*
one's awareness is turned inwards. taijasa *has seven parts and experi-*
ences the dream world via 19 interfaces.

The word *vivikta* is given in Monier-Williams (Ref. 47) as
'separated, kept apart, isolated, alone' and *pra* as 'excessively,
very much' (when used as a prefix to an adjective) so it translates
as 'very much alone', i.e. 'private'. Swami Sivananda in Ref. 22
translates it as [*pra* – differentiated and *vivikta* – from the objects
of the waking state] although I don't see any justification for this
from the dictionary. But it amounts to the same thing as he goes
on to say that objects in the world have reality for everyone,
whereas those in dream have reality only for the dreamer.

Professor Dave (Ref. 21) simply translates it as 'subtle'; i.e. the 'subtle enjoyer' or 'enjoyer of the subtle world'. Swami Paramarthananda also translates as 'subtle' and this is clearly the simplest and most obvious since the second *pAda* is all about the subtle aspect.

taijasa literally means 'consisting of light' or 'the brilliant or luminous one'. It is so-called because it generates its own world inside the mind without the assistance of any external illumination or power. As with *vishva-vaishvAnara-virAT*, the individual Self in the subtle dream world is not only the observer of that world but also the dream world itself. This entire dream world does not consist of external objects but is made up of the light (of the dreamer) himself. No external, gross objects are seen at all. Of course this is much more obvious here, since even non-Advaitins accept that the dream is entirely a product of their own minds and that the 'stuff' of that world is also nothing other than their own minds. (Pedantically, one has to point out that *vishiShTAdvaitin-s* do *not* accept this. They believe that the dream world is just as real as the waking world!) Also, one has to acknowledge that, not only am I the individual microcosmic subtle dreamer, but I am also the macrocosmic aspect, called *hiraNyagarbha*.

In respect of the macrocosmic or *samaShTi* view of the entire creation, *hiraNyagarbha* is the subtle level; *virAT* is the gross and *Ishvara* is the causal level. From the individual or *vyaShTi* aspect of creation, *taijasa* is the subtle, *vishva* the gross and *praj~nA* the causal level. I have never found *hiraNyagarbha* to be a particularly obvious concept, nor a necessary one! Swami Krishnananda says that Ishvara 'becomes' *hiraNyagarbha*:

Teachers of the Vedanta tell us that the coming down of Ishvara to the Hiranyagarbha state and then to the state of Virat is something like the process of painting on a canvas (Note that this is Shankara's metaphor). *The canvas is stiffened with starch for the purpose of drawing outlines on it by the artist. The canvas is the background on which the outlines are drawn.* Hiranyagarbha *is the outline of the cosmos,* Virat *is the fully-colored picture of the cosmos, and the background of this screen is the Supreme Absolute,* brahman, *appearing as* Ishvara, Hiranyagarbha *and* Virat. (Ref. 34)

Thus, there is a sort of 'condensation' of the 'steam' of the causal *Ishvara*, to the 'water' of the subtle *hiraNyagarbha* and then a 'freezing' to the 'ice' of the gross *virAT*, representing a progressive 'grossification' in the apparently manifesting creation.

It (*hiraNyagarbha*) is also equated with the creator-god *brahmA* in some texts, although quite what the connection is I am not sure! And it is described as the golden womb (this is the literal meaning of the word – *hiraNya* means 'gold' and *garbha* is a womb) or egg out of which *brahmA* was born. The *RRig veda saMhitA* (10.121.1) says that: "*In the beginning there appeared* hiraNyagarbha, *born the one lord of all that exists*" (quoted in Ref. 35). It should be understood as the 'universal mind' or 'cosmic intelligence' (*mahA tattva*). Sri Swami Viditatmananda Saraswati of Arsha Vidya Gurukulam compares the stages to a seed (causal, *Ishvara*), a sprout (subtle, *hiraNyagarbha*) and the tree itself (gross, *virAT*). He says: "*Hiranyagarbha, therefore, represents the shining and resplendent form of the universe before its manifestation, which is apparent to us as the creation.*" (http://www. avgsatsang.org/hhsvs/pdf/Hiranyagarbha_and_Mithya.pdf)

Swami Paramarthananda simplifies things to the 'knower' of the subtle dream state being *taijasa* and the 'known', objective dream world being *hiraNyagarbha*, the *samaShTi nAma-rUpa*, universal name and form. Thus, he says (Ref. 5) that I effectively 'divide myself into two'. At first sight, this is easy to understand and the idea of a microcosmic knower, with all of the known being macrocosmic, seems very reasonable. However, whilst this seems obvious at the gross level, it is less so at the subtle level, since it seems that I (the *jIva*) create my dream world, which is not accessible to anyone else (fortunately). We do not do this consciously; it is 'as though' it is created for us.

The seven divisions and nineteen interfaces referred to have the same meaning as in the previous mantra, except that now they refer to the subtle, dream body and ego rather than the gross. We have dream-senses and dream-organs of action etc. to interact with all of the dream objects, which are themselves 'made out of' my past impressions *(vAsanA-s)*. In the dream, this identity has the same seeming reality to us as has our waking body in the gross world, and our imagined dream world totally supplants what we normally call the 'real' world. The waking ego is *vishva*; the dreamer ego is *taijasa*. Who we really are is the *Atman* identifying with first the gross, then the subtle realm. The waking state is the realm of transactional reality, *vyavahAra*; the dream state is the realm of the illusory, *pratibhAsa*.

Shankara's commentary supports what is also the modern scientific view regarding dreams, namely that they are created out of the past impressions that we have gained, together with desires *(kAma)* and fears *(bhaya)* we might have had in the waking state, whether from actual experiences or from things we have read or seen etc. He says that:

> the mind (in dream) without any of the external means, but possessed of the impressions left on it by the waking consciousness, like a piece of canvas with the pictures painted on it, experiences the dream state also as if it were like the waking. This is due to its being under the influence of ignorance, desire and their action." (Ref. 4)

The paintings here should be understood to be super-realistic ones, as opposed to impressionistic or abstract ones, so that we are readily deluded that we are looking at a real world!

Shankara also notes in passing that the objects perceived in the waking state are *'as if external, though (in reality) they are nothing but states of mind'*. This might easily lead someone down the path of idealism, but we should interpret this in the sense of the Chandogya Upanishad's *vAchArambhaNa* sutras.

Swami Nikhilananda (Ref. 4) adds the footnote that *"External objects are nothing but mental existents produced by* avidyA. *There are no such independent external entities as objects; they are creations of the mind."* This reference to *avidyA* is not, in my understanding, what Shankara is saying here – see my essay 'Ignorance – not so obvious!' at http://advaita-academy.org/pages/BlogSingle.asp x?BlogId=16#. One could certainly say, however, that what we call external objects are effectively seen as separate as a result of language. But, at any rate, it sows the seed for later discussions on such topics as the illusory nature of cause and effect. The point of the 'painted canvas' is that we see the dream world in the same way that we see the waking world, and believe it to be just as real at the time of dreaming.

Shankara cites two scriptural references in support of the argument that the dream arises from prior impressions in the waking state. Firstly, Brihadaranyaka Upanishad IV.3.9:

When he dreams, he takes away a little of the (impressions of) this all-embracing world (the waking state), himself puts the body aside and himself creates (a dream body in its place), revealing his own luster by his own light – and dreams. In this state, the man himself becomes the light.

Here, the word for light is the more general *jyotiH*, not *taijasa* but Shankara's commentary on this Upanishad states that:

When, however, that luster consisting of the impressions of the waking state is perceived as an object, then, like a sword drawn from its sheath, the light of the Self, the eternal witness, unrelated to anything and distinct from the body and such organs as the eye, is realized as it is, revealing everything. Hence it is proved that, 'in that state the man himself becomes the light'." (Ref. 32)

Secondly, he quotes the Prashna Upanishad IV.5:

Here, in dream, the deity called mind experiences glory. It sees whatever has been seen before; whatever was heard it hears again; the experiences it had in different countries and directions it experiences again and again. Whatever was seen or not seen, heard or not heard, experienced or not experienced, real or unreal, all that it sees, being itself all.

(Shankara points out here that there cannot be impressions of what has never been experienced so that the references to 'what has not been seen' etc. refer to experiences in previous lives.) (Ref. 33)

Mantra 5

यत्र सुप्तो न कञ्चन कामं कामयते न कञ्चन स्वप्नं पश्यति तत् सुषुप्तम् ।
सुषुप्तस्थान एकिभूतः प्रज्ञानघन एवानन्दमयो ह्यानन्दभुक् चेतोमुखः
प्राज्ञस्तृतीयः पादः ॥ ५ ॥

yatra supto na ka~nchana kAmaM kAmayate na ka~nchana svapnaM
pashyati tat suShuptam |
suShuptasthAna ekibhUtaH praj~nAnaghana evAnandamayo
hyAnandabhuk chetomukhaH prAj~nastRRitIyaH pAdaH || 5 ||

> *tat suShuptam* – That (is called) the deep-sleep state
> *yatra supto* – in which the sleeper
> *kAmyate na ka~nchana kAmaM* – desires nothing (not any
> desired objects) *na pashyati ka~nchana svapnaM* – nor sees any
> dreams.
> *tRRiitIyaH pAdaH* – The third aspect
> *prAj~naH* – (is called) 'the one who knows or understands',
> *suShuptasthAna* – the state of deep sleep.
> *ekibhUtaH* – (In this state), everything is undifferentiated
> (literally 'one element'),
> *praj~nAnaghana eva* – just a homogenous mass of
> Consciousness
> *AnandamayaH* – full of bliss,
> *hi Ananda bhuk* – indeed the 'enjoyer' of bliss.
> *chetomukhaH* – (Literally) it is the one whose mouth is intelli-
> gence.

The third aspect of the Self is prAj~na. *This is the deep-sleep state in*
which one neither desires anything nor sees any dream. Everything is
undifferentiated; simply blissful Consciousness alone, gateway to the
other two cognitive states.

Mantras 5 and 6 are about the third state of consciousness –

deep sleep. Mantra 5 deals with the individual, *vyaShTi* aspect, known as *prAj~na*, while Mantra 6 addresses the universal, *samaShTi* aspect, called *antaryAmin*.

'Sleep' in general is *supta* in Sanskrit but we could be in deep sleep or dreaming and still be 'asleep'. The prefix *su* indicates 'good, excellent, well' and, of course, the most restful sleep is deep sleep – *suShupta* – when there are no dreams to disturb the peace! When I am functioning (or rather resting!) in this state, I am called *prAj~naH*.

The deep-sleep state is one in which we are not aware of anything. But this is not because there is no awareness present, rather because there is nothing there of which we could be aware. The senses are not functioning and the mind itself is effectively 'switched off'. There are no reasoning faculties and no memory – no *manas*, *buddhi* or *chitta*. This is analogous to looking into deep space with the sun behind us. Everything would appear black because there is nothing there to reflect the sun's light. The world and the mind are said to be 'resolved', i.e. in an unmanifest form. Experiences are 'unified', as the Upanishad puts it (*ekibhUtaH*); condensed, as it were, into an 'undifferentiated mass' of Consciousness (*prAj~naHnaghana*). There is no duality. Whereas both waking and dream states are characterized by a subject and an object, whether it be external or internal, in the deep sleep state there is awareness of neither. Whilst there is a 'concealing', *AvaraNa*, of reality in all three states, there is projection of an appearance, *vikShepa*, only in the waking and dream states.

Shankara uses the metaphor of the darkness of night time obscuring the objects around us. Phenomenal objects are 'covered over', as it were, when darkness falls. They are still there but can no longer be seen. Similarly, the imagined world of dream, and the objects of the waking world (which are also nothing other than name and form – effectively thoughts arising in *Ishvara*) become undifferentiated in deep sleep. But they are all still there, waiting to become manifest again when the sun of the waking state or the moon of the dream state illumines them (my images, not Shankara's)! All conscious experiences, then, become a 'mass of Consciousness', because there is nothing to differentiate experience. There is effectively nothing but Consciousness (*eva*, literally 'verily').

The fact that both the waking and dream worlds are 'ready' in unmanifest form, to 'spring out' as soon as Consciousness goes through the gate, to 'look' outwards or inwards, is why the deep sleep state is also known as the 'causal' state, with the other two states its 'effects'. (The word *eva* can apparently also be read as *iva* and translated as 'as it were', meaning that the *ekibhUtaH* nature is only temporary, since the unified Consciousness springs back into apparent multiplicity when we move into waking or dream. (Ref. 21)

Upon waking from deep sleep, we know that we did not know or experience anything; i.e. we acknowledge that there was Consciousness still there but with no object of which we could be aware – the sun shining into the void. It is a state in which we do not desire anything (*na ka~nchana kAmaM*) – equating to the waking state, in which awareness goes out to sense objects – nor do we have any dreams (*ka~nchana svapnaM*) – in which awareness is 'turned inwards' to manufacture an imaginary world based upon past impressions and thoughts.

Because Consciousness is now left to its own devices, with no seeming external element of world or thoughts to distract it, it is now as though in its elemental form of *satyam j~nAnam anantam* and, in so far as there could be said to be any experience, it is one of bliss (*AnandamayaH, hi Anandabhuk*). (Note that the word *maya*, here, means 'consisting of' and has nothing to do with the power of *mAyA*.) It is blissful because that is our real nature and we are taken away from it precisely by those perceived external objects and internal thoughts. The mistaken belief that I am a limited individual, which also clouds the natural bliss, is also absent. The deep sleep state is without distinctions or manifoldness –

nirvikalpa.

We also know that we are not directly aware of the bliss at the time, unlike the bliss of *samAdhi*. The bliss is there because the mind is absent. It is registered by the *kAraNa sharIra* instead of the *sUkShma sharIra* or mind. With the latter, I am aware as it happens but with the former, it is only when we subsequently awake that we are able to appreciate, by comparison of our usual waking feelings with the 'awareness of nothing' that existed during deep sleep, that 'I slept well'. There was nothing present to distract me from my natural state. The deep sleep state is also sometimes equated with the 'sheath of bliss' (*Anandamayakosha*) of the Taittiriya Upanishad and this is the reason why. The 'experience' is not bliss itself, precisely because it is an experience which, by definition, has a beginning and an end – we wake up and are back in the world of temporary happiness and pain. *prAj~naH* is conditioned by the causal *upAdhi* of ignorance. Nevertheless, it is an effortless experience of bliss so the deep sleeper is said to be *Anandabhuk.*

Deep sleep is said to be the mouth or 'gateway' between the waking and dream states. We cannot pass from one to the other without going through the intermediary state of deep sleep. (So says Advaita. I rather think that science says that most of us experience a dream state immediately prior to waking, and this is when we remember our dreams. And that is my own experience also.) Consciousness passes through the gateway, as it were, to re-enter the waking or dream world, prompted by ignorance, *avidyA.* So the bliss remains temporary until the ignorance is dispelled once and for all on enlightenment. Consciousness passes through the gate into the external waking world, where desire for objects takes us away from our natural state of bliss. And it passes through into the inner world to be carried off into the *vAsanA*-manufactured world of dream.

As regards the reason for the term '*prAj~naH*', Shankara offers three reasons (Swami Nikhilananda translation, Ref. 4), although the logic for none of them is really explained:

1. Because it is conscious of the past and future as well as of all objects. There is no further explanation for this surprising claim but it is assumed to refer to the fact that the 'knowledge' of both the other states, whether the earlier ones or the ones to come, is 'contained' (in an unmanifest state) within deep sleep.
2. It is the 'knower par excellence' (or 'best knower', as Prof. Dave puts it in ref. 21) because of its having been so in the two previous states.
3. Because of the undifferentiated feature, whereas the other two states experience variety.

In fact, the meaning of *prAj~naH* in this context – i.e. the 'I' sense identified with the deep sleep state – cannot be arrived at from the *dhAtu 'j~nA'*. The dictionary meaning, which is derived from the *dhAtu* is simply 'one who is wise'.

Mantra 6

एष सर्वेश्वरः एष सर्वज्ञ एषोऽन्तर्याम्येष योनिः सर्वस्य
प्रभवाप्ययौ हि भूतानाम् ॥ ६ ॥

*eSha sarveshvaraH eSha sarvaj~na eSho.antaryAmyeSha yoniH
sarvasya*
prabhavApyayau hi bhUtAnAm || 6 ||

> *eSha* – This (i.e. the universal deep-sleep state)
> *sarva Ishvara* – (is) the Lord of everything;
> *eSha* – this
> *sarvaj~na* – (is) omniscient,
> *antaryAmin* – the 'inner controller'.
> *eSha* – This
> *yoniH sarvasya* – (is) the source of everything;
> *hi* – (is) assuredly
> *prabhava apayayau* – the place of the arising and dissolution
> *bhUtAnAm* – of all beings.

*The macrocosmic deep-sleep state is the Lord of everything, omniscient;
Ishvara, the source of everything; indeed the source and final resting
place of all beings.*

In describing the gross and subtle states - waking and dream -
the Upanishad does not clearly differentiate the micro and
macrocosmic forms. The difference between me, the knower
(waker or dreamer), and the objective universe (gross or subtle)
are clear. In deep sleep, there is no knower-known differentiation, since all is in unmanifest form. Accordingly, a little more
explanation is needed!

Mantra 5 dealt with the individual, or *vyaShti*, aspect of the
deep-sleep state: I, the deep-sleeper. This mantra is concerned
with the objective, deep-sleep universe; the *saMaShti*. Here,

everything is held in potential form, ready for manifesting the waking or dream universes. It is the 'causal form' of everything.

There are two aspects to a 'cause' in the sense of creation. If you imagine the mundane example of creating a painting, for example, there is the painter and there is the paint. The paint itself is the material cause - the physical stuff which is put onto the canvas. But, although anyone may squeeze a tube of oil paint, it requires much more to produce a work of art. It requires knowledge, of such things as color theory and perspective. And it requires skill, in the form of sketching, figure drawing and maybe even building the frame or mixing the pigment.

Obviously, manifesting the universe requires much more of these qualities! Since everything has to be manifested (in both the gross world and the subtle), there must be knowledge of everything - *sarvaj~na*. And there have to be all necessary skills - *sarveshvara*. These represent the efficient or intelligent cause for creation - *nimitta kAraNa*.

Ishvara is both the efficient and material cause of all creation. Everything is name and form of *brahman*; *Ishvara* is *brahman* (as if) wielding the force of *mAyA*. In this sense, He is all-knowing and lord of all; the source of everything. And *Ishvara* 'allocates' bodies for rebirth according to that *karma* designated as coming to fruition for a given being in the next life. He is 'responsible for' the laws which govern the universe and those that live in it, and for the laws which determine the ending of one universe and the beginning of the next; i.e. the birth and death of everyone and everything. Indeed, those laws, in a sense, *are Ishvara*.

If I ask you how a child is made, of course you will be familiar with the mechanism! Clearly, in simplistic terms, the 'instructions' are contained in the DNA that results from combination of the man's sperm and the woman's egg. The material for the baby in the womb comes from the food eaten and processed by the mother. So one could accurately say that mankind himself is the material cause for the creation of a human being. But, equally clearly, the mother does not control the correct positioning of organs in the body and connecting of neurons in the brain. There are immutable physical laws governing all of this - this is *Ishvara* as the efficient cause.

Though all-knowing and all-powerful, *Ishvara* also exercises restraint and control in His creation so that the result is ordered rather than chaotic. *antaryAmin literally means* the 'indwelling' (*antaH* meaning 'inside') 'restrainer' (*yam* means 'to restrain'). Moreover, since everything arises out of *Ishvara* and dissolves back into Him, it follows that everything at the level of empirical reality (including 'me') *is* effectively *Ishvara*, not just before and after but also during creation. The feeling of separate existence is a mistake, resulting from ignorance. Ultimately, even *mAyA* is *mithyA* and, from the perspective of absolute reality, there is only *brahman*.

The 'lord of all' (*sarveshvara*) reference is from the Brihadaranyaka Upanishad (IV.4.22). There, the Self is described as the authority or controller of all, the ruler of all, the lord of all, ruler and protector of all beings, i.e. *Ishvara*. And it is noted that *'the seekers of brahman seek to realize it through study of the Vedas.'* (Ref. 48) The 'inner controller' *antaryAmin* comes from Brihadaranyaka II.7.1 – the *'inner controller who controls this world, the other world and all beings'*. *'He who knows that inner controller, he knows brahman, he knows the worlds, he knows the shining ones, he knows the Vedas, he knows the beings, he knows the Self; he knows everything.'* (Ref. 48)

The 'omniscient' reference (*sarvaj~na*) is from Mundaka Upanishad (I.1.9), as is the 'womb' (*yoni*) as the 'source of all beings (*bhUtayonim*) (I.1.6). By referring to 'this' (*Ishvara*) as the 'source of everything' (*yoniH sarvasya*), as well as that into which the world resolves on dissolution, the Mandukya Upanishad is pointing out that *Ishvara* is the material cause as well as the efficient cause for creation.

Mundaka I.1.9 says that Ishvara is the knower of everything

and uses two words – *sarvaj~na* and *sarvavit*. The former is in the sense that *Ishvara's* knowledge *is* the world, in the same way that the dreams that we have at night are our knowledge. It is not possible for us to dream about something of which we are ignorant, because the information about those things is not present in our mind in order for us to construct them in the dream. The dream is made up out of stuff that we already know, or can imagine based upon that stuff. But *Ishvara* also has the knowledge to manifest everything in creation, which we do not; hence the term *sarvavit*.

One becomes a *sarvaj~na* by realizing that 'everything is *brahman*' and all seemingly separate things are *mithyA*. But we cannot become a *sarvavit* with respect to the universe.

Mundaka Upanishad I.1.6 is an extremely important mantra in the scriptures, explaining how *Ishvara*, which itself is without attributes and beyond perception, brings about the manifestation of everything (*vibhU*) yet without undergoing any change. It doesn't 'become' the world, as that would involve changing into something different. Nor is the world a 'part' of *Ishvara*. In fact, 'everything is *brahman*', as is said in the Chandogya Upanishad (III.14.1).

In addition to being causal, 'holding' the unmanifest state of everything, gross or subtle, in potential form, it is also that into which everything is resolved. At the microcosmic level, the individual mind and senses are resolved when we go into deep sleep or *lAya*; at the macrocosmic level, all is resolved at *pralAya* or dissolution.

It is said that the deep-sleep state is the 'corridor' between waking and dream (*chetomukhaH* in the previous mantra). We cannot go directly from waking to dream, or vice versa. In the waking state, we are identified with the body and mind - a 'waker' ego. In the dream, we are identified with a different, dream body and mind. We have to disidentify with one before we can put on the 'mask' of the other. It is in deep-sleep that we take off our mask and identify with nothing.

This third state is the 'causal state' in the sense that a seed is the cause for a tree. All the 'knowledge' to produce the tree is contained in the seed. All of the knowledge for manifesting the universe is 'contained' within *Ishvara*. But note the choice of word here. Gaudapada points out that there is no actual 'creation'; all of the universe already exists in causal or unmanifest form to begin with. And he later uses this mantra as a launching point for a discussion of some of the theories of creation and refutation of these.

Mantra 7

नान्तःप्रज्ञं न बहिष्प्रज्ञं नोभयतःप्रज्ञं न प्रज्ञानघनं न प्रज्ञं नाप्रज्ञम् ।

अदृष्टमव्यवहार्यमग्राह्यमलक्षणमचिन्त्यमव्यपदेश्यमेकात्मप्रत्ययसारं
प्रपञ्चोपशमं शान्तं शिवमद्वैतं चतुर्थं मन्यन्ते स आत्मा स विज्ञेयः ॥ ७ ॥

*nAntaHpraj~naM na bahiShpraj~naM nobhayataHpraj~naM na
praj~nAnaghanaM na praj~naM nApraj~nam |*

*adRRiShTamavyavahAryamagrAhyamalakShaNamachintyamavyapad
eshyamekAtmapratyayasAraM prapa~nchopashamaM shAntaM
shivamAdvaitaM chaturthaM manyante sa AtmA sa vij~neyaH || 7
||*

*This (consciousness) is known as the 'fourth'. (It is) neither (the
knower of) the internal (world), nor the external. Neither (is it the
knower of) both. (And it is) not (just) a 'mass' of consciousness. (It is)
not consciousness (in the empirical sense of conscious 'of') nor (is it)
unconsciousness. (It is) imperceptible, transaction-less, not 'graspable',
un-inferable, unthinkable, and indescribable. (It is) the essential 'I'-
experience. (It is) the negation of the experience of all plurality of the
universe. (It is) pure, tranquility, and non-dual. This is the Self. This
is to be understood.*

This 7th mantra is possibly the single most important mantra
in the whole of the Vedic scriptures; it attempts to 'describe' the
nature of absolute reality, knowing that such description is
intrinsically impossible.

It first makes it clear that *turIya* is not a 'knower' of any sort
(*pramAta vilakShaNa*); i.e. not the waker, dreamer or deep-sleeper
that have just been described in the previous four mantras, nor
some intermediate or combined state:

- *chaturthaM manyante* – this (i.e. Consciousness) is known as the fourth (*chaturtha* - this is a synonym for *turIya*).
- *nAntaHpraj~naM* – (It is) not (the knower of) the internal, subtle world, i.e. not the dreamer, *taijasa*;
- *na bahiShpraj~naM* – nor (the knower of) the external, gross world of objects (*bahis* means 'outside'), i.e. not the waker, *vishva*;
- *na ubhayataHpraj~naM* – nor (the knower of) both (*ubhaya*), i.e. not some intermediate state, such as day-dreaming;
- *na praj~nAnaghanaM* – and not that (knower) which is a (compact) mass of (*ghana*) consciousness (i.e. not the deep-sleep state, in which the mind is resolved and there is consciousness which is 'conscious of nothing');
- *na praj~naM* – there are two possible interpretations of what is intended here and both are correct. One meaning of *praj~naM* is 'all-consciousness' or 'all-knower', i.e. conscious of everything. This should be understood as meaning that it should not be thought of as God or *Ishvara*. It is 'pure' Consciousness, as opposed to Consciousness qualified by *mAyA*. *Ishvara* can be thought of as the cause of everything but *brahman* has nothing to do with cause and effect.

But the simple meaning is that it is not 'Consciousness'. This would seem to be a contradiction of the usual understanding of the seeker, namely that a synonym for *Atman* or *brahman* or *turIya* is 'Consciousness', with the capital 'c' to denote that it is not the usual (i.e. waking) 'consciousness' but an all-encompassing, eternal variety, which is in fact all that there is. But *turIya-brahman-Atman* is not nameable in any way, pedantically speaking. And the very word implies that there exists something else of which Consciousness is conscious – and, of course, there isn't. Anything that we say about it, or any name we give it, has to be dropped ultimately. What should be understood is that *turIya* is that which is the substratum of everything and, in particular, it is that which 'provides' the consciousness in everything that is conscious.

* *na apraj~naM* – nor is it inert, 'unconsciousness', unawareness or insentience.

We deduce, therefore, that it is consciousness without having any attributes of 'knower-hood'.

Shankara, in his commentary on this mantra, uses the metaphor of rope and snake. Just as we realize the nature of the rope by negating all of the illusory attributes of the snake, so we can come to understand the nature of *turIya* by negating the attributes of knower and known in each of the three states. Just as the rope is revealed as the essence of the snake, when we remove the superimposed attributes, so *turIya* is seen to be the substratum of the states of consciousness. Once this is seen, the *mithyA* nature of the waking and dream worlds are simultaneously appreciated.

We negate the particular attributes of the waker (*na bahiShpraj~nam*), who then becomes the dreamer; we negate the particular attributes of the dreamer (*na antaHprajnam*) who then becomes the deep-sleeper; and we negate those particular attributes (*na praj~nAnaghanam*) too. But Consciousness remains ever the same throughout all of this. This is analogous to the manner in which the bangle may be melted down and remade as a chain and then a ring but all are really only ever gold. Since 'I' am present throughout, as each of the three states come and go, I must be *turIya* and not any of them.

Anandagiri points out here (Ref. 21) that *turIya* is not different in *essence* from *vishva, taijasa* and *prAj~na*. There is an 'apparent' difference but no 'absolute' difference. If *turIya* were completely different, then this presentation of the Upanishad would not help us to realize the truth. Also, if the three states were entirely negated, then we would have to conclude that there was no

Atman at all. This would lead to nihilism or the 'emptiness' (*shUnyata*) of Buddhism.

The mantra next states that *turIya* does not have any attributes of 'known-hood' either; i.e. it is not 'knowable' (*prameya vilakShaNa*). It does this by looking at the various ways by which we come to know of the existence of something. If it is not accessible to any of these, then it cannot be known.

- *adRRiShTam* – imperceptible; (It is) unseen (by any of the senses) [*dRRiShTa* means, seen, perceived, visible, apparent - but the word stands for all the senses]. This negates the *pramANa* of *pratyakSha*, direct perception.
- *avyavahAryam* – unavailable for transactions; It has nothing to do with 'worldly' things [*vyavahAra* is to do with common practice, ordinary life, conduct, behavior etc. i.e. transactions within *vyavahAra*]. This follows, since it is not accessible to senses, mind, organs of action etc. as described by the other words in this section of the mantra.
- *agrAhyam* – not 'graspable' [*grAhya* often means to be perceived, recognized or understood but here it is used in its literal sense and stands for all the five *karmendriya*-s (organs of action) – *grahaNa* literally means to catch, where the organs of action are involved in catching.]
- *alakShaNam* – without any characteristics [*lakShaNa* is an indicatory mark or sign or, more commonly in Advaita, a pointer] also translated as 'un-inferable'. This negates the *pramANa* of inference.
- *achintyam* – unthinkable. Since *turIya* is unavailable for the *pramANa*-s of perception or inference, it is incomprehensible, beyond thought. It follows that whatever you can conceive is not *turIya*!
- *avyapadeshyam* – unspeakable. Since it is not an object of experience, it cannot be described or defined. I.e. it is not available to *shabda pramANa* either. See the main text for a

description of how Advaita and the *sampradAya* tradition manage to talk about that which cannot be described!

If *turIya* is neither the knower nor the known, what then is it and how can we appreciate that it is the only reality?

- *ekAtmapratyayasAraM* – it has to be recognized (*sAra*) to be the one unique (*eka*) 'I'-experience (*Atma-pratyaya*). It is the same Self that is experienced in all three states. We know that the 'feeling of I' that I have remains the same throughout my life. Although the body changes, the mind changes and my personal circumstances continually change, the 'essential I' that I feel myself to be now is the same as that which existed when I was a child and first appreciated myself as an existent entity. The attributes - size, age, health, relations, job, possessions, emotions, beliefs etc. are all transitory attributes but 'I am' – Consciousness – continues unchanged. When all of those attributes are dropped, what remains is my true Self – *Atman*. That is *turIya*. (The 'dropping' is, of course, an intellectual exercise, which has to be done in the waking state.)
- *prapa~nchopashamaM* – that in which all phenomena cease; negation (*ama*) of the experience (*pash*) of all plurality of the universe (*prapa~ncha*). The waking state is that in which we are conscious of the gross universe – *sthUla prapa~ncha*. The dream state is that in which we are conscious of the subtle world projected by the mind – *sUkShma prapa~ncha*. The deep-sleep state is that in which we experience peace and bliss, though the causal world (*svapna prapa~ncha*) is unmanifest. But *turIya* is neither knower nor known. All of those attributes which charac-terize the three states are negated. There is no plurality; no universe; consciousness alone exists without a second –

this word is effectively negating the existence of the world; *turIya* is that which is free from the 'universes' in the three states of consciousness.

As Shankara points out, it is because *turIya* is different from the three states that it is called the fourth; the three are only appearances, whereas *turIya* is the reality. Another, possibly useful metaphor here is that of the three states of H_2O, viz. ice, liquid water and steam. Each of these has H_2O as its substantial reality, though their empirical characteristics differ widely. H_2O is not itself intrinsically any of the states, though it is the only reality of all of them. Although each state changes into the others under differing conditions, H_2O remains the unchanging reality. Similarly, waking dream and deep sleep change, one into the other at appropriate (or inappropriate) times of the day, but *turIya* remains the unchanging reality.

- *shAntaM* – peace, tranquility;
- *shivam* – favorable, propitious, auspicious. Swami Gambhirananda (Ref. 15) translates this as 'absolutely pure; supreme Bliss and Consciousness in essence'. This makes more sense.
- *AdvaitaM* – non-dual;
- *chaturthaM manyante* – they (i.e. ignorant people) consider it to be the fourth (= *turIya*), (because they erroneously think that that waking, dream and deep-sleep states are real, whereas they are actually *mithyA*);
- *sa AtmA* – that is the Self;
- *savij~neyaH* – that is to be understood. I.e. the ignorance of this truth in *vyavahAra* has to be removed. Swami Muni Naryanana Prasad (Ref. 38) says that *j~neyaH* means 'that which is to be known', but *vij~neyaH* provides additional emphasis: 'that which is to be specifically known'. And he cites Bhagavad Gita (VII.8 - 11), where Krishna states that

he is the quality of the taste in water, the light in the sun and moon, fragrance of the earth and the vital essence of all living beings etc. The point is that our minds have to become so trained that, whatever we do or perceive, we are constantly aware that 'everything is *brahman*' (*sarvam khalvidam brahma*) and 'this *Atman* is *brahman*' (*ayam Atmabrahma*).

The upshot of this is that no word can ever describe the nature of reality and, indeed, anything that we predicate of it cannot be true. Even to speak of it as 'Consciousness' or 'non-dual' or '*brahman*' has to be, in the final analysis, merely an attempt to understand it with our feeble mind.

But, by negating the defining characteristics of the three states, we are able to apprehend the nature of the real Self. Shankara compares this to negating the imagined snake, crack in the ground or stick, thus enabling us to realize that their 'substratum' of rope is the only reality. We do not need to look for a separate source of knowledge to tell us about the rope. This explains how it is possible for scripture to function as a *pramANa*.

Mantra 8

सोऽयमात्माऽध्यक्षरमोङ्कारोऽधिमात्रं पादा मात्र मात्राश्च पादा अकार उकारो मकार इति ॥ ८ ॥

so.ayamAtmA.adhyakSharamo~NkAro.adhimAtraM pAdA mAtra
mAtrAshcha pAdA akAra ukAro makAra iti | | 8 | |

> *saH ayam AtmA* - this same *AtmA* (just described in the 7th mantra)
> *adhyakSharam* - *adhi* - concerning (i.e. from the standpoint of) - *akShara* - the syllables
> *o~NkAra* - is *OM*.
> (*adhi* literally means 'making it the basis'. Shankara says that the previous mantras have concentrated on the *abhidheya* meaning 'that which is being spoken of', i.e. the thing named or denoted. OM, therefore, is effectively the *abhidhAna* - name or appellation. What is meant is that *Atman* is equated to OM in the linguistic sense.)
> *adhimAtraM* - from the standpoint of the *mAtra*-s, i.e. the individual parts of *OM*, (note that the literal meaning of *mAtra* is measure; the symbolism of this will become clearer with the 10th mantra)
> *pAdA mAtra* - the (four) aspects (of the Self) are the (four) *mAtra*-s
> *mAtrAshcha pAdA* - and the letters are the aspects.
> *akAra ukAro makAra iti* - In this manner, (the letters are) a, u and m.

This Atma can be equated to OM. The aspects of the Self are the parts of OM and the parts of OM are the aspects. The letters constituting OM are 'a', 'u' and 'm'.

With the 8th *mantra*, we move from investigation into the

Atman, with its four *pada*-s or aspects, into investigation into the syllable OM, with its four 'parts', 'measures' or *mAtra*-s. The Upanishad tells us that there is a one-to-one correspondence between the aspects just discussed in mantras 3 - 7 and the parts of OM. The precise nature of the similarities will be pointed out in the remaining mantras but the associations are as follows:

The letter *a* stands for the waking state of consciousness;
u stands for the dream state and
m for the deep-sleep state.
turIya is symbolized by the silence that follows the sound of OM.

The purpose behind this equation of letters and states is to produce associations in the mind so that, when we think of the *u* of OM, for example, we immediately connect that with the dream state, the dreamer and *hiraNyagarbha*. With these associations firmly established, we may then use the syllable OM as a mantra in meditation.

Anandagiri says that the first part of the Upanishad has explained the nature of reality for the benefit of those of superior, or at least average, intelligence. But those of less intelligence will not be able to cope with this. Accordingly, meditation is prescribed as being a practice designed for those students who are insufficiently bright to assimilate the teaching immediately.

The association of concepts with physical objects such as the cross in Christianity, or sounds as in this syllable OM, helps one to focus the attention in prayer or meditation. Eventually, whenever the object is seen or sound heard, the related idea immediately springs to mind to reinforce the association. In order for the association to function optimally, there should ideally be common features between the two, rather than the choice of symbolism being entirely random. The next three mantras explain these common features and point out the benefits to be gained by the beginning student who is not yet ready for Self-inquiry.

Mantra 9 (and *kArikA* K1.19)

जागरितस्थानो वैश्वानरोऽकारः प्रथमा मात्रऽऽऽतेरादिमत्त्वाद्वाऽऽऽप्नोति ह वै
सर्वान् कामानादिश्च भवति य एवं वेद ॥ ९ ॥

jAgaritasthAno vaishvAnaro.akAraH prathamA
mAtra.a.apteraadimattvaadvA.a.apnoti ha vai sarvAn
kAmAnAdishcha bhavati ya evaM veda || 9 ||

> *prathamA mAtra* - The first *mAtra* (of OM)
> *akAraH* - the letter 'a'
> *vaishvAnara* - is *vaishvAnara*
> *jAgarita sthAno* - the waking state
> *ApteH* - (because of both having the characteristics of) being
> all-pervasive
> *va* - or
> *AdimatvatvAt* - being the first.
> *ya evam veda* - Whoever knows this
> *ha vai Apnoti* - certainly obtains
> *sarvan kAmAn* - all desirable objects
> *cha* - and
> *AdiH bhavati* - becomes the first.

The letter 'a', the first mAtra of OM, is vaishvAnara, the waking state,
because both are first in their respective series and have the character-
istic of all-pervasiveness. Whoever knows this will fulfill all their
desires and be the foremost in their field of endeavor.

It was explained in the introductory Sanskrit section that *a* is
the fundamental sound. We cannot speak any word without
opening the mouth and, when we simply do this and allow the
vocal cord to operate, *a* is the sound which emerges. (Note that
this is the basic sound, as in the word 'that', and not the letter as
pronounced when reciting the alphabet.) Thus, *a* must be

regarded as the first, or primary sound. Furthermore, if this sound is made and allowed to continue sounding, it can be discovered that every other sound is essentially a modification of this original sound. The modifications are made by altering the shape of the mouth and the position of the tongue and lips. Thus, it is also apparent that we can regard this sound as pervading every other sound.

Similarly, we normally regard the waking state as having primacy. We only 'know' of the existence of the dream and deep-sleep states from the vantage point of waking. We have to be awake in order to pursue this enquiry and attain enlightenment. We always consider that we go to sleep and maybe dream; we would never think of our basic state as being in deep sleep or dreaming and that we sometimes wake up.

Also, in the scriptures, *vaishvAnara* is said to pervade the whole of the universe. Krishna, in the Bhagavad Gita (10.33), describing himself (as *Ishvara*) says that 'of all the letters, I am the letter *a*'.

This mantra, then, is advocating meditation on OM, with specific attention to the first letter, *a*. Whilst repeating the mantra mentally, one should be aware of the association with the waking state by virtue of the aspects of similarity, namely that both the letter and the state are the 'first' and are 'all-pervasive'. The value of this practice (*upAsana*) for the meditator will be to satisfy his or her desires and to become the 'first' in whatever worldly pursuits are followed.

Swami Chinmayananda points out in Ref. 3 that it is common practice in the Upanishads to promise significant worldly benefits to beginning students in order to persuade them to take up the related *sAdhana*, knowing that the hidden benefits will help them progress on the spiritual path also.

Swami Muni Narayana Prasad (Ref. 38) has a different view of the meaning here, which is also plausible. He points out that it is never possible to satisfy all worldly desires. As soon as one is satisfied another arises. (The scriptures use the metaphor of 'feeding' a fire.) He suggests that the equating of *vaishvAnara* and *a* enables one to intuit the glory of *Atman* and thereby become detached from pleasurable objects rather than infatuated with them. The mantra's reference to 'obtaining all desired objects' may therefore mean 'attaining the desire-less state', which is effectively equivalent to satisfying all desires.

His view of 'becoming the first' also differs from the most obvious interpretation. He suggests that the fame comes because they are wise men (i.e. *j~nAnI*-s) rather than through any sort of worldly attainment. This does not seem likely since these meditations are provided for those who are not yet ready for *Atma vichAra* so that they are unlikely to become *j~nAnI*-s as a result.

Mahadevan (Ref. 54) points out that, in meditation on OM, *a* is also a mnemonic for *Adi* and *Apti*, the two characteristics highlighted in this *mantra*. Similarly, *u* in the next *mantra* is a mnemonic for *utkarSha* and *ubhayatva*. And finally *m* in the 11th *mantra* is a mnemonic for *miti*.

Mantra 10 (and *kArikA* K1.20)

स्वप्नस्थानस्तैजस उकारो द्वितीया मात्रोत्कर्षादुभयत्वाद्वोत्कर्षति ह वै
ज्ञानसन्ततिं समानश्च भवति नास्याब्रह्मवित्कुले भवति य एवं वेद ॥ १० ॥

svapnasthAnastaijasa ukAro dvitIyA
mAtrotkarShAdubhayatvAdvotkarShati ha vai j~nAnasantati.n
samAnashcha bhavati nAsyaabrahmavitkule bhavAti ya evaM veda | |
10 | |

> *dvitIyA mAtra* - The second *mAtra* (of OM)
> *ukAraH* - the letter 'u'
> *taijasa* - is *taijasa*
> *svapna sthAna* - the dream state
> *utkarShAt* - because it is superior
> *vA* - or
> *ubhayatvAt* - because it is in the middle.
> *ya evaM veda* - Whosoever knows this
> *ha vai* - verily
> *utkarShAti* - increases
> *j~nAna saMtati* - the flow of knowledge
> *cha bhavati* - and becomes
> *samAnaH* - the equal (of anyone).
> *abrahmavit* - (A person who is) not a knower of *brahman*
> *na bhavAti* - is not born
> *asya kule* - in his family.

The letter u, the second mAtra of OM, is taijasa, the dream state,
because both are regarded as superior and also are in the middle of their
respective series. Whoever knows this will become superior in
knowledge and accepted by all. All members of his family will be
j~nAnI-s.

The letter *u* is regarded as superior to *a* because it comes later in the alphabet and, in the sounding of *o*, the *a* 'resolves' into *u*. Whereas *a* was the basic, unadorned sound made by merely opening the mouth, *u* is a more subtle sound requiring that we modify the lips significantly.

The subtle *taijasa* is regarded as superior to *vishva* because subtle is superior to gross. Also, gross can be considered as the 'effect' of the subtle 'cause'. Gross equates to matter, subtle to energy. Mental is superior to physical; it is the quality of our mind that raises us above animals. The gross body returns to earth on death, whereas the subtle and causal bodies continue to rebirth (for the *aj~nAnI*). At the macrocosmic (*samaShTi*) level, at the end of the universe (*pralaya*), the entire gross creation (*virAT*) is subsumed into *hiraNyagarbha*.

Each is the middle of its respective series: *u* comes between *a* and *m*; *taijasa* comes between *vishva* and *prAj~na*.

By meditating on OM, giving attention particularly to the letter *u* and being aware of these associations, the following benefits will accrue to the seeker who is still primarily interested in material benefits: their mental power and corresponding knowledge will increase; they will be treated equally by everyone, yet envied by no one.

Mantra 11 (and *kArikA* K1.21)

सुषुप्तस्थानः प्राज्ञो मकारस्तृतीया मात्र मितेरपीतेर्वा
मिनोति ह वा इदं सर्वमपीतिश्च भवति य एवं वेद ॥ ११ ॥

*suShuptasthAnaH prAj~no makArastRRitIyA mAtra miterapItervA
minoti ha vA idaM sarvamapItishcha bhavati ya evaM veda || 11 ||*

> *tRRitIyA mAtra* - The third *mAtra* (of *OM)*
> *makAra* - the letter '*m*'
> *prAj~na* – (is) *prAj~na*
> *suShupta sthAnaH* - the deep-sleep state
> *miteH* – because (it is like) a 'measure'
> *va* - or
> *apIteH* - on account of absorption.
> *ya evaM veda* - Whosoever knows this
> *ha vai* - verily
> *minoti sarvam* - measures everything
> *cha bhavati* - and becomes
> *apItiH* - (one who) understands.

The letter m, the third mAtra of OM, is prAj~na, the deep-sleep state because both have the characteristic of a measure and are as though absorbed into the final part. Whoever knows this will be able to assimilate and comprehend everything.

miti means a measure, and (according to Shankara) specifically refers to a utensil called a *prastha*, which is used for measuring quantities of (usually) barley or rice. The idea is that the grain is visible in, for example, a sack. You pour the grain into the measure and it (the grain) disappears from view. You take the measure over to the cooking pot and empty it in. The grain then 'reappears' in the pot.

Similarly, at the level of the individual (*vyaShTi*), the waking

288

and dream states as though disappear into the deep-sleep state, *prAj~na* or *laya* (the measure) and emerge once again at some later time. In the deep-sleep state, all the waking or dream state attributes are resolved and we know nothing. We no longer believe ourselves to be a man or a woman, happy or sad, employed or unemployed, etc. But all the relevant characteristics reappear again when we wake up so that they did not actually disappear but were simply rendered unmanifest.

At the macrocosmic (*samaShTi*) level, the gross and subtle worlds (*virAT* and *hiraNyagarbha*) disappear at the end of creation (*pralaya*) into the causal state (*antaryAmin* or *Ishvara*) and reappear at the next creation. Obviously we have to take the scripture's word for this aspect! *m* thus represents the universe in its causal or potential state (i.e. prior to the Big Bang or after the Big Crunch).

In an analogous manner, the sounds *a* and *u*, when chanting OM, disappear when we close the mouth and only the *m* sounds. But they re-appear when the mouth is opened again and the mantra is next sounded.

The word *apIti* means 'becoming one' and refers to the aspect whereby the waking and dream states are both effectively absorbed into deep sleep. It means 'getting merged or united in'. They become an amorphous 'mass of consciousness' (the *prAjnAnaghana* of mantra 4). Similarly, all sounds become the single sound *m* when the mouth is closed.

When this is known and understood, we also are better able to 'measure' or discriminate and ascertain the value of things. Shankara says that we realize ourselves as *Ishvara*, the cause of the universe.

Swami Muni Narayana Prasad points out (Ref. 38) that the benefit of understanding this mantra can be explained as 'seeing oneself in everything and everything in the Self'. *Atman* is the 'measure' of everything (in both the gross and subtle worlds). I.e. one can see everything as non-different from oneself.

Everything merges into the Self in *prAj~na* and there is then only the Self.

Mantra 12

अमात्रश्चतुर्थोऽव्यवहार्यः प्रपञ्चोपशमः शिवो ।आद्वैत
एवमोङ्कार ।
आत्मैव संविशत्यात्मनाऽ ।आत्मनं य एवं वेद य एवं वेद ॥ १२ ॥

amAtrashchaturtho.avyavahAryaH prapa~nchopashamaH
shivo.Advaita
evamo~NkAra .
Atmaiva saMvishatyAtmanA.a.AtmanaM ya evaM veda ya evaM
veda || 12 ||

    chaturtha - The fourth (aspect)
    o~NkAra - *of the syllable OM*
    amAtra – (has) no parts (i.e. is limitless);
    avyavahArya - (is) transcendental (not at the level of empirical transactions),
    prap~nchopashamam - has no phenomenal existence,
    shivaH - is 'all bliss'
    Advaita - (and) non-dual.
    Atma eva - (It is therefore) verily the Self.
    ya evaM veda - Whosoever knows this
    saMvishati atAnaM - merges his self
    AtmanA - into the Self.

The fourth aspect of OM is silence. It is transcendental, without any worldly existence, blissful and non-dual; it is the Self. Whoever knows this realizes his oneness with the Self. Whoever knows this. (This last bit is repeated to emphasize the supreme importance of this pursuit and to leave the reader with this thought as the last statement of the Upanishad. Many of the translations and commentaries omit the repetition for some reason.)

    Just like *turIya*, *amAtra* cannot be described. Any word spoken

would immediately destroy the silence! The identity is emphasized here by using the same words to refer to *amAtra* as were
used in the 7th *mantra* with reference to *turIya*. Both are without
attributes – *nirguNa*; blissful – *shivam*; and non-dual – *Advaitam*.
The three states are associated with their respective universes of
objects: gross, subtle and causal (unmanifest). The three *mAtra*-s
are the 'names' which refer to those universes and observers.
Both *turIya* and *amAtra* are described as *prapa~nchopashama*.
Whereas *turIya* has nothing to do with the worlds of objects,
amAtra has nothing to do with the names (sounds) that refer to
those objects.

There is an implicit reference to the *vAchArambhanaM* sutras
in Chandogya Upanishad again here. (See earlier discussion.) The
sounds are the names of the objects and *amAtra*, the witness of
the sounds is *turIya*, the witness of the three states. Shankara says
that the cause of both speech and mind is ignorance and, since
there is no ignorance in *Atma*, it is not possible either to
comprehend it (*Atma*) or speak about it. Anandagiri clarifies this
by pointing out that 'speech' means 'naming', *abhidhAna*, and
'mind' means 'object', *abhidheya*. *"...for there is no object apart from
mind – they arise because of ignorance, and when ignorance ceases to
exist – speech and mind, the name and the nameable objects all
disappear"* (Ref. 2).

As a result of investigating into the nature of the Self and
analyzing OM, we can come to the realization that everything can
be negated except Consciousness, the witness of all. Just as there
is no bangle, chain or ring, but only gold, so there is no waker,
dreamer or deep-sleeper, only *turIya*. And, once the objects have
been nullified, the words have no further relevance and can also
be dropped. So we are left with only silence and the ever-present
witness of that silence. (Remember the quotation of Shankara
given in the analysis of the first mantra: *"the necessity of understanding their identity arises from the fact that (once this identity is
established,) one can by a single effort eliminate both the name and the*

nameable to realize brahman that is different from all.")

Thus, the benefit of meditation on *amAtra* is ultimately that there is release from *saMsAra*, i.e. no rebirth. The causal element for the gross and subtle aspects is held in *prAj~na*. Once the three states are as though 'merged' into *turIya*, there is no longer any 'seed' (*bIja*) for the 'sprout' (*a~Nkura*) of rebirth. (Gaudapada uses this metaphor in I.13.)

Shankara says that *OM* known in this way has 3 *mAtra*-s and 3 *pAda*-s and that therefore *OM is Atma*.

The message of this Upanishad is further explored by the *kArikA*-s in the first chapter, *AgAma prakAraNa*, and these aspects are covered in the main text.

Appendix 2 – Other States of Consciousness

The Mandukya Upanishad, together with the explanatory *kArikA*-s from Gaudapada have shown that the common, so-called 'states of consciousness' are *mithyA* and our true nature is *turIya* or *brahman*. It is therefore superfluous to consider more, possible states. Nevertheless, it is very possible that you will want to ask questions about other conditions that you might think qualify as states of consciousness. What about the 'hypnotic state' or the state 'experienced' under general anesthesia for example? Accordingly, the following discussion is included 'for interest'.

It is true that most of the scriptures refer to the three states already discussed. These three states are *mithyA* and the reality underlying them is called *turIya*. In the *tattva bodha* (attributed to Shankara), the question is asked: *avasthAtrayaM kim?* – What are the three states? Admittedly, this seems to be presupposing the answer but the answer is given: *jAgratsvapnasuShuptyavasthAH* – they are the waking, dream and deep sleep states – *jAgrat, svapna* and *suShupti*. And it goes on to explain each in turn.

But most seekers will be well aware of the practice of *adhyAropa-apavAda*. Whenever we are told that X is the Advaitin's answer to a particular question, it is quite likely that, when we look into the question more deeply, we will be given a different answer. There is one answer for the beginner and one for the advanced student. And maybe several in between ones, too! This was encountered in the main text in respect of the teaching about creation.

So what other possible states are there?

One of the great champions of Shankara – Sri Swami Satchidanandendra Saraswati (SSSS) – gives two possible answers: '2' and 'invalid'. [This occurs in his book *pa~nchapAdikA chintAmani*, which was written in Kannada but translated, or freely rendered into English, by his pupil D. B. Gangolli. This book is very difficult to obtain, since only 1000 copies were printed in 1986. It is called 'The Magic Jewel of Intuition (The Tri-basic Method of Cognizing the Self)' (Ref. 24). This is a fascinating book, although one which is difficult to read, since it was not edited and Sri Gangolli's command of the English language was not brilliant.]

In answering the question 'How many states?', he first points out that we should consider all the possibilities if the answer is to be final. Accordingly, he mentions wishful thinking, intoxication, insanity, fainting, delirium, sleep-walking, coma, semi-consciousness (just waking up but not quite made it yet – we all recognize this!), unconsciousness, hypnotic trance, samAdhi, mokSha and death. We could argue that these other states are not like waking, dream or deep sleep so ought to be examined.

His first point is that, when we see people in the above conditions, their symptoms are part of our waking state. If something belongs to the world as we see it, then it belongs to the waking state, since the two go together. If there is a state in which we have no knowledge of the world then it is equivalent to the deep sleep state. In fact, we could argue that there are only two states – one in which we experience something external and one in which we do not. Then, waking and dream collapse into a single state and deep sleep is the second state. Wishful thinking and madness would then belong to the first state; deep sleep, unconsciousness, samAdhi, and any other state in which there is no consciousness of anything external, belong to the second state.

Death, he says, is not really a state at all. Our waking state sees other people die but we have no data concerning our own death at this time, so cannot reasonably consider it at all. For seekers, the same applies to mokSha, by definition. And we cannot conceive of any experience other than 'with external knowledge' and 'without external knowledge'.

He then goes on to point out that we cannot describe any sort of 'relationship' between the states, because in order for there to be any sense of one being a cause, and another being an effect, they would have to exist within a common time frame. This they clearly do not, since a dream may encompass years of experience, yet we may return to the waking state to find that only minutes of waking time have elapsed. There is no common time frame in which the concept of causality could have meaning. Therefore, there is no question of any relationship between the states. Rather it is the case that the non-dual reality 'manifests' as the states and each state is nothing but the entire reality. Accordingly, it is the world that appears in the state and not vice versa.

Furthermore, the very idea that there are three states is one that is formed from the vantage point of the waking state. Since it has already been pointed out that the states cannot have any cause-effect relationship because they do not share common time or space, it makes no sense to speak of a 'number' of states at all. We cannot, from the waking state, justly speak of other states at all in relation to ourselves. And, as pointed out above, the supposed states of other people are all part of our waking world only.

He also uses the rope-snake metaphor to conclude that the three states are not really there at all. The rope might be misperceived as a snake, a stream of water or a crack in the ground. When it is seen as one, it is not simultaneously seen as another and, when the reality of the rope is realized, none of the others are seen. Similarly, we are never simultaneously awake and asleep and, on enlightenment, we see everything as *brahman*. Accordingly, the very notion of counting the number of states is something that only has relevance in the waking state.

The State of Swoon, Faint or Coma

vyAsa, on the other hand, in the Brahma Sutra effectively answers '5' to the question of 'how many states are there?'. The states are: waking, dreaming, deep sleep, coma and death. BS III.2.10

considers whether coma (referred to as 'swoon', *mUrChA*) is justified as being a separate state or not. The commentary below is based on the *bhAShya* of Shankara (e.g. see http://www. bharatadesam.com/spiritual/brahma_sutra/brahma_sutra_sanka ra_38113.php). The argument is that coma cannot be considered to be the same as the waking state because, in it, we do not experience any external world. Similarly, it cannot be the same as the dreaming state because we do not experience any internal world. Finally, it cannot be the same as the deep sleep state for several reasons. Sleep is a natural process and its cause is both natural and healthy. We feel happy and refreshed when we come out of a deep sleep. None of these apply to a coma – when we go into a coma, we call for a doctor (or, to be more accurate, someone else does)! In fact, we may well call for a doctor if we *cannot* go to sleep; i.e. we are worried by the *presence* of coma or the *absence* of sleep.

Even the appearance of the person differs. In deep sleep, the features and body will be relaxed, whereas in a coma or faint, the whole body maybe in spasm with labored breathing etc. and the eyes may be open. We can usually awaken the sleeping person quite easily, whereas it may well prove impossible to awaken someone from a coma. Finally, everyone goes to sleep on a regular basis (some more than others) whereas, for most people, unconsciousness is not at all a regular occurrence and is usually caused by some external event, such as a blow to the head.

The question is also asked as to whether *mUrChA* could be included in the state of death (*mAraNa*). The answer to this is also 'no'. Although we may be unconscious, activities of heart, lungs and brain still continue albeit perhaps at a reduced rate. In death, these all cease completely, never to be resumed in that body. And, it is quite normal for the *jIva* to resume life in the same body, even after a prolonged, comatose state. After *mAraNa*, however the *jIva* returns to life in a new body (according to traditional Advaita). If the *jIva* returned to the same body, the state

cannot have been the same as death, because of the very definition of the word.

The actual sutra is *mugdhe.arddhasampattiH parisheShAt*, which
is translated by Swami Sivananda: *In a swoon (in him who is
senseless) there is half union on account of this remaining (as the only
alternative left, as the only possible hypothesis).* So *vyAsa* concludes
that this state is effectively half deep-sleep and half death, i.e. it
is half-union with *brahman*. It can be considered as the doorway
to death. If there is remaining *prArabdha karma*, then the person
will return to consciousness; if not he will die. Shankara
concludes that it is a valid state, although it only happens
occasionally but, since it is a mixture of the two states of deep
sleep and death, it cannot be considered as a separate state.

Lucid Dreaming

This is the situation in which I am dreaming but suddenly *realize*
that I am dreaming. I am then able to manipulate the dream
consciously in whatever way I wish. Most people have probably
not experienced this and may view it with suspicion but I can
confirm that this really is the case. Having read a little on the
subject, it seems that one can actually train oneself to increase the
frequency of lucid dreaming also. But there is no new state here,
according to Advaita. It can be considered as being a special case
of the dream state.

The 'world' that exists for the lucid dreamer is still a mind-
generated one. It is just that the mind is now able to play some
conscious part in the creation of this world and influence the
'actions' of the dream-self. There is no consciousness of the
external, gross universe and the physical body remains in its
relatively inert state, apart from (one presumes) its rapid eye
movements or other characteristics of dream activity (e.g. brain
wave patterns) as perceived by another waker.

There are some claims to experience of lucid dreams in which
the dreamer has access to waking memories, which can be

consulted while the dream is taking place – these are called 'fully lucid'. And, in so-called 'super lucid' dreams, one can dispel the current dream completely and direct the mind to other pursuits, such as consulting Shankara on the subject of lucid dreams, for example!

One could therefore argue that the extremes of lucid dreaming do involve the 'waker' and could be considered to be a mixture of waking and dream states. Even so, these would still fall into the realm of what is referred to in the seventh mantra as *ubhayataHpraj~naM*. And it is pointed out there that the fourth – *turIya* – is not this either.

Any state that we could conceive would still be merely a superimposition upon *Atman* and would be *mithyA* only. *Atman* is always the substrate, and is the only reality.

Appendix 3 – chidAbhAsa

The essay below was originally published on the Advaita
Academy website, http://advaita-academy.org.

The 'real I' Verses the 'Presumed I' – An Examination of chidAbhAsa

Ramana Maharshi's instruction to seekers to ask themselves 'Who
am I?' is lauded by many modern Western teachers as sufficient,
on its own, to lead to enlightenment. I suggest that this is not
strictly true; that what it can do is rather to give us insight into
what we are not and thereby point us in the direction of traditional teachings to learn about our real nature. It is inciting us to
conduct Self-inquiry in the proven manner, i.e. by listening to a
qualified teacher interpret the scriptures, rather than merely
providing a mantra or formula to provide an answer directly.

An explanation of how traditional teaching can lead us to an
understanding of who I am might begin with an analysis of our
three states of consciousness – this is the so-called *avasthA traya
prakriyA* of traditional Advaita.

We almost certainly begin with the belief that who-I-really-am
is only fully present in the waking state. In the dream state, I am
not in command of my mental faculties so that the mind 'free-
wheels' outside of my control even though I am not actually
unconscious. And we no doubt accept the deep sleep state as one
in which mind and body rest and recuperate in order to be ready
for the trials that the next day may bring. According to this interpretation, consciousness in deep sleep is in a resting state, as
indicated by the lowered activity shown by EEG displays. (This
view, also supported by many Western philosophers, claims that
consciousness is a by-product or 'epiphenomenon' of the brain;
an evolutionary advantageous development to enable an animal
to find food and mate more efficiently than before. This is also the

view of the *chArvAka-s* or materialists of thousands of years ago – it is certainly not new!)

But the way that the *mANDUkya upaniShad* and other scriptures view the three states is quite different. The waker-I, or *vishva*, is the name given to Consciousness identified with the gross body, when it is functioning in the external world. The physical senses are turned outwards and we believe that 'I' am the gross, material body.

When dreaming, this body is absent. Instead, our minds conjure up an entirely new, dream world, in which we have a new dream body which may be quite different from our own. This world has its own rules of time and space and the events may contravene all rules of waking physics. The dreamer-I is given the name *taijasa*; Consciousness is identified with the subtle objects of the mind. The physical senses are inoperative and attention is turned inward.

In deep sleep, neither physical nor subtle bodies are evident. We are aware of nothing and it may seem that we only infer that there was something still present after we wake up and see that waking time has elapsed. The deep-sleeper-I is called *prAj~na* and our knowledge is said to be resolved into an undifferentiated state of Consciousness. But Consciousness is not absent during deep sleep; rather it is aware of nothing. And this is quite different.

The *bRRihadAraNyaka upaniShad* (IV.iii.23) states: *"That it does not see in that state is because, though seeing then, it does not see; for the vision of the witness cannot be lost, because it is imperishable. But there is not that second thing separate from it which it can see."* [1] I.e. the reason that we are not aware of anything in deep sleep is simply that there is nothing to be aware *of*. In the waking state the senses are aware of external objects; in the dream state, the 'dream senses' are aware of the 'dream objects' of the mind. In deep sleep, all these are resolved and there are no objects of any kind.

It seems that, being conscious of nothing, I am effectively not there at all. Advaita tells us that this is certainly not the case. When we say that 'I was not there', the 'I' that was absent is the ego. Identification of my true self with the body-mind takes place in the mind so that, since the mind is inactive during deep sleep, there is no identification.

Sureshvara says in his *naiShkarmya siddhi* (II.54): "*One who wakes up from deep sleep says 'I did not know anything in sleep'. Here the term 'I' signifies the pure Self as the ego is suspended in sleep. When we say that the iron burns, we mean that fire, by which the iron has become red-hot, burns, and not the iron as such. Similarly in the sentence, 'I am brahman', the term 'I' signifies the Self and not the Ego.*" [2]

Even after hearing an explanation such as this, it does not alter our experience. We still feel as though this body-mind-ego that I think of as my 'self' is alive and conscious in its own right, as it were. How can it be that the Consciousness that we are – the real 'I' – is actually *brahman*, and therefore not different from the Consciousness that you are?

Shankara uses the metaphor of the sun sending its light out in all directions. We need not be able to see the sun itself to know that it exists because, everything that we see, we see only by virtue of the sunlight reflected from it. Suppose that we are floating in the emptiness of space, with no objects, no planets or other opaque material, within the range of our eyes. If we were facing away from the sun then we would see only blackness. Although the light from the sun continues to stream outwards, there is nothing to illumine so that nothing is seen. And so it is with deep sleep. Although consciousness is still present (after all, it is our true nature), the mind and senses are effectively 'switched off'. Consciousness itself is aware of nothing. It is the reflected consciousness in the mind that perceives objects via the senses. Since these are inactive, we are not aware of anything. But Consciousness is still there, as we realize on awakening because we know that we were aware of nothing whilst we were in the deep sleep state. This is why the Self is called the eternal witness or *sAkshI*; its 'light' is still there even in deep sleep.

So where does this leave us in respect of answering the question 'Who am I?'? The answer is provided by an Advaita concept called *chidAbhAsa* and an extension of the above metaphor. The word *chit* refers to consciousness and *AbhAsa* means "semblance, phantom, phantasm of the imagination; mere appearance, fallacious appearance; reflection; or simply image". *chidAbhAsa* (when the words join, the 't' converts to a 'd') therefore means the 'reflection, image or false appearance of Consciousness'.

Suppose that we have a dark, shuttered room. It is so dark that we are unable to find anything inside it. We are only able to open the door and, although there is bright sunlight outside, this does not penetrate far enough to illumine the interior. There is no electricity and I do not have a torch. I do, however, have a mirror. By positioning myself in the doorway, I can hold the mirror at such an angle that the sunlight reflects in the mirror and illumines the contents of the room. Although the mirror is itself inert, having no light of its own, it becomes a source of light by virtue of reflecting the light from the sun, which does have its own light. This, of course, is also how we get the moonlight by which we can see during the night, when there is a moon in a cloudless sky. The light of the moon is simply the reflected light of the sun.

The parallel can now be made with our own inert equipments and Consciousness. *Bbrahman* is the equivalent of the sun, the only true 'source' of Consciousness. *Bbrahman* 'illumines' the instrument of the mind, which itself is not a source of Consciousness. But, by virtue of this illumination, the mind is able to reflect the Consciousness via the senses into the 'room' of the world and become aware of the objects therein and interact with them (including the body-mind itself).

Furthermore, when we see an object, we register the object itself (i.e. its name, form and attributes) but rarely think that this is only possible because light is being reflected off it from an external source. Similarly, in respect of our actual awareness of objects or of our own body and mind, we register *that* we are aware of something but not that *by which* we are aware, i.e. Consciousness itself. Once I have acknowledged that my feeling of being an aware, conscious being is because Consciousness is reflecting in my (independently) inert mind, I can also acknowledge that it is the same Consciousness reflecting in other independently inert minds that gives the impression of other people.

The 'reflection' theory (or *pratibimba vAda*) was fully developed post-Shankara by the *vivaraNa* school of philosophy as opposed to the theory of 'limitation' or *upAdhi-s* (known as *avachCheda vAda*), which belongs to the *bhAmatI* school. But the origins of both can be found in Shankara's own writing and, in particular, the reflection metaphor is found in his commentary or *bhAShya* on Brahma Sutra II.3.50 (*AbhAsa eva cha*). Shankara says on this:

The individual soul is not directly the highest Atman, because it is seen to be different on account of the upAdhi-s; *nor is it different from the* Atman, *because it is the* Atman *who has entered as the* jIvAtman *in all the bodies. We may call the* jIva *as a mere reflection of the* Atman. *But just as when one image of the sun in some water trembles, the other image in other portions of water need not, even so if one soul is connected with actions and fruits thereof, the others need not be so connected. So there would be no confusion. And, as the reflection itself is the effect of* avidyA, *the whole of the* saMsAra *as connected with this reflection is also the effect of* avidyA. *Naturally, with the destruction of the* avidyA *there will be the destruction of the so-called reflection of the* Atman *on buddhi, and the consequent justification of the instruction that the soul is nothing but the* brahman.[3]

There are many reflections, *jIva-s* or *chidAbhAsa-s* ['reflections of consciousness'], but only one 'original Consciousness', *bimba chaitanya*. The *pratibimba* or reflection is the 'I' that we start off presuming ourselves to be. But this is only the empirical or *vyAvahArika* reflection, otherwise known as the ego or *ahaMkAra*. The real, or *pAramArthika* Consciousness or *chit* on which it is founded – its *adhiShThAna* – is the *sAkshI chaitanya*, the 'witness' Consciousness. And it is this which is the real 'I'. We are the sun, not its reflection in the mind-mirror of the *jIva*. (N.B. Swami Paramarthananda, commenting on Brahma Sutra II.3.49, points out that the metaphor should not be taken too literally – there is no physical separation between Consciousness and its *AbhAsa*, unlike the distance between the sun and mirror.)

The *pa~nchadashI* states that (VII.29) "*chidAbhAsa* with his mind devoted to the worldly existence does not know that he is the self-evident *kUTastha*." [4] Because our attention is constantly turned outwards, it never occurs to us that who-we-think-we-are is not this 'as-if' separate, but actually only reflected, 'individual' consciousness but the immovable, unchanging, absolute spirit (*kUTastha* literally means 'standing at the top'). What happens is that this truth is obscured by ignorance and, instead, we super-impose other ideas such as 'I am the doer, enjoyer' etc.

Accordingly, in the progression of asking 'Who am I?' we start off by believing we are the ego or, we might say, the *ahaMkAra* 'supported by' *sAkshI*. In the end we realize that 'I am the *sAkshI* functioning through the *ahaMkAra*'. The thinking or speaking of this at all, of course, requires both aspects. I am *chidAbhAsa* from the *vyAvahArika* perspective but *chit* from the *pAramArthika*. Without the *sAkshI* Consciousness, the *ahaMkAra* is inert; without the mental equipments, Consciousness does not think or speak, like the sun in deep space metaphor. Whilst we remain identified with the reflection, we continue to believe that we are mortal and limited. As soon as we realize ourselves to be the original, we recognize that we are eternal and forever free.

1. The bRRihadAraNyaka upaniShad, with the Commentary of shaMkarAchArya, Translated by Swami Madhavananda, Advaita Ashrama, 1934. ISBN 81-7505-102-7.
2. naiShkarmya siddhi of Sri sureshvarAchArya, English translation by S. S. Raghavachar, Pasaranga University of Mysore, 1965. No ISBN.
3. Vedanta Explained: Shankara's Commentary on The Brahma Sutras, Volume II, V. H. Date, Munishiram Manharlal Publisher Pvt. Ltd., 1954. No ISBN.
4. pa~nchadashI of Sri Vidyaranya Swami, Translated by Swami Swahananda, Sri Ramakrishna Math, 1967. No ISBN.

The above essay was followed by a further, explanatory essay, also posted to Advaita Academy:

Back in March I wrote an article which looked into the concept of *chidAbhAsa*. This is the idea that the 'notion of I' is a reflection, in the mind, of the non-dual consciousness. The theory is called *pratibimba vAda* in Advaita. It says that there is only one 'real', *pAramArthika* or witnessing Consciousness, although there are many jIva-s; one 'original' (*bimba*) and many 'reflections' (*prati-bimba-s*).

But of course, reality is non-dual, so it makes no sense to talk of a 'Consciousness' *and* a 'reflected Consciousness'! So how do we explain this? In order for there to be a reflection, there have to be two things: an original thing, and some medium in which a reflection can take place. This is obvious in the case of the mirror. We cannot see our face in order to be able to shave or apply make-up by looking into empty space. We cannot even do it by looking at a blank wall. There has to be a mirror or some reflecting medium which can serve as a mirror. Here, we seem to be saying that there is Consciousness *and* a reflecting medium – the mind. But of course if we have these two things, then we're talking about dvaita not Advaita.

Shankara's Advaita introduces the concept of *mAyA* to provide a sort-of explanation for the world-appearance but the Dvaitin may argue that, pedantically, *brahman* and *mAyA* are still two things. Only if we can explain everything in terms of *paramArtha* alone, he might say, can we establish non-duality. Of course, we can be pedantic too – you cannot explain anything in *paramArtha*, only in *vyavahAra*! But we acknowledge that *mAyA* is *mithyA*. In reality, there are no *jIva-s*, no world, no reflections. So, the bottom line is that reality is non-dual, so that we do not really have to justify the theory at all!

But there are useful things to be learned from this criticism. A reflection can only occur if there are two things, namely something having a definite form plus a separate physical medium (with reflecting properties). The Sanskrit for something having 'form', or attributes, is *saguNa*. And yet we (i.e. the Advaitin) state that Consciousness or *brahman* is formless, *nirguNa*. And clearly the mind, which we say is the reflecting medium, is also formless. So how can we get a reflection of something which is formless in a medium which is also formless?

The reply is that we cannot! And a careful restatement of the theory (unfortunately, we are so often a bit careless when we use metaphors!) is that the *chidAbhAsa* is not *actually* a reflection; it is *like* a reflection. Many of the usual similes that we use in the English language function in this way. When we say that something (or someone) is 'as hard as nails', we do not really mean that it (he or she) has a sharp point and can easily be driven into wood; we mean that they are very resistant to damage (literally or, if a person, emotionally). Or if someone is as 'busy as a bee', we do not expect to find them collecting pollen from flowers from dawn till dusk but we do not usually find them lazing around doing nothing.

Swami Paramarthananda, in his talks on the Brahma Sutras (3.2.20 – 1), lists five ways in which *chidAbhAsa* is like a reflection:

- When we see a reflection, it is always in a particular place, such as a mirror, a pool of water, a shop window etc. Similarly, Consciousness always 'occurs' in a body, such that scientists even think that it is a property of the body! (Yet we never conclude that our face is actually 'in' the shaving mirror or that the sun is literally 'in' the pond.)

- The reflection itself has distinct similarities with the original. The make-up mirror is an obvious example. There was also the example that I gave in the linked article above of using a mirror to reflect the sun into a dark place; i.e. the reflection has similar properties to the original. We can also use a mirror to start a fire by focusing the reflection, so the reflection has properties of both heat and light (though obviously not to the same degree!) And Advaita tells us that the Consciousness in the body is 'similar to' 'real Consciousness'. (In fact, of course, it is the same, but that is even better than similar!)

- We know from the example of the shaving or make-up mirror that a dirty mirror does not function so well as a clean, polished one. And if we look into a distorting mirror, our image is distorted. So it is apparent that a reflection takes on some of the attributes of the reflecting medium. Similarly, Consciousness pervades the body; as the body grows, Consciousness effectively grows with it. A new reflection appears when a pond is formed after heavy rain and that in a mirror disappears when the mirror breaks. So a reflection is subject to creation and destruction, dependent on the reflecting medium. Similarly, Consciousness in the *jIva* is born with, and dies with the body.

- A reflection is obviously less real than the original – fortunately, as the earth would not survive for an instant if all of the reflected suns were as real as the sun itself! Similarly, the 'individual' Consciousness is less real than the non-dual, *pAramArthika* Consciousness itself. In fact, both the reflected sun and the *jIva* are *mithyA*. They are not 'unreal', but their reality is dependent upon the original, which is the only reality or *satyam*.

- Although the reflection may be *mithyA*, it nevertheless has utility – otherwise no one would ever buy a shaving mirror! In fact, as Swami Paramarthananda points out (possibly disturbingly), *only* the *mithyA* has utility – *brahman* itself is quite useless! And, of course, we know that Consciousness in our body has utility – I am typing this, you are reading it for starters, both impossible without the reflected consciousness.

And now we can return to the distinction between *saguNa* and *nirguNa*. At the microcosmic or *vyaShTi* level, the individuated consciousness is called the *jIva*; at the macrocosmic or *samaShTi* level, it is called Ishvara. Both are 'with form', *saguNa*, or reflections of Consciousness. And, as has been explained above, both must be *mithyA*. Only the original, formless, *nirguNa* Consciousness is *satyam*. Just as only the original sun is real, while all its reflections, whether in the ocean or in a drop of water, are *mithyA*.

Incidentally, in case you hadn't made the connection, the name we give to the medium in which the metaphorical reflection of Consciousness takes place is *upAdhi*.

Appendix 4 – manonAsha

manonAsha – Not the Literal Death of the Mind

Most seekers who have investigated the teaching of Ramana to even a small extent will be aware of the concept of *manonAsha*. This is often presented as the idea that enlightenment is synonymous with the 'death of the mind'. And indeed this is its literal meaning. Consequently, some writers claim that, following enlightenment, the *j~nAnI* literally no longer has a mind. This goes along with similar ideas such as that, for the *j~nAnI*, the world literally no longer exists.

This way of thinking is unfortunate. Shankara himself emphasized that we should not discount either our experience or reason, when it comes to interpreting the scriptures. And, speaking for myself, whenever I have encountered writings on Advaita which significantly contradicted my perception of what seemed to be 'reasonable', they have always proved to be misguided or incomplete, if not plain wrong (or, of course, I misunderstood what they were saying!).

And so it is in this case. Reason tells us that a *j~nAnI* would not be able to operate – move, eat, speak and so on – without a mind. There would be no motivation to do so either. And since there are no others, and no world, why and how would he teach? This is the *reductio ad absurdum* argument but, if we allow this (and of course the adherents of the mistaken view do not), then how can we understand the concept? What exactly can Ramana have meant when he used the term?

Ramana is perfectly well aware that, from the standpoint of absolute reality, there is only *brahman*. So there cannot be a mind (or body). Therefore the mind cannot be destroyed, since it never really existed to begin with. Despite this awareness, Ramana still uses the word *manonAsha*, so he must necessarily be speaking from the standpoint of empirical reality – our everyday experience of the world-appearance. But even here it cannot be taken literally.

At the level of *paramArtha* (absolute reality), it is the *Atman* that is actionless, not the body-mind (there isn't one!). If we are attempting to speak at the *pAramArthika* level, then all we can say is that there is only *brahman*. (Even that is saying too much!) And at the *vyAvahArika* level, even the enlightened have minds, walk and talk. Anyone who claims otherwise is misrepresenting the fundamentals of Advaita. Everyone is really Consciousness functioning through the reflecting medium of the mind. The simple difference between a *j~nAnI* and an *aj~nAnI* is that the *j~nAnI* knows this to be so. Outwardly, they remain the same, from the point of view of either.

A ratification of this point of view can be found by looking at the Bhagavad Gita: *The balanced person who knows the truth thinks: 'I do nothing at all; it is only the senses relating to their sense objects,' even whilst seeing, hearing, touching, smelling, eating, going, sleeping, breathing, speaking, excreting or grasping; even just opening or closing the eyes* (chapter 5, verses 8-9).

Anyone who has read my *Book of One* may recall that this is one of my favorite quotations, brought to mind especially when cycling up hills! I go on to say:

The Self is that which is behind everything but itself does nothing. The Kena Upanishad speaks of it at length: *'By whom commanded and directed does the mind go towards its objects? Commanded by whom does the life force, the first cause move? At whose will do men utter speech? Which power directs the eye and the ear? It is the ear of the ear, the mind of the mind, the speech of the speech, the life of the life, the eye of the eye. ...There the eye does not go, nor speech, nor mind. We do not know That; we do not understand how it can be taught. It is distinct from the known and also It is beyond the unknown.'* (Ref. 72)

The Self is the reality behind all appearances, itself unknowable. It does nothing, but all apparent activity takes place through its power and against its background. We are the Consciousness, which, by virtue of this body-mind instrument, is capable of seeing, hearing, speaking etc. The body-mind sees, hears, speaks and acts but 'we' do not. Everything takes place within this awareness; but the awareness itself, which is what we truly are, is beyond all movement, beyond space and time. (Ref. 77)

Despite all of this 'doing' that seems to be taking place, the *j~nAnI* knows that he is the Self, who does not do anything. He knows that the body carries on 'doing', even if only breathing and circulating the blood. But he has the knowledge that 'I am not the body or mind'; 'I am that by virtue of which they are able to function'. The identification – *ahaMkAra* – has been 'destroyed' as a result of Self-knowledge.

'Who-we-really are' is the Self, Consciousness or *brahman*. There is no such thing as a body or mind in reality and the 'I' does nothing. There are only the ever changing forms, whose substratum is always *brahman* only. And the key difference between the realized man and the 'ordinary person' is that the former knows this to be so. He knows that '(in reality) I do nothing at all' and, to return to the topic of this article, '(in reality) my mind has no absolute existence: without consciousness, it is as good as dead.' It is alright to leave out those repeated phrases in brackets... but only so long as you understand what is being said.

In the Gita (II.54), the first question which Arjuna asks of Krishna is to describe to him how an enlightened person behaves. (Such a person he calls a *sthitapraj~na* – a man of 'steady wisdom' or firm knowledge; one whose mind remains established in the Self – *samAdhisthasya*. Shankara clarifies that *sthita* means 'well-established' and *praj~na* is the knowledge relating to the ability to discriminate between *Atma* and *anAtma*.) Krishna spends the rest of the chapter (II.55 – 72) answering the question. His first statement (II.55) points directly to the key element of this problem. He says that the enlightened person is one who ignores, or is not in any way distracted by those desires which *arise in the mind* (*manogata*); i.e. such a person still has desires and, more specifically germane to this article, he or she also has a mind in which those desires arise. The desire of Krishna, for example, was to relieve Arjuna of his angst on the battlefield.

So the realized person still has desires but, as they arise in his mind, he is no longer attached to them and is able to let them go without their distracting him. Whereas the ordinary person relies upon the satisfaction of desires for his happiness, the realized man knows he is already complete and unlimited, no longer dependent upon acquisition of worldly things and the like for what could only ever be temporary satisfaction. The ordinary person can be said to be 'bound' by his desires and, if thwarted, they give rise to anger, delusion and ultimate destruction (II.62 – 63). On the other hand, the 'actions' of a realized person, who knows that he does not act, are non-binding.

It is attachment to external things, thinking that one is a doer and an enjoyer, which leads to desire and its dire consequences. This, in turn, is due to ignorance of one's true nature; knowing that one is everything, how could there be desire to attain anything? Accordingly, what we need to do is to negate all of these wrong ideas. What destroys ignorance is Self-knowledge; we need to investigate the Self, via the unfolding of the scriptures through the skills of a qualified teacher. At its successful conclusion when the realization dawns, the mind (in the sense of the dominion of wrong ideas) is effectively destroyed. More specifically, it is the 'I notion' – 'I am this body', 'I am a teacher', etc. which goes. The *ahaMkAra* resolves into the truth of itself – *sat-chit-Ananda*, limitless Existence-Consciousness. Attachment ceases; desire no longer unbalances the mind. This, I suggest, is what is meant by the term *manonAsha*.

II.65 states that 'in tranquility' (i.e. at the dawn of enlightenment), all sorrows are destroyed. The word used here is *hAniH*, nominative singular of the feminine noun *hAni*, meaning 'destruction' or 'injury' (Ref. 73). Destroy the ignorance and the attachments, realize that I am not a doer or enjoyer, and the sorrows, too, are destroyed.

Swami Dayananda says, commenting on this verse:

...the mind of a person with self-knowledge stays. And because the knowledge stays, the mind no longer causes any problem. The knowledge stays because there is nothing to oppose or inhibit it. The mind of such a person becomes a useful instrument. Because the mind is tranquil, it no longer causes trouble. (Ref. 74)

The mind, though still very much present, is now an instrument rather than a controlling force. The dominion of the attachments and aversions (*raga-dveSha-s*) has been forever destroyed. As II.71 says: "*That man who, giving up all attachments, moves about desirelessly, without owning anything, and without egoism—he goes to peace.*" (Ref. 75)

Shankara elaborates on this:

That man of renunciation who, entirely abandoning all desires, goes through life contented with the bare necessities of life, who regards not as his even those things which are needed for mere bodily existence, who is not vain of his knowledge – such a man-of-steady-knowledge, who knows brahman, *attains peace, the end of all the misery of mundane existence. In short, he becomes* brahman. *(Ref. 76)*

manonAsha, then, refers to the figurative death of the *ahaMkAra*, the 'I thought' that identifies with body and mind etc. ('figurative' because there is not actually anything to die in reality). It is 'death' in the sense that this mistaken idea is dissolved as a result of gaining Self-knowledge. But it is a metaphorical death only. Rather, it should be said that the mind 'resolves' into *Atman*. Nothing actually changes, just as the appearance of the wave does not change once we realize that it is only water. The mistaken idea (that I am the body-mind) was in the mind and the Self-knowledge is also in the mind. This is the meaning of 'enlightenment': the event in time when the mind realizes that we are already free.

So it is not true to say that the 'destroyed' mind does not exist. What we should say is that the mind does not exist *separate from its substratum, brahman*. The mind is *mithyA*, as is everything else. *brahman* alone is real.

Appendix 5 – ITRANS

All that this appendix will attempt to do is to explain to you how to pronounce the Sanskrit words used in this book. They have been written (italicized in brackets after what is usually a poor attempt to render the word phonetically in English) in what is called transliterated form, using the ITRANS scheme. Avinash Chopde devised this scheme for use on the Internet. His software, and details about the system, may be downloaded from his website, http://www.aczone.com/itrans/. There already existed at least one widely used scheme for rendering Sanskrit letters in a 'Romanized' way. However, since this used symbols called macrons (lines above letters) and dots above and below letters, it was quite unsuitable for computer keyboards with basic letters and the normal fonts provided with word processors. Accordingly, this scheme uses only the usual letters of our alphabet, together with the occasional special character such as the tilde ~.

General

Sanskrit is an extremely interesting language. It is amazingly logical. There are lots of rules but, once you have learnt them, there are none of the tiresome exceptions found in most languages. Also, once you have learned how to pronounce a letter, it is *always* pronounced in that way. Unfortunately, simply learning the letters is not sufficient to enable you to look up words in the dictionary. Letter combinations can look quite different from the same letters on their own. Also words found in the scriptures usually consist of combinations of many separate words and, when words join, they often change. An example that you will have seen in the book is *sachchidAnanda*. If you did not know this word, you would have to know the rules of these combinations in order to be able to work out that the separate words of which this consists – *sat, chit* and *Ananda* – in order to be able to look them up. You can see that, when a word ending in t combines with one beginning with ch, the t also changes to a ch. And the t at the end of chit becomes a d. Accordingly, you will not find this word in the dictionary under 'sach' but just after 'sat'. This particular word is present in its complete form because it is in such common usage but infrequent combinations will not themselves be listed and you have to break them down into the individual words to find out the meaning. (This is known as euphony or *saMdhi*.)

Finally, it is interesting to note in passing that there is a close parallel between the structure of the language and the Advaita-related myth of the creation. Indeed, some schools of thought, notably in the North of India and Kashmir, believe that the universe was 'spoken' into existence. Though this 'primordial' language is beyond ordinary sound, Sanskrit is its earthly manifestation as it were and embodies many of the 'universal principles'. The language itself is believed to embody the truth of the unity of the Self. Since pure Advaita tells us that there is effectively no such thing as creation, the value of discussing these ideas is ultimately academic. Such studies can help prepare the mind to acknowledge those truths that remain forever beyond its grasp but they can also prove a hindrance. They have more appeal to those whose nature is inclined towards *bhakti yoga* rather than *j~nAna*.

The entire language evolves in an almost mathematical way from a fundamental sound. The laws governing the way that words are constructed, and the grammar used to join them, are strict. It is amazing that the language, though the most ancient known and no longer in general use, remains true to its original form and someone learning it now would be able to communicate perfectly well with someone speaking the language thousands of years ago.

The Five Basic Vowels

The first letter of the alphabet forms the fundamental sound from which all others are derived simply by moving the tongue and lips. It is made by opening the mouth wide and letting the vocal chords operate. The sound which emerges sounds like a cross between the short 'a' in cat and 'u' in but. It is written as '*a*' in ITRANS but the correct letter in the proper script, called *devanAgarI* (meaning city of the gods), is:

अ *a*

This is the first letter of the alphabet and the first vowel or, to use its correct term, *svara*, meaning sound. I will not show the Devanagari for any of the other letters for the reasons already discussed above. If the back of the tongue is now raised slightly towards the back of the roof of the mouth, keeping the front of the tongue down against the back of the lower teeth, and the same short movement of the vocal cord is made, a slightly different sound emerges. This sounds a bit like the short 'i' in bit. It is written as *i* in ITRANS.The next two vowels seem strange to Westerners but follow the logic of the development. The underlying sound for both of these is the *i* sound just covered but the tip of the tongue is first moved further forward in the mouth. If you raise the tip of the tongue until it is almost touching the roof of the mouth and then, make the 'i' sound as before, the next vowel sound emerges. Modern students often actually flick the tongue downwards as the sound is made so that the result sounds something like 'ri' in the word rip, though the rolling 'r' beginning is not clearly enunciated because the tongue never actually touched the roof of the mouth. However, strictly speaking this is not correct. It is written *RRi* in ITRANS (or, in old releases, *R^i*).

This procedure is repeated but now the tip of the tongue moves further forward still, to just behind the front teeth, before the 'i' is sounded. Again, modern speakers often flick the tongue up towards the roof and down so that the sound that actually comes out is 'lri'. Again, not strictly correct but it hardly matters since there is only one word in the language that uses this letter! It is written *LLi* in ITRANS (or, in old releases, *L^i*).

Continuing the development, the emphasis finally shifts to the lips (labial position), having begun in the throat (guttural position), moved to at the back of the mouth (palatal), then to the roof of the mouth (cerebral) and then the teeth (dental). If a circle is formed of the lips but without any tension and the basic sound is made, a short 'oo' sound comes out as in soot or cut. This is the last of the simple vowels, written *u*.

These five vowels with their characteristic mouth positions effectively head up the five main groups of consonants. Consonants all effectively still sound the basic 'a' but 'stop' it from coming out in that simple way by varying the position of the tongue and lips in the way dictated by the vowel at the head of the group.

The Long Vowels

The basic five vowels above are all *short* vowels – *hrasva*. This means that, when pronounced, the sound is made as short as possible whilst still being distinguishable – really quite short! Each of these vowels *can* be sounded long. The length is actually very precise. If the short form is treated as one measure, then the long form should be two measures. The long form is called *dIrgha*. In ITRANS, the vowel is shown as long either by putting two of them, as with the *ii* in *diirgha* or by capitalizing it thus: – *dIrgha*. The latter form has been used as standard in this book.

When the vowels become long, the pronunciation naturally changes slightly, too. Thus, the short *a* becomes *aa* or *A* and sounds like the 'a' in calm. The short *i* becomes *ii* or *I* and sounds like the double 'ee' sound in words like sleep. The short *RRi* becomes *RRI* (or *R^I* in old releases of ITRANS). Here there is no option of having two small i's. The *dIrgha* vowel is sounded as for the *hrasva* form but with the ending 'ee' instead of 'i'. Similarly, the short *LLi* becomes *LLI* (or *L^I* in the old releases of ITRANS) but, since there are no words at all known to contain it, this hardly seems to matter! Finally, short *u* becomes long *uu* or *U* and sounds like the double 'oo' in root.

The vowels can be sounded for longer than two measures, in which case they are called *pluta* – prolonged. In this case they are written with a number '3' below and just to the right of the letter, both in *devanAgarI* and in the Romanized version. This form cannot be represented in ITRANS.

The Compound Vowels

Now, if the sound *a* is made and continues to sound while the mouth is slowly closed, the sound made before the lips come together is *u*. If these two sounds are made together or, more practically speaking, if the sound corresponding to the mid-point between these two is made, the sound that emerges is *o* (as in 'boat'). This new letter is called a compound vowel. Similarly, when *a* combines with *i*, it forms the compound vowel *e*. If you sound a prolonged a_3, and then raise the back of the tongue towards the *i* position, but stop before you get there, you should hear the *e* sound. It's a bit like the 'a' in 'hate' but not as open as we would pronounce this. If, after making the above sound for *e*, you relax the tongue back towards the *a* position but again stop before you get there, there is another sound formed as a compound between *a* and *e* which sounds like the 'ie' in 'die'. It is written *ai*.

In a similar way to that described above, if the mouth moves from the *a* (open-mouthed) position to the *o* (partially closed) position but stops half-way, there is a sound similar to 'ow' in 'brown'. This is written *au* in ITRANS.

These, then are the fourteen vowels but there are two final letters to be added to complete the group of sixteen, so-called *mAtRRikA*. They are not really part of the alphabet but act as modifications to a preceding vowel. (Note that, because of this, if they are sounded as letters in their own right, they assume an 'a' before rather than after.)

The first of these is called an *anusvAra*. It is written as *M* and causes the preceding vowel to be sounded through the nose. The precise nasal sound is determined by the consonant that follows it, in that it uses the mouth position corresponding to that for the consonant so that the effect is something like the nasal consonant (*anunAsika*) described below.

The other special letter, not really part of the alphabet, also modifies the sound of the preceding vowel, is written *H* and it has the effect of adding a brief, breathing out, 'unvoiced' sound after the vowel. It is as though there were a word beginning with 'h' immediately following and you start to sound it as soon as you finish the preceding letter (i.e. without changing the mouth position) but then realize your mistake and stop before the word itself starts to sound. It is called a *visarga*.

So, to recap, the 16 vowels, or *mAtRRikA*, are as follows:

a   A   i   I   u   U   RRi   RRI   LLi   LLI   e   o   ai
au   aM   aH

The First Group of Consonants (Guttural)

The Sanskrit term for consonants is *vya~njana*, meaning a 'decoration' (of the basic vowel sound). Twenty-five of these are grouped in five sets of five 'underneath' the five basic vowels described above. They are formed by positioning the mouth (tongue or lips) in such a way as to 'stop' the sound of the vowel in some way. The first group uses the mouth position of the *a* sound for decorating. This all takes place at the back of the mouth where it becomes the throat – the 'guttural' position.

Strictly speaking it is not possible to pronounce a consonant on its own. It is in itself only a positioning of the mouth to 'stop' the sound made by a vowel. Accordingly, when speaking the alphabet, the sound of *a* is used by default after each letter. The first consonant of this group is written *k*, sounded (with *a*) 'ka' as in cat.

When talking about the letter on its own, the sound 'a' is automatically assumed after it, since it cannot be sounded on its own without a vowel. Clearly it could occur at the end of the word (as 'k' in 'rack' for example). In this case it would have an additional mark under the letter, called a 'halant', which means 'don't make any vowel sound after this'. This used to be written *k.h* – *.h* after any consonant in ITRANS means that it is followed by a halant and 'a' is not sounded after it. In fact, it is no longer necessary in ITRANS to do this – if the letter is written on its own, a halant is inserted automatically.

The second consonant in the guttural group is written *kh*. Its pronunciation is much like the preceding one but with the addition of a slight breathy sound caused by actually letting out some air immediately following the 'k' sound. It is often sounded as though it were 'k-h' in an imaginary word 'k-hat' but there is much too much emphasis in this – it is really more subtle. Consonants such as *k* are said to be 'with little breath' (*alpaprANa*) while ones like *kh* are 'with much breath' (*mahAprANa*).

The third in this group is written *g*, sounded 'g' as in gap (*alpaprANa*). The fourth is written *gh* and, like 'kh' is *mahAprANa* and sounds like 'gh' in doghouse.

The final consonant in this group is the first of the type mentioned briefly above – *anunAsika*, meaning that the sound is made through the nose. It is written ~*N*. There are four n-related sounds; hence the need for the tilde and capitalization. It has the sound of 'ng' made at the back of the throat and sounding through the nose, like 'sing' but with the ending further back in the throat like someone being strangled rather than singing!

The Second Group of Consonants (Palatal)

This second group forms the sounds in the back part of the mouth but not the throat. Based on the *i* vowel, these use the back of the tongue and the rear of the mouth; they are called 'palatal'. They follow the same pattern as the previous group (as do all five of these groups of consonants, you will be pleased to know!) in that the first and third members are *alpaprANa*, the second and fourth are *mahAprANa*, and the fifth is *anunAsika*. The first, then is written *ch* and is sounded like the 'cha' in chap but, whereas English pronounces this by using the *front* of the tongue near the *front* of the roof of the mouth, Sanskrit uses the *rear* parts.

The second character is written *Ch* (or *chh* in older versions). Since I have already said that the pattern of the first group is repeated in the others, you might guess that this is sounded pretty much like *ch* but with some added breath – and you would be right! Just remember not to make it too pronounced so that it comes out like 'ch-ha' and it should be fine.

The third is written *j* and pronounced more or less as would expect, like the 'ja' in 'jam' spoken as far back in the mouth as you can without injuring yourself. It uses minimum breath again as for all in this third 'row' of the main consonants. The fourth is written *jh* and you can work out now how it should sound – like 'j-ha' but not too much so.

The final letter in this group the second of the *anunAsika* characters (the 'n' type sounds made through the nose). It is written ~n and has a sort of 'ny' sound, as in canyon. However, whereas the latter is made by the front of the tongue at the front of the mouth, you have to try to make this sound with the back of the tongue at the rear of the mouth.

The Third Group of Consonants (Cerebral)

This third group has now moved the mouth position another step forward so that the tip of the tongue is used, pointing up to the roof of the mouth. To construct the main consonants, the tongue actually touches the roof. It is called the cerebral position. The first is written *T*. All of this third, (middle) group are written as capital letters to differentiate them from the fourth group. (In the Romanized transliteration, the letters have a dot beneath them.) *T* is pronounced as the 't' in tub but instead of having the tongue forward of the roof of the mouth, put it right up to the roof as you say it. That should have been spoken 'with only a small breath' as usual (*alpaprANa*). The second letter is the same but with more breath as you make the sound (*mahAprANa*), a bit like 'po-th-ole' (pothole). It is written *Th*.

The next is written *D* and pronounced like 'd' in dot but, as before, with the tip of the tongue right up in the roof of the mouth. The fourth letter sounds the same as the third but with more breath (e.g. go-dh-ead) and is written *Dh*. The last in the group is another 'na' sound but with the tongue in the roof of the mouth. Written, as you already know, *N*.

The Fourth Group of Consonants (Dental)

This group of consonants are sounded just behind the teeth and called, unsurprisingly, dental. The first is *t*. It is sounded just like our t, as in 'tip'. Then comes the equivalent letter, but with more breath (*mahAprANa*), *th*, as in 'butthead'. Next is *d* as in 'dog' and the breathy equivalent *dh*, as in 'redhead'. Finally, in this group, is the one sounded through the nose (*anunAsika*) *n*, as in ...er 'nose'.

The Fifth Group of Consonants (Labial)

And so, at last, the final group of the main consonants sounded at the lips and called labial. The first is *p* just like our p, as in 'put'. Then comes the corresponding breathy *ph*, as in uphill. Next is *b*, as in 'bad' and the *mahAprANa bh*, as in 'clubhouse'. And finally the *anunAsika* in this group is *m*, as in 'man'.

Table of Basic Consonants

The table of the five groups of consonants, with the corresponding vowel shown in Column 1 for reference, is as shown below:

Guttural	*a*	*k*	*kh*	*g*	*Gh*	*~N*
Palatal	*i*	*ch*	*Ch*	*j*	*Jh*	*~n*
Cerebral	*RRi*	*T*	*Th*	*D*	*Dh*	*N*
Dental	*LLi*	*t*	*th*	*d*	*Dh*	*n*
Labial	*u*	*p*	*ph*	*b*	*Bh*	*m*

The Semi-Vowels

There are two small groups of letters left. The first of these is the group of four so-called 'semi-vowels'. They are formed by combining the four main vowels other than 'a' with 'a'. Thus, if you sound *i* and then immediately move to the *a* sound, what emerges sounds like 'ya' and this is the first semi-vowel or *antaHsthA*: – *y* as in 'yap'. If you sound *RRi* and move to *a*, you get *r* as in 'rap'. If you sound *LLi* and move to *a*, you get *l* as in 'lap'. Finally, if you sound *u* and move to *a*, you get *v* as in 'wag'. Note that Americans seem to prefer to ignore this logical derivation and pronounce it as 'va' in 'van'. Since it is somewhat illogical to write it as beginning with a 'v' while sounding it as a 'w', I suppose both sides of the Atlantic have a case.

The Sibilants

Almost last of all, there are three sibilants or sss-sounds. (A sibilant is called *USHman* in Sanskrit.) These are in the palatal, cerebral and dental positions. (In theory there are also ones in the other two positions but these are so rare that they are usually ignored.) In the palatal position, there is *sh* sounded by making a shh sound in that mouth position; it comes out like the ending of a soft German 'ich' with the default *a* ending of course. The second, in the cerebral position, is *Sh* (or *shh* in older releases) made by sounding 'sha' with the tongue up to the roof of the mouth. Finally is the dental *s*, sounding like the normal 's' in 'sand'.

h

This leaves the last letter in the alphabet, *h*, sounding, as you would expect, as 'h' in 'hat'. It is sometimes considered to be another sibilant and is also called *UShman*, which literally means 'heated'.

The Complete Alphabet

The order of the alphabet, if you want to look up a word in the dictionary, is pretty much the order used here in introducing the letters. The 16 *mAtRRikA* are at the beginning, followed by the basic consonants – guttural, palatal, cerebral, dental and labial. Then come the four semi-vowels (*antaHsthA*) and the three sibilants and finally *h*.

Further Study

As you will certainly have realized by now, in order to learn how to sound these correctly, you really need to listen to someone who knows. Since it is unlikely that you will be sufficiently interested to go into it this deeply, however, just follow the instructions and don't worry about how it feels. We are unused to making full use of our mouth and tongue in speaking and, since Sanskrit makes almost scientific use, we will find much of it peculiar and initially uncomfortable. If you want a more thorough introduction, my book *Sanskrit for Seekers* (Ref. 78) expands upon this to give you a more thorough grounding but without going into too much detail. Its aim is to teach you the rudiments of Sanskrit in order to enable you to read the script, pronounce words and look them up in a dictionary.

Appendix 6 – Similarity of Waking and Dream – an Apparent Contradiction

In his commentary on Brahmasutra II.ii.29, Shankara seems to contradict what he has said in the *kArikA* commentary. The sutra itself says that: *"And because of the difference in nature (the waking state is) not (false) like dream etc."* Shankara says (Gambhirananda translation, Ref.67) that: *"It has been said by those who deny the existence of external things that perceptions of things like a pillar etc. in the waking state occur even in the absence of external things, just as they do in a dream; for as perceptions they are similar. That has to be refuted. With regard to this we say the perceptions of the waking state cannot be classed with those in a dream."*

Later, he makes the very clear statement, in direct contradiction to the *kArikA* commentary:

> *...it cannot be asserted by a man... that the perception of the waking state is false, merely on the ground that it is a perception like the perception in a dream. (And it is not logical for those who consider themselves intelligent to deny their own experience.)*

Sri S. N. Sastri, a Sanskrit scholar, explains (in the Advaitin Email discussion group) that such a confusion as this comes about because of the failure to appreciate the correct meaning of the Sanskrit term used:

> [Referring to Shankara's commentary on K2.4] The word in Sanskrit, which has been translated as 'having the feature of being perceived' is *dRRishyatvam*. This word is derived from the verb *dRRik*, meaning 'to see' and so it has been translated as 'being perceived'. But actually what is meant by the word *dRRishyatvam* here is ' the feature of being objectified'. This is in contrast to *adRRishyam*, which is one of the words used to

describe *brahman*. That has been interpreted in the *bhAShya* as: `what cannot be objectified'.

Brahman is always the subject and can never be objectified. Everything other than *brahman* can be objectified and is therefore *dRRishyam*. In dream also, various objects become the objects of the witnessing consciousness, and so they are also *dRRishyam*, though they are not seen by the eye. In the waking state sounds, smell, etc., are also experienced, and these are also called *dRRishyam*, because they are all objects of the witnessing consciousness. Thus your question as to how the same word *dRRishyam* can be used for dream as well as waking experiences is answered.

What Shankara says in K2.4 is that *dRRishyatvam* and unreality are common to both the states and so they are similar. Everything that is *dRRishyam* is unreal, because it is different from *brahman* which alone is *adRRishyam* and real. Here he does not go into the difference between the two states. This he brings out only in BSB. II.ii.29. So there is actually no contradiction. The similarity alone is pointed out in K2.4. The difference is pointed out in BSB II.ii.29.

Appendix 7 – eka-jIva-vAda – 'One *jIva'* Theory

The translations and interpretations of K2.16 are many. It seems clear that Gaudapada is saying that *Atman* creates the *jIva* first, and then *Atman* creates the objects. But some of the translations of Shankara's commentary suggest that this *jIva* itself imagines the subsequent world. If the *Atman/turIya* does the creating, we have the normal scenario of *Ishvara* plus *mAyA* being the 'creator' from the standpoint of transactional reality with a 'realism' scenario. But if the *jIva* imagines the world, we have idealism.

But I could find no commentaries that continue with the idealistic implications, that it is the *jIva* who effectively 'creates' the waking world according to his mental make-up. The idea that it is our 'naming' of 'forms' that brings about seeming separation has already been mentioned (the *vAchArambhaNa* mantras from the Chandogya Upanishad). But the creation theory of *dRRiShTi-sRRiShTi-vAda* has not been referred to. This says that the seeming existence of the world is simultaneous with our perception of it; i.e. there is no real external world; it exists in our mind and is 'as if' brought about in accordance with our thoughts and desires.

This theory also has further implications in that it implies that all the (other) *jIva*-s, too, are 'imagined' by us; that in fact there is only one *jIva*. This theory is called *eka-jIva-vAda*. This theory, objectionable though it might seem at first sight, has clear advantages over the normal view of things. If it is assumed that there are many *jIva*-s (that theory is called *aneka-jIva-vAda* or *nAnAjIva-vAda*), then there arises a thorny problem as regards the successive enlightenment of these *jIva*-s. The traditional teaching is that unenlightened *jIva*-s are reborn and the bodies into which they are born are determined by accumulated *karma* and may be vegetable or animal. Once a human attains enlightenment, he or she is not reborn. Therefore, the total number of *jIva*-s on the earth will gradually diminish over time as they become enlightened. Logically, there will come a time when there are so few *jIvas*-s remaining that there will be insufficient food to keep them alive, because all of the vegetable and animal *jIva*-s will have graduated to human form and dropped out of *saMsAra*!

Under the one-*jIva* theory, as soon as that *jIva* gains Self-knowledge, all other (imaginary) *jIva*-s will disappear and creation will immediately come to an end, in the same way that the characters in our dream disappear when we wake up.

Of course, Gaudapada is not really interested in any of this, since he is proving in the *kArikA*-s that there is no creation at all, so there is not even a single *jIva*. Arguing whether there is one or many is therefore of no more interest than discussing whether one was paid the correct salary for the work one did in last night's dream. Both waking and dream worlds have only relative reality; one comes and the other goes. The dream is real in the dream; the waking world is real while I am awake. Both are *mithyA* and each derives its seeming reality from me, the *turIya-Atman*. All objects are *mithyA*; only the ultimate subject on which they all depend – I the *Atman* – is *satyam*.

Presumably because of the easier rationale to explain what happens when 'all' are enlightened, the *eka-jIva-vAda* theory has become more popular in recent times. (By 'recent', I mean around the sixteenth century AD, when it was specifically advocated by a highly respected writer, *appayya dikShita*, in his work *siddhAnta lesha saMgraha*.) It is also associated these days with the teaching of Ramana Maharshi (again). One notable aspect of the theory is that it obviates the need for *Ishvara* as creator of the universe; so it might appeal particularly to those who find the notion of a god difficult to accept. But it was never a theory advocated by Shankara, who remains, in my mind at least, the authority on all topics relating to the optimal teaching of Advaita. The non-dual

Consciousness, which is the only reality, has nothing to do with realism or idealism; it is beyond such *mithyA* concepts.

Glossary – Sanskrit Terminology

Each word is presented in the following format:

Typical English Spelling (*ITRANS representation*, **Devanagari Script)** – meaning.

Words appear in order of the English (Roman) alphabet, not the Sanskrit alphabet.

(This section is based upon the Glossary in Ref. 63.)

a (*a*, अ) – as a prefix to another word, it changes it into the negative. E.g. vidya – knowledge, avidya – ignorance.

abhasa (*AbhAsa*, आभास) – semblance, phantom, phantasm of the imagination; mere appearance, fallacious appearance; reflection; or simply image.

abhava (*abhAva*, अभाव) – non-existence, absence. See anupalabdhi.

abhyAsa (*abhyAsa*, अभ्यास) – exercise, discipline; in Raja Yoga, this refers to "the effort of the mind to remain in its unmodified condition of purity (*sattva*)." Ramana Maharshi sometimes refers to a spiritual aspirant as an *abhyAsI* – i.e. one who practices.

acharya (*AchArya*, आचार्य) – a spiritual guide or teacher. See Shankaracharya.

achintya (*achintya*, अचिन्त्य) – inconceivable or beyond thought.

adhama (*adhama*, अधम) – lowest, vilest, worst.

adhibhautika (*adhibhautika*, अधिभौतिक) – (resulting) from such things as wars, disagreements, natural disasters. *adhi* means from, from the presence; *bhautika* means anything elemental or material.

adhidaivika (*adhidaivika*, अधिदैविक) – (resulting) from the presence of divine or supernatural forces. *adhi* means from, from the presence; *daivika* is the adjective from *deva* (god) meaning coming from the gods, divine.

adhikari (*adhikArin* or *adhikArI*, अधिकारिन् or अधिकारी) – a seeker who is mentally prepared (see *chatuShTaya sampatti*) and therefore ready to receive the final teaching from the guru; literally "possessing authority, entitled to, fit for."

adhisthana (*adhiShThAna*, अधिष्ठान) – substratum; literally basis, support, that upon which something rests.

adhyaropa (*adhyAropa*, अध्यारोप) – erroneously attributing one thing to another.

(*adhyAropa-apavAda*, अध्यारोप अपवाद) – One of the principal methods of teaching Advaita, whereby an attribute is applied to brahman initially (and erroneously – hence *adhyAropa*) but is later taken back, once the point has been understood. *apavAda* means denial or contradiction.

adhyasa (*adhyAsa*, अध्यास) – used to refer to the "mistake" that we make when we "superimpose" a false appearance upon the reality or mix up the real and the unreal. The classical example is when we see a snake instead of a rope, which is used as a metaphor for seeing the world of objects instead of the reality of the Self. This concept is fundamental to Advaita and Shankara devotes a separate section to it at the beginning of his commentary on the Brahmasutra.

adhyaya (*adhyAya*, अध्याय) – lesson, lecture or chapter.

adhyatmika (*adhyAtmika*, अध्यात्मिक) – resulting from self, i.e. problems such as pain and mental suffering. *adhi* means from, from the presence; *Atmika* means relating to self.

adrishta (*adRRiShTa*, अदृष्ट) – unseen (this stands for not being accessible to any of the senses).

Advaita (*advaita*, अद्वैत) – not (*a*) two (*dvaita*); non-dual philosophy. (Adjective – *advitIya* – unique, without a second.)

agama (*Agama*, आगम) – acquisition of knowledge, science; traditional doctrine; anything handed down and fixed by tradition.

agamin (*AgAmin*, आगामिन्) – That type of sanskara which is generated in reaction to current situations and which will not bear fruit until sometime in the future. It literally means "impending," "approaching" or "coming." Also called *kriyamANa*, which means "being done." See prarabdha, sanchita, sanskara.

agni (*agni*, अग्नि) – fire.

agocara (*agochara*, अगोचर) – (literally) imperceptible by the senses but treated as anything that is unavailable to any *pramANa* other than *shabda* (i.e. scriptures).

agrahya (*agrAhya*, अग्राह्य) – ungraspable (i.e. inaccessible to the organs of action).

aham (*aham*, अहम्) – I am.

aham vritti (*aham vRRitti*, अहम् वृत्ति) – the thought "I am" as opposed to thoughts about objects, feelings etc. – idam vritti. See vritti.

ahankara (*ahaMkAra*, अहंकार) – the making, kara (*kAra*), of the utterance "I," aham (*aham*) – this is the equivalent of what we would call the "ego" but specifically refers to the identification or attachment of our true Self with something else, usually the body or mind but can be much more specific e.g. I am a teacher, I am a woman. It is one of the "organs" of the mind in classical Advaita – see antakarana.

ahimsa (*ahiMsA*, अहिंसा) – not injuring anything (one of the yamas).

aikya (*aikya*, ऐक्य) – unity, oneness; in Advaita specifically the identity of *Atman* and *brahman*.

aja (*aja*, अज) – unborn.

ajati (*ajAti*, अजाति) – *a* – no or not; *jAti* – creation; the principle that the world and everything in it, including these mind-body appearances were never created or 'brought into existence'. Most clearly stated by Gaudapada in his karika on the Mandukya Upanishad. *jAta* is the adjective, meaning born, brought into existence. The theory that there has never been any creation is called either *ajAta vAda* or *ajAti vAda*.

ajnana (*aj~nAna*, अज्ञान) – (spiritual) ignorance. See jnana. An *aj~nAnI* is one who is not enlightened, i.e. still (spiritually) ignorant.

akasha (*AkAsha*, आकाश) – space, ether or sky; one of the five elements in the Upanishads, the subtle fluid supposed to pervade the universe. Associated with sound and hearing.

akhaNDAkAra vRRitti (अखण्डाकार वृत्ति) – the mental 'occurrence' which effectively causes enlightenment. This is the vRRitti (thought) in the form of (AkAra) the formless or undivided (akhaNDa).

akshara (*akShara*, अक्षर) – imperishable, unchangeable.

alakshana (*alakShaNa*, अलक्षण) – without any characteristics.

alAtashAnti (*alAtashAnti*, अलातशान्ति) – the fourth topic in *gauDapAda*'s *kArikA* on the *mANDUkya upaniShad* – "On the Quenching of the firebrand." *alAta* is a firebrand or coal; *shAnti* is "peace."

amatra (*amAtra*, अमात्र) – without measure, limitless; used to refer to the silence between chants of OM.

amsha (*aMsha*, अंश) – part or portion.

amurta (*amUrta*, अमूर्त) – unmanifest, formless, shapeless.

anadi (*anAdi*, अनादि) – without any beginning, often used to refer to 'ignorance'.

ananda (*Ananda*, आनन्द) – "true" happiness; usually called "bliss" to differentiate it from the transient variety that always alternates with pain or misery. It is an aspect of our true nature and is often combined with the other elements of our real nature – sat and chit – into a single word, satchidananda. See sat, chit and satchidananda.

anandamayakosha (*Anandamayakosha*, आनन्दमयकोश) – the sheath made of bliss (one of the "five Coverings" that surround our true essence).

ananta (*ananta*, अनन्त) – eternal, without end.

anatman (*anAtman*, अनात्मन्) – something other than spirit or soul (not Self or atman); perceptible world. See atman.

anavastha (*anavastha*, अनवस्थ) – logical error of infinite regress.

anichcha (*anichChA*, अनिच्छा) – without desire. See prArabdha.

anirvachaniya (*anirvachanIya*, अनिर्वचनीय) – not able to be categorized; literally: unutterable, indescribable, not to be mentioned. Used to describe nature of reality etc.

anitya (*anitya*, अनित्य) – transient. Also **anityatva** (*anityatva*, अनित्यत्व) – transient or limited existence (mortality).

ankura (*a~Nkura*, अङ्कुर) – sprout (i.e. plant growing from a seed, *bIja*).

Annamayakosha (*annamayakosha*, अन्नमयकोश) – the sheath made of food, *anna*. (One of the "five Coverings" that surround our true essence).

anta (*anta*, अन्त) – end, conclusion, death etc.

antakarana (*antaHkaraNa*, अन्तःकरण) – used to refer to the overall "organ" of mind; the seat of thought and feeling. It derives from *antar* – within, interior – and *karaNa*, which means "instrument" or sense-organ (an alternative for indriya). It consists of a number of separate functions – see manas, buddhi, chitta and ahankara.

antaranga (*antara~Nga*, अन्तरङ्ग) – essential to, internal, interior as opposed to *bahira~Nga*, external or worldly (in relation to spiritual displines).

antaryamin (*antaryAmin*, अन्तर्यामिन्) – the soul, "internal ruler." The known causal (*kAraNa*) universe, *Ishvara*; macrocosmic form of *prAj~na*.

anubhava (*anubhAva*, अनुभाव) – perception, understanding, experience; knowledge derived from personal observation. Intuition as (opposed to reasoning – *yukti*).

anubhuti (*anubhUti*, अनुभूति) – knowledge gained by means of the *pramANa*-s.

anugraha (*anugraha*, अनुग्रह) – grace; literally showing favor or kindness, conferring benefits.

anumana (*anumAna*, अनुमान) – inference (in logic); one of the six means of obtaining knowledge. See pramana.

anupalabdhi (*anupalabdhi*, अनुपलब्धि) – non-perception, nonrecognition; one of the six means of obtaining knowledge. See pramana.

anvaya-vyatireka (*anvaya-vyatireka*, अन्वय व्यतिरेक) – a method in logic for determining the truth of something. For example, is the clay or the pot real? *anvaya* establishes the logical connection that "when the pot **is**, the clay **is**." *vyatireka* establishes the logical discontinuity that "when the pot **is not**, the clay **is**." Therefore the clay is *satya*, the pot is *mithyA*. *anvaya* means "connection, association"; *vyatireka* means "distinction, separateness, exclusion."

anyonya ashyraya (*anyonya Ashraya*, अन्योन्य आश्रय) – mutual dependence in a "cause-effect" situation such as the chicken and egg example.

ap (*ap*, अप्) – water – one of the five elements or *pa~nchabhUta*. Associated with taste.

apana (*apAna*, अपान) – one of the five "vital airs," relating to excretion. More generally refers to rejection of irrelevant material gained from perception etc. and to the formation of limited views.

aparoksha (*apArokSha*, अपारोक्ष) – immediate (relating to gaining of knowledge, i.e. does not require application of reason).

aparokshanubhuti (*apArokShAnubhUti*, अपारोक्षानुभूति) – one of the works attributed to Shankara. The word means "knowledge acquired directly by one of the valid *pramANa*-s."

apaurusheya (*apauruSheya*, अपौरुषेय) – literally "not coming from men"; used to refer to the shruti – scriptural texts passed on verbatim from generation to generation since their original observation by realized sages. See shruti.

apta-vakya (*Apta vAkya*, आप्त वाक्य) – something reported by another in whom one has faith. Literally "a correct sentence." *Apta* means "respected, trustworthy"; vAkya means "statement, declaration."

arambha (*Arambha*, आरम्भ) – literally "beginning,

commencement" but encountered in the context of a material cause in which the effect is clearly distinguishable from its cause but has not actually been transformed, e.g. cloth made from cotton as opposed to butter made from milk.

arambha vada (*Arambha vAda*, आरम्भ वाद) – the theory that the world (i.e. universe) is the result of the coming together of atoms.

arankyaka (*Aranyaka*, आरन्यक) – a class of religious or philosophical writings closely connected with the *brAhmaNa*-s and so-called because they were written or studied in the forest.

artha (*artha*, अर्थ) – acquisition of wealth. One of the four *puruShArtha*-s. See purushartha.

artha-adhyasa (*artha-adhyAsa*, अर्थ-अध्यास) – superimposition of an object onto a substratum, like the snake on the rope.

arthapatti (*arthApatti*, अर्थापत्ति) – inference from circumstances, presumption; one of the 6 means of obtaining knowledge. See pramana.

asanga (*asa~Nga*, असङ्ग) – free from ties, having no attachment or interest in.

asat (*asat*, असत्) – non-existent. See sat.

asatkarya vada (*asatkArya vAda*, असत्कार्य वाद) – the doctrine which denies that the effect pre-exists in the cause (usually in reference to the creation).

ashrama (*Ashrama*, आश्रम) – generic term for one of the four "stages" in the life of a Hindu brahmin, viz. *brahmacharya*, *gRRihastha*, *saMnyAsa*, *vanaprastha*.

asparsha (*asparsha*, अस्पर्श) – intangible, touchless; Gaudapada's term for the fact that there is never any contact of Consciousness (*turIya*) with anything, because there is nothing else.

astika (*Astika*, आस्तिक) – literally "there is or exists"; used to refer to one who believes in the existence of God or, more specifically, one who defers to the authority of the Vedas. See nastika, veda.

atma (*Atma*, आत्म) – see atman.

atmabodha (*Atmabodha*, आत्मबोध) – knowledge of Self or supreme spirit; a book attributed to Shankara.

atman (*Atman*, आत्मन्) – the Self. Usually used to refer to one's true (individual) nature or consciousness but Advaita tells us that there is no such thing as an 'individual' and that this atman is the same as the universal Consciousness, Brahman. see also jiva.

atmavicara (*AtmavichAra*, आत्मविचार) – *vicAra* in this context means reflection or examination upon the *Atman*, the Self. See atman.

avacheda-vada (*avachCheda-vAda*, अवच्छेद वाद) – theory that the Self is limited by ignorance in the forms of *upAdhi*-s. *avachCheda* means "cut-off." See upadhi.

avarana (*AvaraNa*, आवरण) – the veiling power of maya. In the rope-snake metaphor, this prevents us from seeing the reality of the rope. See maya, vikshepa.

avastha (*avasthA*, अवस्था) – state; literally "to stay, abide, exist, remain or continue doing (anything)." In Advaita, it is most frequently encountered as *avasthA traya* – the three states of waking, dreaming and deep sleep.

avidya (*avidyA*, अविद्या) – ignorance (in a spiritual sense) i.e. that which prevents us from realizing the Self. See also maya.

avyakta (*avyakta*, अव्यक्त) – unmanifest, imperceptible, invisible; the universal spirit (paramAtman).

avyapadeshya (*avyapadeshya*, अव्यपदेश्य) – indefinable.

avyavaharya (*avyavahArya*, अव्यवहार्य) – nothing to do with 'worldly' transaction.

badha (*bAdha*, बाध) – sublation or subration. This is the process by which an accepted point of view or understanding is superseded by a totally different one when some new information is received. An example is seeing a lake in the desert and then realizing that it is only a mirage. The adjective is *bAdhita*, meaning negated, contradictory, absurd, false.

bandha or bandhana (*bandha* or *bandhana*, बन्ध or बन्धन) – bondage, attachment to the world.

(*bhAga tyAga lakShaNa*, भाग त्याग लक्षण) – a technique used by the scriptures to point to aspects that cannot be explained directly in words. The oneness that is pointed to (*lakShaNa*) is understood by "giving up" (*tyAga*) the contradictory parts (*bhAga*). An example would be in the apparent contradiction of the *jIva* being "created" while *Ishvara* is the "creator." Both are given up in order to recognize their identity as *brahman*.

Bhagavad (*bhagavat*, भगवत्) – holy; prosperous, happy; illustrious, divine. In the context of Bhagavad Gita, it refers to the God, Krishna and Bhagavad Gita means Krishna's Song (the *t* changes to a *d* when the words join). See below.

Bhagavad Gita (*bhagavadgItA*, भगवद्गीता) – the scriptural text forming part of the Hindu epic, the Mahabarata. It is a dialogue between Krishna, the charioteer/God, representing the Self and the warrior Arjuna, representing you and me, on the battlefield of Kurukshetra prior to the commencement of battle. The scripture is regarded as smriti. See Bhagavad, smriti.

bhakta (*bhakta*, भक्त) – one who practices bhakti yoga. See bhakti yoga.

bhakti (*bhakti*, भक्ति) **yoga** – devotion or worship as a means to enlightenment. See also karma and jnana.

bhamiti (*bhAmatI*, भामती) – literally "lustrous"; name of one of the two schools of Advaita, also called the *vAchaspati* school, after the philosopher *vAchaspati mishra*. The other school is the *vivaraNa* school

Bhartihari (*bhartRRihari*, भर्तृहरि) – poet and grammarian in seventh century AD, composer of *vAkyapadIya*.

bhashya (*bhAShya*, भाष्य) – explanatory work, exposition or commentary on some other scriptural document. Thus Shankara, for example, has written bhashyas on a number of Upanishads, the Bhagavad Gita and the Brahmasutra.

bhashyakara (*bhAShyakAra*, भाष्यकार) – various commentators (on a philosophy).

bhava (*bhAva*, भाव) – condition or state of body or mind.

bhavana (*bhAvana*, भावन) – reflection, contemplation.

bhoktri (*bhoktRRi*, भोक्तृ) – one who enjoys, an experiencer or feeler.

bhrama (*bhrama*, भ्रम) – confusion, perplexity, mistake (N.B. Not to be confused with brahma or brahman!).

bija (*bIja*, बीज) – seed (of a plant).

bodha (*bodha*, बोध) – knowing, understanding.

Brahma (*brahma*, ब्रह्म) – God as the creator of the universe in Hindu mythology (the others are Vishnu, *viShNu*, the preserver and Shiva, *shiva*, the destroyer). N.B. Not to be confused with Brahman!

brahmacharya (*brahmacharya*, ब्रह्मचर्य) – the first stage of the traditional Hindu spiritual path, in which the Brahman begins his life as an unmarried, religious and chaste student. (*charya* means 'due observance of all rites and customs'.) One of the five *yama*-s in Raja yoga. See also grihasta, sanyasa, vanaprastha.

Brahman (*brahman*, ब्रह्मन्) – the universal Self, Absolute or God. There is only Brahman. It derives from the Sanskrit root *bRRih*, meaning to grow great or strong and could be thought of as the adjective 'big' made into a noun, implying that which is greater than anything. See also atman, Brahma, jiva, jivatman, paramatman.

brahmana (*brAhmaNa*, ब्राह्मण) – an aspirant; a member of the first of the traditional four castes in India (also called Brahmin); alternatively a portion of the Vedas, containing information relating to the use of mantras and hymns in sacrifices.

brahmanishta (*brahmaniShTha*, ब्रह्मनिष्ठ) – one who is absorbed in contemplating brahman and committed only to that purpose. *niShTha* means "devoted to."

Brahma Sutra (*brahmasUtra*, ब्रह्मसूत्र) – a book (in sutra form,

which is terse verse!) by Vyasa. This book is the best known of
the third accepted source of knowledge (nyaya prasthana).
Effectively, it attempts to summarize the Upanishads. It has
been extensively commented on by the three main philosophical branches of Indian thought, dvaita, advaita and
vishishtadvaita, and the proponents of each claim that it
substantiates their beliefs. Shankara has commented on it and
provided extensive arguments against any interpretation
other than that of Advaita. See bhashya, nyaya prasthana,
sruti, smriti.

brahmavidya (*brahmavidyA*, ब्रह्मविद्या) – knowledge of the one
Self. (Also *brahmavitva*, with someone with this knowledge
being called a *brahmavit*.) See brahman.

Brihadaranyaka (*bRRihadAraNyaka*, बृहदारण्यक) – one of the
major Upanishads (and possibly the oldest). The word derives
from *bRRihat* – great, large, wide, tall etc. and *Aranyaka* –
produced in (or relating to) a forest. See Upanishad.

buddhi (*buddhi*, बुद्धि) – the organ of mind responsible for discrimination and judgment, perhaps nearest equated to the intellect
in Western usage. See also, ahankara, antakarana, manas and
chitta.

Chandogya (*chhAndogya*, छान्दोग्य) – one of the major
Upanishads. See Upanishad.

Charvaka (*chArvAka*, चार्वाक) – materialist philosopher or a
follower of him.

chaturtha (*chaturtha*, चतुर्थ) – the ordinal number 'fourth' (*chatur*
is the numeral '4').

chatushtaya sampatti (*chatuShTaya sampatti*, चतुष्टय सम्पत्ति) – the
fourfold pre-requisites specified by Shankara as needed by a
seeker before he can achieve Self-realisation. *chatuShTaya*
means "fourfold"; *sampatti* means success or accomplishment.
See sadhana, vairagya, viveka, mumukshutvam.

chetana (*chetana*, चेतन) – consciousness, intelligence etc.

chidabhasa (*chidAbhAsa*, चिदाभास) – false appearance or reflection (*AbhAsa*) of consciousness (*chit*) – i.e. the ego.

chin mudra (*chin mudrA*, चिन् मुद्रा) – hand sign symbolizing the three states of consciousness and reality (*chin* means Consciousness and *mudrA* means sign).

chit (*chit*, चित्) – pure thought or Consciousness. See ananda, sat, satchidananda.

chitta (*chitta*, चित्त) – the organ (part) of mind responsible for memory. See antakarana, ahankara, buddhi, manas.

Dakshinamurti (*dakShiNAmUrti*, दक्षिणामूर्ति) – Sage who is said to be the first teacher of Vedanta. As such, he was the head of the teaching *sampradAya* and did not himself have a teacher – i.e. he was already fully enlightened.

dama (*dama*, दम) – self-restraint but understood as control over the senses; one of the six qualities that form part of Shankara's chatushtaya sampatti. See chatushtaya sampatti, *shamAdi shhaTka sampatti*.

darshana (*darshana*, दर्शन) – audience or meeting (with a guru); viewpoint; one of the six classical Indian philosophical systems (purvamimamsa, uttaramimamsa, nyaya, vaisheshika, samkhya, yoga).

deha (*deha*, देह) – person, individual, outward form or appearance (body).

deva (*deva*, देव) – (pl. noun) the gods; (adj.) heavenly, divine.

Devanagari (*devanAgarI*, देवनागरी) – the script used in Sanskrit representation. The word literally means "city of the Gods" (deva – gods; nAgara – belonging or relating to a town or city).

devadatta (*devadatta*, देवदत्त) – fellow, common noun for "man" used in philosophy; literally "god-given."

dharma (*dharma*, धर्म) – customary practice, conduct, duty, justice and morality. One of the four *puruShArtha*-s. The favored meaning of most traditional teachers is, however, "nature, character, essential quality," which they often translate as "essence." Our own dharma (*svadharma*) is what we ought to do with our lives in order to dissolve our accumulation of sanskara. See sanskara, karma.

dhuma (*dhUma*, धूम) – smoke.

dhyana (*dhyAna*, ध्यान) – meditation, usually in the sense of the mechanical act using a mantra as opposed to *nididhyAsana*.

dravya (*dravya*, द्रव्य) – substance.

drg-drsya-viveka (*dRRigdRRishya viveka*, दृग्दृश्य विवेक) – "Discrimination between the Seer and the Seen" – a work attributed to Shankara. *dRRik* is the seer or perceiver and *dRRishya* that which is seen or which can be objectified.

drishtanta (*dRRiShTAnta*, दृष्टान्त) – the end or aim of what is seen, example or instance.

drishti-srishti-vada (*dRRiShTisRRiShTivAda*, दृष्टिसृष्टिवाद) – the theory that our mistaken view of the world arises from a mental image (based on memory and sense data) superimposed upon the reality. *dRRiShTi* means "seeing"; *sRRiShTi* means "creation"; *vAda* means "thesis" or "doctrine." See also adhyasa, ajati, srishti-drishti-vada.

drishya (*dRRishya*, दृश्य) – visible; seen; i.e. objects of experience.

dukha (*duHkha*, दुःख) – pain, sorrow, trouble.

dvaita (*dvaita*, द्वैत) – duality, philosophy of dualism; belief that God and the atman are separate entities. Madhva is the scholar most often associated with this philosophy.

dvayakala (*dvayakAla*, द्वयकाल) – term used to refer to the fact that waking objects continue to exist when I am not actually observing them (i.e. at two separate points in time); this differentiates waking experiences from dream experience (which are *chittakAlAh*, lasting only so long as the mind of the dreamer imagines them).

dvesha (*dveSha*, द्वेष) – hatred, dislike.

ekagra (*ekAgra*, एकाग्र) – one-pointed, fixing one's attention on one point. *ekAgratA* – intentness in the pursuit of one object.

eka-jiva-vada (*eka-jIva-vAda*, एक-जीव-वाद) – theory that there is only one *jIva* who 'imagines' the world.

Gaudapada (*gauDapAda*, गौडपाद) – The author of the commentary (karika) on the Mandukya Upanishad. He is said to have been the teacher of Shankara's teacher. See karika, Mandukya, Upanishad.

gita (*gIta*, गीत) – a sacred song or poem but more usually refers to philosophical or religious doctrines in verse form (*gIta* means "sung"). The most famous are the Bhagavad Gita and Astavakra Gita. If the word is used on its own, it will be referring to the former. See Bhagavad, Astavakra.

grantha (*grantha*, ग्रन्थ) – hatred, dislike.

grihasta (*gRRihastha*, गृहस्थ) – this is the second stage of the traditional Hindu spiritual path, called the period of the householder, in which the Brahman performs the duties of master of the house and father of a family. See also brahmacharya, grihasta, sanyasa, vanaprastha.

guna (*guNa*, गुण) – According to classical Advaita, creation is made up of three "qualities," sattva, rajas and tamas. Everything - matter, thoughts, feelings – is "made up of" these three in varying degrees and it is the relative proportions that determine the nature of the thing in question. See sattwa, rajas and tamas for more details.

guru (*guru*, गुरु) – literally "heavy"; used to refer to one's elders or a person of reverence but more commonly in the West to indicate one's spiritual teacher.

hetu (*hetu*, हेतु) – cause or reason; the logical reason or argument in a syllogism.

Hinayana (*hinayAna*, हिनयान) – One of the two original branches of Buddhism; survives in Sri Lanka as the Theravada school.

hiranyagarbha (*hiraNyagarbha*, हिरण्यगर्भ) – the known subtle (*sUkShma*) universe; macrocosmic form of *taijasa*. (Literally 'golden womb' or 'egg'.)

iccha (*ichChA*, इच्छा) – wish, desire, inclination.

idam vritti (*idam vRRitti*, इदम् वृत्ति) – thoughts of objects, concepts, feelings etc., as opposed to aham vritti – the thought

"I am." See vritti.

indriya (*indriya,* इन्द्रिय) – the number five symbolizing the five senses. The five sense organs are called j~nAnendriya-s and the five "organs" of action are the karmendriya-s.

Isha Upanishad (*IshopaniShad,* ईशोपनिषद्) – also known as the Isavasya Upanishad, because its first verse begins: OM IshA vAsyamidam{\m+} sarvaM. IshAvAsya means "pervaded by the lord."

ishta (*iShTa,* इष्ट) – wished, desired, liked, beloved.

Isvara (*Ishvara,* ईश्वर) – the Lord; creator of the phenomenal universe. See saguna Brahman.

jada (*jaDa,* जड) – inert, lifeless.

jagat (*jagat,* जगत्) – the world (earth), mankind etc.

jagrat (*jAgrat,* जाग्रत्) – the waking state of consciousness. The "waker ego" is called vishva. See also, sushupti, svapna, turiya.

janma (*janma,* जन्म) – birth.

japa (*japa,* जप) – the simple repetition of a mantra; usually associated with the initial stage of meditation. See mantra.

jati (*jAti,* जाति) – birth, the form of existence (as man, animal etc.); genus or species.

jiva (*jIva,* जीव) – the identification of the atman with a body and mind; sometimes spoken of as "the embodied atman." See atman.

jivanmukta (*jIvanmukta,* जीवन्मुक्त) – someone liberated (in this life) from all future births; i.e. self-realized. (*mukta* is the adjective – liberated; *mukti* is the noun – liberation)

jivatman (*jIvAtman,* जीवात्मन्) – another word for atman, to emphasize that we are referring to the *Atman* in this embodied state, as opposed to the *paramAtman,* the "supreme Self." In the Sri Dakshinamurti Stotram of Shankara, *jIvatman* is equated with Consciousness and *paramAtman* with Existence. (All are, of course, equivalent.) See atman.

jnana (*j~nAna,* ज्ञान) **yoga** – yoga based on the acquisition of true knowledge (j~nAna means "knowledge") i.e. knowledge of the Self as opposed to mere information about the world of appearances. See also bhakti, karma.

jnana-adhyasa (*j~nAna-adhyAsa*, ज्ञान-अध्यास) – superimposition of the knowledge of an object onto its substratum, like realizing that the pot is only clay.

jnana kanda (*j~nAna kANDa*, ज्ञान काण्ड) – those sections of the Vedas concerned with knowledge, i.e. the Upanishads.

jnanendriya (*j~nAnendriya*, ज्ञानेन्द्रिय) – an organ of perception (eye, ear, nose, tongue, skin), plural *j~nAnendryAni*.

jnani or jnanin (*j~nAnI or j~nAnin*, ज्ञानी or ज्ञानिन्) – one who practices jnana yoga. (*j~nAnin* is the *prAtipadika*; *j~nAnI* is the nominative singular *pada*.) See jnana yoga.

jnatri (*j~nAtRRi*, ज्ञातृ) – a knower.

jneya (*j~neya*, ज्ञेय) – something to be known.

kaivalya (*kaivalya*, कैवल्य) – absolute unity, detachment of the soul from further transmigration, leading to eternal happiness or emancipation.

kama (*kAma*, काम) – desire, longing; one of the four *puruShArtha*-s. Not to be confused with karma. Shankara differentiates this from *rAga*: *rAga* is attachment to something one already has whereas *kAma* is wanting something one doesn't have. See purushartha.

kanda (*kANDa*, काण्ड) – part or section, division of a work or book, especially relating to the Vedas.

karana (*karaNa*, करण) – "instrument" in the context of causality. *karaNa kAraNa* – instrumental cause. (The first "a" is short.)

karana (*kAraNa*, कारण) – cause (noun) as in *nimitta kAraNa* or causal (adj.) as in *kAraNa sharIra*. Literally "a cause (in philosophy i.e. that which is invariably antecedent to some product)." (The first "a" is long.)

karika (*kArikA*, कारिका) – (strictly speaking) a concise philosophical statement in verse. The most well known is that by Gaudapada on the Mandukya Upanishad. (Not to be confused with *karika*, which is an elephant!). See Gaudapada, Mandukya, Upanishad.

karma (*karma*, कर्म) – literally "action" but generally used to refer to the "law" whereby actions carried out now will have their lawful effects in the future (and this may be in future lives). Note that karma yoga is something different – see below. See also sanskara.

karmakanda (*karmakANDa*, कर्मकाण्ड) – that portion of the Vedas relating to ceremonial acts, the rituals we should follow, sacrificial rites and so on.

karmaphala (*karmaphala*, कर्मफल) – the fruit (*phala*) of action; i.e. the result or consequence of our actions.

karma yoga (*karma yoga*, कर्म योग) – the practice of acting in such a way as not to incur karma, by carrying out "right" actions, not "good" or "bad" ones. See bhakti, karma, jnana.

karmendriya (*karmendriya*, कर्मेन्द्रिय) – an organ of action, plural karmendriyAni. These are hand, foot, larynx, organ of generation and organ of excretion.

kartri (*kartRRi*, कर्तृ) – one who makes, does or acts; the agent of an action.

karya (*kArya*, कार्य) – effect or result.

kashaya (*kaShAya*, कार्य) – literally means 'stain' and is that negative state of the mind in which latent desires 'take over' our thoughts.

Katha Upanishad (*kaThopaniShad*, कठोपनिषद्) – one of the 108+ Upanishads and one of the 10 major ones. *kaTha* was a sage and founder of a branch of the Yajur Veda. See Upanishad.

Kena Upanishad (*kenopaniShad*, केनोपनिषद्) – one of the 108+ Upanishads and another one of the 10 major ones. *kena* means "whence?" ("how?," "why?" etc.) and is the first word of this Upanishad. See Upanishad.

khalvidam (*khalvidam*, खल्विदम्) – in the statement sarvam kahlvidam brahma – all this is verily Brahman. *khalu* means "indeed, verily," *idam* is "this" (neutral pronoun).

kosha (*kosha,* कोश) – literally "sheath" as in the scabbard of a sword; one of the five layers of identification that cover up our true nature.

kripana (*kRRipaNa,* कृपण) – narrow-minded, miserly, wretched, pitiable.

krodha (*krodha,* क्रोध) – anger, passion.

kshanika vada (*kShaNika vAda,* क्षणिक वाद) – theory that Consciousness is 'momentary', arising and disappearing in each moment. This is the belief of the Yogachara or *vij~nAna vAda* Buddhist.

kutastha (*kUTastha,* कूटस्थ) – the immovable, unchanging spirit (literally "standing at the top."

lakshana (*lakShaNa,* लक्षण) – pointer; indicating or expressing indirectly; accurate description or definition.

lakshya (*lakShya,* लक्ष्य) – that which is to be characterized, defined, indicated or expressed.

laukika (*laukika,* लौकिक) – worldly, belonging to or occurring in ordinary life. *laukika anumAna* is inference by scientific reasoning, based on observation.

laya (*laya,* लय) – literally "dissolution" (and the last stage in the cycle of creation, preservation and destruction of the universe).

lila (*lIlA,* लीला) – literally "play," "amusement" or "pastime"; the idea that the apparent creation is a diversion for a creator – a means for Him to enjoy Himself. He plays all the parts in such a way that they are ignorant of their real nature and believe themselves separate.

linga (*li~Nga,* लिङ्ग) – sign, mark or badge; evidence. Sometimes used as *li~Nga sharIra* to describe the subtle body.

loka (*loka,* लोक) – world, universe, sky or heaven etc. (adjective laukika).

lokottara (*lokottara,* लोकोत्तर) – beyond worldly experience; effectively without either subject or object; i.e. the deep-sleep state.

Madhva (*madhva,* मध्व) – founder of the school of dvaita philosophy.

mahavakyas (*mahAvAkya*, महावाक्य) – *maha* means "great"; *vAkya* means "speech, saying or statement." The four "great sayings" from the Vedas are: "Consciousness is Brahman," "That thou art," "This Self is Brahman" and "I am Brahman."

Mahayana (*mahAyAna*, महायान) – One of the two original branches of Buddhism; the main school in China, Tibet, Japan and Korea.

manana (*manana*, मनन) – reflecting upon what has been heard (shravana). This is the second stage of the classical spiritual path, to remove any doubts about the knowledge that has been received via shravana. See also samshaya, shravana, nididhyasana.

manas (*manas*, मनस्) – the "organ" of mind acting as intermediary between the senses and the intellect (buddhi) on the way in and the intellect and the organs of action on the way out. These are its primary functions and "thinking" ought to consist only of the processing of data on behalf of the intellect. Unfortunately, it usually tries to take on the role of the intellect itself and this is when thinking becomes a problem. See ahankara, antakarana, buddhi and chitta.

Mandukya (*mANDUkya*, माण्डूक्य) – One of the major Upanishads and possibly the single most important, when considered in conjunction with the karika written by Gaudapada. (In many versions of this Upanishad, there is no distinction made between the original and the additions made by Gaudapada and there is some argument over which is which.) See Gaudapada, karika, Upanishad.

manomayakosha (*manomayakosha*, मनोमयकोश) – the mental sheath (one of the "five Coverings" that surround our true essence).

manonasha (*manonAsha*, मनोनाश) – literally 'death of the mind'; the idea being that the mind is the cause of our seeing duality and we gain enlightenment by putting an end to this. The intended meaning is only figurative.

manonigraha (*manonigrAhA*, मनोनिग्राहा) – control of the mind (can be understood as equivalent to *nididhyAsana*).

mantra (*mantra*, मन्त्र) – a group of words (or sometimes only one or more syllables), traditionally having some mystical significance, being in many religions an actual 'name of God' or a short prayer. Often used in meditation (always in Transcendental Meditation). See japa.

marana (*mAraNa*, मारण) – death, destruction.

marga (*mArga*, मार्ग) – path, track, way. *vichAra mArga* is translated as "Direct Path," referring to the particular method of teaching Advaita.

math or matha (*maTha*, मठ) – (religious) college or temple.

matra (*mAtrA*, मात्रा) – a measure of any kind. In Sanskrit, the short vowel is said to be 1 *mAtrA* and the long vowel 2, i.e. sounded for twice the length.

maya (*mAyA*, माया) – literally "magic" or "witchcraft," often personified in Hindu mythology. The "force" used to explain how it is that we come to be deceived into believing that there is a creation with separate objects and living creatures etc. See also avarana and vikshepa.

mayakara (*mAyAkAra*, मायाकार) – a maker of magic i.e. a conjurer or magician. See maya.

mimamsa (*mImAMsA*, मीमांसा) – profound thought, reflection, examination. See purvamimamsa, utteramimamsa.

mithya (*mithyA*, मिथ्या) – dependent reality; literally "incorrectly" or "improperly," used in the sense of "false, untrue." It is, however, more frequently used in the sense of "depending upon something else for its existence." It is ascribed to objects etc., meaning that these are not altogether unreal but not strictly real either i.e. they are our imposition of name and form upon the undifferentiated Self. See adhyasa.

moksha (*mokSha*, मोक्ष) – liberation, enlightenment, Self-realization; one of the four *puruShArtha*-s.

mudra (*mudrA*, मुद्रा) – particular positions or intertwinings of the fingers, commonly practiced in religious worship.

mukti (*mukti*, मुक्ति) – setting or becoming free, final liberation. (*mukta* is the adjective – liberated).

mula (*mUla*, मूल) – original, primary, root; e.g. original cause – *mUla kAraNa*.

mumukshu (*mumukShu*, मुमुक्षु) – one for whom the desires to achieve enlightenment is the predominant goal in life; a seeker.

mumukshutva (*mumukShutva*, मुमुक्षुत्व) – the desire to achieve enlightenment, to the exclusion of all other desires. See sadhana, chatushtaya sampatti.

Mundaka Upanishad (*muNDakopaniShad*, मुण्डकोपनिषद्) – Another one of the 108+ Upanishads and also one of the 10 major ones – but not to be confused with the Mandukya. *muNDa* means "having a shaved head" and the Upanishad is so called because everyone who comprehends its sacred doctrine is "shorn," i.e. liberated from all error. See Upanishad.

murcha (*mUrChA*, मूर्छा) – fainting, swoon, stupor, hallucination.

murta (*mUrta*, मूर्त) – manifest, material, embodied.

naimittika (*naimittika*, नैमित्तिक) – occasional, special. *naimittika karma* are those occasional duties that we have to perform, such as helping a neighbor who has helped one in the past.

Naiyayika (*naiyAyika*, नैयायिक) – a follower of the *nyAya* philosophy.

nama-rupa (*nAma-rUpa*, नामरूप) – name and form.

nara (*nara*, नर) – man, humanity; see *vaishvAnara*.

nasha (*nAsha*, नाश) – loss, destruction, annihilation, death.

nastika (*nAstika*, नास्तिक) – atheist, unbeliever; usually refers to one who does not recognise the authority of the Vedas.

neti (*neti*, नेति) – not this (*na* – not; *iti* – this). From the Brihadaranyaka Upanishad (2.3.6). Used by the intellect whenever it is thought that the Self might be some "thing" observed e.g. body, mind etc. The Self cannot be anything that is seen, thought or known. See Brihadaranyaka, Upanishad.

nididhyasana (*nididhyAsana*, निदिध्यासन) – meditating upon the essence of what has now been intellectually understood until there is total conviction. The third stage of the classical spiritual path. See also shravana and manana. It is to be understood as "right apprehension" (*vij~nAna*) rather than simply mechanical as *dhyAna* might be construed.

nidra (*nidrA*, निद्रा) – sleep – the 'individual' power of *mAyA*.

nigraha (*nigraha*, निग्रह) – restraint, control.

nimitta (*nimitta*, निमित्त) – literally the "instrumental or efficient cause" but normally used (*nimitta kAraNa*) as meaning the latter, which is also referred to as 'intelligent cause'.

nirguna (*nirguNa*, निर्गुण) – "without qualities"; usually referring to Brahman and meaning that it is beyond any description or thought. Since there is only Brahman, any word would imply limitation or duality. See. Brahman, saguna, Isvara.

nirodha (*nirodha*, निरोध) – restraint.

nirupadhika (*nirupAdhika*, निरुपाधिक) – without attributes or qualities. *nirupAdhika adhyAsa* is superimposition as of the snake on the rope, as opposed to *sopAdhika adhyAsa* e.g. the sunrise, which is still seen even when the mistake is realized.

nirvikalpa (*nirvikalpa*, निर्विकल्प) – (referring to samadhi) 'without' doubts about one's identity with the one Self. See savikalpa, samadhi, vikalpa.

nirvishesha (*nirvisheSha*, निर्विशेष) – making or showing no difference. *nirvisheShaNa* – attributeless.

nishkama (*niShkAma*, निष्काम) – desireless, disinterested. *niShkAma karma* is so-called "right action," performed in response to the need, neither selfishly nor unselfishly – it generates no *saMskAra*.

nishtha (*niShTha*, निष्ठ) – committed or devoted to; having a basis or grounding in. *niShThA* is the noun, meaning firmness, steadiness, devotion.

nitya (*nitya*, नित्य) – eternal. It also means "ordinary, usual, necessary, obligatory." It is used in this latter sense in connection with action. *nitya karma* are those daily duties that we have to perform, such as looking after one's children.

nivritti (*nivRRitti*, निवृत्ति) – giving up, abstaining, renouncing (esp. of desires in the path to enlightenment – *nivRRitti mArga*).

nyaya (*nyAya*, न्याय) – logical argument; literally, "that into which a thing goes back," a "standard" or "rule"; one of the six classical Indian philosophical systems, whose principal exponent was Gautama in the third century BC. So called because the system "goes into" all physical and metaphysical subjects in a very logical manner.

nyaya prasthana (*nyAya prasthAna*, न्याय प्रस्थान) – refers to logical and inferential material based upon the Vedas, of which the most well known is the Brahmasutra of Vyasa (*nyAya* can also mean method, axiom, logical argument etc.). See pramana, prasthana-traya, smriti, sruti.

omkara (*omkAra*, ओम्कार) – the syllable OM.

pada (*pAda*, पाद) – quarter, i.e. one of the 'three states + *turIya*'.

paksha (*pakSha*, पक्ष) – subject of the discussion, proposition to be proved.

panchabuta (*pa~nchabhUta*, पञ्चभूत) – the five elements, viz. earth – *pRRithivI*; water – *ap*; fire – *tejas*; air – *vAyu*; space or ether – *AkAsha*.

Panchadashi (*pa~nchadashI*, पञ्चदशी) – literally means "fifteen" because it has this many chapters – a book written by Vidyaranya (*vidyAraNya*), based upon the Upanishads. It discusses many Advaitic truths and uses some original metaphors to illustrate the concepts.

panchakosha (*pa~ncha kosha*, पञ्च कोश) – the five sheaths.

pandita (*paNDita*, पण्डित) – literally "wise" as an adjective or "scholar, teacher, philosopher" as a noun and used in this way in the scriptures. However, it has come to mean someone who knows a lot of theory but does very little practice. We sometimes use the word "pundit" in our language – the word "sophist" would probably be a good synonym.

papa (*pApa*, पाप) – literally "bad" or "wicked" but used in the sense of the "sin" that accrues (according to the theory of karma) from performing "bad" actions, i.e. those done with a selfish motive. See also punya.

parama (*parama*, परम) – chief, highest, most prominent, best etc.

paramartha (noun), (*paramArtha*, परमार्थ);

paramarthika (adj.), (*pAramArthika* (adj.), पारमार्थिक – the highest truth or reality; the noumenal as opposed to the phenomenal world of appearances (vyavaharika). See pratibhasika and vyavaharika.

paramatman (*paramAtman*, परमात्मन्) – usually translated as the "supreme Self" as opposed to the atman in the embodied state, the jivatman. Swami Dayananda insists that it actually means "limitless" in the sense of not limited by time or place and therefore changeless (Ref. 58). See atman.

parampara (*paramparA*, परम्परा) – literally "proceeding from one to another"; "guru parampara" refers to the tradition of guru – disciple passing on wisdom through the ages. See also sampradaya.

parechcha (*parechChA*, परेच्छा) – relating to the desires of others – see prArabdha.

parichinna (*parichChinna*, परिच्छिन्न) – finite.

parinama (*pariNAma*, परिणाम) – literally "change, transformation into"; encountered in the context of a material cause in which the effect is a transformation from its cause as opposed to simply distinguishable from, e.g. butter made from milk as opposed to cloth made from cotton.

parinama vada (*pariNAma vAda*, परिणाम वाद) – the doctrine of creation as proposed by *sAMkhya* philosophy.

paroksha (*pArokSha*, पारोक्ष) – remote, mysterious, invisible, hidden (also *pArokShya*); opposite of *pratyakSha*.

Patanjali (*pata~njali*, पतञ्जलि) – philosopher, writer of the "Yoga Sutras" and responsible for *aShTA~Nga* or *rAja yoga*.

phala (*phala*, फल) – fruit; often used in the context of the consequences that necessarily follow as a result of action. See *karmaphala*.

pradhana (*pradhAna*, प्रधान) – primary nature or matter (belief of *sAMkhya* philosophy).

prajna (*praj~nA*, प्रज्ञा) – (verb) to know or understand, find out, perceive or learn; (noun) wisdom, intelligence, knowledge. Not to be confused with *prAj~na* below.

prajna (*prAj~na*, प्राज्ञ) – the "deep sleep ego" in the deep sleep state of consciousness, sushupti. Literally, "wise, clever" (adj.) or "a wise man" or "intelligence dependent on individuality." See also vishva, taijasa.

prajnana (*praj~nAna*, प्रज्ञान) – consciousness.

pralaya (*pralaya*, प्रलय) – the destruction of the world at the end of a kalpa. See kalpa.

prakarana (*prakaraNa*, प्रकरण) – subject, topic, treatise etc. but especially opening chapter or prologue.

prakarana grantha (*prakaraNa grantha*, प्रकरण ग्रन्थ) – this is the term used to refer to authoritative commentaries on the scripture but which are not part of the *prasthAna traya*. It is frequently used in respect of the works attributed to Shankara such as *upadesha sAhasrI*, *vivekachUDAmaNi* etc. The word *grantha* literally means "tying or stringing together" though can itself mean composition or treatise.

prakriti (*prakRRiti*, प्रकृति) – literally the original or natural form or condition of anything; generally used to refer to what we would call "nature."

prakriya (*prakriyA*, प्रक्रिया) – a methodology of teaching; literally a chapter (esp. the introductory chapter of a work).

pralaya (*pralaya*, प्रलय) – dissolution, destruction, annihilation, specifically relating to the universe at the end of a *kalpa*.

prama (*pramA*, प्रमा) – true knowledge, basis or foundation.

pramana (*pramANa*, प्रमाण) – valid means for acquiring knowledge. There are six of these in Vedanta: perception (*pratyakSha*), inference (*anumAna*), scriptural or verbal testimony (*shabda* or *Agama shruti*), analogy (*upamAna*), presumption (*arthApatti*) and non-apprehension (*anupalabdhi*). The first three are the major ones referred to by Shankara.

pramatri or pramata (*pramAtRRi or pramAtA*, प्रमातृ or प्रमाता) – the subject of knowledge obtained via a *pramANa*; authority, one who has a correct notion or idea.

prameya (*prameya*, प्रमेय) – the object of knowledge obtained via a *pramANa*; also "thing to be proven" or "topic to be discussed."

prana (*prANa*, प्राण) – literally the "breath of life"; the vital force in the body with which we identify in the "vital sheath."

pranamayakosha (*prANamayakosha*, प्राणमयकोश) – the sheath made of breath (one of the "five Coverings" that surround our true essence).

pranava (*praNava*, प्रणव) – mystical or sacred symbol (OM); OM is usually called *praNava shabda*, though either word separately can also be use with the same meaning. *praNu* means "to make a humming or droning sound."

pranayama (*prANayAma*, प्रानयाम) – usually understood to mean control of breathing in advanced yoga techniques or as a prelude to meditation. According to Swami Chinmayananda, however, it does not mean this but relates to the five "departments" of active life as described in the chapter on Spiritual Practices.

prapanchopashamam (*prapa~nchopashamam*, प्रपञ्चोपशमम्) – negation (*ama*) of the experience (*pash*) of the universe (*prapa~ncha*). This confirms the status of the world as *mithyA* or *vaitathya* and thereby negates it.

prarabdha (*prArabdha*, प्रारब्ध) – This literally means "begun" or "undertaken." It is the fruit of all of our past action that is now having its effect. This is one of the three types of sanskara. See agamin, sanchita, sanskara. Also, there are three types of prArabdha karma – *ichChA*, *anichChA* and *parechChA* (personally desired, without desire and due to others' desire).

prasthana-traya (*prasthAna traya*, प्रस्थान त्रय) – *prasthAna* means "system" or "course" in the sense of a journey; *traya* just means "threefold." It refers to the three sources of knowledge of the Self (*shabda*), nyaya prasthana, sruti and smriti. See nyaya prasthana, shabda, sruti, smriti.

pratibhasa (noun) (*pratibhAsa*, प्रतिभास);

pratibhasika (adj.) (*prAtibhAsika*, प्रातिभासिक) – appearing or occurring to the mind, existing only in appearance, an illusion. See paramartha, vyavahara.

pratibimba (*pratibimba*, प्रतिबिम्ब) – a reflection. In logic, *bimba* is the object itself, with the *pratibimba* being the counterpart with which it is compared.

pratibimba-vada (*pratibimba vAda*, प्रतिबिम्ब वाद) – the theory that the jiva is a reflection of the atman, similar to a the reflection of an object in a mirror.

pratijna (*pratij~nA*, प्रतिज्ञा) – (in logic) an assertion or proposition to be proved.

(*pratipAdya – pratipAdaka sambandha*, प्रतिपाद्य प्रतिपादुक सम्बन्ध) – refers to that type of knowledge where the knowledge itself brings about the goal without the need for any action. *pratipAdya* means "that which is to be explained or revealed"; *pratipAdaka* means "that which reveals, explaining or demonstrating"; *sambandha* means "relationship."

pratyabhijna (*pratyabhij~nA*, प्रत्यभिज्ञा) – recognition

pratyaksha (*pratyakSha*, प्रत्यक्ष) – "present before the eyes, clear, distinct etc." but particularly "direct perception or apprehension" as a valid source of knowledge. Opposite of *pArokSha*, hidden. See pramana.

pratyagatman (*pratyagAtman*, प्रत्यगात्मन्) – the individual soul.

pratyaya (*pratyaya*, प्रत्यय) – belief, firm conviction, certainty; basis or cause of anything.

pravritti (*pravRRitti*, प्रवृत्ति) – active life, following one's desires (*pravRRitti mArga* as opposed to the path to enlightenment – *nivRRitti mArga*).

prayojana (*prayojana*, प्रयोजन) – motive or purpose.

punya (*puNya*, पुण्य) – literally "good" or "virtuous"; used to refer to the "reward" that accrues to us (according to the theory of karma) through the performing of unselfish actions. See also papa.

purna (*pUrNa*, पूर्ण) – full, complete, satisfied, perfect.

purusha (*puruSha*, पुरुष) – person (usually male), spirit.

purushartha (*puruShArtha*, पुरुषार्थ) – The general meaning of this term is "any object of human pursuit" but it is used here in the sense of human (i.e. self) effort to overcome "fate," the fruit of one's past actions. The four classical pursuits are kAma, artha, dharma and mokSha. *puruShArtha-labha* is fulfillment of those pursuits. See karma, sanskara.

purva (*pUrva*, पूर्व) – former, preceding.

purvapaksha (*pUrvapakSha*, पूर्वपक्ष) – objection; view of the 'opponent' in a philosophical discussion. A common technique used in philosophical presentations.

Purva mimamsa, (*pUrva mImAMsA*, पूर्व मीमांसा) – the philosophical system based upon the first part of the Vedas and attributed to Jaimini. Mainly concerned with enquiring into the nature of dharma or right action. See mimamsa, uttaramimamsa.

raga (*rAga*, राग) – any feeling or passion but especially vehement desire; interest in, attachment. Shankara differentiates this from *kAma*: *rAga* is attachment to something one already has whereas *kAma* is wanting something one doesn't have. *rAga-dveSha* is love-hatred.

rajas (*rajas*, रजस्) – the second of the three guna. Associated with animals and activity, emotions, desire, selfishness and passion. Adjective – rajassic (Eng.); *rAjasa* or *rAjasika* (Sansk.) See guna.

Ramanuja (*rAmAnuja*, रामानुज) – founder of the *vishiShTAdvaita* school of philosophy.

rishi (*RRiShi*, ऋषि) – author or singer of sacred Vedic hymns but now more generally used to refer to a saint or Sage.

rupa (*rUpa*, रूप) – form, outward appearance.

sadhaka (*sAdhaka*, साधक) – a seeker or, more pedantically, a worshipper.

sadhana (*sAdhana*, साधन) – literally "leading straight to a goal"; refers to the spiritual disciplines followed as part of a "path" toward Self-realization. See also chatushtaya sampatti.

sadhu (*sAdhu*, साधु) – a sage, saint, holy man; literally leading straight to the goal, hitting the mark.

sadhya (*sAdhya*, साध्य) – (that which is) to be concluded, proved or demonstrated.

saguna (*saguNa*, सगुण) – "with qualities." The term is usually used to refer to Brahman personified as the creator, Iswara, to symbolise the most spiritual aspect of the world of appearances. See Brahman, Isvara, nirguna.

sahaja sthiti (*sahaja sthiti*, सहज स्थिति) – Once Self-realisation has been attained, there is full and lasting knowledge of the Self. "*sahaja*" means "state" but this stage of samadhi is not a state – it is our true nature. It is permanent (*sthiti* meaning "steady" or "remaining"), unlike the earlier stages of samadhi. See nirvikalpa, samadhi, savikalpa, vikalpa.

sakshin (*sAkShin*, साक्षिन्) – a witness, the ego or subject as opposed to the object (also *sAkshi*).

sakshibhava (*sAkshibhAva*, साक्षिभाव) – being or becoming (*bhAva*) a "witness" (*sAkshin*).

samadhana (*samAdhAna*, समाधान) – contemplation, profound meditation; more usually translated as concentration; one of the "six qualities" that form part of Shankara's chatushtaya sampatti. See chatushtaya sampatti, *shamAdi shhaTka sampatti*.

samadhi (*samAdhi*, समाधि) – the state of total peace and stillness achieved during deep meditation. Several "stages" are defined – see vikalpa, savikalpa samadhi, nirvikalpa samadhi and sahaja sthiti.

samana (*samAna*, समान) – one of the five "vital airs," concerned with the digestive system. More generally, relates to assimilation and integration of perceptions with existing knowledge.

samanya (*sAmAnya*, सामान्य) – general, universal, opposite of specific; genus as opposed to species.

samashti (*samaShTi*, समष्टि) – totality, as opposed to *vyaShTi*, the individual.

samavaya (*samavAya*, समवाय) – inseparable connection (inherence) between two things, particularly between a substance and its properties.

sambandha (*sambandha*, सम्बन्ध) – relationship, literally "union, association, conjunction."

samkhya (*sAMkhya*, सांख्य) – one of the three main divisions of Hindu philosophy and one of the six darshanas; attributed to Kapila.

sampradaya (*sampradAya*, सम्प्रदाय) – the tradition or established doctrine of teaching from master to pupil through the ages. See also parampara.

samsara (*saMsAra*, संसार) – the continual cycle of death and rebirth, transmigration etc. to which we are supposedly subject in the phenomenal world until we become enlightened and escape. *saMsArin* – one who is bound to the cycle of birth and death.

samshaya (*saMshaya*, संशय) – uncertainty, irresolution, hesitation or doubt. See manana.

sanchita (*saMchita*, संचित) – one of the three types of sanskara, literally meaning "collected" or "piled up." That sanskara, which has been accumulated from past action but has still not manifest. See agamin, prarabdha, sanskara.

sanga (*sa~Nga*, सङ्ग) – assembly, association, company. See satsanga.

sankalpa (*saMkalpa*, संकल्प) – conception, idea or notion formed in the mind (or heart); will, volition, desire, purpose, intention.

sanskara (*saMskAra*, संस्कार) – Whenever an action is performed with the desire for a specific result (whether for oneself or another), sanskara is created for that person. These accumulate and determine the situations with which we will be presented in the future and will influence the scope of future actions. There are three "types" – agamin, sanchita and prarabdha. The accumulation of sanskara (sanchita) dictates the tendencies that we have to act in a particular way (vasanas). This is all part of the mechanism of karma. See agamin, karma, prarabdha, sanchita and karma.

sanyasa (*saMnyAsa*, संन्यास) – the final stage of the traditional Hindu spiritual path; involves complete renunciation. The word literally means "putting or throwing down, laying aside"; i.e. becoming a professional ascetic. One who does so is called a sanyasin (*saMnyAsin*). See also brahmacharya, grihasta, vanaprastha.

sarvajna (*sarvaj~na*, सर्वज्ञ) – all knowing (of Ishvara).

sat (*sat*, सत्) – existence, reality, truth (to mention a few). See also ananda, chit, satchitananda.

satchitananda (*sat-chit-Ananda* or *sachchidAnanda*, सचिदानन्द) – the oft used word to describe our true nature, in so far as this can be put into words (which it can't). It translates as being-consciousness-bliss but see the separate bits for more detail.

satkarya vada (*satkArya vAda*, सत्कार्य वाद) – the doctrine of the effect actually pre-existing in the cause (usually in reference to the creation).

satsanga (*satsa~Nga*, सत्सङ्ग) – association with the good; keeping "good company"; most commonly used now to refer to a group of people gathered together to discuss (Advaita) philosophy.

sattva (*sattva*, सत्त्व) – the highest of the three guna; associated with stillness, peace, truth, wisdom, unselfishness and spirituality, representing the highest aspirations of man. Adjective – sattwic (Eng.); *sAttva* or *sAttvika* (Sansk.). See guna.

satya (*satya*, सत्य) – true, real. *satyam* – truth. Also one of the *yama*-s – truthfulness, sincerity.

savikalpa (*savikalpa*, सविकल्प) – (referring to samadhi) still "with" doubts about one's identity with the one Self. See nirvikalpa, samadhi, vikalpa.

shabda (*shabda*, शब्द) – scriptural or verbal testimony. See pramana, nyaya prasthana, prasthana-traya, sruti, smRRiti

shama (*shama*, शम) – literally tranquillity, absence of passion but more usually translated as mental discipline or self-control; one of the *shamAdi shhaTka sampatti* or "six qualities" that form part of Shankara"s chatushtaya sampatti. See chatushtaya sampatti, *shamAdi shhaTka sampatti*.

(shamAdi ShaTka sampatti, शमादि षट्क सम्पत्ति) – the six qualities that form part of Shankara"s chatushtaya sampatti. These are *shama, dama, uparati, titikShA, samAdhAna* and *shraddhA*.

Shankara (*shaMkara*, शंकर) – eighth-century Indian philosopher responsible for firmly establishing the principles of Advaita. Though he died at an early age (32?), he commented on a number of major Upanishads, the Bhagavad Gita and the Brahmasutras, as well as being attributed as the author of a number of famous works, such as Atmabodha, Bhaja Govindam and Vivekachudamani.

Shankaracharya (*shaMkarAchArya*, शंकराचार्य) – The title given to one of the four teachers (see acharya) following the tradition in India established by Shankara (see Shankara). He set up four positions, North, South, East and West, to be held by realized men, who would take on the role of teacher and could be consulted by anyone having problems or questions of a spiritual nature.

shanti (*shAnti*, शान्ति) – peace, tranquility.

shanti patha (*shAnti pATha*, शान्ति पाठ) – a traditional prayer for peace (*pATha* means recitation, reading and study of sacred texts etc.)

sharira (*sharIra*, शरीर) – one's body (divided into gross, subtle and causal aspects); literally "that which is easily destroyed or dissolved."

shastra (*shAstra*, शास्त्र) – order, teaching, instruction; any sacred book or composition that has divine authority.

shastriya anumana (*shAstrIya anumAna*, शास्त्रीय अनुमान) – inference based upon the material contained in the scriptures.

shishya (*shiShya*, शिष्य) – pupil, scholar, disciple.

shraddha (*shraddhA*, श्रद्धा) – faith, trust or belief (in the absence of direct personal experience); the student needs this initially in respect of what he is told by the guru or reads in the scriptures; one of the "six qualities" that form part of Shankara's chatushtaya sampatti. See chatushtaya sampatti, *shamAdi shhaTka sampatti*.

shravana (*shravaNa*, श्रवण) – hearing the truth from a sage or reading about it in such works as the Upanishads; first of the three key stages in the classical spiritual path. See also manana, nididhyasana.

shrotriya (*shrotriya*, श्रोत्रिय) – someone (usually a *brAhmaNa*) who is well-versed in the scriptures.

shruti (*shruti*, श्रुति) – refers to the Vedas, incorporating the Upanishads. Literally means "hearing" and refers to the belief that the books contain orally transmitted, sacred wisdom from the dawn of time. See nyaya prasthana, pramana, smriti.

shuddha laukika (*shuddha laukika*, शुद्ध लौकिक) – pure worldly; without objects; i.e. the dream state.

shunya (*shunya*, शुन्य) – literally 'empty' or 'void'. This is associated with the beliefs of the *mAdhyamika* branch of Mahayana Buddhists.

siddha (*siddha*, सिद्ध) – literally 'accomplished' or 'perfected'; used to refer to one who has practiced Yoga for many years and acquired special powers.

siddhanta (*siddhAnta*, सिद्धान्त) – final end or purpose; conclusion of an argument.

smriti (*smRRiti*, स्मृति) – refers to material "remembered" and subsequently written down. In practice, it refers to books of law (in the sense of guidance for living) which were written and based upon the knowledge in the Vedas, i.e. the so-called *dharma-shAstra*-s – Manu, Yajnavalkya, Parashara. In the context of nyaya prasthana, it is used to refer to just one of these books – the Bhagavad Gita. See pramana, nyaya prasthana, sruti.

sopadhika (*sopAdhika*, सोपाधिक) – *nirupAdhika adhyAsa* is super-imposition as of the snake on the rope, as opposed to *sopAdhika adhyAsa* e.g. the sunrise, which is still seen even when the mistake is realized.

spandana (*spandana*, स्पन्दन) – vibration (of the mind in the context of Advaita).

sri (*shrI*, श्री) – used as a title, c.f. "reverend," to signify an eminent person. May also be used in a similar manner to refer to revered objects or works of scripture, for example.

srishti (*sRRiShTi*, सृष्टि) – creation.

srishti-drishti-vada (*sRRiShTidRRiShTivAda*, सृष्टिदृष्टिवाद) – the theory that the world is separate from ourselves, having been created (by God or big-bang) and evolving independently of ourselves, i.e. the "common sense" view of things. See also adhyasa, ajati, drishti-srishti-vada.

sthula (*sthUla*, स्थूल) – large, thick, coarse, dense; the gross body (*sthUla sharIra*).

sukha (*sukha*, सुख) – comfortable, happy, prosperous etc. *sukham* – pleasure, happiness.

sukshma (*sUkShma*, सूक्ष्म) – subtle, as in the subtle body – *sUkShma sharIra*.

sushupti (*suShupti*, सुषुप्ति) – the deep-sleep state of consciousness. The "sleeper ego" is called prajna. See also, jagrat, svapna, turiya.

sutra (*sUtra*, सूत्र) – an especially abbreviated verse in which the fewest possible words are used to convey the message (literally 'thread').

sva (*sva*, स्व) – one's own.

svabhava (*svabhAva*, स्वभाव) – one's natural disposition.

svadharma (*svadharma*, स्वधर्म) – one's own dharma. See dharma.

svapna (*svapna*, स्वप्न) – the dream state of consciousness. The "dreamer ego" is called taijasa. See also, jagrat, sushupti, turiya.

svarga (*svarga*, स्वर्ग) – heaven.

svarupa (*svarUpa*, स्वरूप) – one's own character or nature and, e.g., *svarUpAnanda* – one's own Ananda (limitless bliss).

taijasa (*taijasa*, तैजस) – the "dreamer ego" in the dream state of consciousness, svapna. See also visva, prajna.

Taittiriya (*taittirIya*, तैत्तिरीय) – one of the principal Upanishads. (*taittirIya* was one of the schools of the Yajur Veda.)

tamas (*tamas*, तमस्) – the "lowest" of the three guna. Associated with matter and carrying characteristics such as inertia, laziness, heedlessness and death. It literally means "darkness" or "gloom." Adjective – tamasic (Eng.); *tAmasa* or *tAmasika* (Sansk.). See guna.

tarka (*tarka*, तर्क) – reasoning, speculation, philosophical system or doctrine.

tarkika (*tArkika*, तार्किक) – logician or philosopher.

tatastha (*taTastha*, तटस्थ) – a property distinct from the nature of the body and yet that by which it is known. An example would be telling someone that the house they are referring to in the street ahead is the one with the crow on the chimney. The house is what the listener is interested in but the crow is a *taTastha lakShaNa*, i.e. that by which it is known.

tatratatra (*tatratatra*, तत्रतत्र) – here and there, everywhere (e.g. wherever there is smoke, there is invariably fire).

tejas (*tejas*, तेजस्) – fire (or light) – one of the five elements or *pa~nchabhUta.* Associated with sight.

titiksha (*titikShA*, तितिक्षा) – forbearance or patience; one of the "six qualities" that form part of Shankara's *chatuShTaya sampatti.* See chatushtaya sampatti, *shamAdi shhaTka sampatti.*

trikalatita (*trikAlAtIta*, त्रिकालातीत) – that which transcends past, present and future (describing the Self).

tucha (*tuchCha*, तुच्छ) – completely unreal, e.g. son of a barren woman.

turiya (*turIya*, तुरीय) – the "fourth" state of consciousness (turiya means "fourth"). In fact, some (e.g. Sri Atmananda Krishna Menon) define it rather as the background against which the other states (waking, dream and deep sleep) take place. In this latter case, it is also our true nature. (If defined merely as the highest "state" then our true nature is called turiyatita.

udana (*udAna*, उदान) – one of the five "vital airs," associated with the throat. More generally relates to the understanding that has been gained from past experience.

udaharana (*udAharaNa*, उदाहरण) – prior example (in a logical syllogism).

upadana (*upAdAna*, उपादान) – literally "the act of taking for oneself"; used to refer to the "material cause" in logic (*upAdAna karaNa*).

upadesha (*upadesha*, उपदेश) – instruction or teaching.

upadesha sahasri (*upadesha sAhasrI*, उपदेश साहस्त्री) – "A Thousand Teachings" – book attributed to Shankara (with more certainty than most). *sAhasrika* means "consisting of a thousand."

upadhi (*upAdhi*, उपाधि) – Literally, this means something that is put in place of another thing; a substitute, phantom or disguise. In Vedanta, it is commonly referred to as a "limitation" or "limiting adjunct" i.e. one of the "identifications" made by *ahaMkAra* that prevents us from realizing the Self.

upamana (*upamAna*, उपमान) – comparison, resemblance, analogy.

upanishad (*upaniShad,* उपनिषद्) – one of the (108+) books forming part (usually the end) of one of the four Vedas. The parts of the word mean: to sit (*Shad*) near a master (*upa*) at his feet (*ni*), so that the idea is that we sit at the feet of a master to listen to his words. Monier-Williams (Ref. 5) states that, "according to native authorities, upanishad means "setting at rest ignorance by revealing the knowledge of the supreme spirit." See Vedanta.

uparama (*uparama,* उपरम) – see uparati.

uparati (*uparati,* उपरति) – desisting from sensual enjoyment; "revelling" in that which is "near" i.e. one's own Self; also translated as following one"s dharma or duty; one of the "six qualities" that form part of Shankara"s chatushtaya sampatti. See chatushtaya sampatti, *shamAdi shhaTka sampatti.*

upasana (*upAsana,* उपासन) – worship, homage, waiting upon; literally the act of sitting or being near to; sometimes used in the sense of "meditation."

upeya (*upeya,* उपेय) – the 'end' or 'aim' for which the 'means' are *upAya.*

uttama (*uttama,* उत्तम) – uppermost, excellent, highest.

Uttara mimamsa (*uttara mImAMsA,* उत्तर मीमांसा) – the Vedanta philosophy, based on the latter (uttara) part of the Vedas rather than the earlier (purva). Its founder was Badarayana, who authored the Brahmasutras. There are three main schools – dvaita, advaita and vishishtadvaita. See Brahmasutras, mimamsa, purvamimamsa, veda.

vacharambhana (*vAchArambhaNa,* वाचारम्भण) – depending on mere words or some merely verbal difference. From the Chandogya Upanishad 6.1.4 – 6. (These sutras explain how we effectively create the world by notionally separating out forms and giving them names.)

Vachaspati (*vAchaspati,* वाचस्पति) – name of one of the two schools of Advaita, after the philosopher *vAchaspati mishra.* It is also called the *bhAmati* school. The other school is the *vivaraNa* school.

vak (*vAch*, वाच्) – speech, language sound; speech personified as the Goddess, wife of *prajApati* (lord of creatures).

vada (*vAda*, वाद) – speech, proposition, discourse, argument, discussion, explanation or exposition (of scriptures etc.)

vairagya (*vairAgya*, वैराग्य) – detachment or dispassion; indifference to the pleasure that result from success or the disappointment that result from failure. Literally to be "deprived of" (*vai*) "passion or desire" (*rAga*). See sadhana, chatushtaya sampatti.

vaisheshika (*vaisheShika*, वैशेषिक) – one of the six classical Indian Philosophies, a later development of nyaya by the theologian, Kanada; named after the nine "essentially different substances" believed to constitute matter. See darshana, vishesha.

vaishvanara (*vaishvAnara*, वैश्वानर) – the gross physical condition, or waking state of man (more usually known as *vishva*). brahman "located in" the bodily form. Literally means "relating to or belonging to all men, universal."

vaishya (*vaishya*, वैश्य) – a working man, trader or farmer – the third of the traditional four castes in India.

vaitathya (*vaitathya*, वैतथ्य) – falseness; *vaitathya prakaraNa* is chapter 2 of Gaudapada's *kArikA* on the Mandukya Upanishad and means 'a chapter about the unreality' of the universe. It is a synonym for *mithyA*.

vanaprastha (*vanaprastha*, वनप्रस्थ) – the third stage of the traditional Hindu spiritual path, in which the Brahman retires from life and becomes a "forest dweller," living as a hermit. Traditionally speaking, "a properly initiated *dvija* or twice-born." See also brahmacharya, grihasta, sanyasa, vanaprastha.

vasana (*vAsanA*, वासना) – literally "desiring" or "wishing" – latent behavioural tendency in one's nature brought about through past action (karma) and the sanskara that resulted from this. See karma, sanskara.

Vasishta (*vAsiShTha,* वासिष्ठ) – eponymous sage of the "Yoga Vasishta" one of the classical works of Advaita.

vastu (*vastu,* वस्तु) – a thing that exists, object, subject matter. Strictly speaking, there is only one vastu – Atman. Everything else is incidental – it comes and goes. Only Consciousness is always there, intrinsic.

vastu-tantra (*vastu-tantra,* वस्तुतन्त्र) – objective, dependent on things.

vayu (*vAyu,* वाय) – air (or wind) – one of the five elements or *pa~nchabhUta.* Associated with touch.

veda (*veda,* वेद) – knowledge, but the word is normally only used to refer to one of the four Vedas (see Vedanta) and vidya is used for knowledge per se. See vidya.

Vedanta (*vedAnta,* वेदान्त) – literally "end" or "culmination" (*anta*) of knowledge (*veda*) but veda in this context refers to the four Vedas, the Hindu equivalents of the Christian bible (called Rig, *RRig* Veda; Sama, *sama* Veda; Atharva, *atharva* Veda; Yajur, *yajur* Veda). Traditionally, the last part of the vedas (i.e. "end") is devoted to the Upanishads. See upanishad.

vichara (*vichAra,* विचार) – consideration, reflection, deliberation, investigation. *vichAra mArga* is translated as "Direct Path,"

vidya (*vidyA,* विद्या) – knowledge, science, learning, philosophy. *Atma-vidyA* or *brahma-vidyA* is knowledge of the Self.

Vidyaranya (*vidyAraNya,* विद्यारण्य) – author of the Panchadashi

vijnana (*vij~nAna,* विज्ञान) – discerning, understanding, comprehending; "right apprehension" in the case of *nididhyAsana* as opposed to *dhyAna.* *vij~nAna vAda* is the philosophical theory of Idealism , held by the Yogachara Buddhists.

vijnanamayakosha (*vij~nAnamayakosha,* विज्ञानमयकोश) – the intellectual sheath (one of the five "coverings" that surround our true essence).

vikalpa (*vikalpa,* विकल्प) – doubt, uncertainty or indecision; division or manifoldness.

vikara (*vikAra*, विकार) – transformation, modification, change of form or nature. Also *vikAratva* – the state of change; and *vikAravat* – undergoing changes.

vikshepa (*vikShepa*, विक्षेप) – the "projecting" power of *mAyA*. In the rope-snake metaphor, this superimposes the image of the snake upon the rope. See avarana, maya.

vilakshana (*vilakShaNa*, विलक्षण) –differing from; not possible to define exactly; one definition of *mithyA* is *sad-asad-vilakShaNa*.

virat (*virAT*, विराट्) – objective, gross, physical universe; macrocosmic form of *vishva*.

vishaya (*viShaya*, विषय) – object of sensory perception; any subject or topic; the subject of an argument. The word *viSha* from which it derives means 'poison' or 'venom.'

vishesha (*visheSha*, विशेष) – literally "distinction" or "difference between"; particular or specific. The Vaisheshika philosophy believes that the material universe is made up of nine substances, each of which is "essentially different" from any other. See Vaisheshika.

visheshya (*visheShya*, विशेष्य) – noun; that which is to be distinguished (from something else).

vishishta (*vishiShTa*, विशिष्ट) – distinguished, particular, excellent.

vishishtadvaita (*vishiShTAdvaita*, विशिष्टाद्वैत) – qualified non-dualism; belief that God and the atman are distinct but not separate. Ramanuja is the scholar most often associated with this philosophy. See advaita, dvaita.

vishva (*vishva*, विश्व) – the "waker ego" in the waking state of consciousness, jagrat. Also sometimes referred to as *vaishvAnara*. See also taijasa, prajna.

vivarana (*vivaraNa*, विवरण) – literally "explanation" or "interpretation"; name of one of the two schools of Advaita. The other school is the *vAcaspati or bhAmati* school.

vivarta (*vivarta*, विवर्त) – an apparent or illusory form; unreality caused by avidya.

vivarta vada (*vivarta vAda*, विवर्त वाद) – the theory that the world is only an apparent projection of Ishvara (i.e. an illusion); apparent transformation only; manifestation not creation.

viveka (*viveka*, विवेक) – discrimination; the function of buddhi, having the ability to differentiate between the unreal and the real. See sadhana, chatushtaya sampatti.

Vivekachudamani (*vivekachUDAmaNi*, विवेकचूडामणि) – the title of a book attributed to Shankara. *chUDAmaNi* is the name given to the jewel worn on top of the head. An English version of the book is called "The Crest Jewel of Discrimination."

vritti (*vRRitti*, वृत्ति) – in the context of Vedanta, this means a mental disposition. In general, it can mean a mode of conduct or behaviour, character or disposition, business or profession etc. See aham vritti and idam vritti.

vyakta (*vyakta*, व्यक्त) – manifested, apparent, visible, perceptible to the senses as opposed to avyakta – transcendental.

vyana (*vyAna*, व्यान) – one of the five "vital airs," concerned with the circulatory system. More generally, alludes to the discriminatory faculties, evaluating and judging etc.

vyapti (*vyApti*, व्याप्ति) – inseparable presence of one thing in another, invariable concomitance (as in e.g. no smoke without fire).

vyashti (*vyaShTi*, व्यष्टि) – the individual or "individuality" as opposed to the totality, *samaShTi*.

vyavahara (noun) (*vyavahAra*, व्यवहार);

vyavaharika (adj.), (*vyAvahArika*, व्यावहारिक) – the "relative," "practical," or phenomenal world of appearances; the normal world in which we live and which we usually believe to be real; as opposed to *pAramArthika* (reality) and *prAtibhAsika* (illusory). See paramarthika and pratibhasika.

yatrayatra (*yatrayatra*, यत्रयत्र) – wherever (e.g. wherever there is smoke, there is invariably fire).

yoga (*yoga*, योग) – literally "joining" or "attaching" (our word "yoke" derives from this). It is used generally to refer to any system whose aim is to "join" our "individual self" back to the "universal Self." The Yoga system pedantically refers to that specified by Patanjali. See bhakti, jnana, karma.

Yogachara (*yogAchAra*, योगाचार) – branch of Hinayana Buddhism; also known as *vij~nAna vAda*.

yukti (*yukti*, युक्ति) – reasoning, argument, induction, deduction (as opposed to intuition – *anubhava*).

Annotated Bibliography

Ref. 1   **Mandukya Karika Of Gaudapada, Vidyavachaspati V. Panoli**

This is a basic translation of the Upanishad and kArikA-s, without Devanagari or transliteration. It is downloadable from the (Celextel) Vedanta Spiritual Library (which has versions of all Upanishads and many other texts) – http://www.celextel.org/upanishads/atharva_veda/man dukya.html.

Ref. 2   **The Mandukyopanishad With Gaudapada's Karikas and the Bhashya of Shankara, Manilal N. Dvivedi, Kessinger Publishing. ISBN 1428643060.** (This is a reprint of the original publication by Tookaram Tatya, F.T.S. in 1894)

This is a modern reprint of an old book. Originally published in 1894 for the Bombay Theosophical Society, it is one of the scanned publications by Kessinger Rare Reprints. Whether it is a partial consequence of 'archaic' English, or simply a too-literal translation, the complete rendition of Shankara's commentary is not very readable. There is no Devanagari and no transliteration, so it is not possible to check which Sanskrit words have been translated (or mistranslated). In fact there are very few Sanskrit terms used at all, which can certainly cause problems. As an example just encountered, the phrase 'inverted cognition' is used (I.11 and I.14) when what is meant is 'misperception', 'mistake', or 'error'. Accordingly, I would suggest that it has its use when you want to read an alternative rendition of Shankara's bhAshya but otherwise it is best ignored.

Ref. 3   **Discourses on Mandukya Upanishad with Gaudapada's Karika, Swami Chinmayananda, Central Chinmaya Mission Trust, 1953. No ISBN.**

After the Nikhilananda version (Ref. 4), this is probably the easiest to obtain (although you may have to contact a Chinmaya Mission for a copy). It is also by far the most readable; in fact, it may suffer from being a bit too verbose! A concise, carefully worded explanation may succeed whereas a long one may lose or divert us. That said, the interpretation may usually be relied upon, since Swami Chinmayananda is a solid, traditional teacher.

Each verse has Devanagari followed by transliteration and a translation (not word by word). There is then a lengthy commentary (the whole book is 430 pages).

This was not originally written material but has been recon-structed from notes taken by attendees of the 91-day session of the talks. These were subsequently checked by Swamiji with amendments being made as necessary but clearly the final result does not bear comparison with a formally edited manuscript. Nevertheless, if the reader wishes to purchase only one of the books in this bibliography, this probably ought to be it.

Ref. 4 **The Mandukya Upanishad with Gaudapada's Karika and Shankara's Commentary, Translated by Swami Nikhilananda, Advaita Ashrama, 1932. No ISBN.**

This is the translation that you are most likely to find in your specialist bookstore (of course you do not find any Advaita-related books in most High Street bookstores). Swami Nikhilananda is well-known and was a highly respected monk in the Ramakrishna Order. The book was first published in 1932. For many years, this was the only version I had and I attempted to read it several times, intrigued with its content and finding lucid pearls amongst rather more impenetrable material.

Its format is to present the Devanagari, followed by a simple translation without transliteration or word by word inter-pretation. This is then followed by Shankara's commentary.

Any observations of the author are relegated to notes at the bottom of the page in small font. These notes often merely reword the comments of Shankara and do not really add much to the translation. Any Sanskrit reference in these notes is in Devanagari only, so the reader is definitely expected to be able to read the script!

This version really does emphasize the need for a suitably qualified teacher to present the material. This is so that the seeker may benefit from hundreds of years of sampradAya methodology on how best to interpret the original for ease of understanding.

Ref. 5   Classes on Mandukya Upanishad and Karikas, H. H. Swami Paramarthananda, Vedanta Vidyarthi Sangha. No ISBN.

These are brilliant – no other adjective seems suitable. There is lots of Sanskrit but so much is explained, and with such clarity that it is worth listening to them many times if necessary. They are in the form of around 80 hours worth of mp3-format talks on CD. They are available from Shastraprakashika Trust in Chennai. Unfortunately, if you live outside of India, you will probably need to find someone who can purchase them on your behalf and forward them. I realized that this is probably my fault, as I tried to persuade Swamiji to allow me to post the talks on the Internet (even though many were already available without his permission). He said that he did not want to do this, as the recordings were really for the purpose of revision by those who had already attended the talks. After all, he points out, one should only study this Upanishad after studying the other major Upanishads, and only then under the guidance of a qualified teacher. I believe it was after this that the Trust ceased to export the talks. Most of the other sources on the Internet seem to have dried up.

Ref. 6   Mandukyopanishad: A Summary of Gaudapada's

Karika, Swami Sharvananda, Sri Ramakrishna Math, 1982. No. ISBN.

This is a very small book in two parts. The first part is a translation, with brief notes, on the Upanishad. There is Devanagari followed by transliteration and phrase by phrase translation. Apart from the inevitable, (neo-Vedanta version) mention of samAdhi, the commentary is good. The second part (Appendix) is an essay of twenty-odd pages on the kArikA-s by Swami Tyagisanada. This presents a good summary of the main points of each chapter, including a very reasonable explanation for the Buddhist tendencies.

Ref. 7   **The Agamashastra of Gaudapada, Edited by Vidushekhara Bhattacharya, Motilal Banarsidass, 1943. ISBN 81-208-0652-2.**

Of all the books I have ever seen, I think this takes the prize as having the most unattractive set of fonts and poorest editing and layout in general. The preface and introduction take up a third of the book – up to page cxlvi! There are 9 separate indexes and 18 pages of 'Addenda et corrigenda' at the end!

There is no Devanagari but extensive transliterated Sanskrit, usually in brackets after the English. The style is extremely academic, with very many references to obscure texts and authors, sometimes even quoting Sanskrit verses without translation, clearly expecting his readers to be proficient. It is also the only commentary I am aware of that lists all the various source Manuscripts for the Gaudapada text and includes an appendix indicating the 'variants'. It is very much a book for someone studying the scripture as part of a university course rather than as a seeker. I would be surprised if anyone else succeeds in reading more than a few pages. Certainly I didn't!

There is no real commentary on the kArikA itself or discussion of Advaita philosophy as presented. The author sets out to present an alternative interpretation to that of Shankara, especially showing the many influences of mahayAna *Buddhism on Gaudapada's text. Although it clearly does this well, given the extent to which other authors address his arguments, it is obviously not a book to recommend here.*

Ref. 8 **Gaudapada Mandkyakarika: The Metaphysical Path of Vedanta, Translation and commentary by Raphael, Aurea Vidya, 2002. ISBN 1-931406-04-9.**

Raphael is the founder of the Italian 'Ashram Vidya Order'. He no longer teaches but has written many books. Although a number of these are well-known Advaita texts (in addition to this, there are also dRRigdRRishya viveka, vivekachUDAmaNi *and the* bhagavadgItA *for example), he has also written books on Plato and the philosophers of the 'Orphic' tradition. His books often promote a synthesis of this background wisdom. This is useful if the reader wants to gain an understanding of the truth regardless of its source but less so if he or she wishes to understand a particular text and the meaning intended by its author, or to adhere to a strictly traditional Advaita context.*

In the main part of the book, verses are presented as English translation only, without either Devanagari or transliteration (there is an appendix containing just the transliterated Sanskrit without translation). Some of the verses are followed by the author's commentary. And one has to say that some of the comments have a mystical ring to them and are difficult to make sense of.

Ref. 9 **Dispelling Illusion: Gaudapada's Alatashanti, Translation and Introduction Douglas A. Fox, State University of New York Press, 1993. ISBN 0-7914-1502-3.**

One of the books by Western authors, this specifically addresses the fourth chapter of the kArikA-s. *Part 2 of the book contains a translation of this, followed by a detailed commentary. Part 1 is concerned with supplying a background by looking briefly at the historical context and, in particular, the place of Buddhism in the development of the ideas. There follows a brief look at* pramANa-s, *a summary of the content of the first three chapters and then a more detailed summary of the material in the fourth chapter and the arguments for* ajAti vAda. *Douglas Fox was Professor of Religion at The Colorado College at the time of writing, so the book is aimed at the academic reader. It is nevertheless readable, with some useful material. There is no Devanagari and only a very little transliterated Sanskrit.*

Ref. 10   The Mandukya Upanishad: An Exposition, Swami Krishnananda, The Divine Life Trust Society, 1981. ISBN 81-7052-100-9.

This is available as a thin (96 page) paperback or it can be downloaded electronically from http://www.swami-krishnananda.org/mand_0.html. There is a direct translation of the Upanishad (including Devanagari and transliteration without diacritical marks). This is followed by chapters on what he sees as the main topics covered by the Upanishad (e.g. 'The Mystery of Dream and Sleep', 'The God of the Universe').

This is a traditionally based (completely non-academic) treatment of the Upanishad. I found the chapter on 'The Universal Vaisvanara' very confusing however. As soon as one confuses virAT *and* Ishvara, *gross and causal become confused and the entire explanation breaks down. Similarly, the chapter on the seventh mantra, addressing the 'description' of* turIya, *talks about 'God in His essence'. This is not helpful when trying to discriminate between relative and absolute.*

Ref. 11   Asparsha Yoga: A Study of Gaudapada's Mandukya Karika, Colin A. Cole, Motilal Banarsidass, 1982.

ISBN 81-208-1992-6.

As the title implies, this book is specifically concerned with the practical aspects of the kArikA-s – the 'spiritual instructions' (upadesha) for attaining mokSha. *As such, it concentrates on III.29-48 and selected verses from chapter IV (the English translations of these are given in Appendices). There are short chapters on Gaudapada himself and the kArikA-s in general, and there are chapters on the philosophy in general and the style in which this is presented, on the 'phenomenology and meta-psychology', and on the overall synthesis of philosophy and religion. By far the longest chapter, however, nearly half of the book, is devoted to 'soteriology', the 'doctrine of salvation' as the dictionary has it. The book is readable and well articulated, with some good explanations. Transliterated Sanskrit terms are given where appropriate and there are lots of references to scriptural and other sources in footnotes. Although written as a Masters Thesis, it is clear that the author's interest goes far deeper and he has succeeded in producing a work which is accessible to those who do not have extensive prior exposure to Advaita.*

Ref. 12 **The Philosophy of Mandukya Karika, Caterina Conio, Bharatiya Vidya Prakashan, 1971.**

This is another one of the versions that you are unlikely to find. It was published in Varanasi in 1971 in a poor-quality hardback and I do not think it has been republished since. It is not a straight commentary and does not address the Upanishad itself. Rather it looks at Gaudapada's philosophy, as represented by the kArikA and "evaluates its significance to contemporary philosophy both in and out of India". It is written in an academic style, with lots of footnotes.

It has chapters on how Gaudapada presents the various categories of philosophy, viz. logic, causality, epistemology, religious. There is a chapter on the kArikA-s in general and one on the first chapter specifically, looking at the problem of creation. There is also a chapter on Shankara's bhAShya *and a final chapter on the interpretation of other schools of Vedanta.*

There is no Devanagari, and Sanskrit quotations, where given, are in transliterated form without translation.

Ref. 13 **The Method of Early Advaita Vedanta: A Study of Gaudapada, Shankara, Sureshvara and Padmapada, Michael Comans, Motilal Banarsidass, 2000. ISBN 81-208-1722-2.**

The first third of the book is devoted to Gaudapada. There are 3 chapters, with the first being a running commentary on the kArikA-s. Michael Comans is a direct disciple of Swami Dayananda (and now goes by the name of Sri Vasudevacharya). Accordingly, this is a very reliable interpretation and is clearly written, with 'academic' elements being relegated to notes at the end of each chapter. The second chapter summarizes the philosophy and deals with the relation to Buddhist thought, while the third chapter is entitled 'Gaudapada on Liberation and the Means to Liberation'. The entire book is highly recommended.

Ref. 14 **Early Advaita Vedanta and Buddhism: The Mahayana Context of the Gaudapadiya-Karika, Richard King, Sri Satguru Publications, 1997. ISBN 8170305586.**

This book looks at the philosophy of early Advaita and examines its relationship to the various schools of Buddhism that were extant at the time. There is an early claim to the effect that a 'proper understanding of Gaudapadian thought requires... a comprehensive grasp of the philosophical texts of Mahayana Buddhism' so that King also claims that any book lacking this is bound to be deficient. From an academic point of view, this of course may be true but I, along with all of the other authors of books on the subject, must disagree with the implication that one cannot understand the material in an Advaita context.

Following a 'date and authorship' chapter, the next part of the book deals with the background to the kArikA-s, and that dealing with the 'Vedantic Heritage' has some very useful material on other Upanishads and discussions in the Brahma Sutras. The next chapter on the 'Abhidarma Context' is awash with Buddhist terminology and largely incomprehensible to someone with only a background of Advaita (such as myself).

Subsequent chapters deal with ajAtivAda and asparsha yoga (some very good descriptions in both of these) before concluding with two more Buddhist-related chapters. There is then a useful summary translation of the kArikA-s before the many pages of Notes and comprehensive index and bibliography.

There is no Devanagari. There is frequent use of transliterated Sanskrit terms, but these usually appear in brackets after the English translation. As noted, there are many (Buddhist) terms with which students of only Advaita will not be familiar. The conclusion has to be that, if you want to study Gaudapada to understand where he is coming from then you do need to be aware of the Buddhist context. In that case, this book is essential. If you only (!) want to understand what Gaudapada is saying in an Advaita context, then it may be best to ignore this book.

Ref. 15 **Eight Upanishads, with the commentary of Shankaracharya, translated by Swami Gambhirananda, Advaita Ashrama, 1958. ISBN 81-7505-015-2.**

Swami Gambhirananda was a monk with the Ramakrishna Mission, who died in 1988. He is well-known for his translations and commentaries, which can be more readily purchased than most versions. These eight major Upanishads are contained in two volumes. The Mandukya is in Volume 2 and takes up about half the book (around 240 pages), since it

covers the kArikA-s as well.
Each verse has the Devanagari without transliteration.
There then follows his translation (not word by word).
Shankara's commentary follows. This often translates
specific words and these are presented in transliterated form.
Swami Gambhirananda's notes appear as footnotes but,
unlike the Swami Nikhilananda version, there are not many
of these.
Other commentaries have clearly been taken into account in
providing Shankara's translation since, for example,
Anandagiri's interpretation is sometimes used. Also, where
Shankara quotes from the scriptures, complete reference to
source has been added. This addition makes the book an
indispensable reference.

Ref. 16 **A New Approach to Gaudapadakarika, N. Aiyaswami Sastri, published in Bulletin of Tibetology, vol. 8, no. 1, Feb. 1971.** Downloadable from http://www. dspace.cam.ac.uk/retrieve/637017/bot_08_01_02.pdf.
Aiyaswami compares aspects of the kArikA presentations
variously to Yogachara, Madhyamika and Mahayana
Buddhist teaching, as he summarizes the content. He takes
for consideration a number of Sanskrit terms used by
Gaudapada and looks at their usage compared to those in the
various Buddhist schools. He concludes that Gaudapada
adopted dialectics from Nagarjuna and a number of other
Buddhist authors and adapted them for his own teaching.
This is an academic presentation, using both Devanagari
and transliterated Sanskrit (not usually together, and not
always translated) and is not recommended unless you are
interested in the Buddhist angle.

Ref. 17 **Gaudapada Karika, Raghunath Damodar Karmarkar, Bhandarkar Oriental Research Institute, 1953.**
Downloadable from http://archive.org/details/Gaudapada-Karika.English. (in various formats). According to his

preface, this book was written expressly to criticize the arguments of Prof Bhattacharya in Ref. 7 "so that a balanced view of Gaudapada's philosophy could be taken". He specifically objects to the Buddhist interpretations, believing that Gaudapada was a traditional Vedantist.

There are some 50 pages of introductory material, followed by the text and translation of the kArikA-s. The text is in Devanagari without any transliteration and the translation does not cross-reference the Sanskrit. There are then around 90 pages of notes on the four chapters followed by two indexes.

The text is effectively impossible to read for those who do not understand Sanskrit. Whereas most writers give all the Sanskrit terms in transliterated form, Karmarkar uses only Devanagari, even though many terms are followed by the English in brackets. Often there will be long quotations in Devanagari, without translation. Some English sentences have interpolated, and untranslated, Devanagari words.

Clearly another book that will appeal to very, very few readers.

Ref. 18   Upanishads Retold Vol. 2, V. H. Date, Munshiram Manoharlal, 1999. ISBN 81-215-0874-6.

This is what the publisher calls a 'free rendering' and is similar to the author's presentation of the Brahma Sutras. The idea is to reword the material so as to present the essence of the teaching in clear English, thus avoiding the stilted wording of literal translation. These Upanishad volumes have no Devanagari or transliteration of mantras (the Brahmasutra version has both) and only essential Sanskrit terms are used. And they are very good.

The Mandukya version here also covers the kArikA-s and the essence of Shankara's comments. The other Upanishads covered by Volume 2 are Chandogya, Aitareya, Taittiriya, Shvetashvatara, Kaushitaka, Maitri and Jabala.

Ref. 19   Ten Upanishads of Four Vedas, Researched and Edited by Ram K. Piparaiya, Bharatiya Vidya Bhavan, 2003. ISBN 81-7276-298-4.

This a large (and very expensive!) hardback book with an unusual format. It assumes no prior exposure to Vedanta and Part 1 of the book explains what the Upanishads are and extols their virtues. There are chapters devoted to the metaphors and parables used and a selection of key dialogs and maxims.

Part 2 contains ten of the most significant Upanishads and occupies most of the book (over 500 pages). Each is presented as English translation, without either Devanagari or transliteration, and the number of Sanskrit terms used is much smaller than usual and always translated. The most significant difference is that the text of each Upanishad is preceded by a 'simplified synopsis' and followed by several different 'focused' commentaries.

The Mandukya appears mainly without the kArikA* and occupies only 23 pages but includes notes on the commentaries of Shankara (as translated by Swami Nikhilananda), S. Radhakrishnan, Swami Krishnananda, Sri Madhava, Rohit Mehta (a Gujurati philosopher who died in 1995) and N. A. Nikam (another twentieth-century Indian philosopher). [*The translation of the first chapter of the kArikA-s is given with a few notes by Swami Nikhilananda.] Comments have been made elsewhere in this bibliography on theNikhilananda and Krishnananda commentaries. The other commentaries are not at all helpful and overall, despite its interesting format, this version cannot be recommended. It cannot be overemphasized how easy it is to be taken in by seemingly authoritative statements encountered in a book. The fact that it is written down does not make it reliable! The best guideline is to look for the influence of an accepted sampradAya, *in which there is a careful methodology*

behind the introduction of material (and its later rescission)!
In case it has not been realized by now, my own influence is
principally through Swami Dayananda and his disciples.

Ref. 20 Mandukya Upanishad (with Gaudapada's Karika),
Swami Lokeswarananda, The Ramakrishna Mission
of Culture, 1995. ISBN 81-85843-71-6.

At first sight, this appears to be a text to recommend. It has
large, clear type and the language used is also straight-
forward and readable. Each verse appears in Devanagari,
followed by Romanized transliteration and then a translation
of each word or phrase. And there is a paragraph or more of
commentary on each verse.

Unfortunately, the translations and commentary cannot be
relied upon. They are often very 'free' and can be positively
misleading for someone who does not already have a good
understanding of Advaita such that they are able to spot the
inconsistencies and inaccuracies.

Some of these are subtle. For example, in mantra 7, he trans-
lates alakShaNam *as 'beyond perception by any organ'. But*
this aspect has already been covered by adRRishTam. *By*
repeating this, he misses the pramANa *of inference.*
lakShaNa *is an 'indicatory mark' or 'pointer', not directly*
relevant to organs of perception. But there are more signif-
icant errors stemming from neo-Vedanta. The main one of
these is treating turIya *as a state. He says, for example, "You*
attain this turIya *state, the fourth and real aspect of the Self,*
through samAdhi, *through a transcendental experience." If*
the real Self is 'attained', who attains it and how could this
not be duality?

Nevertheless, there are some insightful explanations and,
because of its readability, the Devanagari and word transla-
tions, it is an essential addition to the library!

Ref. 21 Thirteen Principal Upanishads, Vol. II Mandukya

Upanishad with Gaudapa Karikas, Prof. Jayantkrishna H. Dave, Bharatiya Vidya Bhavan, 1990.

This is a hardback book published in India in 1990 and my copy, at least, does not have very sound binding! It is quite long at 370 pages and has an index which appears to have been computer generated in that each keyword has very many entries and is singularly unhelpful!

On the plus side, this is one of the few books that explicitly takes into account Anandagiri's commentary (TIkA) on Shankara's commentary (bhAshya) on Gaudapada (kArikA) and even some commentaries from other interpreters. (The flysheet of the cover records that there are notes from kUranArAyana from the Ramanuja School, madhva and shriniVasa from the madhva School, and puruShottama goswAmI from the Vallabha School.)

Unfortunately, references to who said what, or even to scriptural quotations, are few. This is a significant omission, since it means the reader cannot easily find and read the original in order to gain more understanding. There is also a lot of repetition, rather than clarification. This means that the translation of Shankara's commentary is often followed by 'comments' which are virtually identical. Many Sanskrit terms are used, mostly without translation and the English, though quite good, does not seem to have been edited. Both Devanagari script and transliteration are presented for each verse.

Despite its shortcomings, this is the version that I found myself using most frequently, in order to ascertain the most accurate rendering of Shankara's commentary and to find any additional Anandagiri material. It is a book that is very difficult to find, however.

Ref. 22 **Meditation on OM and Mandukya Upanishad, Swami Sivananda, The Divine Life Society, 1941,**

ISBN 81-7052-043-6.

This little book does contain a translation of the Mandukya Upanishad – about 25 pages, complete with Devanagari script and a transliteration (albeit without any diacritical marks). The comments are based upon translation of individual words and it is generally good. (As an aside, his translation and commentary on the Brahma Sutras is particularly recommended.)

The rest of the book is concerned with other 'OM-related' material. There is a chapter containing extracts from other Upanishads which refer to OM. There are meditations, songs and kirtans. The introductory chapter is on the 'Philosophy of OM', sometimes useful, sometimes mystical and repetitive. There are also some non-traditional Advaita statements (e.g. there are '16 states of consciousness' and turIya 'has to be realized through meditation'). This is understandable, since Sivananda's teaching was a mix of Yoga and Vedanta. [Note that some much later, minor Upanishads multiply the number of states. Since there is really only non-dual Consciousness, one wonders what is served by making things more, rather than less complicated!]

Ref. 23 Notes On Mandukya Upanishad And Karika, Kuntimaddi Sadananda, Posts to Advaitin List, 2006 .

These notes were based upon talks given by Swami Chinmayananda and two of his disciples as well as those by Swami Paramarthananda. Acharya Sadananda teaches as the Chinmaya Mission, Washington. They are an introduction only, since the series was never completed. Nevertheless, this introduction is over 30,000 words long and also covers the first two mantras of the Upanishad, so is well worth reading.

Ref. 24 The Magic Jewel of Intuition (The Tri-Basic Method of Cognizing the Self), D. B. Gangolli, Adhyatma Prakasha Karyalaya, 1986. No ISBN.

This is not actually a commentary on either the Upanishad or the kArikA-s. The entire book, however, is on the subject of the three states and the nature of the ultimate reality (its subtitle indicates this, although the term 'tri-basic' may not be familiar). It was written by Sri Satchidanandendra Saraswati Swami (SSSS) in the Kannada language and has been loosely translated into English, and considerably extended, by his disciple D. B. Gangolli.

It is a very poor quality paperback and the quality of English also leaves much to be desired. Together, these make this a difficult book to read; this is a great pity because the subject matter is very interesting. There are also some challenging ideas and convincing explanations. There is not too much Sanskrit but, where there is, it is not in any recognized transliteration since the printing obviously did not permit either Devanagari or diacritical marks.

All of this is largely academic, though, since there were only 1000 copies printed in 1986 and it is extremely unlikely that you will find one anywhere now. As far as I know, there is no electronic copy available.

Ref. 25 Vedanta or The Science of Reality, K. A. Krishnaswamy Iyer, Adhyatma Prakasha Karyalaya, 1957. No ISBN.

Krishnaswamy Iyer was the guru of SSSS (see Ref. 24), who provides an introduction to the second edition. This book, dedicated to Shankara, was written in 1930 and principally examines many Western philosophers and religions, highlighting their Vedanta-like insights and revealing their errors.

The writing is 'flowery' but often quite humorous and ironic, and there are clear explanations of some difficult topics. Some of the major ones are reality versus appearance, mAyA, idealism versus realism, perception; and, throughout, there is referral back to the key prakriyA of avasthA traya – the analysis of the three states of consciousness.

Ref. 26 **The Self and its States, Andrew O. Fort, Motilal Manarsidass, 1990. ISBN 81-208-0633-6.**

This is another of the few books by Western authors and, as its title implies, it only deals with the material from the Upanishad itself and the first chapter of the kArikA-s. It also takes into account Shankara's commentary and Part II actually translates these three elements. But only two of the seven chapters in Part I address these aspects. The remaining ones look at the treatment of states of consciousness in early Advaita and in post-Shankara philosophy through to modern psychology. The book is academically oriented (as opposed to being written for a spiritual seeker). This is to be expected as Andrew Fort was, at the time of writing, Assistant Professor of Asian Religions at Texas Christian University. It follows that it is well-researched, with lots of useful references. It is also well-written and readable, with some useful descriptions. I did have one or two queries on his interpretations, however. The scriptural material appears in Devanagari and is not transliterated. Some transliterated Sanskrit appears throughout the rest of the book.

Ref. 27 **Sixty Upanishads of the Veda, Volume-II, Paul Deussen, translated V. M. Bedekar and G. B. Palsule, Motilal Banarsidass, 1980. ISBN 978-81-208-1469-1.**

The Mandukya, together with the kArikA is covered in this volume, taking up 33 pages of the 995. There is a five-page introduction but then the verses are simply presented in a translated form without Devanagari or transliteration. The verses of the kArikA are given in the form of poetry (as are the original Sanskrit). Thankfully, there is no attempt to provide any rhymes but the struggle to find suitable words means that the translations sometimes seem contrived and certainly cannot be relied upon for accuracy. Having been converted from Sanskrit to German to English, it is simply hopeless.

Ref. 28 **The World as Dream, Arvind Sharma, D.K. Printworld (P) Ltd., 2006. ISBN. 8124603650.**

Sharma also has books on the Rope-snake metaphor and the shell-silver but it is this one that is particularly relevant to this book. It addresses many aspects and occurrences of the metaphor in different contexts, with chapters on its usage by Ramana Maharshi, Nisargadatta, Western religion and modern dream research. There are a number of references to Gaudapada, and the material in general makes for interesting reading, but it should be noted that Sharma derives the Gaudapada-related material from Ref. 54.

Ref. 29 **The Essential Gaudapada, Swami Satchidanandendra Saraswati, Translated by D. B. Gangolli, Adhyatma Prakasha Karyalaya, 1997. No ISBN.**

Similar comments apply as for Ref. 24: the author of that is the translator of this. Much of it is very difficult to read, with sentences extending over many lines so that the sense is lost before one reaches the end. But there were only 500 copies printed so you are unlikely to find a copy anyway!

The format is generally to present the Devanagari of the verse from the kArikA, without transliteration but with a 'meaning' rather than pure translation. There are then likely to be headings and general discussion on the related topic before moving on to the next verse. Important points are rendered in bold font, which is useful.

As with the other material from SSSS, much is valuable if one can follow it. It is obvious that the translator is making considerable effort to use correct English and convey the concepts clearly but unfortunately his command of the vernacular is outdated and inadequate for the task.

Ref. 30 **The Ten Principal Upanishads, translated Sri Purohit Swami and W. B. Yeats, Faber and Faber, 1937. ISBN 0-571-09363-9.**

Only 3 pages of this short book are devoted to the Mandukya. Translations are poetic-inspirational and not at all literal, so this book should be purchased for that purpose and not to uncover the meaning through any reasoned manner. This version is also the one used for the spoken interludes in the following reference.

Ref. 31 **Mandukya Upanishad: A Musical Experience of OM, Pandit Jasraj, Times Music, 2001.**

Three CDs of Pandit Jasraj singing the Sanskrit mantras of the Upanishad to the accompaniment of sitar etc. If you like this sort of music, the performance is electrifying.

Ref. 32 **The Brihadaranyaka Upanishad with the commentary of Shankaracharya, Translated by Swami Madhavananda, Advaita Ashrama, 4ᵗʰ Edition, 1965. ISBN 81-7505-102-7.**

Included because of quoted reference. This seems to be the most authoritative version of the Br. U. that I have seen. It has the Devanagari (without transliteration or word by word translation) followed by Shankara's commentary, with just the occasional note by the translator as a footnote.

The version by Som Raj Gupta ("The Word Speaks to the Faustian Man", Vol V Parts 1 &2) looks very good, accurate but more readable, but is much larger and much more expensive.

Ref. 33 **Thirteen Principal Upanishads, Vol. I Prasna and Mundaka Upanishads, Prof. Jayantkrishna H. Dave, Bharatiya Vidya Bhavan, 1988. No ISBN.**

Included because of quoted reference. The same general comments apply as for Ref. 21, since this is part of the same series. A more readable version of the prashna upaniShad *is that by Swami Muni Naryana Prasad, but the Dave version has the full Shankara* bhAShya *and authoritative notes.*

Ref 34 **The Epistemology of Yoga, Swami Krishnananda, Divine Life Society. ISBN 978-8170522287.**

(Free download from www.swami-krishnananda.org.)
Included because of quoted reference.

Ref. 35   **ShvetAshvataropaniShad: The knowledge that liberates, translated and commentary by Devadatta Kali, Nicholas-Hays Inc., 2011. ISBN 978-0-89254-166-9.**

Not directly relevant; included because of the quotation. This is a huge book – nearly 500 pages – and looks very authoritative and well-presented. A nice touch is that mantras in the main body of the book are given in Devanagari, followed by transliteration, followed by translation; but the entire text in Devanagari is presented word by word with translation in an Appendix. Unfortunately, I cannot comment on the content as I have not yet read it!

Ref. 36   **A History of Early Vedanta Philosophy, Part 2, Hajime Nakamura, Translated into English by Hajime Nakamura, Trevor Leggett and others, Motilal Banarsidass, 2004. ISBN 81-208-1963-2.**

The whole of Part VI of this book is devoted to the Mandukya kArikA – 172 pages. A first observation has to be that I have never encountered such a complex layout of the material in a book before. There are sections, sub-sections and appendices within each chapter and the same source material seems to be covered in several different places. It is most confusing!

The headings addressed by the chapters are: 'Interpretation of some words and phrases', 'Textual analysis' and 'Thought'. Within each sub-section, the author looks separately at how the ideas are conveyed by the Upanishad itself and by each chapter of the kArikA. Since some commentators claim that each chapter was actually written by someone different, this approach may well be justified but it certainly does not make for a comfortable reading experience. This is compounded by the fact that, since this is an academic text, there are masses of notes, references and transliterated Sanskrit without translation.

This sort of approach certainly has its value. For example, in the first chapter, it is pointed out that the word alakShana *is translated as 'without form' by Chinese translators of Buddhist texts. And Nakamura says that Shankara's translation as* ali~Nga *(without any characteristic mark) is 'contrived'. Personally, I feel that lack of form is covered by* adRRiShTam *and that he has missed the implication of* turIya *not being available to the* pramANa-s *(and its translation as 'un-inferable').*

Ref. 37   **Mandukya Upanishad with Gaudapada Karikas and Shankara's Commentary, translated by M Srinivasa Rao, The Vedanta Kesari, Chennai, volumes XVIII – XXI (1931 – 35).**

There are about 30 separate articles published periodically over the five years. There is no Devanagari, transliteration or word by word translation. This version presents a simple translation of each mantra or shloka without further commentary.

The Vedanta Kesari 96-year archive may be purchased on DVD from Sri Ramakrishna Math, Chennai – http://www.chennaimath.org/istore/product/96-years-of-the-vedanta-kesari-a-dvd-collection/.

Ref. 38   **Isavasya and Mandukya Upanisads, Translation and Commentary by Swami Muni Narayana Prasad, D. K. Printworld (P) Ltd, 2009. ISBN 078-81-246-0492-2.**

This only covers the Upanishad and not the kArikA-s *(although you get the added bonus of the* Isha *commentary also). Swami Prasad is a very good commentator indeed and this is no exception. There are over 60 pages of writing on the 12 mantras. Intelligent and valuable observations are combined with useful notes on the derivation and meaning of Sanskrit words. There are also numerous quotations from his teacher, Narayana Guru. Highly recommended.*

Ref. 39 **The Mandukya Upanisad and the Agama Sastra: An Investigation into the Meaning of the Vedanta, Thomas E. Wood, Motilal Banarsidass, 1992. ISBN 81-208-0930-0.**

This is not a 'straight' commentary on the Upanishad and kArikA-s but a book with an agenda! The introduction explains that the purpose is to argue a number of issues: 1) that the whole is a single work and not four separate pieces, possibly by different authors; 2) that it was probably not written by the teacher of Shankara's teacher and 3) that Shankara's commentary was not written by Shankara.

He attempts to demonstrate that the world is real (though still ultimately non-dual) and that brahman experiences this world (although it transcends them).

Finally, he proposes a theory that Ishvara *should not be equated with the* samaShTi *causal state, as Shankara would have it but with the 4th 'state' of turIya. This seems to be because of mantra 6 in the Upanishad, which he believes ought to be associated with mantra 7, as opposed to being associated with mantra 5 by most other writers. Accordingly, this may be a very interesting book for a reader already familiar with the work but is not to be recommended for someone wishing to read and learn about it for the first time.*

I have to say that his 'translation' of the mantras of the Upanishad does not inspire confidence.

Ref. 40 **In Search of Reality: A layman's journey through Indian philosophy, O. N. Krishnan, Motilal Banarsidass, 2004. ISBN 81-208-2021-5.**

This book provides a mixed bag of topics. The first two parts look at some of the major concepts in Vedanta such as creation, karma, brahman, mokSha *and* sAdhana. *The third part examines the teaching of the various schools of Buddhism. Part 4 looks specifically at Gaudapada's kArikAs and part 5 at Shankara's teaching. The final part provides an overall review and has the title 'Ultimate Truth'.*

It is clearly a 'Buddhist' text rather than a Vedantic one. Krishnan states in the final chapter: "A pure absolute unchanging entity cannot account for the dynamic world process and the world of imperfections resulting therefrom. The questions as to how the real brahman can support the unreal world... have not been satisfactorily answered in their (GK and Shankara's) philosophies." And the chapter on Gaudapada is constantly compared to Buddhist thought and writers.

Ref. 41 **Svetasvataropanisad: The Knowledge that Liberates, Translation and Commentary by Devadatta Kali, Nicolas-Hays, 2011. ISBN 078-0-89254-166-9.**

Included because of quoted reference.

Ref. 42 **Preceptors of Advaita, ed. Pujyasri Jayendra Saraswathi Swamigal Peetarohana, Samata Books, 2003. ISBN 81-85208-51-4.**

There is a 19-page chapter on Gaudapada, written by T. M. P. Mahadevan. Apart from a brief introduction, this is concerned only with the Mandukya kArikA-s. (The book itself consists of 61 chapters, each addressing a different teacher, from Vasishtha down to Jagadguru Sri Chandrasekharendra Sarasvati, with various authors for the material.) This is a useful summary of the essential points, together with footnote references to the source verses. But obviously one would not buy the book unless also interested in the other teachers. Although I have not yet read any of the other chapters myself, the book looks very good indeed.

Ref. 43 **Encyclopedia of Indian Philosophies, Vol. III Advaita Vedanta up to Samkara and his Pupils, Karl H. Potter, Motilal Banarsidass, 1981. ISBN 978-81-208-0310-7.**

This is a remarkably readable book (considering the title!), very well-written in an accessible, and occasionally amusing *way. And he is brilliant at summarizing 'who said what' on Advaita topics. This volume covers Advaita from 'inception' through to Shankara's disciples. (There is another volume for Post-Shankara.) Most of the book covers the key scriptural texts and, again, summarizes what each chapter/verse says rather than the usual literal translation and commentary. Intelligent, seemingly authoritative and, above all, readable! The only trouble is that it is $114 from Amazon US! Shop around the Indian outlets for a more reasonable price.*

There are only 12 pages devoted to the kArikA-s. The material summarizes groups of verses according to the topic which they address. Accordingly, there is no Devanagari, transliteration or translation but key terms are referenced in transliterated form in brackets, after an English rendering. This is all extremely useful for providing an overview.

Other key texts, such as all the Shankara commentaries and attributed texts, as well as those written by his direct disciples, and Mandana Mishra's 'Brahmasiddhi' are treated in a similar fashion. So, if you want to gain a good understanding of what any of these are about without having to find a specific translation and commentary, this is possibly the book for you!

Ref. 44   The Upanishads, SrI Aurobindo, SrI Aurobindo Ashram Publication Department, 1970. ISBN 81-7058-003-X.

Included for reference in main text. Contains all of the translations and commentaries on the Upanishads, divided into three sections − those after 1910, those before 1910 and incomplete/fragmentary translations. (From 1910, he devoted himself entirely to Yoga philosophy.) The Mandukya occupies only three pages, merely translating the Upanishad itself. It provides the Devanagari text without transliteration and the translation is not literal.

Ref. 45   Indian philosophy volume 2, S Radhakrishnan,

Oxford University press, 1923. ISBN 019563820-4.

Included for reference in main text. This two-volume work is a 'must' if you want to study all the various branches of Indian philosophy. Radhakrishnan is a very good writer and is extremely knowledgeable. This second volume has a chapter of over 200 pages on Shankara's Advaita which explains some aspects very well. There are also lots of quotable sentences. (But note the negative comments against his book on the Upanishads below.)

Ref. 46 **Mandukya Upanishad, Discourses by Swami Nikhilananda, Regional Head, Chinmaya Mission, New Delhi. MP3 format. No ISBN.**

These are the recordings of a 7-day series of talks given on the Upanishad and the related verses from Chapter 1 of the kArikA-s. The emphasis is therefore on explaining the three states and turIya, with just the last part discussing the use of the parts of OM for upAsana. It is therefore useful if you only wish to learn about those aspects, being easy to listen to (although a disproportionate amount of time seems to be spent chanting the mantras!) (Note that, obviously, this is not the same Swami Nikhilananda who authored Ref. 4.)

Ref. 47 **A Sanskrit English Dictionary, M. Monier-Williams, Motilal Banarsidass, 1899. ISBN 81-208-0065-6.**

This is the standard dictionary for Sanskrit to English. Very expensive to purchase in the West, it can be obtained much more cheaply from India. (Also, you do have to be able to read the Devanagari script, even if you don't understand it! There are also versions available electronically at no cost – see my website – http://www.Advaita.org.uk/sanskrit/sanskrit.htm. You do not need to be able to read the script for these.)

Ref. 48 **The Brihadaranyaka Upanishad (3 volumes), Nitya Chaitanya Yati, D.K. Printworld (P) Ltd., 1995. ISBN 81-246-0008-2.**

Included because of quoted reference. It is thought that this

Upanishad (probably the oldest) was a principal source for the ideas in the kArikA-s. *In the fourth chapter, Yajnavalka speaks to Janaka about the states of consciousness with the object of discovering the nature of* turIya.

This version is in 3-volumes. It is very readable but does not indicate original sources for what is said. The author is a disciple of Nataraja Guru and, based upon books I have read by Swami Muni Narayana Prasad, should be reliable. There is no Devanagari but transliteration and word meanings are given. (The direct translation of the mantras is remarkably close to those by Swami Madhavananda.) Again, it is an expensive outlay, however.

Ref. 49 **Maandookya Upanyaasa Manjari, Sri Satchidanandendra Saraswati, compiled by Sri H. S. Lakshminarasimha Murthy, Bangalore, 2005.**

This is a 40,500 word document acquired electronically. It was emailed to me by a correspondent but does not seem to be available anywhere on the Internet. It is essentially a commentary on the 12 mantras of the Upanishad. Unfortunately, as seems usually to be the case with the translations of SSS's material, the English is very poor and it is often difficult to understand what is being said. This is a pity since, as is usually the case with this author, some interesting points are made.

Ref. 50 **Three states and one reality – a reflective psychology from the Mandukya Upanishad, Ananda Wood,** download from https://sites.google.com/site/Advaitaen quiry/3States%261Reality.pdf?attredirects=0.

Ref. 51 **'Om' – three states and one reality (An interpretation of the Mandukya Upanishad), Ananda Wood,** download from http://www.Advaita.org.uk/discour ses/downloads/om.pdf.

Ref. 52 **Mandukya Upanishad, Notes from talks by Ramananda Saraswati and Rangananthananda**

Saraswati, download from https://sites.google.com/ site/allaboutvedanta/upanishad/mandukya-upanishad.

Ref. 53 **Philosophia Ultima: Discourses on the Mandukya Upanishad, Talks given from 11/12/80 am to 26/12/80, Osho, Rajneesh Foundation International, 1983. ISBN 978-0880506175.** Also download from http://www. oshoworld.com/e-books/search.asp?pdf_id=100 _Philosophia_Ultima.pdf&download=Yes. *This is not one of Osho's better discourse series! There is always a tendency for him to intersperse jokes amongst his unfoldment of scriptural texts; maybe the intention is to keep his listeners awake. In this particular set of talks, however, the order seems reversed and it is difficult to find any Mandukya-related discourse amongst the mass of irrelevant and usually puerile stories.*

Ref. 54 **Gaudapada: A Study in Early Advaita, T. M. P. Mahadevan, University of Madras, 1954. No ISBN.** *This may be downloaded in DJVU format from http:// archive.org/details/Gaudapada-A.Study.in.Early.Advaita- by.T.M.P.Mahadevan. An excellent (free) DJVU reader (for PC or MAC) may be downloaded from http://windjview. sourceforge.net/. You can also obtain readers for Android and Windows mobile devices. The interface is very clean and I personally find reading on-line with this is much better than with PDF files.*

Mahadevan is a very good writer so this is certainly worth obtaining by any serious Gaudapada student. There is no Devanagari. Transliterated Sanskrit terms are used where necessary, with the English translation following in brackets. The first three chapters deal with Gaudapada's identity and methodology; the 9th looks specifically at the Buddhist problem and the 10th summarizes his value in the chronology of Advaita. The remaining chapters are more directly relevant to the kArikA content, looking at the topics of the 3 states, non-duality, ajAti vAda, *the illusoriness of the world and the practical aspects of Self-realization. Elements of the Upanishad and* kArikA-s *are addressed with an excellent free translation cum commentary and the relevant sources are referenced in footnotes. Highly recommended!*

Ref. 55 **God-Realization Through Reason, Swami Iswarananda, Sri Ramakrishna Ashrama, Trichur, 1959. No ISBN.**

Not specifically related to the Mandukya Upanishad, this book aims to use reason to expound the principles of Advaita and demonstrate the truth of non-duality. The first part contains his main arguments and the second substantiates these through reference to five of the Upanishads (of which one is the Mandukya) and the Brahmasutra bhAsya.

It is included here because the author is particularly interested in the deep-sleep state and he argues that this is identical with turIya. *(Of course the deep-sleep state is* turIya, *but then so are waking and dream, just as bangle, chain and ring are gold.) But* turIya *is not the deep-sleep state. If it were, one would only need to go to sleep to attain* mokSha. turIya *is characterized by neither ignorance nor error, whereas the deep-sleep state is total ignorance.*

Ref. 56 **The Principal Upanishads, S. Radhakrishnan, HarperCollins, 1994, ISBN 81-7223-124-5.**

A thick paperback – nearly 1000 pages – containing a long introduction, followed by translation and notes on 17 of the Upanishads. The Mandukya occupies just 15 pages but, since these cover only the Upanishad, the notes are quite extensive. There is transliterated text without Devanagari and just a translation of each mantra (not word by word).

Unfortunately, the comments are not aimed at elucidating the text according to Advaita but rather in demonstrating the erudition of the author, with references to Christian and Taoist ideas, Parmenides, Plotinus, Augustine, Plato,

Hegel... And there are statements such as: "From him (Ishvara) proceeds hiraNyagarbha who, as Demiurge, fashions the world."

All in all, I would advise that Radhakrishnan be avoided for accurate understanding of the traditional viewpoint.

Ref. 57 Gaudapada and Vasistha: A comparative survey of their philosophy, B. L. Atreya, Darshana International, Volume XIII, January 1973, Number 1.
This may be downloaded from http://theosnet.ning.com/for um/attachment/download?id=3055387%3AUploadedFile%3 A100947.

Ref. 58 The Gaudapadakarikas and Buddhism, Prf. N. B. Purohit, Proceedings and Transactions of the Eighth All-India Oriental Conference, Mysore, Dec. 1935.
This may be downloaded from http://theosnet.ning.com/for um/attachment/download?id=3055387%3AUploadedFile%3 A100949.

Ref. 59 Gaudapada's Asparshayoga and Shankara's Jnanavada, P. C. Divanji, The Poona Orientalist, January 1940.
This may be downloaded from http://theosnet.ning.com/for um/attachment/download?id=3055387%3AUploadedFile%3 A101036.

Ref. 60 The Place of Reason and Revelation in the Philosophy of an Early Advaitin, T. M. P. Mahadevan, Proceedings of the Tenth International Congress of Philosophy, Amsterdam, August 1948.
This may be downloaded from http://theosnet.ning.com/for um/attachment/download?id=3055387%3AUploadedFile%3 A100848.

Ref. 61 Gaudapada: His Works and Views, Nirod Baran Chakraborty, The Calcutta Review, Vol. 145, October 1957. *This may be downloaded from http://theosnet.ning. com/forum/attachment/download?id=3055387%3AUploade dFile%3A101040.*

Ref. 62 **The Book of One: The Ancient Wisdom of Advaita, Dennis Waite, O-Books, 2010. ISBN 978-1846943478.**
Included because of quoted reference.

Ref. 63 **Back to the Truth, Dennis Waite, O Books, 2007. ISBN 1905047614.**
Included because of quoted reference.

Ref.64 **Introduction to Vedanta (The Vedic View and Way of Life), H. H. Swami Paramarthananda Saraswati, Yogamalika, 2005. No ISBN.**
Included because of quoted reference.

Ref. 65 **Tat Tvam Asi: The Universal Message in the Bhagavadgita (Vol. 1), Pathikonda Viswambara Nath, Motilal Banarsidass, 1998. ISBN 81-208-1585-8.**
Included because of quoted reference.

Ref. 66 **The Word Speaks to the Faustian Man, Vol.2, Som Raj Gupta, Motilal Banarsidass, 1995. ISBN 81-208-1175-5.**
I only discovered this book (by accident), about a third the way through writing; hence its late appearance in this bibliography. It is a commentary on the Mundaka and Mandukya Upanishads. The 2-part volume which deals with the Brihadaranyaka Upanishad was mentioned above. There are other volumes, too – the aim is to provide commentaries on all the works of the prasthAna traya *and Shankara's commentaries thereon.*

It is a hefty, hard-back book which I was fortunate to find second-hand. I have to say that I think the title was ill-chosen since readers such as myself, looking for specific commentaries, are unlikely to find it with this title. The Mandukya part takes up about 340 pages, the Mundaka less than 150.There is a Sanskrit glossary and a comprehensive index. One excellent innovation is that the kArikA *reference is given at the top of every page so that there is no need to hunt for verses.*

Each verse is given in transliterated form, followed by trans-
lation. There is no Devanagari and no word-by-word trans-
lation. Shankara's bhAShya *is given, where relevant, in very*
good, modern English and this is then followed by Som Raj
Gupta's extensive commentary. As an example, K2.20 does
not receive many words from most commentators. Shankara
himself did not comment at all, saying that it served no
purpose. But here, there are over four pages of comments with
Som Raj Gupta 'waxing lyrical' on the merits of Sankhya
philosophy. This is not intended as a criticism, since eluci-
dation is what we are looking for in a book of this sort. But
there is a clear danger of overwhelming the reader with his
enthusiasm!

I had intended to read from start to finish but I'm afraid the
flowery style has defeated me. Here is a random sample (from
K2.21): "This participatory mode of being must be
deepened into ecstasy, the ecstasy in which words turn
into sound, pure and wordless, and the world into a
happy dance. When man becomes that song, that
exalted song, then he and the world die into what we
mortals call eternity, immortality, beatitude,
redemption."

But reading the commentary for key verses can be very
worthwhile, as the author may well make observations that
have been missed by others.

Ref. 67 **Brahma Sutra Bhashya of Shankaracharya, translated**
by Sami Gambhirananda, Advaita Ashrama, 1996.
ISBN 81-7505-105-1.

Included because of quoted reference. There are numerous
versions available and I would not especially recommend this
over others. It just happened to be the only one I had when the
quotation was made.

Ref. 68 **From Early Vedanta to Kashmir Shaivism:**
Gaudapada, Bhartrhari, and Abhinavagupta, Natalia

Isayeva, Sri Satguru Publications, 1997. ISBN 81-7030-556-X.

Around 50 pages of this nearly 200 page book are devoted to Gaudapada's 'Life and Works' and most of this discusses the content of the kArikA-s. The aim of the work as the title suggests, is to compare the three philosophers. Combined with the fact that it was originally published by the State University of New York, it will be appreciated that this is an academic presentation rather than one written for the seeker. There are lots of footnotes and references, though fewer than some of the other books referenced above.

The material is quite readable and 'modern' (e.g. using computer analogies) but, despite the seeming authority, there are erroneous statements, e.g. that 'the fourth stage is a state of consciousness' and 'a closer approach towards the nature of the Atman'.

Ref. 69 Mandukya Upanishad with Gaudapada Karika and Shankara Bhashya, as taught by **Swami Dayananda Saraswati** during the three-year course in Vedanta and Sanskrit beginning in 1993 at Anaikatti, Tamil Nadu, India. **Compiled by John Warne.**

I only acquired this after I had already written a third of this book. It is unquestionably the definitive version. It is in letter-sized, cone-bound format and 527 pages long. Complete transcription of all verses and Shankara's bhAShya are provided and Swami Dayananda gives extensive, authoritative commentary on all of them.

There are a few drawbacks: there is no content list, index or glossary. There is no numbering of kArikA-s, so the first thing to be done is to go through the entire work writing in verse references at the top of each right-hand page so that it is possible to locate a specific commentary. The most serious problem of all for many potential readers is that the Sanskrit content of the commentary is extremely high. Most sentences contain at least one Sanskrit term and many of these will not have been encountered previously by most Western seekers. It is necessary to have alongside the 'Vedanta Glossary from class with Swami Dayananda' (also compiled by John Warne). Fortunately, with the help of this, most terms can be translated. (An on-line dictionary should solve the remainder.)

Providing that you are prepared to cope with these issues however, the effort proves to be more than worthwhile, with Swami Dayananda bringing his usual clarity of explanation, presented with reason and humor. This is the version to be studied by any serious seeker.

Ref. 70 **The Bhagavad Gita, translated by Winthrop Sargeant, State University of New York Press, 1994. ISBN 0-87395-830-6.**

Included because of quoted reference. There are very many versions available. I do recommend this for translation, however – each word is given its correct part of speech and meaning, and the Devanagari is also included. But there is no commentary at all.

Ref. 71 **A Concise Dictionary of Indian Philosophy, John Grimes, Indica Books, 2009. ISBN 81-86569-80-4.**

The book I always recommend for discovering the meaning of Sanskrit words encountered in the above books. It is rare indeed to encounter a word which is not covered and the explanations are always concise and accurate. An indispensable reference book.

Ref. 72 *Four Upanishads. Swami Paramananda. Sri Ramakrishna Math, Madras, 1974. ISBN 81-7120-233-0, Part 1 verses 1 – 3.*

Ref. 73 **Critical Word-Index to the Bhagavad Gita, Prahlad C. Divanji, Munshiram Manoharlal Publishers Pvt Ltd. 1993. ISBN 81-215-0545-3.**

Ref. 74 **Bhagavad Gita Home Study Course Vol.2, Swami**

Dayananda Saraswati, Arsha Vidya Research and Publication Trust, 2011, ISBN 978-93-80049-39-7 (9 volume set).

Ref. 75 Bhagavad Gita, Nitya Chaitanya Yati, D. K. Printworld (P) Ltd, 1993. ISBN 81-246-0010-4.

Ref. 76 The Holy Geeta, Commentary by Swami Chinmayananda, Central Chinmaya Mission Trust, 1996. No ISBN.

Ref. 77 The Book of One, Dennis Waite, O-Books, 2010. ISBN 978-1-84694-347-8.

Ref. 78 Sanskrit for Seekers, Dennis Waite, Mantra Books, 2014. ISBN 978-1-78279-227-7.

Ref. 79 Advaita Made Easy, Dennis Waite, Mantra Books, 2012. ISBN 978-1-78099-184-9.

Ref. 80 Maitrayaniya Upanishad, with the commentary of Ramatirtha, translated by E. B. Cowell, Bharatiya Kala Prakashan, 2007. ISBN 978-81-8090-155-6.

Ref. 81 Brahmas Sutras: Sanskrit Text and Commentary by Sankaracharya (2 volumes), George Thibault, Bharatiya Kala Prakashan, 2004. ISBN: 978-81-8090-040-2.

Index

there cannot be a root cause, 115

Dakshinamurthy, 158, 224
Date, V. H., 137, 197, 214
Dave, Prof. J. H., 252
day and night metaphor, 73
Dayananda, Swami, 195
Dayananda, Swami, 314
death, 113, 296
deep sleeper, 43
deep-sleep state, 49, 264
Descartes, 75
describability, criteria for, 57
Devanagari, 318
difference, 181
discrimination, 222
dispassion, 222
DNA, 135
dream state, 48
  similarity with waking, 327
  unreality of, 73
dream tiger metaphor, 131
dreamer, 41
dreams
  belief that they are real, 81, 137
  mechanism for, 75
  objectively real for dreamer, 82
dRRiShTAnta, 33
dRRiShTi-sRRiShTi-vAda, 329
dRRishyam, 327
dualism, criticism of, 94
duality
  how does it come about?, 170

interim explanation, 106
only an appearance, 165
why does Advaita teach?, 166
dvaita, 116
  criticism of, 94
dvayakAla, 87

effect, pre-existent in cause, 110
eka-jIva-vAda, 329
elephant in rut story, 95
elephants in will story, 69
empirical reality, 71
enlightenment, 50, 121, 188
  concept of 'path', 206
  does not make us free, 190
  waking from the dream, 198
  what happens, 183
error, 67
essential nature, 112
existence
  depends on knower, 46
  theories of, 201
experience, 44

faint, 296
faith, 28, 140
fire on hill, example of inference, 33
firebrand metaphor, 19, 109, 173
five sheaths metaphor, 104
footprints of birds metaphor, 232
Fox, Douglas, 50
fruit of knowledge, 210

**MANTRA
BOOKS**

We publish books on Eastern religions and philosophies.
Books that aim to inform and explore the various
traditions, that began rooted in East and
have migrated West.